D1272700

LIFE IN THE NORTH DURING THE CIVIL WAR

A SOURCE HISTORY

LIFE IN THE NORTH DURING THE CIVIL WAR

A SOURCE HISTORY

by George Winston Smith

& Charles Judah

THE UNIVERSITY OF NEW MEXICO PRESS

© THE UNIVERSITY OF NEW MEXICO PRESS 1966

ALL RIGHTS RESERVED

Composed, printed and bound

at the University of New Mexico Printing Plant

Albuquerque, New Mexico, U.S.A.

973.7
S

67 1336
45 0669
PENINSULA PUBLIC LIBRARY

Library of Congress Catalog Card Number 66-14776

First Edition

for Karin

&

Victoria

Contents

Illustrations

Acknowledgments

WE WISH to thank the many librarians and archivists whose helpfulness made our research tasks less burdensome. We should especially like to mention: Ruth H. Davis and Herbert J. Tepper of The State Historical Society of Wisconsin; Ruth Miller, R. N. Williams II, and Nicholas B. Wainwright of The Historical Society of Pennsylvania; Genevieve Porterfield, Dorothy A. Wonsmos, Charles Warren, Robert B. Harness, and Arthur L. DeVolder of the University of New Mexico Library; Stanley F. Dunnetski of the Chicago Public Library; Mrs. Ruth Bleecker and Mrs. Cynthia Fedders of the Boston Public Library; Dr. Clifford K. Shipton and Kimball C. Elkins of the Harvard University Archives; Dr. Stephen T. Riley of the Massachusetts Historical Society; and Dr. C. Percy Powell, of the Manuscript Division, and Peter Ho, of the Newspaper Reference Division, Library of Congress.

Gerald B. Snedeker and Buford Rowland, of Washington, D.C., gave valuable assistance and advice; also William Owings of Albuquerque, Dr. Myra Alice Jenkins, of Santa Fe, New Mexico, and our colleague, the late Dr. Dorothy Woodward of the University of New Mexico.

The research was partially financed by two grants from the Social Science Research Council, and one from the Sandia Foundation. We also acknowledge a typing grant from the Organized Research Fund, University of New Mexico.

Special permissions to cite material under copyright have been received from G. P. Putnam's Sons, to quote from Frederic Bancroft, ed., *Speeches, Correspondence and Political Papers of Carl*

Schurz; from Houghton Mifflin Company to cite, Worthington Chauncey Ford, ed., *A Cycle of Adams Letters;* and from Columbia University Press, to quote from Ralph L. Rusk, ed., *The Letters of Ralph Waldo Emerson.* The Historical Society of Pennsylvania very kindly permitted citations from the Salmon P. Chase and Henry C. Carey MSS in its possession.

Our sincere appreciation is due to Roland Dickey, the able director of the University of New Mexico Press, and to his efficient staff for their many hours spent with this manuscript. Most of all we acknowledge the indispensable help of Mrs. Helen M. Smith, who has worked with us ceaselessly at every stage of this project.

Introduction

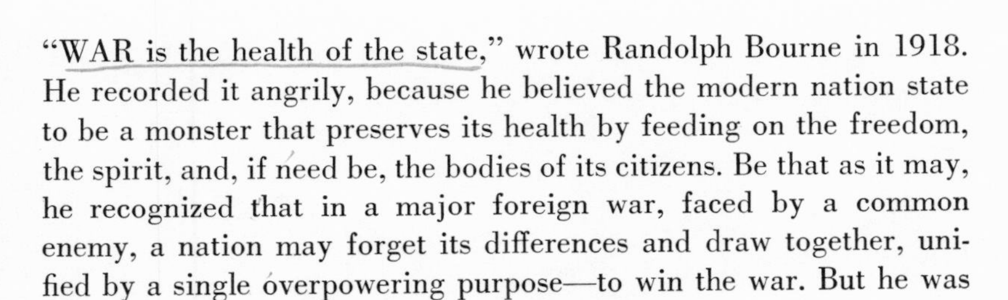

"WAR is the health of the state," wrote Randolph Bourne in 1918. He recorded it angrily, because he believed the modern nation state to be a monster that preserves its health by feeding on the freedom, the spirit, and, if need be, the bodies of its citizens. Be that as it may, he recognized that in a major foreign war, faced by a common enemy, a nation may forget its differences and draw together, unified by a single overpowering purpose—to win the war. But he was observing and writing about war between nations.

Civil war is the sickness of the state. It is brought on by poison distilled of festering antagonism, conflicting interest, willful ignorance, stubborn dogmatism, jealousy, greed and, in the end, hate. It does not unify; it divides. The citizens do not stand together; they stand apart. They do not destroy a common enemy; they kill one another. Sometimes, as in the case of the American Civil War, bloodletting alleviates the sickness and the patient survives. But even in such cases the illness which has eaten deep into the bone lingers on, to be passed on from generation to generation until, eventually, time heals and a final cure is effected.

It was a civil war, and after the nature of civil wars it divided the country. From 1861 to 1865 the American people warred upon one another. The great division was between the North and the South. In general, physical combat was confined to the armies representing those sections. But there was no ideological wall along the Mason-Dixon Line, or on either bank of the Ohio River, on one side of which stood a unified North, on the other a united South. On the contrary, there was civil discord in both sections.

In the North a state of ambivalence prevailed. There was emotional fervor and hell-for-leather enthusiasm, but neither the one nor the other sealed over the deep fissures within the society. Instead

Columbia Awake at Last

the conflict opened new ones. No community escaped the impact and the awareness of war, yet at no time was there complete mobilization, and by and large civilians insisted on luxuries (if they could afford them, and more could) and diversions and business as usual. Great sacrifices brushed elbows with craven rejection of responsibility, honesty with gross malfeasance and profiteering. Business boomed—prosperity derived from shoddy was nonetheless prosperity—while poverty enshrouded the jobless and underpaid whose ill-condition anteceded the war. The draft riots in New York City were not directed solely against conscription. Though brutal and bestial, they were not reasonless; the mudsills of the North that Southern pro-slavery propagandists had been pointing to for decades were in revolt. And discontent was not confined to the poverty-stricken city rabble. More than one observer speculated on the possibility of agrarian grievances leading to secession of the West from the East should the South succeed in its effort to shatter the Union, while among those most determined on total victory were many who wished to wrest the government from the hands of Abraham Lincoln in order to put it into those of Major General George B. McClellan.

Nor was the Northern division only political and economic. An overwhelming majority of the people were united on the need to preserve the Union, but this was the extent of agreement. Some insisted that the abolition of slavery should be an irrevocable war aim; others would accept slavery on the South's terms as the price for peace and unity; still others (Lincoln was among these) would save the Union with or without slavery as circumstances might dictate. Radical Republicans were determined to destroy not only slavery but the slaveholding aristocracy and the social system the latter had created as well. Conservative Republicans and Democrats opposed this.

There was more agreement about the Negro. Practically everyone held him in contempt as a member of an inferior race. Moreover, labor feared him as a source of cheap competition. Thus the opposition to the extension of slavery was engendered more by the determination to keep the "niggers" out than by disapproval of slavery as an institution. Nonetheless, a majority in the North did abhor human slavery as a violation of both Christian and democratic principles, and although they regarded the abolitionists as troublemakers raising a whirlwind of passion, disunion, and war, circumstances might —and did—arise that would cause most of them to support emancipation and thus further intensify factionalism.

Even military unity was molded slowly. The Northern soldier fought, suffered, died, and won, and deserved all the glory and many of the benefits to be heaped upon him by a grateful nation. But before the glory there was humiliation, before victory defeat, before tribute criticism and doubts. The army was composed of many elements—volunteers, conscripts, bounty jumpers. Only hardship, combat, and leadership—that for many months eluded Lincoln—could weld these elements into a great army.

The credos of the North were also in conflict. The war itself—was it a holy crusade, an unfortunate and unchristian necessity, or an unredeemed evil? What of the arts in war time? Could the customary tributes continue to be paid at their several shrines, or must they be abandoned while the nation rendered undivided homage before the altar of Mars? Or should they be hitched to the war god's chariot? Learning? Did the embattled armies represent in some measure the newly recognized forces of evolution, or were they relics of barbarism not yet conquered by civilization? Were the economic overlords of an emerging industrial capitalism the product of immutable economic law, or was war siring a new type of monster, more respectable but as cruel as Simon Legree? On all these questions, Northern opinion differed.

Thus the North entered the war deeply divided, and at its end it was still divided on many fundamental issues. Nonetheless, Abraham Lincoln twisted two strands of unity, the determination to preserve the Union and the abhorrence of chattel slavery, into a rope strong enough to bind it together sufficiently to overwhelm a South which after four years of epic resistance found its strength unable to sustain further effort—the grinding effort of guerrilla warfare carried on over decades if need be by a defeated but unconquered people confronted by an intolerable tyranny.

It is, then, with the North, at war with itself yet fumblingly and awkwardly pulling itself together, that the following pages deal. We have let it tell its own tale, with editorial effort confined to an attempt to give some sort of cohesion and continuity to a necessarily diverse whole.

I

The North in the Secession Crisis

IN MAY of 1860 the Republican National Convention adopted a platform containing a plank that pledged opposition to any further extension of slavery. It nominated Abraham Lincoln to run on that platform. Reaction in the South was violent. "It makes little difference whether we are governed by a gentleman or ruled by a baboon, but with Lincoln comes something worse," screamed one editor. This was not the voice of the whole South, but it was that of an influential segment of it, and it warned that should a Black Republican be elected the South would secede. But the people of the North were obdurate. On November 6, 1860, they elected Lincoln. This did not make secession inevitable, but it did make it a very real possibility, and when on December 20 the South Carolina secession convention adopted an ordinance of secession, the possibility of at least the lower South following her example became a probability. The North's dilemma was complex. Should it wait and see, doing nothing? Should it attempt conciliation through concession? Should it call the South's bluff by means of an exhibition of firmness? And if it was not a bluff? If the South did secede? What then? Northern opinion was deeply divided.

Some said let the South go in peace. Their reasons were varied: the federal government had no constitutional authority to hold a state in the Union against its will; the Union was a voluntary one of mind and heart—broken, it could not be held together by force for the simple reason that it no longer existed; Northern acquiescence to secession would stifle the aggressiveness of the Black Republicans and reassure the South, thus paving the way for a compromise that would reestablish the Union on a foundation of mutual understanding; secession of the cotton states of the deep South would put an end to the recurrent crises that disturbed the economic as well as the political equilibrium of the nation—with them gone, the North would be free to build a sound economy on a foundation of protective tariffs and internal improvements. Eventually an economically crippled and chastened South would limp back into the Union.

Horace Greeley was a staunch Republican; he had supported Lincoln in the presidential election of 1860. But he had a profound respect for the Jeffersonian principle that governments derive their just powers from the consent of the governed. He believed the North would be violating this principle if it did not allow the Southern people to express themselves, even in secession. Later he became honestly convinced, or rationalized himself into the opinion, that the clamor for secession was not the voice of the Southern people—but that was later. In an editorial in his paper, the New York Tribune *of December 17, 1860, he said:*

. . . If seven or eight contiguous States shall present themselves authentically at Washington, saying, "We hate the Federal Union; we have withdrawn from it; we give you the choice between acquiescing in our secession and arranging amicably all incidental questions on the one hand, and attempting to subdue us on the other,"—we could not stand up for coercion, for subjugation, for we do not think it would be just. We hold the right of Self-Government sacred, even when invoked in behalf of those who deny it to others. So much for the question of Principle.

Now as to the matter of Policy:

South Carolina will certainly secede. Several other Cotton States will probably follow her example. The Border States are evidently reluctant to do likewise. South Carolina has grossly insulted them by her dictatorial, reckless course. What she expects and desires is a clash of arms with the Federal government, which will at once commend her to the sympathy and cooperation of every Slave State, and to the sympathy (at least) of the Pro-Slavery minority in the Free States. It is not difficult to see that this would speedily work a political revolution, which would restore to slavery all, and more than all, it has lost by the canvass of 1860. We want to obviate this. We would

HARPER'S WEEKLY.
A JOURNAL OF CIVILIZATION.
VOL. V.—No. 218.] NEW YORK, SATURDAY, MARCH 2, 1861. [PRICE FIVE CENTS.
Entered according to Act of Congress, in the Year 1861, by Harper & Brothers, in the Clerk's Office of the District Court for the Southern District of New York.

ABRAHAM LINCOLN, THE PRESIDENT ELECT, ADDRESSING THE PEOPLE FROM THE ASTOR HOUSE BALCONY, FEBRUARY 19, 1861

expose the seceders to odium as dis-unionists, not commend them to pity as the gallant though mistaken upholders of the rights of their section in an unequal military conflict.

We fully realize that the dilemma of the incoming administration will be a critical one. It must endeavor to uphold and enforce the laws, as well against rebellious slaveholders as fugitive slaves. The new President must fulfill the obligations assumed in his inauguration oath, no matter how shamefully his predecessor may have defied them. We fear the Southern madness may precipitate a bloody collision that all must deplore. But if ever "seven or eight States" send agents to Washington to say, "We want to get out of the Union," we shall feel constrained by our devotion to Human Liberty to say, "Let them go!" And we do not see how we could take the other side without coming in direct conflict with those Rights of Man which we hold paramount to all political arrangements, however convenient and advantageous.[1]

Henry C. Carey, the brilliant Philadelphia political economist, was also a Republican. For many years he had been a high-tariff advocate. To him secession of the lower South offered the remainder of the nation surcease from recurrent political crises and the opportunity to put into effect a sound economic policy. In a letter begun December 20—the day South Carolina seceded—and finished on the twenty-first, he included the following notation from a Missouri newspaper:"Let them go, we shall then have internal improvements & a protective tariff," and added in his own words, "So say I—let them go, peacefully, as fast as they see fit to go. It would be a fitting exit for the wildest men the world has yet seen." On the same day, December 21, he wrote in another letter that "South Carolina has at length seceded & others are to follow her. I say let them go, *quietly and peaceably. When a man and his wife cannot live quietly together in one house, it is best they should separate."*

During the next three months he continued to advocate peaceful secession of the lower South, but the Border States and Upper South he would keep in the Union. In January he observed:

"The Cotton States have gone out, and so entirely willing am I that they should stay out, that I would not move a finger to induce them to return. Now, however, that they have done their worst, it is

for our interest to stay the work of secession, and thus retain the powers to enforce the laws, & bring order out of chaos. . . ." His attempt to link the protective tariff with the future of the Union came a month later, when he wrote in a public letter addressed to William H. Seward:

. . . Had the [protectionist] tariff of 1842 been maintained the South would now be filled with furnaces and factories, our production would be treble what it is, and the strength and harmony of the Union would be greater than they have ever been.

. . . . .

Our fourteen years of free-trade policy had so far weakened us, [the United States] while strengthening them [Great Britain] that in the Union, as it existed three months since, the only effect of any attempt at resistance must have been that of tightening and strengthening the cord we had allowed to be thrown about our limbs. Happily for us, however, if we know how to profit from the lesson we have received, the Cotton States have now seceded, and have thus left us free to pursue the policy by means of which alone we may repair the damage done. . . . Let us profit now by the Secession of the Cotton States, and we shall, one year hence, have reason to return our thanks to heaven for it, as having been the means of saving the Union. Let us once again establish our independence [by a protective tariff], and the day will not then be far distant when the Union will again comprise the whole of the existing states. . . .[2]

Greeley's plea to let the South go in peace was based on Jeffersonian principle, Henry C. Carey's on a peculiarly inverted form of economic nationalism; both spoke with the voice of reason. Not so William Lloyd Garrison. Garrison was probably the best known of all the Abolitionists; for thirty years his newspaper, The Liberator, *had been the mouthpiece of abolitionist extremists. His was the voice of outraged morality. Only major surgery—the amputation of the South and its fountains of poison—could save the North. In January 1861, he wrote in an editorial:*

Under these circumstances, what is the true course to be pursued by the people of the North? Is it to vindicate the sovereignty by the sword till the treason is quelled and allegiance restored? Constitutionally, the sword may be wielded to this extent, and must be, whether by President Buchanan or President Lincoln, if the Union is to be preserved. The Federal Government must not pretend to be in actual operation, embracing thirty-four States, and then allow the seceding States to trample upon its flag, steal its property, and defy its authority with impunity; for it would then be (as it is at this moment) a mockery and a laughing-stock. Nevertheless, to think of whipping the South (for she will be a unit on the question of slavery) into subjection, and extorting allegiance from millions of people at the cannon's mouth, is utterly chimerical. True, it is in the power of the North to deluge her soil with blood, and inflict upon her the most terrible sufferings; but not to conquer her spirit, or change her determination.

What, then, ought to be done? The people of the North should recognize the fact that THE UNION IS DISSSOLVED, and act accordingly. They should see, in the madness of the South, the hand of God, liberating them from "a covenant with death and an agreement with hell," made in a time of terrible peril, and without a conception of its inevitable consequences, and which has corrupted their morals, poisoned their religion, petrified their humanity as towards the millions in bondage, tarnished their character, harassed their peace, burdened them with taxation, shackled their prosperity, and brought them into abject vassalage. . . .

Now, then, let there be a CONVENTION OF THE FREE STATES called to organize an independent government on free and just principles; and let them say to the slave States—"Though you are without excuse for your treasonable conduct, depart in peace! Though you have laid piratical hands upon property not your own, we surrender it all in the spirit of magnanimity! And if nothing but the possession of the Capitol will appease you, take even that, without a struggle! Let the line be drawn between us where free institutions end and slave institutions begin! Organize your own confederacy, if you will, based on violence, tyranny, and blood, and relieve us from all responsibility for your evil course!"[3]

Sixteen days after South Carolina's secession another voice was heard in the North. It was as loud and bitter as Garrison's, but without Garrison's fanatical moral fervor to justify it. It was that of Fer-

nando Wood. Wood was the Democratic mayor of New York City. He was at war with a state Republican legislature and governor. To him emancipation from Albany was more important than the emancipation of Southern slaves; the city's commerce must not suffer though the Union fall into pieces. He would even assist in its shattering. On January 6 he said in an address to the New York City Common Council:

To the Honorable the Common Council:

. . . It would seem that the dissolution of the Federal Union is inevitable. Having been formed originally upon the basis of general and mutual protection, but separate local independence—each State reserving the entire and absolute control of its own domestic affairs, it is evidently impossible to keep them together longer than they deem themselves fairly treated by each other, or longer than the interests, honor and fraternity of the people of the several States are satisfied. Being a Government created by *opinion,* its continuance is dependent upon the continuance of the sentiment which formed it. It cannot be preserved by coercion or held together by force. A resort to this last dreadful alternative would of itself destroy not only the Government, but the lives and property of the people.

. . . . .

With our aggrieved brethren of the slave States, we have friendly relations and a common sympathy. We have not participated in the warfare upon their constitutional rights or their domestic institutions. While other portions of our State have unfortunately been imbued with the fanatical spirit which actuates a portion of the people of New England, the City of New York has unfalteringly preserved the integrity of its principles in adherence to the compromises of the Constitution and the equal rights of the people of all the States. We have respected the local interests of every section, at no time oppressing, but all the while aiding in the development of the resources of the whole country. Our ships have penetrated to every clime, and so have New York capital, energy and enterprise found their way to every State, and, indeed, to almost every county and town of the American Union. If we have derived sustenance from the Union, so have we in return disseminated blessings for the common benefit of all. Therefore, New York has a right to expect, and should endeavor to preserve a continuance of uninterrupted intercourse with every section.

. . . . . .

Much, no doubt, can be said in favor of the justice and policy of a separation. It may be said that secession or revolution in any of the United States would be a subversion of all Federal authority, and, so far as the Central Government is concerned, the resolving of the community into its original elements—that, if part of the States form new combinations and Governments, other States may do the same. California and her sisters of the Pacific will no doubt set up an independent republic and husband their own rich mineral resources. The Western States, equally rich in cereals and other agricultural products, will probably do the same. Then it may be said, why should not New York city, instead of supporting by her contributions in revenue two-thirds the expenses of the United States, become also equally independent? As a free city, with but nominal duty on imports, her local government could be supported without taxation upon her people. Thus we could live free from taxes, and have cheap goods nearly duty free. In this she would have the whole and united support of the Southern States, as well as of all other States, to whose interests and rights under the Constitution she has always been true. . . . If the Confederacy is broken up the Government is dissolved, and it behooves every distinct community, as well as every individual, to take care of themselves.

When Disunion has become a fixed and certain fact, why may not New York disrupt the bands which bind her to a venal and corrupt master—to a people and a party that have plundered her revenues, attempted to ruin her commerce, taken away the power of self-government, and destroyed the Confederacy of which she was the proud Empire City? Amid the gloom which the present and prospective condition of things must cast over the country, New York as a *Free City*, may shed the only light and hope for a future reconstruction of our once blessed Confederacy. . . .[4]

Fantastic as Wood's proposal may seem in the perspective of history, in January 1861 it was not without respectable support. It had been delivered with the approval of August Belmont, prominent in New York financial, political, and social circles; it was discussed gravely and with a measure of approval in a New York Journal of Commerce *editorial that reveals the depths of dissension that existed in the North.*

. . . It is peculiarly appropriate for the Chief Magistrate of New York, on occasions like the present, to point out the abuses which have grown up, the usurpations which have been practiced, and the inroads upon vested rights which have been made by the Legislature. These abuses, usurpations and inroads, can never be justified, even upon the plea that they are designed to promote the welfare of the people of the city, but when notoriously if not avowedly designed to promote partizan ends, and to subject the independent citizens of this city to the domination of a central power, whose strength is to be perpetuated and success promoted by the control of the great amount of patronage thus placed at its disposal, they become simply oppressions, which may be resisted in every lawful and appropriate form until redress is obtained.

The Mayor seems to anticipate, in the disturbed state of the country, and the disintegration going on about us, the approach of the period when the people of the city of New York may throw off the burdens which oppress them, and assume independent existence as a "free city." That there is every probability of a disruption of the Union, and the separation of section from section, is indeed apparent. That such a breaking up of the confederacy may introduce new elements into our system, lead to new complications, and inaugurate with reference to ourselves a new policy, is not at all improbable. Deprecating as we should such a calamity, and hoping to the last for some method of averting it, we cannot, in the present condition of public affairs, refuse to recognize impending dangers, nor do we wonder that the thoughts and minds of our citizens are turned towards measures of self-protection and future security. If the Union shall indeed be broken up, it is not within the compass of man's wisdom to say where the work of disruption shall end. We have already seen its beginning, but its termination can no man understand, until the problem shall have been worked out before his eyes. . . .[5]

New York Democrats held their State Convention in late January 1861. Horace Greeley ironically described it as "the most imposing assemblage of delegates ever convened within the State." Among those present were thirty delegates who had been elected to Congress and a former New York governor; Samuel F. B. Morse, the inventor of the telegraph also was there. He was president of the American Society for Promoting National Unity in the Crisis, a conservative organization which professed itself to be against such nonconformists as "dreamers of abolitionism, of women's rights—free love, spiritualists—socialism—agrarianism—and similar visionary schemes."

James S. Thayer, a former Whig, addressed this distinguished assembly. He expressed the views of those Northern Democrats who were pro-Southern from conviction, politics, self-interest, or emotion. They were to oppose Lincoln's war policies and to be branded as Copperheads. Although Thayer undoubtedly was more extreme in his views than most of the convention delegates, the speech was applauded.

. . . We can at least, in an authoritative way and a practical manner, arrive at the basis of a peaceable separation (renewed cheers); we can at least by discussion enlighten, settle, and concentrate the public sentiment in the State of New York upon this question, and save it from that fearful current, that circuitously, but certainly, sweeps madly on, through the narrow gorge of "the enforcement of the laws" to the shoreless ocean of civil war. (Cheers) Against this, under all circumstances, in every place and form, we must now and at all times oppose a resolute and unfaltering resistance. The public mind will bear the avowal, and let us make it—that if a revolution of force is to begin, *it shall be inaugurated at home.* (Cheers) And if the incoming Administration shall attempt to carry out the line of policy that has been foreshadowed, we announce that, when the hand of Black Republicanism turns to blood-red, and seeks from the fragment of the Constitution to construct a scaffolding for coercion —another name for execution—we will reverse the order of the French Revolution, and save the blood of the people by making those who would inaugurate a reign of terror the first victims of a national guillotine. . . .

The Democratic and Union party at the North made the issue at the last election with the Republican party that, in the event of their success, and the establishment of their policy, the Southern States not only would go out of the Union but would have adequate cause for doing so. (Applause) Who of us believed that, with the government in the hands of a party whose avowed policy was no more slave States, no further extension of Slavery, and asserting the power and duty of Congress to prohibit it in all the territories, that the Southern States *would* remain in the Union? It seems to me, thus encompassed and menaced, they could not, with safety to their largest interest, and any prudent consideration for their future condition and welfare, continue in the confederacy. What would become, in twenty-five years, of 8,000,000 of white people and 4,000,000 of slaves, with their natural increase, walled in by congressional prohibition, besieged and threatened by a party holding the seats of Federal power and patronage, that, according to the doctrine of the President-elect, must "arrest the further spread of Slavery," and place the institution itself "where the public mind will rest satisfied in the belief that it is in the course of ultimate extinction?"

This is the position I took, with 313,000 voters in the State of New York on the sixth of November last. I shall not recede from it; having admitted that, in a certain contingency, the Slave States would have just and adequate causes for a separation. Now that the contingency has happened, I shall not withdraw that admission, because they have been unwise or unreasonable in the "time, mode, and measure of redress." (Applause)

Aside from particular acts that do not admit of any justification, those who imagine that the Southern States do not well know what they are about, forget that they have been for fifteen years looking at this thing with all its importance to their larger interest, as well as to their safety, and mistake the deep and deliberate movement of a revolution for the mere accidents and incidents which always accompany it. (Applause) There are some Democrats and Union men who, when the fever for a fight has subsided, will wake up and wonder that they mistook the madness of passion for the glow of patriotism. Again: we should consider that, whatever may be our construction of the Constitution under which we live, as to any right under it for one or more States to get out of the Union, when six States by the deliberate, formal, authoritative action of their people, dissolve their connection with the government, and nine others say that the dissolution shall be final if the seceding members so choose, announcing to the North, "No interference; we stand between you and them." Can you bring them back? No! Enforcement of the laws in six States is a war with fifteen. And, after all, to speak plainly on this subject, and reveal the true secret of the utter repugnance of the people to resort to any coërcive measures, it is within their plain judgment and practical common sense, that the very moment you go outside the narrow circle of the written letter and provisions of the Constitution of the United States, you are confronted with the great world of facts, and find this is not a consolidated government; not a government of the whole people in the sense and meaning now attached to it. (Applause.)

. . . It is announced that the Republican Administration will enforce the laws against and in all the seceding states. A nice discrimination must be exercised in the performance of this duty; not a hair's breadth outside the mark. You remember the story of William Tell, who, when the condition was imposed upon him to shoot an apple from the head of his own child, after he had performed the task, he let fall an arrow. "For what is that?" said Gesler. "To kill thee, tyrant, had I slain my boy!" (Cheers) Let one arrow winged by the Federal bow strike the heart of an American citizen, and who can number the avenging darts that will cloud the heavens in the conflict that will ensue? (Prolonged applause) What, then, is the duty of the State of New York? What shall we say to our people when we come to meet this state of facts? That the Union must be preserved. But if that cannot be, what then? *Peaceable separation.* (Applause) Painful and humiliating as it is, let us temper it with all we can of love and kindness, so that we may yet be left in a comparatively prosperous condition, in friendly relations with another Confederacy. (Cheers) [6]

Meanwhile, as state after Southern state seceded and strident voices in the North said, "let them go," the President of the United States was a caretaker executive. James Buchanan was not spineless, but personally he had been repudiated by a large segment of his own Democratic party, and that party had suffered division and defeat in 1860. When the breakup of his cabinet followed the resignation of its Southern members, Buchanan replaced them with staunch

Unionists; he refused to traffic with South Carolina's would-be commissioners; he declared secession to be unconstitutional, and he authorized the sending of an unarmed merchant steamer the Star of the West, *with reinforcements to Major Robert Anderson in Charleston harbor. But James Buchanan did not make any other move when the* Star of the West *was turned away from Fort Sumter by South Carolinian artillery fire, and he steadfastly insisted that the federal government had no constitutional power to aggressively constrain a state. Instead he handed over to Congress the task of policy-making. His Special Message of January 8, 1861, to the Senate and House, classifies Buchanan among those who would let the South "go in peace" rather than use coercive force against the seceding states. The President had been a "doughface" (a Northerner who supported Southern policies), but he was not, nor was he ever to be, a Copperhead. During the war he gave money to soldier relief and supported conscription.*

. . . In my annual message I expressed the conviction, which I have long deliberately held, and which recent reflection has only tended to deepen and confirm, that no State has a right by its own act to secede from the Union or throw off its federal obligations at pleasure. I also declared my opinion to be that even if that right existed and should be exercised by any State of the Confederacy the executive department of this Government had no authority under the Constitution to recognize its validity by acknowledging the independence of such State. This left me no alternative, as the chief executive officer under the Constitution of the United States, but to collect the public revenues and to protect the public property so far as this might be practicable under existing laws. This is still my purpose. My province is to execute and not to make the laws. It belongs to Congress exclusively to repeal, to modify, or to enlarge their provisions to meet exigencies as they may occur. I possess no dispensing power.

I certainly had no right to make aggressive war upon any State, and I am perfectly satisfied that the Constitution has wisely withheld that power even from Congress. But the right and duty to use military force defensively against those who resist the Federal officers in the execution of their legal functions and against those who assail the property of the Federal Government is clear and undeniable.

But the dangerous and hostile attitude of the States toward each other has already far transcended and cast in the shade the ordinary executive duties already provided for by law, and has assumed such vast and alarming proportions as to place the subject entirely above and beyond Executive control. The fact can not be disguised that we are in the midst of a great revolution. In all its various bearings, therefore, I commend the question to Congress as the only human tribunal under Providence possessing the power to meet the existing emergency. To them exclusively belongs the power to declare war or to authorize the employment of military force in all cases contemplated by the Constitution, and they alone possess the power to remove grievances which might lead to war and to secure peace and union to this distracted country. On them, and on them alone, rests the responsibility.

. . . . .

A common ground on which conciliation and harmony can be produced is surely not unattainable. The proposition to compromise by letting the North have exclusive control of the territory above a certain line and to give Southern institutions protection below that line ought to receive universal approbation. In itself, indeed, it may not be entirely satisfactory, but when the alternative is between a reasonable concession on both sides and a destruction of the Union it is an imputation upon the patriotism of Congress to assert that its members will hesitate for a moment.

Even now the danger is upon us. In several of the States which have not yet seceded the forts, arsenals, and magazines of the United States have been seized. This is by far the most serious step which has been taken since the commencement of the troubles. This public property has long been left without garrisons and troops for its protection, because no person doubted its security under the flag of the country in any State in the Union. Besides, our small Army has scarcely been sufficient to guard our remote frontiers against Indian incursions. The seizure of this property, from all appearances, has been purely aggressive, and not in resistance to any attempt to coerce a state or States to remain in the Union.

At the beginning of these unhappy troubles I determined that no act of mine should increase the excitement in either section of the country. If the political conflict were to end in a civil war, it was my determined purpose not to commence it nor even to furnish an excuse for it by any act of this Government. My opinion remains unchanged that justice as well as sound policy requires us still to seek a peaceful solution of the questions at issue between the North and the South. Entertaining this conviction, I refrained even from sending reenforcements to Major Anderson, who commanded the forts in Charleston Harbor, until an absolute necessity for doing so should make itself apparent, lest it might unjustly be regarded as a menace of military coercion, and thus furnish, if not a provocation, at least a pretext for an outbreak on the part of South Carolina. . . .[7]

The "let them go in peace" faction was vociferous. During the war it was to be a divisive influence in the North. But it was only a small minority. Most Northerners would have agreed with Ralph Waldo Emerson that "the imbecility of men is always inviting the impudence of power." To these, "peaceful acquiescence" was an imbecility that would only encourage the impudence of secession. Yet, civil war, too, was an imbecility, so naturally there was a demand for preservation of the Union through conciliation. An editorial, "What Is to be Done," published in the Philadelphia Press, *December 27, 1860, expressed this demand and the reasoning leading to it.*

. . . But the North has a vital interest in the preservation of the Union on its own account. The well being of our millions of men and women is not to be endangered or thrown away upon a sentiment of doubtful philanthropy, to result in a state of things which can do no good in any way to the objects for which the sacrifice is made. Our trade with the slaveholding states is much greater than is commonly thought. Every man in business, and every laborer depending upon full employment for his daily bread, now feels the mischief which a temporary suspension of trade and credit between the sections has the power to inflict upon him. . . . In 1859 we exported to foreign countries thirty-four millions worth of manufactured commodities, which would leave nineteen hundred and sixty-six millions worth that must find a home market and home consumption. If the South supplies herself with only one-tenth of this amount, and consumes only one-fourth of them, she gives the Northern States a market for two hundred and ninety-six millions of her manufactures. We do not stop to inquire now how the balance of agricultural exchanges stands between the sections. The Northern farmer has his share of this trade in manufactures of which we are now speaking, and participates largely in its profits, and as largely in its losses and suspensions. It is enough that, without pretending to statistical accuracy, we show a market for our surplus manufactures in the South nine times larger than all the world besides affords us. The foreign exports of all the free States of every kind, do not average more than one hundred and twenty millions a year; their sales to the Southern States are more than twice that amount. The slave State trade is of as great value annually to the free States as that of the Union is to all Europe, Asia, and South America.

Is it any wonder that our prosperity and our labor decline twenty-five per cent, in present value, when so large a commerce as this is interrupted, and the commercial confidence of the parties is shaken?

We present the claims of trade as a motive to conciliation. . . .[8]

This was a voice from Philadelphia. Similar sentiments were more widely held and strongly expressed in the Ohio Valley of the Trans-Appalachian West where ties of kinship, proximity, and above all commerce, seemed to many to make peace imperative. For this no price was too high. The case was presented a few months prior to the outbreak of the war in an editorial, "Cincinnati and the Southern Troubles," published in The [*Columbus, Ohio*] Crisis. The Crisis *was published by Samuel Medary, who was to become an outstanding Peace Democrat.*

No great city in the West, and certainly no commercial point in Ohio, is so deeply and so fearfully affected by our sectional difficulties as Cincinnati. She has been termed the "Queen City," but if her river and Southern trade is cut off, she can be the "Queen City" no longer. Her every interest is identified with the Southern trade, and such has been the fact since the first house was built within her corporate limits.

When we first saw the city it contained a population of about 25,000, all told. She now numbers near 200,000, with 500,000 more outside her city government, identified with her trade and dependent upon her thrift and commercial prosperity. The disturbing elements now afflicting the country come home to her in a fearful volume. If these troubles are prosecuted to a bloody issue, Cincinnati will be converted into a camp of soldiers instead of a busy mart of peace and prosperous commerce. With the Ohio river only dividing her from a hostile foe, she will be exposed to the shell and the ball from the overlooking hills beyond. Fear and absolute safety would compel thousands to remove to a more distant point, and give the city up to camp life and all the ills that follow. And for what are we to be driven to this desolate condition? Can any one answer?

As long as peace is preserved we have everything to hope; when that is discarded all hope of restoration of order and a return to duty as good citizens is lost, in all reasonable calculation, for ever.

Cincinnati cannot live as a border town. Her prosperity is the result of peaceful avocations; her pride is in her sound commercial transactions, her name is honored by the arts and sciences, her hopes are in her own uninterrupted course of self-reliance. And why should all these be disturbed? The very tide of trade and commerce will bind the river cities together. "Those whom God has joined together let no man put asunder." The law of communion will do more in a very brief period to restore fellowship, force trade into its legitimate channels, open a correspondence of business and kindly sentiments, test the folly of attempting to do without each other, than all the armies. . . .

. . . If war and blood and desolation must come, let them come in their own good time, when all else fails, when our crimes are sufficiently great for the Ruler of all things to give us over to self destruction, and thus hustle us out of the family of nations as unfit to remain. . . .[9]

There was action as well as talk. In early December, Union-saving committees were appointed in both Houses of Congress. To that of the Senate, Senator John J. Crittenden of Kentucky offered five unamendable amendments to the Constitution and four resolutions. One of the latter, a recommendation for more effective enforcement of the African slave trade ban, was a sop to Northern antislavery feeling; the rest represented appeasement of the South. Its heart was the reestablishment of the old 36°30′ line with slavery to be protected in all territory south of it. The Senator defended his proposal.

. . . Mr. President, great dangers surround us. The Union of these States is dear to the people of the United States. The long experience of its blessings, the mighty hopes of the future, have made it dear to the hearts of the American people. What ever politicians may say; whatever of dissension may, in the heat of party politics, be created among our people, when you come down to the question of the existence of the Constitution, that is a question beyond all party politics; that is a question of life and death. The Constitution and the Union are the life of this great people—yes, sir, the life of life. We all desire to preserve them, North and South; that is the universal desire. But some of the southern States smarting under what they conceive to be aggressions of their northern brethren and of the northern States, are not contented to continue this Union, and are taking steps, formidable steps, towards a dissolution of the Union, and towards the anarchy and bloodshed, I fear, that are to follow. I say, sir, we are in the presence of great events. We must elevate ourselves to the level of the great occasion. No party warfare about mere party questions or party measures ought now to engage our attention. They are left behind; they are as dust in the balance. The life, the existence of our country, of our Union, is the mighty question; and we must elevate ourselves to all those considerations which belong to this high subject.

. . . . .

History is to record us. Is it to record that when the destruction of the Union was imminent; when we saw it tottering to its fall; when we saw brothers arming their hands for hostility with one another, we stood quarreling about points of party politics; about questions which we attempted to sanctify and to consecrate by appealing to our conscience as the source of them? Are we to allow such fearful catastrophies to occur while we stand trifling away our time? While we stand thus, showing our inferiority to the great and mighty dead, showing our inferiority to the high positions which we occupy, the country may be destroyed and ruined; and to the amazement of all the world, the great Republic may fall prostrate and in ruins, carrying with it the very hope of that liberty which we have heretofore enjoyed; carrying with it, in place of the peace we have enjoyed, nothing but revolution and havoc and anarchy. . . . Can it be that our name is to rest in history with this everlasting stigma and blot upon it?

Sir, I wish to God it was in my power to preserve this Union by renouncing or agreeing to give up every conscientious and other opinion. I might not be able to discard it from my mind; I am under no obligation to do that. I may retain the opinion, but if I can do so great a good as to preserve my country and give it peace, and its institutions and its Union stability, I will forego any action upon my opinions. Well now, my friends (addressing the Republican Senators), that is all that is asked of you. Consider it well, and I do not distrust the result. As to the rest of this body, the gentlemen from the South, I would say to them, can you ask more than this? Are you bent on revolution, bent on disunion? God forbid it. I cannot believe that such madness possesses the American people. . . .[10]

The Crittenden proposals were acceptable to border state members of the committee, but Republicans, in close liaison with Lincoln, rejected it. To accept would have been to repudiate their party platform and quite possibly kill the party in its infancy.

On January 14, Thomas Corwin of Ohio offered an amendment to the Crittenden proposals.

"No amendment shall be made to the Constitution which will authorize or give to Congress the power to abolish or interfere, within any State, with the domestic institutions thereof, including that of persons held to labor or service by the laws of said State."

Inasmuch as the Republican party platform had pledged that slavery in the states (as opposed to the territories) should not be interfered with, the Corwin amendment was acceptable to both sides. It was passed by Congress and sent to the states. War intervened before it could be acted upon. Even if it had been ratified by the necessary three-fourths of the states, it would have settled nothing since it dealt with only the one area upon which there was already substantial agreement, offering nothing in regard to the issues that were tearing the nation apart.

The last great effort at compromise was the Border States Peace Convention which assembled in Washington on February 4, the very day that the Montgomery convention was assembling to create the

Confederacy. Delegates from twenty-one states attended, but the lower South was not represented. Neither were Michigan, Wisconsin, Minnesota, California, and Oregon, while other Northern states, such as Massachusetts, sent "stiff-backed men," opposed to compromise. Under such circumstances it is not strange that the conference failed. It adjourned February 27, after sending to Congress proposals resembling the Crittenden resolutions. These were rejected by the Republicans.

One other Northern voice raised in behalf of conciliation needs to be noted. It represented the view of conservative Republicans and those Democrats who were later to give wholehearted support to the Northern war effort. It was that of Senator William H. Seward of New York. Until Lincoln's nomination for the presidency the previous summer, Seward had been the Republicans' best known and most distinguished leader. The national party convention had rejected him as its nominee in part because he was more radical on the slavery issue than Lincoln. But in a speech delivered in the Senate on January 12, 1861, he was conciliatory—at least too conciliatory to please radical Republicans, some of whom, such as Ben Wade, Zack Chandler, and Lyman Trumbull, were already accepting coercion as an effective means of saving the Union and the Republican party. There was little ground for such disapproval. Seward urged his fellow Republicans to put national above party interest; he declared himself ready to meet "violence with the right hand of peace." But he would "surrender no principle," and the proposals he offered as a basis for conciliation were those already rejected by Southern secessionists. In a long speech he said in part:

. . . The Union cannot be saved by mutual criminations concerning our respective share of responsibility for the present evils. He whose conscience acquits him will naturally be slow to accuse others whose cooperation he needs. History only can adjust the great account.

A continuance of the debate on the constitutional power of Congress over the subject of slavery in the Territories will not save the Union. The opinions of parties and sections on that question have become dogmatical, and it is this circumstance that has produced the existing alienation. A truce, at least during the debate on the Union, is essential to reconciliation.

The Union cannot be saved by proving that secession is illegal or unconstitutional. Persons bent on that fearful step will not stand long enough on forms of law to be dislodged; and loyal men do not need such narrow ground to stand upon.

I fear that little more will be gained from discussing the right of the Federal Government to coerce seceding States into obedience. If disunion is to go on, this question will give place to the more practical one, whether many seceding States have a right to coerce the remaining members to acquiesce in a dissolution.

I dread, as in my innermost soul I abhor, civil war. I do not know what the Union would be worth if saved by the use of the sword. Yet, for all this, I do not agree with those who, with a desire to avert that great calamity, advise a conventional or unopposed separation, with a view to what they call a reconstruction. It is enough for me, first, that in this plan, destruction goes before reconstruction; and secondly, that the strength of the vase in which the hopes of the nation are held consists chiefly in its remaining unbroken.

Congressional compromises are not likely to save the Union. I know, indeed, that tradition favors this form of remedy. But it is essential to its success, in any case, that there be found a preponderating mass of citizens, so far neutral on the issue which separates parties, that they can intervene, strike down clashing weapons, and compel an accommodation. Moderate concessions are not customarily asked by a force with its guns in battery; nor are liberal concessions apt to be given by an opposing force not less confident of its own right and its own strength. I think, also, that there is a prevailing conviction that legislative compromises which sacrifice honestly cherished principles, while they anticipate future exigencies, even if they do not assume extra-constitutional powers, are less sure to avert imminent evils than they are certain to produce ultimately even greater dangers.

Indeed, Mr. President, I think it will be wise to discard two prevalent ideas or prejudices, namely: first, that the Union is to be saved by somebody in particular; and secondly, that it is to be saved by some cunning and insincere compact of pacification. If I remember rightly, I said something like this so long ago as 1850, and afterwards in 1854.

. . . . . .

Congress, in the present case, ought not to be impassive. It ought, if it can, to redress any real grievances of the offended States, and then it ought to supply the President with all the means necessary to maintain the Union in the full exhibition and discreet exercise of its authority. Beyond this, with the proper activity on the part of the Executive, the responsibility of saving this Union belongs to the people, and they are abundantly competent to discharge it.

. . . . . .

Beyond a doubt, Union is vitally important to the Republican citizens of the United States; but it is just as important to the whole people. Republicanism and the Union are, therefore, not controvertible terms. Republicanism is subordinate to Union, as everything else is and ought to be—Republicanism, Democracy and every other political name and thing; all are subordinate—and they ought to disappear in the presence of the great question of Union. So far as I am concerned, it shall be so; it should be so if the question were sure to be tried as it ought only to be determined, by the peaceful ordeal of the ballot. It shall be so all the more since there is on one side preparedness to refer it to the arbitrament of civil war. I have such faith in this republican system of ours, that there is no political good which I desire that I am not content to seek through its peaceful forms of administration without invoking revolutionary action. If others shall invoke that form of action to oppose and overthrow Government, they shall not, so far as it depends on me, have the excuse that I obstinately left myself to be misunderstood. In such a case I can afford to meet prejudice with conciliation, exaction with concession which surrenders no principle, and violence with the right hand of peace. Therefore, sir, so far as the abstract question whether, by the Constitution of the United States, the bondsman, who is made such by the laws of a State, is still a man or only property, I answer that, within that State, its laws on that subject are supreme; that when he has escaped from that State into another, the Constitution regards him as a bondsman who may not, by any law or regulation of that State, be discharged from his service, but shall be delivered up, on claim, to the party to whom his service is due. While prudence and justice would combine in persuading you to modify the acts of Congress on that subject so as not to oblige private persons to assist in their execution, and to protect freemen from being, by abuse of the laws, carried into slavery, I agree that all laws of the States, whether free States or slave States, which relate to this class of persons, or any others recently coming from or resident in other States, and which laws contravene the Constitution of the United States, or any law of Congress passed in conformity thereto, ought to be repealed.

Secondly. Experience in public affairs has confirmed my opinion, that domestic slavery, existing in any State, is wisely left by the Constitution of the United States exclusively to the care, management, and disposition of that State; and if it were in my power, I would not alter the Constitution in that respect. If misapprehension of my position needs so strong a remedy, I am willing to vote for an amendment of the Constitution, declaring that it shall not, by any future amendment, be so altered as to confer on Congress a power to abolish or interfere with slavery in any State.

Thirdly. While I think that Congress has exclusive and sovereign authority to legislate on all subjects whatever, in the common Territories of the United States; and while I certainly shall never, directly or indirectly, give my vote to establish or sanction slavery in such Territories, or anywhere else in the world, yet the question what constitutional laws shall at any time be passed in regard to the Territories, is, like every other question, to be determined on practical grounds. I voted for enabling acts in the cases of Oregon, Minnesota, and Kansas, without being able to secure in them such provisions as I would have preferred; and yet I voted wisely. So now, I am well satisfied that, under existing circumstances, a happy and satisfactory solution of the difficulties in the remaining Territories would be obtained by similar laws, providing for their organization, if such organization were otherwise practicable. If, therefore, Kansas were admitted as a State, under the Wyandotte constitution, as I think she ought to be, and if the organic laws of all other Territories could be repealed, I could vote to authorize the organization and admission of two new States which should include them, reserving the right to effect subdivisions of them whenever necessary into several convenient States; but I do not find that such reservations could be constitutionally made. Without them, the ulterior embarrassments which would result from the hasty incorporation of States of such vast extent and various interests and character would outweigh all the immediate advantages of such a measure. But if the measure were practicable, I should prefer a different course, namely: when the eccentric movements of secession and disunion shall have ended, in whatever form that end may come, and the angry excitements of the hour shall have subsided, and calmness once more shall have resumed its accustomed sway over the public mind, then, and not until then—one, two or three years hence—I should cheerfully advise a convention of the people, to be assembled in pursuance of the Constitution, to consider and decide whether any and what amendments of the organic national law ought to be made. . . .

Fourthly. I hold myself ready now, as always heretofore, to vote for any properly-guarded laws which shall be deemed necessary to prevent mutual invasions of States by citizens of other States, and punish those who shall aid and abet them.

Fifthly. . . . I remain of the opinion that physical bonds, such as highways, railroads, rivers, and canals, are vastly more powerful for holding civil communities together than any mere covenants, though written on parchment or engraved upon iron. I remain, therefore, constant in my purpose to secure, if possible, the construction of two Pacific railways, one of which shall connect the ports around the mouths of the Mississippi, and the other the towns on the Missouri and the Lakes, with the harbors on our western coast.

. . . I learned early from Jefferson, that in political affairs we cannot always do what seems to us absolutely best. . . . We must be content to lead when we can, and to follow when we cannot lead; and if we cannot at any time do for our country all the good that we would wish, we must be satisfied with doing for her all the good we can. . . .[11]

But even Seward's mild gesture toward conciliation was unacceptable to many, perhaps a majority, of Northerners. Their motives were mixed. Republican politicians regarded Lincoln's election as a mandate and were determined to carry out the party pledges in the interest of both the voters who elected them and their own and their party's political future. Merchants and manufacturers feared and were opposed to the emergence of an independent Confederacy dedicated to free trade and purchasing its manufactured goods from the workshops of Europe, or perhaps even developing its own industries. Ordinary citizens, and these were the most numerous, who envisaged no immediate impact on their lives as a consequence of secession were nevertheless united by conviction and emotion on two points—the Union must be preserved and anarchy must be avoided. At least among the 1,865,593 voters who cast their ballots for Lincoln in 1860, it is reasonable to assume that there were many who were determined there should be no further extension of slavery.

Thaddeus Stevens, congressman from Pennsylvania and destined to be the leader of congressional radicals, expressed the Northern extremists' fear of and opposition to compromise of any sort. In a letter to Salmon P. Chase dated February 3, 1861, he wrote:

I fear that the party will soon cease to exist. Mr. Seward's course has mortified and discouraged me. That coupled with the apostasy of [Simon] Cameron, who is his echo, seems to indicate that our platform and principles are to be sacrificed to peace. The belief that they are to be two of the cabinet (Seward certainly) makes all the mercenary (Legions) preach submission. Can we stand up against such a Prime Minister? Will Lincoln have nerve enough to resist? Will he have a cabinet who will resist? You may possibly view Mr. Seward's course differently from me. . . . I have but little hope that we shall be able to survive the next election. If when Mr. Lincoln comes into power, he should imitate Jackson and set vigorously about coercing disobedience, the people will admire and rally again to the republican standard. If he seeks to purchase peace by concessions, and ignoring platforms *a la mode* Seward, I shall give up the fight, being too old for another seven (or thirty) years war. . . .[12]

Ten days earlier John Jay, grandson of the jurist and statesman, an abolitionist and one of the founders of the Republican party, had written to Senator Charles Sumner:

. . . No surer political destruction ever awaited a northern representative than that which awaits every man in the Senate or the

House who devotes to Slavery the Territory of the American people, in the wretched hope of conciliating rebels who have gained a temporary advantage by the meanest treachery & theft. . . .[13]

Preston King, junior senator from New York, wrote at about the same time:

. . . I hope we shall get through here without compromise but nothing is certain and the present state of public affairs makes it more difficult to calculate on what will happen than usual. But there is an apparent firmness in the great body of our folks that is most gratifying and all we hear of Lincoln contributes to this steadiness. My faith is strong that our Country will go through this most dangerous passage and find firmer and safer foundations for her free institutions than they have ever had. *We are now encountering the single great danger which the original founders feared.* If we can once overcome the lawless giant which has so long ruled the Government and threatened liberty and the public peace we may hope for a return to the early policy of the whole Country which looked to the ultimate extinction of Slavery. We must do our whole duty, and have faith in the wise Providence that overrules the affairs of men and nations. I am happy in a faith that defies despair.[14]

Justin S. Morrill, later the author of the Morrill Land Grant Bill which favorably influenced the development of the Land Grant Colleges and Universities, was a congressman from Vermont. In December of 1860 he wrote to his wife:

You will see that I am on the great committee to save the Union but I do not think it can be saved and I shall on Monday decline to serve. . . . There can be no compromise short of an entire surrender of our convictions of right and wrong, and I do not propose to make that surrender. All that can be done will not satisfy the cotton states. Nothing short of legalizing and introducing slavery in the north would satisfy them. By making any offers of compromise we shall only incur disgrace at home and have our humble offerings rejected at last. I regret the facts but we must accept the truth that there is an "irrepressible conflict"—between our systems of civilization. I look for much suffering in all parts of the Union for the year to come. . . .[15]

Morrill was a member of the Congressional Committee of Thirty-Three which considered proposals to save the Union, but his personal opposition to compromise did not diminish. On February 18, 1861, in a speech in the House he said in part:

. . . Against the Government established by Washington, a rebellion, formidable in its proportions and portentous in its results, is even now buckling on its armor, and with vigorous diplomacy courting allies. . . .

Recognizing the fact that there appeared to be an organized plan to revolutionize and break up the Government, a conspiracy to blot out the Declaration of Independence and subvert the Constitution, I voted in favor of raising the committee of thirty-three, when it was proposed, in order to give those who represented that portion of our country loudest in their complaints an opportunity to be heard to the utmost latitude; and not because any real grievance was visible to me—always excepting that some men were about to go out of office, and others were about to come in. . . .

It is undeniably true that, if the late election had resulted in the defeat of Mr. Lincoln, no revolution would have been precipitated, and no new guarantees to slavery would have been required at our hands. But, while we have been victorious in the campaign, we are invited to submit to what would not even have been suggested had we been defeated; aye, and invited to submit to what nearly two-thirds of the popular vote of the Democratic party itself rejected. . . . Under these circumstances, the demand made is a humiliation to which no party can submit. . . . That verdict of the people cannot be reversed, except by the people themselves, four years hence. I trust it may never be reversed. . . . If the South did not mean to abide by the result—only on the principle of "heads I win, tails you lose"—they should not have courted the issue, nor made the appeal to the ballot-box. . . .

. . . Anything like compromise has never been possible for a moment. Compromises are under the ban of all parties, and to the advocates of secession, who mean revolution, more odious than to any other. . . .[16]

The West, too, was heard from, for although prior to the outbreak of the war the voice of appeasement was loud in the Ohio Valley, it was muted beyond the reaching fingers of the rivers. Few Southerners migrated to Michigan and Wisconsin; the commerce of these states with the South was a thin trickle compared to that of Ohio, Indiana and Illinois. So it is not surprising that their spokesman rejected compromise, or even that in their more belligerent moods they cried for blood.

Michigan's Senator Zachariah Chandler was such a spokesman. In a letter of February 11, 1861 he wrote to the state's governor, Austin Blair, that: "Some of the manufacturing States think a fight would be awful. Without a little blood-letting, this Union will not, in my estimation, be worth a rush." He expanded his views in a Senate speech which despite its bombast probably expressed the sentiments of a solid majority of his constituents.

This is not a question of compromise. It is a question whether we have or have not a government. If we have a government it is capable of making itself respected abroad and at home. If we have not a government, let this miserable rope of sand which purports to be a government perish, and I will shed no tears over its destruction. Sir, General Washington reasoned not so when the whiskey rebellion broke out in Pennsylvania; he called out the *posse comitatus* and enforced the laws. General Jackson reasoned not so when South Carolina in 1832 raised the black flag of rebellion; he said: "By the Eternal, I will hang them"; and he would have done it.

After these illustrious examples, we are told that six States have seceded, and the Union is broken up, and all we can do is to send commissioners to treat with traitors with arms in hands; treat with men who have fired upon your flag; treat with men who have seized your custom-houses, who have erected batteries upon your great navigable waters, and who now stand defying your authority! What will be the result of such a treaty? You would stand disgraced before the nations of the earth, your naval officers would be insulted by the Algerines, your bonds would not be worth the paper on which they are written, to-morrow. If you submitted to this degradation your government would stand upon a par with the governments of South America and the Central American States.

Sir, I will never submit to this degradation. If the right is conceded to any State to secede from the Union, without the consent of the other States, I am for immediate dissolution; and if the State which I have the honor in part to represent will not follow that advice, I, for one, upon my own responsibility and alone, will resign my seat in this body, and leave this government, so soon as I can prepare the small matters I shall have to arrange, *for emigration to some country where they have a government.* I would rather join the Comanches; *I will never live under a government that has not the power to enforce its laws.* . . . I see before me some of those men who have been fighting this corrupt organization (the Democratic party) for the last twenty years, who now turn about in dismay at the threatened disruption of the government. Why are they terror-stricken? Why do they not stand firm and denounce you as infamously connected with a plundered treasury instead of cowering before your threats? This thing has gone far enough . . . Sir, this Union is to stand; it will stand when your great-grandchildren and mine shall have grown gray—aye, when they shall have gone to their last account, and their great-grandchildren shall have grown gray. But the traitors who are to-day plotting against this Union are to die. I do not say, literally, that they are all to die personally and absolutely; but they are soon to pass from the stage, and better and purer men are to take their places. God grant that that consummation, "so devoutly to be wished," may be early accomplished! . . .

For the Union-loving men of this nation, for the true patriots of the land, there is no reasonable concession that I would not most cheerfully make: but for those men who profess to be Union men and who are Union men with an "if"; who will take all the concessions we will give them—all that they demand—and then turn about and say "your Union is dissolved," I have no respect; and for them I will do nothing. For the men who love this Union, who are prepared to march to the support of the Union, who will stand up in defense of the old flag under which their fathers fought and gloriously triumphed, I have not only the most profound respect, but to their demands I can scarce conceive anything that I would not yield. But, sir, when traitorous States come here and say, unless you yield this or that established principle or right, we will dissolve the Union, I would answer in brief words—no concession, no compromise; aye, give us strife even to blood before yielding to the demands of traitorous insolence.[17]

On February 26, 1861, a Confederate Statute, passed by the Provisional Congress, repealed the federal laws which excluded foreign vessels from the American coasting trade. Lorenzo Sherwood, a New York observer of the commercial scene saw this as a disaster to Northern commerce. He commented:

Suppose one part of the union to become foreign to the other—a vessel coming from Europe to this port with foreign goods—from this [port] South [ward] to some port in the Southern confederacy with a mixed cargo of domestic & debenture goods—from thence to Europe with cotton. This would bring from Europe a competing force that under its arrangements would nearly impoverish our coasting trade. Then again, European vessels could go from Southern ports to ports on the Pacific with entire facility. I should much fear this foreign competition in connection with that exasperated feeling, South, that would not scruple to break down either the commerce or mechanism of the country. . . .[18]

Even more serious than the loss of the Yankee monopoly in the coasting trade was the threatened loss of revenue from import duties. This would lead to nothing less than financial disaster. In an editorial entitled "Self Protection," a Chicago Tribune *writer warned:*

The revenue rights of the Government cannot be legally impaired or destroyed by the usurpation of the insurgents. The imports are to the Government what food is to the human being. It has practically no other means of existing. Should it resort to direct taxation after allowing the rebels to absorb the revenue from duties, resistance and revolution would instantly take place in all the loyal States, and the Administration would be quickly hurled from power, and another would replace it instructed by the people to collect imports in the southern as well as northern ports.

The national existence of the Government depends upon the collection of the imports and consequently that is its first and highest duty. To preserve peace by permitting a usurper to seize its revenues is to make war on itself, is to connive at robbery of the loyal citizens, is to be guilty of treason against the sacred trusts reposed in its hands by the people; is to commit suicide and end its existence with its own hands. When a government declines to collect its revenues it begins to die as a man begins to die when he refuses to eat. The sort of 'peace' which will be obtained by the non-collection of Federal duties in Southern ports, will be the peace of the grave yard . . . ; if Lincoln's administration fails to collect the revenue throughout the whole Union, it will cease to be. Jeff. Davis' government will collect them and reign in its stead. The whole matter resolves itself into the simple question of which of these governments shall collect the revenues in the Southern ports. The one that doesn't, dies. The one that does, rules. . . .[19]

The opposition to compromise deriving primarily from economic interest was not motivated solely by the desire merely to preserve the status quo. It stemmed in part from a determination to expand the North's economy into the West and even the South. Those holding this view did not oppose slavery because it would spread into the North, but rather because it checked the spread of free labor. A dynamic free labor system thus was challenging the moribund slave-based economy, and in this sense the North rather than the South was the aggressor. This attitude is manifest in a speech prepared for delivery in Congress by Elijah Babbitt, a representative from Pennsylvania.

. . . I have shown that there is nothing in the allegation, that by excluding slavery from the Territories we would establish an inequality of rights between the North and the South. But on the other hand, I say, that the southern design to Africanize the Territories by forcing slavery into them, is as effectually to exclude the free laborers of the North from them as would be a provision in the Constitution that they should never go there; because slave labor is found to degrade the free laborer in his social position, wherever the two exist together and slave laborers are anywise numerous; and because freemen cannot enjoy life and expand in mind and improve their knowledge of men and things without an enlarged and liberal freedom of speech and of the press. . . .

Now, the northern free laborer cannot, at all times, keep a lock on his mind, a bridle in his mouth, and fetters on his pen. He must think and speak and write what he thinks with freedom, and therefore cannot live in a slave State with the terrors of lynch law constantly in his view. And, therefore, to admit slavery into the Territories is to exclude the white free laborer from them. And why should our southern brethren desire to do this? With about one third of the population, they have about two thirds of the area of the organized States of this Union. And when we take into consideration the superior fertility of its soil, and mildness of its climate, it is, I doubt not, capable of sustaining a population at least fourfold more numerous than that which the present area of the free States can support. Indeed, I have heard a distinguished member of Congress from the South aver, that the area of the organized slave States was capable, in addition to its present population, of sustaining the entire population of Europe; and I believe it is so. . . . But free labor has not room enough; it needs more scope and breadth. Why then, oh, why, will our southern brethren try to shut us in on every side? Why, when they now have so much more land than they can possibly cultivate for two centuries to come, will they not allow to the free laborer a small sunny spot south of 36°30′, where, if the fancy takes him, he may literally sit beneath his own vine and fig tree, where the fig tree can grow? Why wish to press him northward, beyond the line of annual six months' snows and ice? The allegation that a white man cannot labor in the South is a flimsy, false pretense, invented by lazy white men as an excuse for whipping labor out of the naturally still more indolent negro. White men labor and thrive in southern Italy, Greece, and Spain—where flourish the fig and the orange—where the flowers ever bloom; where, though in not as low a southern latitude, the climate and productions are far more southern than those of our most southern Territory. The hardy American descendant of the Anglo-Saxon can live and labor wherever mortal man, of any race, can do so. And thousands of them have lived and labored in every southern State of the Union. And it is the blight of slavery, and not of the climate, that drives them thence. . . .

My district, Mr. Speaker, is located in northwestern Pennsylvania, on the northern frontier of the Union. Thirty miles of lake separates it from Queen Victoria's Canadian domain. If we start from this frontier and travel south, about one hundred and fifty miles will bring us to the land of the negro slave. Still moving south, for a thousand miles, bating some mountain region, we will pass over a wide land, fertile and sunny, but sparsely populated, and not cultivated up to one twentieth part of its capacity for production; still the land of the negro slave. Stretching far, far away, on our right and on our left, as we pass on, is still the mild climate, the fertile soil, and thinly populated land of the slave. Now, let us return. We come to the one hundred and fifty miles allowed to the free laborer, looking as though it was squeezed back against the Canadian frontier. Let us pass over it. We find it densely populated, mainly with a rural people. Thickly planted, each on its own few acres, we behold the unpretentious but neat and comfortable, dwellings of free laboring farmers, with as many tradesmen, manufacturers, and mechanics, mostly located in the villages, as the wants of the region require. And here we behold the free laboring man—the peer of every other man—proudly and joyously earning his bread by the sweat of his face. In willing obedience to the first command of God to man, he is also multiplying. But his land will not expand in proportion; and, therefore, he wants more room whereon to labor. His arm is strong, his will is good, to guide the plow, to ply the hoe, to herd his flocks, to wield the hammer, drive the saw, or push the plane; but he wants more room and must have it. The young mother, as she presses to her bosom her first-born son, the pride of her eyes and joy of her heart, knows that, like all his fathers before him, he is born to labor, and, like them, will labor, with a strong arm and glad heart. But she knows there is not room for his labor in the land of his birth. Sadly but hopefully she looks to the Territories of the West and Southwest, and says, in her heart, there is a region provided by God for my son to labor in, where there is room enough. . . . She would despise herself for being the means, in the hand of God, of bringing him into the world if she thought he would have to labor beside the lash-driven slave, with a lock upon his lips. She will never agree, if truckling men would, that these Territories shall be covered and cursed with the blight of African slavery. Does it not, I ask, better comport with truth, to say that free labor is aggressed upon rather than that it is aggressive? . . .[20]

Another point of view, economic in origin and found most frequently in the Southern section of the "old Northwest," may be best expressed as "a curse on both your houses."

Hamilton Smith was a prominent businessman of Cannelton, a

Union Mass Meeting in Union Square, April 20, 1861

town on the Ohio River in southern Indiana. He was a Democrat in politics but his anger and frustration were nonpartisan. A letter written in December 1860, shows desperation inspired by the fear of the disintegration of the Union and subsequent anarchy.

I see no sign of concession or compromise between the north & south. God seems to have afflicted the extremists on both sides with incurable madness & we of the middle states are in a state of stupid apathy. S[outh] Car[olina] & Mass[achusetts] are to beat the gongs & sound the trumpets, far in the rear & out of danger, while we do the fighting. In the meantime our agriculture suffers, our commerce languishes & our manufactures are destroyed. . . . We in Indiana are getting ready to set up for ourselves when the smash comes. We won't tie ourselves to the tail of the Cotton States & we won't subscribe to the creeds manufactured in The Tremont Temple & we won't agree to be governed by the "Albany Regency."[21]

Finally there was the voice of Abraham Lincoln. On March 4, 1861, it did not express the convictions of the whole North, for the North was divided, but even then it was that of the majority of the people who had elected him to the presidency. His political genius is nowhere more manifest than in his patient, and ultimately successful, effort to overcome dissension and unify an ever increasing majority behind the principles expressed in his first inaugural address. The central theme was the preservation of the Union.

. . . Apprehension seems to exist among the people of the Southern States, that by the accession of a Republican Administration, their property, and their peace, and personal security, are to be endangered. There has never been any reasonable cause for such apprehension. Indeed, the most ample evidence to the contrary has all the while existed, and been open to their inspection. It is found in nearly all the published speeches of him who now addresses you. I do but quote from one of those speeches when I declare that "I have no purpose, directly or indirectly, to interfere with the institution of slavery in the States where it exists. I believe I have no lawful right to do so, and have no inclination to do so." Those who nominated and elected me did so with full knowledge that I had made this, and many similar declarations, and had never recanted them. And more than this, they placed in the platform, for my acceptance, and as a law to themselves, and to me, the clear and emphatic resolution which I now read:

"*Resolved,* That the maintenance inviolate of the rights of the States, and especially the right of each State to order and control its own domestic institutions according to its own judgment exclusively, is essential to that balance of power on which the perfection and endurance of our political fabric depend; and we denounce the lawless invasion by armed force of the soil of any State or Territory, no matter under what pretext, as among the gravest of crimes."

I now reiterate these sentiments: and in doing so, I only press upon the public attention the most conclusive evidence of which the case is susceptible, that the property, peace and security of no section are to be in anywise endangered by the now incoming Administration. I add too, that all the protection which, consistently with the Constitution and the laws, can be given, will be cheerfully given to all the States when lawfully demanded, for whatever cause—as cheerfully to one section, as to another.

. . . . .

It is seventy-two years since the first inauguration of a President under our national Constitution. During that period fifteen different and greatly distinguished citizens, have, in succession, administered the executive branch of the government. They have conducted it through many perils; and, generally, with great success. Yet, with all this scope for precedent, I now enter upon the same task for the brief constitutional term of four years, under great and peculiar difficulty. A disruption of the Federal Union heretofore only menaced, is now formidably attempted.

I hold, that in contemplation of universal law, and of the Constitution, the Union of these States is perpetual. Perpetuity is implied, if not expressed, in the fundamental law of all national governments. It is safe to assert that no government proper, ever had a provision in its organic law for its own termination. Continue to execute all the express provisions of our national Constitution, and the Union will endure forever—it being impossible to destroy it, except by some action not provided for in the instrument itself.

II

Citizens as Soldiers

STATESMEN, editors, and other elected or self-appointed spokesmen of the people might debate the issues of war and peace, but when the talking was done with and war was the verdict, the future of the Union rested with the Army of the North.

It was a citizens' army. At the beginning of the war the regulars consisted of 1,098 officers and 15,304 enlisted men. Of these, slightly over one third of the former and almost nine per cent of the latter were absent. Presumably most of these would fight for the Confederacy. Thus, in April 1861, 14,657 soldiers were present and available for duty. Four years later, in April 1865, the aggregate strength of the Army of the North was 1,052,038 fighting men. Fighting men, but not professionally trained warriors, they came from the whole body of the citizenry, and it was they who not only fought and won the war but also paid the price of victory. Union soldiers killed in action numbered 359,528. Of these, 353,730 were volunteers. For it was not only a citizens' army, it was a volunteer army. True, there was a draft, diluted by commutation, but it contributed only 46,347 men. The remainder volunteered. Most of them accepted bounty payments for their services, but their motives generally were those that have sent men to war throughout history. Duty, patriotism, the quest for glory or adventure, frustration as a civilian, devotion to a cause —singly or in combination—called men to arms. And if the call was not loud enough, shame, the fear of being branded a coward or lacking in love of the Union, added its nagging voice to prick the laggard to the recruiting office.

"THE VOLUNTEER'S WIFE TO HER HUSBAND."

Don't stop a moment to think, John,
  Your country calls—then go;
Don't think of me or the children, John,
  I'll care for them, you know.
Leave the corn upon the stalks, John,
  Potatoes on the hill,
And the pumpkins on the vines, John—
  I'll gather them with a will.
But take your gun and go, John,
  Take your gun and go,
For Ruth can drive the oxen, John,
  And I can use the hoe.

I've heard my grandsire tell, John,
  (He fought at Bunker Hill,)
How he counted all his life and wealth
  His country's offering still.
Shall we shame the brave old blood, John,
  That flowed on Monmouth plain?
No! take your gun and go, John,
  If you ne'er return again.
Then take your gun and go, John,
  Take your gun and go,
For Ruth can drive the oxen, John,
  And I can use the hoe.[1]

. . . . .

The "Volunteer's Wife" as a poet is hardly memorable, but she does express sentiments that pervaded much of the North at the outbreak of the war. Ulysses S. Grant recalls in his Memoirs *a meeting in Galena, Illinois.*

As soon as the news of the call for volunteers reached Galena, posters were stuck up calling for a meeting of the citizens at the court-house in the evening. Business ceased entirely; all was excitement; for a time there were no party distinctions; all were Union

"He Shouldn't Go to the Horrid War, Away from his 'Wifey, Tifey.'
He Shall Have a Petticoat and a Broom, and Stay at Home."

men, determined to avenge the insult to the national flag. In the evening the court-house was packed. Although a comparative stranger I was called upon to preside; the sole reason, possibly, was that I had been in the army and had seen service. With much embarrassment and some prompting I made out to announce the object of the meeting. Speeches were in order, but it is doubtful whether it would have been safe just then to make other than patriotic ones. There was probably no one in the house, however, who felt like making any other. The two principal speeches were by B. B. Howard, the postmaster and a Breckenridge Democrat at the November election the fall before, and John A. Rawlins, an elector on the Douglas ticket. E. B. Washburne, with whom I was not acquainted at that time, came in after the meeting had been organized and expressed, I understood afterwards, a little surprise that Galena could not furnish a presiding officer for such an occasion without taking a stranger. He came forward and was introduced, and made a speech appealing to the patriotism of the meeting.

After the speaking was over volunteers were called for to form a company. The quota of Illinois had been fixed at six regiments; and it was supposed that one company would be as much as would be accepted from Galena. The company was raised and the officers and non-commissioned officers elected before the meeting adjourned. I declined the captaincy before the balloting, but announced that I would aid the company in every way I could and would be found in the service in some position if there should be a war. I never went into our leather store after that meeting, to put up a package or do other business.

The ladies of Galena were quite as patriotic as the men. They could not enlist, but they conceived the idea of sending their first company to the field uniformed. They came to me to get a description of the United States uniform for infantry; subscribed and bought the material; procured tailors to cut out the garments, and the ladies made them up. In a few days the company was in uniform and ready to report to the State capital for assignment. The men all turned out the morning after their enlistment, and I took charge, divided them into squads and superintended their drill. When they were ready to go to Springfield I went with them and remained there until they were assigned to a regiment.

There were so many more volunteers than had been called for that the question whom to accept was quite embarrassing to the governor, Richard Yates. The legislature was in session at the time, however, and came to his relief. A law was enacted authorizing the governor to accept the services of ten additional regiments, one from each congressional district, for one month, to be paid by the State, but pledged to go into the service of the United States if there should be a further call during their term. Even with this relief the governor was still very much embarrassed. Before the war was over he was like the President when he was taken with the varioloid: "at last he had something he could give to all who wanted it."

In time the Galena company was mustered into the United States service, forming a part of the 11th Illinois volunteer infantry. . . .[2]

The Galena meeting was typical of hundreds of others being held in village, town, and city. The spirit of war prevailed throughout the country. William Howard Russell, famous war correspondent of the London Times, *witnessed its effects in New York City.*

. . . At about nine A.M., the train reached New York . . . and . . . the first thing which struck me was the changed aspect of the streets. Instead of peaceful citizens, men in military uniforms thronged the pathways, and such multitudes of United States' flags floated from the windows and roofs of the houses as to convey the impression that this was a great holiday festival. . . . Fully a third of the people carried arms, and were dressed in some kind of martial garb.

The walls are covered with placards from military companies offering inducements to recruits. An outburst of military tailors has taken place in the streets; shops are devoted to militia equipments; rifles, pistols, swords, plumes, long boots, saddles, bridles, camp beds, canteens, tents, knapsacks, have usurped the place of the ordinary articles of traffic. Pictures and engravings—bad, and very bad—of the "battles" of Big Bethel and Vienna, full of furious charges, smoke and dismembered bodies, have driven the French prints out of the windows. Innumerable "General Scotts" glower at you from every turn, making the General look wiser than he or any man ever was. Ellsworths in almost equal proportion, Grebles and Winthrops—the Union martyrs—and Tompkins, the temporary hero of Fairfax courthouse. . . .

What would become of all these pseudo-Zouaves who have come out like an eruption over the States, and are in no respect, not even in their baggy breeches, like their great originals, if this war were not to go on? . . .

They are overrunning society, and the streets here, and the dress which becomes the broad-chested, stumpy, short-legged Celt, who seems specially intended for it, is singularly unbecoming to the tall and slightly-built American. Songs "On to glory," "Our country," new versions of "Hail Columbia," which certainly cannot be considered by even American complacency a "happy land" when its inhabitants are preparing to cut each other's throats; of the "star-spangled banner," are displayed in booksellers' and music-shop windows, and patriotic sentences emblazoned on flags float from many houses. The ridiculous habit of dressing up children and young people up to ten and twelve years of age as Zouaves and vivandières has been caught up by the old people, and Mars would die with laughter if he saw some of the abdominous, bespectacled light infantry men who are hobbling along the pavement. . . .

I was desirous of learning how far the tone of conversation "in the city" had altered, and soon after breakfast I went down Broadway to Pine Street and Wall Street. The street in all its length was most draped with flags—the warlike character of the shops was intensified. In front of one shop window there was a large crowd gazing with interest at some object which I at last succeeded in feasting my eyes upon. A grey cap with a tinsel badge in front, and the cloth stained with blood was displayed with the words, "Cap of Secession officer killed in action." On my way I observed another crowd of women, some with children in their arms standing in front of a large house and gazing up earnestly and angrily at the windows. I found they were wives, mothers, and sisters, and daughters of volunteers who had gone off and left them destitute. . . .[3]

From Ohio, Governor William Dennison reported to the War Department a surge of war spirit so ardent that he believed the morale of the people would be adversely affected were it checked.

Owing to an unavoidable confusion in the first hurry and enthusiasm of the movement of our people in Ohio in defense of the Government, I find that I have already accepted, and have in camp, or ready to march instantly to it, a larger force than the thirteen regiments named as the contingent of Ohio under the late requisition of the President. Indeed, without seriously repressing the ardor of the people, I can hardly stop short of twenty regiments.

. . . . .

Let me know what I may expect in regard to this subject, and if the number of regiments is increased, let me know also what increase it will make in the number of general officers.

In the meantime I will let the organization be made to cover the twenty regiments, and have them make all the progress in drill they can. I need not impress upon you the demoralizing results of disbanding the surplus regiments. . . .[4]

New York City, later to be the scene of the draft riots, furnished its full quota of volunteers and its full share of enthusiasm. The New York Tribune *of April 24, 1861, described the departure of the the city's 69th Regiment, "composed entirely of Irishmen."*

. . . At an early hour the entire street was taken possession of by the regiment and its friends, and the distribution of muskets, blankets, etc., commenced. In front of Col. Corcoran's dwelling, No. 5 Prince street, a large truck, loaded with blankets, was stationed, and the recruits were required to file by this truck one by one. The rush at this point was perfectly tremendous, so eager were the men to obtain their equipments. The Captain of each company was stationed on the vehicle; and here the acceptance or rejection of the recruits occurred. . . . Passing the blanket wagon, where a blanket was thrown [to] the accepted ones, they were passed to another man, who seized their head covering and crowned them with the regimental cap.

Still another individual placed a musket in their hands, while others furnished them with a tin plate, knife, fork, and tin cup. It was not until 2 o'clock in the afternoon that all the men were equipped, after which the companies were formed, and, accompanied by the enthusiastic crowd, marched to Great Jones streeet, from which point the regiment were [*sic*] to start. For several hours there had been an assemblage of men, women and children in Broadway, mostly Irish, which had effectually driven every vehicle from that thoroughfare. Housetops and windows were crowded with enthusiastic women, who waved their handkerchiefs incessantly to the crowd beneath. Several Irish civic societies, comprising about 2,000 persons, with waving banners—the harp of Erin kissing the stars and stripes—had formed in procession in Broadway, as an escort, and patiently waited for the regiment to move.

About 3 o'clock the order to march was received, and the entire procession, civic and military, moved down Broadway. The march was a perfect triumph for the Irish citizens, vindicating their loyalty and patriotism in a most substantial manner. Col. Corcoran, who arose from a bed of sickness to accompany his regiment, was nearly killed by kindness. He occupied a carriage with one or two friends, and it became necessary for the police to protect him from the crowd which pressed upon him from all sides.

When the procession arrived at Pier No. 4 North River, where the James Adger was waiting to receive them, an attempt was made to shut off the crowd and prevent their passing the gates, but the efforts of the police were unavailing. The throng pressed in, and soon the pier was a scene of the utmost confusion. The soldiers were forced from the ranks, and speedily becoming identified with the crowd had to fight their way to the steamer's gang-plank. For at least an hour the rush of soldiers and citizens toward the steamer, was terrific. Patriotic Irishmen were determined to bid their friends good-bye, and in their efforts to do so were knocked down and trampled under foot, kicked, bayoneted and otherwise maltreated; but they heeded it not. Regaining their feet with a "hurrah for the 69th" they again entered upon the contest. Several soldiers were served in the same manner, others lost their muskets or caps in the scramble; but all eventually got on board alive.

At 6½ o'clock the Adger steamed away from the dock amid the most uproarious cheering. If the friends of the Jeff. Davis Government ever reckoned upon any assistance from the Irish population of the North, the display of yesterday must convince them that they were mistaken. The harp of Erin floats beside the Stars and Stripes in perfect union, and will do so throughout the present struggle. If more troops are needed by the Government the Irish of this city will furnish five times the number they already have done. . . .[5]

The towns and villages of the West did not lag behind Eastern cities in volunteering citizen soldiers. The Prairie Du Chien Courier *reported on the raising of troops in Wisconsin.*

APRIL 20TH, 1861.

An impromptu Union Meeting was gathered up this evening at Union Hall, attended by the citizens *en masse.*

Rev. A. Brunson was called to the Chair, and O. B. Thomas chosen Secretary.

The Chairman stated the object of the meeting to be an expression of the people upon the present alarming condition of the country, closing with an eloquent and stirring appeal to support the Government.

D. H. Johnson, John Lawler, O. B. Thomas, J. H. Greene, Rufus King, Wm. D. Merrell, and many other gentlemen addressed the meeting, urging the people, in forcible and eloquent terms, to support the Government, the Constitution and the Flag of the Union, without distinction of party.

On motion, the following resolutions were unanimously adopted:

1st. *Resolved.* That in the day of peril to our Government, we will stand by it with unflinching firmness, and cheerfully bear any burthen that may be necessary to carry our Government triumphantly through this contest with treason.

2d. *Resolved.* That Messrs. Partridge, Fonda and Hooe be appointed to organize a volunteer company.

3d. *Resolved.* That a committee of five be appointed for the purpose of soliciting subscriptions, to be used in defraying the expenses of organizing said company, and that the subscription paper be opened immediately.

Messrs. Fay, Beach, Thomas, Parish and Brower were appointed such committee and fully authorized to raise and expend subscriptions.

The song of the "Star Spangled Banner" was sung by Messrs. Jackson, Lester, Coval and Batchelder, with great effect.—Three cheers were given for the Stars and Stripes.

An Enlistment Roll and also a subscription paper was opened, both of which commenced rapidly filling up. Those gentlemen who were so situated that it was impossible for them to volunteer, made (many of them) munificent donations; among whom may be mentioned John Lawler, P. Dorr, Horace Beach and T. L. Brower, and many with promptness placed their names on the volunteer roll. Great enthusiasm and determination to support the Government prevailed, without regard to party.

APRIL 25, 1861.

Last Friday evening, after only an hour's notice, Union Hall was crowded with the most enthusiastic audience ever assembled in Prairie du Chien. It was composed of the most substantial citizens of this vicinity, representing every class and every interest, every opinion and every party. They all seemed to be fully aroused to the importance of the events now transpiring, and had met together with one will to counsel and hear the suggestions of patriotic and practical men. Several speakers, including the venerable Chairman, spoke to the people calmly, deliberately, and determinedly, but without rashness. The fact of a general CIVIL WAR being already commenced, was freely discussed and fearlessly confronted. The only sentiment of all was a common cause in support of the Government, the Constitution, and the Flag of the Union. Resolutions loyal to the Government were unanimously adopted; volunteers enlisted, and a subscription of over THREE HUNDRED DOLLARS subscribed to begin the work of organization. The feeling here is all on the side of sustaining the Government in the enforcement of all constitutional law.

MAY 9, 1861.

The call from the General Government for troops, specified *one* Regiment from Wisconsin. Some 69 companies have been organized and the strife among them to get into the Regiment called is great. The Madison *Patriot* thus speaks of the matter: "Every morning when we are in Secretary Watson's room for a time, we hear gentlemen from various parts of the State complaining that good Companies organized in their towns are not placed in the first regiments instead of the fourth, fifth, or sixth. They were reported full at an early day, but the trouble is that other companies were a little before them.

One gentleman from Prairie du Chien was complaining this morning that the company formed there was not in a higher regiment than the sixth. It was reported full on the 29th of April and yet there were over 50 Companies ahead. He stated that the company was well drilled and commanded by a gentleman who was perfectly educated as a military man, and had seen service. He had been untiring in drilling the company, and it was now in a high state of efficiency, and the gentleman spoke highly of the discipline of the men and their appearance, and said that it was too bad after the citizens had kept them at their own expense for two weeks, such a company should be disbanded.

Yet so it is all over the State, and altho' it must be mortifying to those in authority to let such brave men disband, yet when so many good men all over the State are anxious to meet the enemy there seems to be no other alternative, as up to the present time many more than enough for a much more severe crisis have offered."

JUNE 27, 1861.

The Volunteers have gone, and among them are the sons, brothers, and friends of many in this town and county. They leave us with the best wishes of our citizens for their honor and success. The orders were received by Capt. Hooe to be ready for the early Express train Tuesday morning and the intelligence was enthusiastically received by every man in the Company. On Tuesday morning the company paraded through the streets escorted by the citizens, the German brass band, and the Guard's cannon. An immense crowd was assembled at the depot to see the boys off, and bid them good-bye. Fathers and mothers were there to say a last farewell to some whom they had watched over from infancy, and rejoicing that they could offer such precious offerings on the altar of their country and for its defence. Loving sisters—and sweethearts too, perhaps—were there to say a fond farewell to loved ones with whom they had passed many happy hours. Others there were among the Volunteers who had no fathers, no mothers, no sisters, no loving heart from which to take a fond adieu—but the people gathered around them and with a hearty grasp of the hand bid them "good bye, Alick, goodbye," and none could leave us without a heart beat at the parting. How could we see the gallant fellows leave without feeling that we were parting with friends—some uncouth 'tis true—still, they have honest hearts, and—they go to fight for us. We know not what may be in store for them; but we do know that where their young Captain leads, the Prairie du Chien Volunteers will follow, and when he falls if fall he must, it will be in battling nobly for the Union, the Constitution and the preservation of the Government, and his death will be avenged. The men all love their brave leader, and he is worthy of their confidence. The sympathies of those who remain, follow the Volunteers. They go to fight, not only their own battles, but ours. Heaven bless and protect the Volunteers, and may the laurels of Victory ever be theirs.[6]

The transformation of citizen into fighting man was a pause between the heady excitement of enlistment and departure, and the eventual trial by combat. An observer found life at Camp Randall, in Wisconsin, brisk and somewhat dull.

Camp Randall presents a decidedly lively, if not very warlike appearance. These fine afternoons the volunteers are out in squads and companies drilling as much as they can without arms and equipments. They appear willing and anxious to learn; are assiduous and untiring in exercise, but it is dull work. Members of the uniformed companies that came are in all sorts of rig, some in blue, some in gray, and with all sorts of stripes and badges. Those who have recently enlisted are as various in their styles of dress as any crowd would be, picked up at random. Of course the proficiency of men so variously "rigged" does not appear, and considerable proficiency in drilling would not be noticed in men dressed so oddly. We venture that when their uniforms are donned, their discipline will appear fifty per cent better.

A better place for a rendezvous cannot be found in the State. The entire regiment can drill in squads and companies without interfering with each other, and the grounds are admirably adapted to all varieties of practice.

The eating quarters carry the old sign *"Operative Machinery"* which forms the constant subject of jest. We looked through Maj. McGonigal's ample kitchen and found everything in excellent order, the tables and utensils clean, good cooks at work, and cleanliness and order prevailing.

The volunteers are a set of readers.—Over a hundred copies of the *Argus and Democrat* are taken there, and the war news is, of course, read with thrilling interest.

The companies are all well officered, and the gentlemen in office devote themselves unweariedly to pefecting [*sic*] their troops in discipline. What will be done with the regiment, how soon they will be called for, and how many will go for the required three years, are yet matters of uncertainty.[7]

But what of the volunteers themselves? How did they feel as the bands blared and the people shouted? There is no typical volunteer or composite one, but the emotions and experiences of Warren Lee Goss, a private in a Massachusetts regiment, were shared by many others as they enlisted and marched to war.

It was the news that the 6th Massachusetts regiment had been mobbed by roughs on their passage through Baltimore which gave me the war fever. And yet when I read Governor John A. Andrew's instructions to have the hero martyrs "preserved in ice and tenderly sent forward," somehow, though I felt the pathos of it, I could not reconcile myself to the ice. Ice in connection with patriotism did not give me agreeable impressions of war, and when I came to think of it, the stoning of the heroic "Sixth" didn't suit me; it detracted from my desire to die a soldier's death.

I lay awake all night thinking the matter over, with the "ice" and "brick-bats" before my mind. However, the fever culminated that night, and I resolved to enlist.

"Cold chills" ran up and down my back as I got out of bed after the sleepless night, and shaved preparatory to other desperate deeds of valor. I was twenty years of age, and when anything unusual was to be done, like fighting or courting, I shaved.

With a nervous tremor convulsing my system, and my heart thumping like muffled drum-beats, I stood before the door of the recruiting-office, and before turning the knob to enter, read and re-read the advertisement for recruits posted thereon, until I knew all its peculiarities. The promised chances for "travel and promotion" seemed good, and I thought I might have made a mistake in considering war so serious after all. "Chances for travel!" I must confess now, after four years of soldiering, that the "chances for travel" were no myth; but "promotion" was a little uncertain and slow.

I was in no hurry to open the door. Though determined to enlist, I was half inclined to put it off awhile; I had a fluctuation of desires; I was fainthearted and brave; I wanted to enlist, and yet—Here

I turned the knob, and was relieved. I had been more prompt, with all my hesitation, than the officer in his duty; he wasn't in. Finally he came, and said: "What do you want, my boy?" "I want to enlist," I responded, blushing deeply with upwelling patriotism and bashfulness. Then the surgeon came to strip and examine me. In justice to myself, it must be stated that I signed the rolls without a tremor. It is common to the most of humanity, I believe, that, when confronted with actual danger, men have less fear than in its contemplation. I will, however, make one exception in favor of the first shell I heard uttering its bloodcurdling hisses, as though a steam locomotive were traveling the air. With this exception I have found the actual dangers of war always less terrible face to face than on the night before the battle.

My first uniform was a bad fit: my trousers were too long by three or four inches; the flannel shirt was coarse and unpleasant, too large at the neck and too short elsewhere. The forage cap was an ungainly bag with pasteboard top and leather visor; the blouse was the only part which seemed decent; while the overcoat made me feel like a little nubbin of corn in a large preponderance of husk. Nothing except "Virginia mud" ever took down my ideas of military pomp quite so low.

After enlisting I did not seem of so much consequence as I had expected. There was not so much excitement on account of my military appearance as I deemed justly my due. I was taught my facings, and at the time I thought the drillmaster needlessly fussy about shouldering, ordering, and presenting arms. At this time men were often drilled in company and regimental evolutions long before they learned the manual of arms, because of the difficulty of obtaining muskets. These we obtained at an early day, but we would willingly have resigned them after carrying them a few hours. The musket, after an hour's drill, seemed heavier and less ornamental than it had looked to be. The first day I went out to drill, getting tired of doing the same things over and over, I said to the drill-sergeant: "Let's stop this fooling and go over to the grocery." His only reply was addressed to a corporal: "Corporal, take this man out and drill him like h—l"; and the corporal did! I found that suggestions were not so well appreciated in the army as in private life, and that no wisdom was equal to a drill-master's "Right face," "Left wheel," and "Right, oblique, march." It takes a raw recruit some time to learn that he is not to think or suggest, but obey. Some never do learn. I acquired it at last, in humility and mud, but it was tough. Yet I doubt if my patriotism, during my first three weeks' drill, was quite knee-high. Drilling looks easy to a spectator, but it isn't. Old soldiers who read this will remember their green recruithood and smile assent. After a time I had cut down my uniform so that I could see out of it, and had conquered the drill sufficiently to see through it. Then the word came: On to Washington! . . .[8]

Charles Francis Adams, Jr., being an Adams of the Braintree (Massachusetts) Adamses, was certainly not an example of the average volunteer. But even an Adams is not totally atypical. His reactions were probably shared by many an introvert troubled by conscience and frustrated by the failure to find life as he was living it rewarding. He analyzed his motives mercilessly and reported them to his father, then United States minister to Great Britain.

. . . I don't know whether you will be surprised or disgusted or annoyed or distressed by the information that I have gone into the army, but such is the fact. Before this reaches you I shall be an officer of the 1st Massachusetts Cavalry and probably in Carlisle Barracks. . . .

For going I have many reasons. I do not think myself a soldier by nature. I am not sure I am doing that which is best for myself; but I feel that if I go, I shall be better satisfied with myself, and as I said to you before, I do not think it right that our family, so prominent in this matter while it is a contest of words, should be wholly unrepresented when it has grown to be a conflict of blows. You say there is neither glory nor honor to be won in civil strife. I answer, that it cannot be otherwise than right for me to fight to maintain that which my ancestors passed their whole lives in establishing. These however are general arguments which I have advanced to you before, but there are others nearer home. I have completely failed in my profession and I long to cut myself clear of it. I have indeed derived an income this summer from my office, but not from the law, and that I have made up my mind to give up. This mortifies me and the army must cover my defeat. My future must be business and literature, and I do not see why the army should not educate me for both, for its routine is that of business and it will go hard if my pen is idle while history is to be written or events are to be described. Thus my decision not only closes one career in which I have failed, but it opens others in which experience teaches me I can succeed if at all. . . .[9]

At first, volunteers were plentiful. But it was a civil conflict, and the divisiveness that marked its prelude was not washed away, as is the case in some foreign wars, by the flowing tide of enthusiasm that greeted its outbreak. Many, convinced that it was an unnecessary war fought in a bad cause, hung back sullenly. Others were simply unwilling to assume the burden of fighting it. In 1863 a draft was imposed. There were four calls in all—July 1863, and March, July, and December 1864. Although generally accepted, it was bitterly denounced by a section of the press and its enforcement resisted in many areas. In the hilly backwoods of the Ohio Valley—in Ohio and Indiana—men "hid out" and in a few cases murdered the conscription officers. Such a shooting was reported to the Provost Marshal General in the following dispatch:

I regret to inform you that two of the officers employed in carrying out the enrollment act were murdered yesterday [June 10, 1863] in Rush County. . . . The facts, so far as known and reported to me by the provost-marshal of that district are as follows:

On Tuesday last one of the enrolling officers of Rush County was fired upon from the woods while in the performance of his duties, and returned to the headquarters of the district and reported the fact to the provost-marshal, who proposed to send one of his deputies and a squad of men with the enrolling officer to the same neighborhood where the firing took place. Mr. John F. Stephens, one of the deputy marshals for the district, advised, however, that it would be better not to send any force and proposed to go himself, taking with him only one or perhaps two detectives and the enrolling officer. He expressed the opinion that the shooting was done not with the intention of taking the life of the officer, but for the purpose of intimidating him and insisted on going without any other assistance than that before mentioned.

The provost-marshal agreed that the course advised by Mr. Stephens should be pursued, and accordingly on Tuesday morning he started with the enrolling officer, and I think two detectives. Mr. Stephens and one of the detectives traveled in a buggy and the enrolling officer and the other detective were on horseback.

Yesterday about noon, in the same neighborhood in which the previous shooting had taken place, the party came to a house situated a short distance from the road. The enrolling officer dismounted and went into the house and was making inquiries as to the persons residing there subject to enrollment, when some ten or twelve men rose from their place of concealment in a wheat field and fired upon the two men in the buggy, killing Mr. Stephens immediately and mortally wounding the other man, whose name was Craycraft. . . .[10]

In Schuylkill County, Pennsylvania, the enforcement of the draft offered a tragicomic episode worthy of Shakespeare's Falstaff. The deposition of an enrolling officer recounted his troubles.

Peter W. Kutz, of Eldred Township, in said Schuylkill County, being duly sworn in, says: That he is enrolling officer for sub-district No. 23 . . . duly appointed under the act of Congress entitled "An act for enrolling and calling out the national forces and for other purposes," approved 3d of March, 1863; that as such officer he began to enroll in Hegins Township early in the morning of Thursday, the 4th day of June, 1863, and continued enrolling until between 4 and 5 o'clock in the afternoon; that he came to Israel Stutzman's shoemaker shop in said township at about 4 o'clock in the afternoon, and there enrolled said Stutzman, and soon after he was in he was followed by Christian Stutzman and Abraham Bressler. That said Abraham Bressler then and there told him that it was the best for him that he did not come in his, said Bressler's, house, or he, said Bressler, would have killed him or broken his bones for him; that he could stop enrolling and go home, that would be the best for him; that he should not take the enrollment there, nor anybody else, and also, "if this was in my house," he said, "I would give it to you in the right way; but I have got no right here, I know that." That said Israel Stutzman and Christian Stutzman both joined in with said Bressler and laughed at what he said, and both of them said, "Lincoln ought to go in this war," and said Israel Stutzman also called the deponent a negro catcher; that when he left the shop and proceeded on further to make the enrollment the said three persons above named all came out of the shop also and followed him for a considerable distance, all of them together, and shouting at and quarreling with him as they went, and the said Abraham Bressler, also, all the time had a stone in his hand. . . . they were all angry and seemed to be threatening him and he was afraid of being hurt by them, and so desisted and was driven off from enrolling any further there and went home. That when he had gone from them about a mile on his way home, he came across two men together whom he did not know and cannot name, in the woods by the roadside, and they hailed him and told him the best way for him would be to go home and not enroll there any more. And that when he had gone yet a half a mile or so still farther on his road home, he met three other men in the road, no one he knew or can name, and one of them had a gun in his hands, and they too all told him the best way for him would be to go home; and that, by reason of what he has stated above, he was deterred from enrolling any more then or since in said Hegins Township, and believes he is in danger of his life or of bodily injury if he does so. And further he says not.[11]

Kutz resigned as enrolling officer and presumably continued to live. But other scenes were more disastrous. There were draft riots in a number of cities and towns, ranging all the way from Massachusetts to Wisconsin. The most violent of these, and the only one permitted to get completely out of hand, occurred in New York City.

The New York draft riots were not wholly a protest against conscription. They were bred in part by the squalid filth of the tenements and a blind sense of economic injustice. Most inexcusably of all, the city's partisan Democratic press ignited and fanned the fires of racial hatred against unoffending Negroes by stridently shrieking that white men were being pressed into service and driven to death in a war to free Negroes who would ultimately come North to take their jobs away from them. The seeds thus sown bore fruit in mid-July. The New York Times *described the harvest.*

The initiation of the draft on Saturday in the Ninth Congressional District was characterized by so much order and good feeling as to well nigh dispel the forebodings of tumult and violence which many entertained in connection with the enforcement of the conscription in this City. Very few, then, were prepared for the riotous demonstrations which yesterday, from 10 in the morning until late at night, prevailed almost unchecked in our streets. The authorities had counted upon more or less resistance to this measure of the Government after the draft was completed and the conscripts were required to take their place in the ranks, and at that time they would have been fully prepared to meet it; but no one anticipated resistance at so early a stage in the execution of the law, and consequently, both the City and National authorities were totally unprepared to meet it. The abettors of the riot knew this, and in it they saw their opportunity. We say abettors of the riot, for it is abundantly manifest that the whole affair was concocted on Sunday last by a few wire-pullers, who, after they saw the ball fairly in motion yesterday morning prudently kept in the background. Proof of this is found in the fact that as early as 9 o'clock, some laborers employed by two or three railroad companies, and in the iron foundries on the eastern side of the City, formed in procession in the Twenty-second Ward, and visited the different workshops in the upper wards, where large numbers were employed, and compelled them, by threats in some instances, to cease their work. As the crowd augmented, their shouts and disorderly demonstrations became more formidable. The number of men who thus started out in their career of violence and blood, did not probably at first exceed threescore. Scarcely had two dozen names been called, when a crowd, numbering perhaps 500, suddenly made an irruption in front of the building (corner of Third Avenue and Forty-sixth street,) attacking it with clubs, stones, brickbats and other missiles. . . . Following these missiles, the mob rushed furiously into the office on the first floor, where the draft was going on, seizing the books, papers, records, lists, &c., all of which they destroyed, except those contained in a large iron safe. The drafting officers were set upon with stones and clubs, and, with the reporters for the Press and others, had to make a hasty exit through the rear.

. . . . .

At 11 A.M. word reached the Park Barracks of the disturbance, and Lieut. Ried and a detachment of the Invalid corps immediately repaired to the scene of the riot. They went by the Third avenue route, the party occupying one car. On the way up, crowds of men, women and children gathered at the street corners, hissed and jeered them, and some even went so far as to pick up stones, which they defiantly threatened to throw at the car. When near the scene of the disturbance, Lieut. Ried and command alighted, and formed in company line, in which order they marched up to the mob. Facing the rioters the men were ordered to fire, which many of them did, the shots being blank cartridges, but the smoke had scarce cleared away when the company (which did not number more than fifty men, if as many) were attacked and completely demoralized by the mob, who were armed with clubs, sticks, swords and other implements. The soldiers had their bayonets taken away, and they themselves were compelled [to] seek refuge in the side streets, but in attempting to flee thither, several, it is said, were killed, while those that escaped, did so only to be hunted like dogs, but in a more inhuman and brutal manner. They were chased by the mob, who divided themselves into squads, and frequently a single soldier would be caught in a side street, with each end blocked up by the rioters. The houses and stores were all closed (excepting a few liquor shops, which had their shutters up, but kept the back door open,) no retreat was, therefore, open for him, and the poor fellow would be beaten almost to death. . . .

Elated with success, the mob, which by this time had been largely reinforced, next formed themselves into marauding parties, and paraded through the neighboring streets, looking more like so many infuriated demons, the men being more or less intoxicated, dirty and half clothed. . . . The streets were thronged with women and children, many of whom instigated the men to further work of blood.

. . . . .

As soon as the Provost-Marshal's office had been gutted of its contents, and the adjoining building—a wheelwright's shop, in which there was much combustible material—had been fired, the telegraph wires were cut. Parties and bands of men and boys then visited the various workshops in the vicinity, and compelled the men to leave their work and join. . . .

By this time the Fire Department of the District arrived on the ground, and were preparing to work on the fire; but were prevented from doing so by the mob, who threatened them with instant death if their orders were disobeyed. The cars were stopped from running either way; the horses in several instances were killed, and the cars broken to pieces. . . .

The fire, which had now consumed the wheelwright's shop, had extended to the Provost-Marshal's office, which was soon enveloped in flames, from which issued a large and dark volume of smoke.

The rioters meantime danced with fiendish delight before the burning building, . . . sent showers of stones against the office, smashing in the doors and windows. . . . The murky atmosphere and the heavy black clouds which lined the horizon, formed a strange, weird spectacle, which was made the more complete by the demoniac yells of the mobs.

Ruins of the Provost-Marshall's Office

. . . . .

The Orphan Asylum for Colored Children was visited by the mob about 4 o'clock. This Institution is situated on Fifth-avenue, and the building, with the grounds and gardens adjoining, extended from Forty-third to Forty-fourth street. Hundreds, and perhaps thousands of the rioters, the majority of whom were women and children, entered the premises, and in the most excited and violent manner they ransacked and plundered the building from cellar to garret. The building was located in the most pleasant and healthy portion of the City. It was purely a charitable institution. In it there are on an average 600 or 800 homeless colored orphans. The building was a large four-story one, with two wings of three stories each.

. . . . .

After the entire building had been ransacked, and every article deemed worth carrying away had been taken—and this included even the little garments for the orphans, which were contributed by the benevolent ladies of this City—the premises were fired on the first floor. . . .

. . . The institution was destined to be burned, and after an hour and a half of labor on the part of the mob, it was in flames in all parts. . . . There is now scarcely one brick left upon another of the Orphan Asylum.

. . . . .

Among the most cowardly features of the riot, and one which indicated its political *animus* . . . was the causeless and inhuman treatment of the negroes of the City. It seemed to be an understood thing throughout the City that the negroes should be attacked wherever found, whether then [*sic*] offered any provocation or not. As soon as one of these unfortunate people was spied, whether on a cart, a railroad car, or in the street, he was immediately set upon by a crowd of men and boys, and unless some man of pluck came to his rescue, or he was fortunate enough to escape into a building, he was inhumanly beaten and perhaps killed. There were probably not less than a dozen negroes beaten to death in different parts of the City during the day. Among the most diabolical of these outrages . . . is that of a negro cartman living in Carmine street. About 8 o'clock in the evening as he was coming out of the stable, after having put up his horses, he was attacked by a crowd of about

400 men and boys, who beat him with clubs and paving-stones till he was lifeless, and then hung him to a tree opposite the burying-ground. Not being yet satisfied with their devilish work, they set fire to his clothes and danced and yelled and swore their horrid oaths around his burning corpse. The charred body of the poor victim was still hanging upon the tree at a late hour last evening.

Early in the afternoon the proprietors of such saloons and other places of business as had negroes in their employ, were obliged to close up for fear that the rioters would destroy their premises. In

Hanging a Negro in Clarkson Street

Sacking Brooks' Clothing Store

most of them the negroes were compelled to remain over night, not daring to go home lest they be mobbed on the way. . . .[12]

The draft was made even more unpopular by the provision that a draftee might be exempted from service by procuring a substitute to take his place or by paying three hundred dollars to the federal government as a commutation fee. This gave ammunition to the opponents of the war, as well as to those who disapproved of Lincoln's management of it. Even among the President's supporters there was dissatisfaction. It was charged that while patriots volunteered and the poor man was drafted, the rich man could buy a substitute to do his fighting and perhaps even his dying.

Further dissatisfaction was aroused by maladministration. Under the act, the commutation money was paid to the Provost Marshal's

dollars of the three hundred to which they were entitled. We hear that the brokers who are permitted to cheat the volunteers—and the city—in this scandalous manner, boast of their ill-gotten wealth. One of these rogues has been heard to declare that he has made twenty-five thousand dollars in this business.

There is no excuse for the men in authority who have permitted such disgraceful rascality. The Supervisors are responsible for the proper administration of the bounty fund; that fund is intended not for the volunteers to waste, but for them to apply in a proper way to the support of their families, or for their own benefit. The broker who cheats a volunteer cheats the city also, which will presently be called on to support the families which, if the bounty fund had been properly administered, would have been above need, for a time at least. It cannot be said in excuse that it is no part of the Supervisor's duty to look after the rights of the volunteers. That is their duty, and the most important part of it.

The plan which has been adopted by them is the same by which seamen have for so many years been made the profitable prey of a set of land-sharks. But there is not the poor excuse for it, in this case, that can really be urged for it in the case of the seamen. They receive their "advance" money days, and even weeks, before their ship sails, and of course need some person to act as "security" for this advance. But the volunteer does not receive his bounty till he has enlisted; and after that he is at once sent to the military depot, and is immediately and thenceforth in the charge of the military authorities, who are responsible for him. Why cannot the Supervisors establish a proper agent in every deputy Provost-Marshal's office, with authority to pay over to the recruit himself, as soon as he has enlisted, and in exchange for the formal certificate to that effect, the entire sum of bounty money? Then the occupation of these brokers and security-mongers would be gone, and the city would not be cheated and disgraced by such stories as are now told to the injury of the service. Public opinion will hold the Supervisors responsible for the outrages practiced on recruits; and they will do well at once to adopt some system by which volunteers will get their rights, else it will presently come to be thought that those who administer the bounty fund are in some way in collusion with the brokers who grab so large a share of it.[13]

Nonetheless, although criticizing the administration, the New York Evening Post *defended the principle of commutation. In doing so it probably reflected the views of a majority in Congress and "the large middle class" for whose benefit the bounty system was devised.*

. . . Concerning the three hundred dollar exemption clause there is much difference of opinion; we still hold the belief, after considerable inquiry, that it should be retained. There is no doubt that it is a boon to the large middle class of industrious mechanics and farmers, who, just beginning life, with families of young children dependent upon them, cannot, in many cases, serve under arms without serious distress to those whom they leave unprovided for at home. Almost every one of this class whose presence at home is really necessary to his family, can raise the sum of 300 dollars to secure his exemption. But repeal this clause, and force every man to go or procure a substitute, and these men become at once the prey of sharpers and brokers, or are compelled, at every sacrifice, to serve in person. Now this class, which mainly carries on the varied industry of the free states and creates their prosperity, deserves the most careful consideration at the hands of legislators. . . .[14]

Bounty jumping was a monstrosity sired by commutation. This was the practice of enlisting, taking the bounty money, and deserting, often to repeat the maneuver at another time in another place. In 1863, Frank Wilkeson, a sixteen-year-old New York state farm boy, seized by "war fever," ran away from home to volunteer. After the war was over, bitterly disillusioned, he wrote a description of his shattering experiences. It included a vivid account of the tricks of the bounty jumpers and the brutal countermeasures they evoked.

. . . The war fever seized me in 1863. All the summer and fall I had fretted and burned to be off. That winter, and before I was sixteen years old, I ran away from my father's high-lying Hudson River valley farm. I went to Albany and enlisted in the Eleventh New York Battery, then at the front in Virginia, and was promptly sent out to the penitentiary building. There, to my utter astonishment, I found eight hundred or one thousand ruffians, closely guarded by heavy lines of sentinels, who paced to and fro, day and night, rifle in hand, to keep them from running away. When I entered the barracks these recruits gathered around me and asked, "How much bounty did you get?" "How many times have you jumped the bounty?"

. . . . .

Before I left the barracks I saw the guards roughly haul straw-littered, dust-coated men out of mattresses, which they had cut open and crawled into to hide. Other men were jerked out of the water-closets. Still others were drawn by the feet from beneath bunks. One man, who had burrowed into the contents of a water-tight swill box, which stood in the hall and into which we threw our waste food and coffee slops, was fished out, covered with coffee grounds and bits of bread and shreds of meat, and kicked down stairs and out of the building. . . . Cuffed, prodded with bayonets, and heartily cursed, we fell into line in front of the barracks. An officer stepped in front of us and said in a loud voice that any man who attempted to escape would be shot. A double line of guards quickly took their proper positions around us. We were faced to the right and marched through a room, where the men were paid their bounties. Some men received $500, others less; but I heard of no man who received less than $400. I got nothing. As the men passed through the room they were formed into columns by fours. When all the recruits had been paid, and the column formed, we started to march into Albany, guarded by a double line of sentinels. . . .

Previous to my enlistment I had imagined that the population of Albany would line the sidewalks to see the defenders of the nation march proudly by, bound for the front, and that we would be cheered, and would unbend sufficiently to accept floral offerings from beautiful maidens. How was it? No exultant cheers arose from the column. The people who saw us did not cheer. The faces of the recruits plainly expressed the profound disgust they felt at the disastrous outcome of what had promised to be a remunerative financial enterprise. Small boys derided us. Mud balls were thrown at us. One small lad, who was greatly excited by the unwonted spectacle, rushed to a street corner, and after placing his hands to his mouth, yelled to a distant and loved comrade: "Hi, Johnnie, come see de bounty-jumpers!" He was promptly joined by an exasperating, red-headed, sharp-tongued little wretch, whom I desired to destroy long before we arrived at the steamboat landing. Men and women openly laughed at us. Fingers, indicative of derision, were pointed at us. Yes, a large portion of the populace of Albany gathered together to see us; but they were mostly young males, called guttersnipes. They jeered us, and were exceedingly loth to leave us. It was as though the congress of American wonders were parading in the streets preparatory to aerial flights under tented canvas.

Once on the steamboat, we were herded on the lower deck, where freight is usually carried, like cattle.

. . . . .

Morning came, and we disembarked in New York, and were marched, still heavily guarded, to the low, white barracks, which then stood where the post-office now stands. There we were securely penned and decently fed. The men fretted and fumed, and burned to escape. Many of them had previously jumped bounties in New York. They knew the slums of the city. They knew where to hide in safety. Dozens of them said that if they could get out of the barracks they would be safe. But they could not get out. This time they were going to the front. The officers and men, in whose charge we were, were resolute in their intention to deliver one consignment of bounty-jumpers to the commands they belonged to. That afternoon five days' cooked rations were issued to us, and we were escorted by a heavy double line of guards down Broadway to the Battery. There we turned to march along a street that led to a dock where an ocean steamer lay. The head of the column was opposite the dock, when four recruits shed their knapsacks and ran for the freedom they coveted. One of these men marched two files in front of me. He dashed past the guard who walked by my side at the top of his speed. Not a word was said to him. The column halted at command. The guard near me turned on his heels quickly, threw his heavy rifle to his shoulder, covered the running man, and shot him dead. Two of the remaining three fell dead as other rifles cracked. The fourth man ran through the shower of balls safely. I thought he was going to escape; but a tall, lithe officer ran after him, pistol in hand. He overtook the fugitive just as he was about to turn a street corner. He made no attempt to arrest the deserter, but placed his pistol to the back of the runaway's head and blew his brains out as he ran. The dead man fell in a pile at the base of a lamppost. That ended all attempts to escape. We marched on board the steamer, a propeller, and descended narrow stairs to between decks, where the light was dim and the air heavy with a smell as of damp sea-weed. . . .[15]

Draft riots and bounty jumping constituted the seamy side of the citizens' army. They were not uncommon and are a part of the picture of the North at war—a picture of civil strife. But they are ugly details forming only a small portion of the total canvas. Most of the men of the Army of the North volunteered and, even though they accepted bounty money, by far the greater number fulfilled their obligation loyally and fought as well as their comrades. What sort of army, then, was this army of volunteers? Views differed. One of its staunchest supporters was Secretary of War Simon Cameron. He wrote:

. . . I cannot forbear to speak favorably of the volunteer system as a substitute for a cumbrous and dangerous standing army. It has heretofore by many been deemed unreliable and inefficient in a sudden emergency, but actual facts have proved the contrary. If it be urged that the enemies of order have gained some slight advantages at remote points by reason of the absence of a sufficient regular force, the unexampled rapidity of concentration of volunteers already witnessed is an ample refutation of the argument. A Government whose every citizen stands ready to march to its defense can never be overthrown, for none is so strong as that whose foundations rest immovably in the hearts of the people. The spectacle of more than a quarter of a million of citizens rushing to the field in defense of the Constitution must ever take rank among the most extroardinary facts of history. Its interest is vastly heightened by the lavish out-pouring of States and individuals of voluntary contributions of money, reaching an aggregate thus far of more than ten millions of dollars.

But a few weeks since the men composing this great army were pursuing the avocations of peace. They gathered from the farm, from the workshop, from the factory, from the mine. The minister came from his pulpit, the merchant from his counting-room, the professor and student from the college, the teacher and pupil from the common schools. Young men of fortune left luxurious homes for the tent and the camp. Native and foreign born alike came forward with a kindred enthusiasm. That a well-disciplined, homogeneous, and efficient force should be formed out of such a seemingly heterogeneous mass appears almost incredible. But what is the actual fact? Experienced men, who have had ample opportunity to familiarize themselves with the condition of European armies, concede that in point of personnel this patriot army is fully equal to the finest regular troops of the Old World. A more intelligent body of men, or one actuated by purer motives, was never before marshaled in the field.

The calling forth of this large and admirable force in vindication of the Constitution and the laws is in strict accordance with a wise prudence and economy, and at the same time in perfect harmony with the uniform practice of the Government. . . .[16]

From September 1861 to July 1862, accompanied by two nephews who were aides-de-camp to Major General George B. McClellan, the French Prince de Joinville observed the Army of the Potomac at firsthand. His description and analysis of an army composed of volunteers from an egalitarian society is penetrating.

. . . The American volunteer is richly paid. His pay is $13—more than 65 francs—per month. . . . One may imagine what such an army must cost. This would not matter if even at such an expense the country were well served. It is not so, however. It is ill served for want of discipline, not that the military laws and regulations were not severe enough; but they were not enforced, and could not be, in consequence of the primary organization of the regiment, and of the composition of its corps of officers. And here we come to the essential vice of an American army.

How is a regiment of volunteers actually formed? As soon as Congress has voted the number of men, they calculate at Washington the quota which each State must furnish, according to its resources and population. This calculation being made, each Governor announces that there are to be so many regiments raised within the limits of his jurisdiction. The regiment of one battalion only, is the American military unit. Affairs are managed in this way:

Persons present themselves offering to raise a regiment. Each sets

VISITING THE SUTLER'S STORE

forth his claims, his influence in the State, or among a certain portion of the population, which will enable him to procure easily the necessary number of men, his devotion to the party in power, etc. From among the persons thus presented the Governor makes his choice. Generally the person upon whom the choice falls has laid it down as a condition precedent that he shall have the command of the regiment; and thus Mr. So-and-So, a lawyer or a doctor, never having handled a sword, but feeling within himself an improvised vocation, becomes a colonel at the start, and puts himself in connection with all the recruiting agencies and with all the furnishers of equipment and clothing supplies for the future regiment. The next thing is to find the soldiers; this is not so easy, for there is a great deal of rivalry. They apply to all their comrades, traverse the country, and resort to various plans. This is done quickly and well in America, for the Americans have an inventive mind. Most frequently they find friends who, seized with the same martial ardor, promise to bring so many recruits if they be made—the one captain, the other lieutenant, another sergeant, and so forth. The framework is formed and is partly filled up; it only remains to complete it. It is then that recourse is had to extraordinary measures—to those gigantic posters which set forth in pompous terms all the advantages to be gained by joining the corps. They go among the Catholic priests to procure Irishmen, and give the coveted privilege of sutlership to the individual who promises the necessary complement of men. Thus the regiment finds itself organized, and the lists are carried to the Governor, who approves everything. The regiment is mustered, clothed and equipped, and forwarded by railroad to the seat of the war. Sometimes, even frequently, the grades are made to depend on election; but that is generally only a formality, as everything has been arranged beforehand by those interested.

The inconveniences of this system are obvious. The officers, from the colonel down to the lowest in rank, do not know the first word of the military art, and if they had any real aptitude for it and any war-like qualities, these are still to be proved. The soldiers have no illusions on this point. "They know no more about it than we do, we are well acquainted with them," they say of those who command them. Hence, there is no superiority of knowledge on the part of the officer over the soldier, and no superiority of social position in a country where no such superiority is recognized. Most frequently, also, it is with an idea of being a candidate for political office that the officer has taken up arms. It is to make himself a name in the eyes of the voters. And these future voters are the soldiers. What would become of the popularity he seeks to enjoy if he were rough to the soldiers, or showed himself too exacting in the service? All these causes bring about the want of authority with officers, and the want of respect among soldiers. Of course, then, there can be neither hierarchy nor discipline. All this has been ameliorated by force of necessity, and in the school of experience. Even from the beginning there were exceptions to it; some colonels, impelled by a real vocation, or animated by ardent patriotism, succeeded in overcoming the obstacles placed in their path. Sometimes an officer of the regular army, desirous of distinguishing himself, and having influence enough in his State, raised a regiment and obtained from it an admirable result.

. . . Generally, however, the chief is simply a comrade who wears a different costume. He is obeyed in every day routine, but voluntarily. In the same way the soldiers don't trouble themselves about him when circumstances become serious. From the point of view of American equality, there is no good reason to obey him. Besides, in the eyes of the greater number this title of volunteer does not signify the soldier who devotes himself generously and voluntarily to save the country or to acquire glory, but rather the well-paid soldier, who only does what he wishes and pleases. This is so true that, although the pay and time of service are the same for volunteers and regulars, the recruiting of regulars has become almost impossible. All that class of men who enlisted when regulars alone existed, from a taste for camp life, now join the volunteers. On one side is license, on the other discipline—the choice is easily made. The habits created by universal suffrage also play their part and are reproduced on the field of battle. By a tacit agreement the regiment marches against the enemy, advances under fire and begins to deliver its volleys; the men are brave, very brave; they are killed and wounded in great numbers, and then, when by a tacit agreement they think they have done enough for military honor, they all march off together. The colonel perhaps attempts to give a direction, an impulse, but generally his efforts are in vain. As to the officers, they never think of it. Why should they attempt it, and why should they be obeyed if the majority of the regiment has made up its mind to retreat? . . . Nevertheless, the Government put its hand on an immense mass of armed men, a multitude of regiments; for the country has responded unanimously and vigorously to the call for volunteers. Never, we believe, has any nation created, of herself, by her own will, by her single resources, without coercion of any kind, without government pressure, and in such a short space of time, so considerable an armament. Free governments, whatever may be their faults and the excesses to which they may give rise, always preserve an elasticity and creative power which nothing can equal. Only, the vices of organization which we pointed out singularly impaired the value of this military gathering. . . .[17]

Another foreign observer, an Englishman, was less favorably impressed.

. . . On the road from St. Louis to Cincinnati we passed through numerous camps; the siege of Vicksburg then being in progress, these served as a base of operations and supplies. There was no appearance of military order or discipline about them, though they were guarded by sentries and cannon, and implements of war and soldiers accoutrements were abundant. Some of the sentries carried their rifles under their arms like umbrellas, others carried the butt over the shoulder and the muzzle downwards, some of them had stuck the bayonet of the rifle into the ground and, chin in hand, were leaning their elbows on the stock, others less ingenious had deposited their muskets against the trees and were lying down reading newspapers. Some of them were good enough materials for working into soldiers, but the majority were either too old or too young; and it was not uncommon to see a grey-headed, white-bearded old man standing next to a boy who could hardly shoulder his rifle. Besides this, there was no attempt at sizing the men, and you could frequently see a tall six foot lath of a Yankee standing next to a mannikin, who in our service would be rejected as undersized. . . .[18]

A detailed analysis of the citizen as a soldier was made by Jacob Dolson Cox. Cox was an Ohio lawyer who at the outbreak of the war helped to organize a regiment and received a commission as Brigadier General of Volunteers. He fought under Generals McClellan and Sherman. He was at Antietam, the bloodiest one-day battle of the war.

The work of sifting the material for an army which went on through the winter of 1861-1862, naturally suggests an analysis of the classes of men who composed both parts of the military force of the nation—the volunteers and the regulars. I need add nothing to what I have already said of the unexampled excellence of the rank and file in the regiments raised by the first volunteering. Later in the war, when "bounty jumping" and substitution for conscripts came into play, the character of the material, especially that recruited in the great cities and seaports, was much lower. I think, however, that the volunteers were always better men, man for man, than the average of those recruited for the regular army. The rigidity of discipline did not differ so much between good volunteer regiments and regulars, as the mode of enforcing it. There were plenty of volunteer regiments that could not be excelled in drill, in the performance of camp duty, or in the finish and exactness of all the forms of parades and of routine. But it was generally brought about by much milder methods of discipline. A captain of volunteers was usually followed by his neighbors and relatives. The patriotic zeal of the men of the company as well as their self-respect made them easily amenable to military rule so far as it tended to fit them better to do the noble work they had volunteered for, and on which their hearts were as fully set as the hearts of their colonels or generals. In the regular army, officers and men belonged to different castes, and a practically impassible barrier was between them. Most of the men who had enlisted in the long years of domestic peace were, for one cause or another, outcasts, to whom life had been a failure and who followed the recruiting sergeant as a last desperate resource when every door to a livelihood was shut. The war made some change in this, but the habits and methods of the officers had been formed before that time and under the old surroundings. The rule was arbitrary, despotic, often tyrannical, and it was notorious that the official bearing and the language used toward the regular soldier was out of the question in a volunteer organization. Exceptions could be found in both parts of the service, but there could be no doubt as to the custom and the rule. To know how to command volunteers was explicitly recognized by our leading generals as a quality not found in many regular officers, and worth noting when found. A volunteer regiment might have a "free and easy" look to the eye of a regular drill sergeant, but in every essential for good conduct and ready manoeuvre on the field of battle, or for heroic efforts in the crisis of a desperate engagement, it could not be excelled if its officers had been reasonably competent and faithful. There was inevitable loss of time in the organization and instruction of a new army of volunteers; but after the first year in the field, in every quality which tends to give victory in battle to a popular cause, the volunteer regiment was, in my judgment, unquestionably superior. It is necessary to say this, because there has been a fashion of speaking of regular regiments or brigades in the civil war as though they were capable of accomplishing more in proportion to their numbers or one some occasion of peculiar peril than the volunteers. I did not find it so.

The material in the line, then, was as good as could be; the weakness was in the officers, and it was here that the sifting was necessary. Most of these officers had themselves enlisted as privates, and their patriotic zeal was not to be questioned. They had been chosen to be lieutenants, captains, and even colonels by their men because of faith in their ability to lead, or to recognize their influence in raising the troops. Yet a considerable part of them proved incompetent to command. The disqualifications were various. Some lacked physical strength and stamina. Some had or quickly developed intemperate habits. Some lacked the education and intelligence needful for official responsibility. Some were too indolent to apply themselves to the work of disciplining themselves or their men. Fitness for command is a very general term, yet it implies a set of qualities which intelligent people easily understand and attach to the phrase. Self-command is proverbially one of the chief. Courage and presence of mind are indispensable. Ability to decide and firmness to stick to a decision are necessary. Intelligence enough to understand the duties demanded of him and to instruct his subordinates in theirs is another requisite. But beside all these, there is a constitution of body and mind for which we can find no better name than military aptitude. For lack of it many estimable, intelligent, and brave men failed as officers. Again, not every good captain made a good colonel, and not every good brigade commander was fit for a division or a larger command. There was a constantly widening test of capacity, and a rapid thinning of the numbers found fit for great responsibilities until the command of great armies was reached, when two or three names are all that we can enumerate as having been proven during the four years of our civil strife to be fully equal to the task.

Besides the indications of unfitness for the subordinate commands which I have mentioned, another classification may be made. In an agricultural community (and the greater part of our population was and is agricultural), a middle-aged farmer who had been thrifty in business and had been a country magistrate or a representative in the legislature, would be the natural leader in his town or county, and if his patriotism prompted him to set the example of enlisting, he would probably be chosen to a company office, and perhaps to a field office in the regiment. Absolutely ignorant of tactics, he would find that his habits of mind and body were too fixed, and that he could not learn the new business into which he had plunged. He would be abashed at the very thought of standing before a company and shouting the word of command. The tactical lessons conned in his tent would vanish in a sort of stage-fright when he tried to practise them in public. Some would overcome the difficulty by perseverance, others would give it up in despair and resign, still others would hold on from pride or shame, until some pressure from above or below would force them to retire. Some men of this stamp had personal fighting qualities which kept them in the service in spite of their tactical ignorance, like brave old Wolford of Kentucky, of whom it used to be jocosely said, that the command by which he rallied his cavalry regiment was "Huddle on the Hill, boys!"

A man wholly without business training would always be in embarrassment, though his other qualifications for military life were good. Even a company has a good deal of administrative business to do. Accounts are to be kept, rations, clothing, arms, accoutrements, and ammunition are to be receipted and accounted for. Returns of various kinds are to be made, applications for furlough, musters, rolls, and the like make a good deal of clerical work, and though most of it may fall on the first sergeant, the captain and commissioned officers must know how it should be done and when it is well done, or they are sure to get into trouble. It was a very rare thing for a man of middle age to make a good company officer. A good many who tried it at the beginning had to be eliminated from the service in one way or another. In a less degree the same was found to hold true of the regimental field officers. Some men retain flexibility of mind and body longer than others, and could more easily adapt themselves to new circumstances and a new occupation. Of course such would succeed best. But it is also true that in the larger and broader commands solidity of judgment and weight of character were more essential than in the company, and the experience of older men was a more valuable quality. Such reasons will account for the fact that youth seemed to be an almost essential requisite for a company officer, whilst it was not so in the same degree in the higher positions.

It was astonishing to see the rapidity with which well-educated and earnest young men progressed as officers. They were alert in both mind and body. They quickly grasped the principles of their new profession, and with very little instruction made themselves masters of tactics and of administrative routine. Add to this, bravery of the highest type and a burning zeal in the cause they were fighting for, and a campaign or two made them the peers of any officers of their grade in our own or any other army.

Another class which cannot be omitted and which is yet very hard to define accurately, is that of the "political appointments."

Of the learned professions, the lawyers were of course most strongly represented among officers of the line. The medical men were so greatly needed in their own professional department that it was hard to find a sufficient number of suitable age and proper skill to supply the regiments with surgeons and the hospitals with a proper staff. The clergy were non-combatants by profession, and a few only were found in other than chaplain's duty. Civil engineers, railroad contractors, architects, and manufacturers were well represented and were valuable men. Scarce any single qualification was more useful in organizing the army than that of using and handling considerable bodies of men such as mechanics and railway employees.

The profession of the law is in our country so closely allied to political activity that the lawyers who put on the uniform were most likely to be classed among political appointments. The term was first applied to men like Banks, Butler, Baker, Logan, and Blair, most of whom left seats in Congress to serve in the army. If they had not done so, it would have been easy for critics to say that the prominent politicians took care to keep their own bodies out of harm's way. Most of them won hard-earned and well-deserved fame as able soldiers before the war was over. In an armed struggle which grew out of a great political contest, it was inevitable that eager political partisans should be among the most active in the new volunteer organizations. They called meetings, addressed the people to rouse their enthusiasm, urged enlistments, and often set the example by enrolling their own names first. It must be kept constantly in mind that we had no militia organization that bore any appreciable proportion to the greatness of the country's need, and that at any rate the policy of relying upon volunteering at the beginning was adopted by the government. It was a foregone conclusion that popular leaders of all grades must largely officer the new troops. Such men might be national leaders or leaders of country neighborhoods; but big or little, they were the necessity of the time. It was the application of the old Yankee story, "If the Lord *will* have a church in Paxton, he must take *sech as ther' be* for deacons." . . .[19]

But the volunteer officers of the army were not without their problems. Trying to enforce discipline upon the citizen-soldiers often led to scenes such as the one described by Lieutenant Colonel John Beatty of the Third Ohio Volunteer Infantry.

January 5 [1862] General Mitchel has issued an immense number of orders, and of course holds the commandants of regiments responsible for their execution. I have, as in duty bound, done my best to enforce them, and the men think me unnecessarily severe.

Today a soldier, about half drunk, was arrested for leaving camp without permission; brought to my quarters; he had two canteens of whisky on his person. I remonstrated with him mildly, but he grew saucy, insubordinate, and finally insolent and insulting; he said he did not care a damn for what I thought or did, and was ready to go to the guardhouse—in fact wanted to go there. Finally becoming exasperated, I took the canteens from him, poured out the whisky, and directed Captain Patterson to strap him to a tree until he cooled off somewhat. The captain failing in his efforts to fasten him securely, I took my saddle girth, backed him up to the tree, buckled him to it, and returned to my quarters. This proved to be the last straw that broke the unfortunate camel's back. It was a highhanded outrage upon the person of a volunteer soldier, the last and worst of the many arbitrary and severe acts of which I had been guilty. The regiment seemed to arise *en masse* and, led on by a few reckless men who had long disliked me, advanced with threats and

Reading the War News on Broadway, New York

fearful oaths toward my tent. The bitter hatred that the men entertained for me had now culminated. It being Sunday the whole regiment was off duty, and while some, and perhaps many, of the boys had no desire to resort to violent measures, yet all evidently sympathized with the prisoner and regarded my action as arbitrary and cruel. The position of the soldier was a humiliating one, but it gave him no bodily pain. Possibly I had no authority for punishing him in this way; and had I taken time for reflection it is more than probable I should have found some other and less objectionable mode; confinement in the guardhouse, however, would have been no punishment for such a man; on the contrary, it would have afforded him that relief from disagreeable duty which he desired. At any rate the act, whether right or wrong, had been done, and I must either stand by it now or abandon all hope of controlling the regiment hereafter.

I watched the mob, unobserved by it, from an opening in my tent door. Saw it gather, consult, advance, and could hear the boisterous and threatening language very plainly. Buckling my pistol belt under my coat where it could not be seen, I stepped out just as the leaders advanced to the tree for the purpose of releasing the man. I asked them very quietly what they proposed to do. Then I explained to them how the soldier had violated orders, which I was bound by my oath to enforce; how, when I undertook to remonstrate kindly against such unsoldierly conduct, he had insulted and defied me. Then I continued as calmly as I ever spoke: "I understand you have come here to untie him; let the man who desires to undertake the work begin—if there be a dozen men here who have it in their minds to do this thing—let them step forward—I dare them to do it." They saw before them a quiet, plain man who was ready to die if need be; they could not doubt his honesty of purpose. He gave them time to act and answer; they stood irresolute and silent; with a wave of the hand he bade them go to their quarters, and they went.

General Mitchel hearing of my trouble sent for me. I explained to him the difficulties under which I was laboring, told him what I had done and why I had done it. He said he understood my position fully, that I must go ahead, do my duty and he would stand by me, and, if necessary, sustain me with his whole division. I replied that

I needed no assistance, that the officers, with but few exceptions, were my friends, and that I believed there were enough good, sensible soldiers in the regiment to see me through. He talked very kindly to me; but I feel greatly discouraged. The colonel has practically abandoned the regiment in this period of bad weather, when rigorous discipline is to be enforced, and the boys seem to feel that I am taking advantage of his absence to display my authority, and require from them performance of hard and unnecessary tasks. Many non-commissioned officers have been reduced to the ranks by court-martial for being absent without leave, and many privates have been punished in various ways for the same reason. It was my duty to approve or disapprove the finding of the court. Disapproval in the majority of cases would have been subversive of all discipline. Approval has brought down upon me not only the hatred and curses of the soldiers tried and punished but in some instances the ill will also of their fathers, who for years were my neighbors and friends.

Very many of these soldiers think they should be allowed to work when they please, play when they please, and in short do as they please. Until this idea is expelled from their minds the regiment will be but little if any better than a mob.[20]

Viewed from the jaundiced eye of a defeated general, the volunteer army that ran away at the first battle of Bull Run was a sorry thing. In a letter to John Bigelow, coeditor with William Cullen Bryant of the New York Evening Post, *Brigadier General Irvin McDowell unburdened himself.*

Many thousand thanks for your kind note. It is my chief consolation at this time, that my friends seem warmer towards me than ever. I have many evidences that they do not give me up to the tender mercies of the *dear press!* though I must say for the latter that they are not as savage as I expected. For the most part they have dealt fairly by me, and where they have erred, have not done so intentionally.

It is certainly a great consolation to get such notes as yours and Prof. Mahan's and it encourages me to try again even with such a vicious system as that we are now working under—the Volunteers.

Most of my subordinate commanders, however, are in despair and so are many of the regimental and company officers.

One N.Y. Regt. is so entirely demoralized that the best thing we can do with it will be to send it home as worthless. In another, all the field officers have resigned.

When the regts. were repulsed, the officers could not be found to take care of their men!

The first Zouaves are scattered every where and are worthless!

Is not this a cheering state of affairs?[21]

Bull Run was the baptism. During the next year the raw volunteers were baked in the merciless fires of combat. George Augustus Sala, correspondent of the London Telegraph, *reported the transition to modern warfare that occurred during the American Civil War.*

. . . A more painful account of what civilians imagine to be a scene of bustle, cheering, drumming, and trumpeting, "fights for the standard" after the style of Mr. Ansdell's picture, and hand-to-hand combats à la Coburg melodrama, I heard from an officer who was actively engaged in the dreadful fight of Spottsylvania Court House. All day long the corps to which he belonged was posted on the skirts of a wood. From hour to hour whole regiments were sent into this wood. Reinforcement succeeded reinforcement. A dull booming sound of cannonading never ceased; and, as the doomed men went in, fatigue parties continued to come out, bearing shattered and mutilated forms on stretchers. Was not this going into the jaws of Death and the mouth of Hell? There was no excitement, no sensational melodrama. When your time came you went in to be killed. "And the dead in that wood," added my informant, "have never been buried." To have stood firm through that awful day, "waiting for death," and calmly obeying the grim summons when it came, argues the possession, I think, of a higher grade of personal bravery than is displayed in rushing, amidst the applause of one's comrades, into the embrasure of a fort, or even heading a forlorn hope. The truth is that, since the introduction of arms of precision and artillery of long range, fighting under cover has become the almost invariable rule in America, as it must become when —God avert the evil day!—war breaks out in Europe. The slaughter, even in ambush, is frightful enough; but in the open—as after the explosion of the mine at Petersburg—it would be aggravated to a perfect *battue*. And here let it be sorrowfully noted that an illusion long entertained by the fanatics for Peace—of whom the subscriber hopes that he is one; the humblest, but not the least earnest—has been dispelled. It was long represented that the perfection of offensive weapons—of Miniés, and Armstrongs, and Whitworths—must have a tendency gradually but surely to discourage war; and, at last, by increasing the chances of mutual destruction in a ratio too frightful for contemplation, render war impossible, and abrogate it altogether. When each side could do no more in devising means of annihilation—when the irresistable force met the immovable body—the result was to be inertia. But the Devil is not to be so easily outflanked. His resources are infinite. In proportion as weapons are becoming more formidable, defenses against them are becoming stronger. Whole fleets and armies go into panoply of proof. The loss of human life is much greater than of yore, but it is not in excess of proportion to the means of destruction brought to bear. An average army in the last generation, which, fighting a hundred miles from its base, had lost ten thousand men, was virtually ruined; but now, within a dozen hours, a dozen railway trains can reinforce it to twice the amount of its casualties. Like a witch's prayer—a saintly orison read backwards—the phenomena of modern warfare present a horrible parody of the doctrine of compensation. More men can be killed than in the old time; but more men can be procured to be killed, and they can hold out much longer before they *are* killed. Soldiers are fain to become earthclads, as, on the ocean, sailors trust in ironclads. Analogically, the difference is very slight between plating the sides of your ship and burrowing in the earth like a mole. Almost the first proceeding of an advancing corps is to throw up earth-works, and these, the tools being carried with them, are constructed with wonderful speed. The opposing force has done the same, and then both parties "blaze away." If one side can't stand the fire, they retire, and entrench themselves somewhere else; the other side feel their way into the abandoned pits; this is called "carrying the earthworks in gallant style." The movements of the cavalry are as mysterious as those of the infantry. The real use of the American dragoons is for the marauding expeditions known as raids. For burning houses, cutting railroads, gutting stores, and destroying crops, they are invaluable; but very little employment can be found for them in a pitched battle, and nothing is more common than to dismount them, leaving their horses picketed in charge of a few of their number, and send them into ambuscade to "blaze away." The sabre they are scarcely ever called upon to use.

I have now done my best to describe what, at the risk of paradox, I may term the indescribability of Transatlantic warfare, in which the opposing elements are not only angry and resolute men, but Dahlgrens and Parrotts, Sharps' rifles, and mounds of earth. And these elements, I apprehend, conspire to make scientific warfare more venomous and more persistent than the old hand-to-hand fighting. No little David can come out to the Philistine front to challenge Goliath of Gath to the duello. The "gentlemen of the guard" fire first, and whenever they have an opportunity, without waiting for an invitation. The slaughter of human beings has come to be a mere matter of settled calculation and mute volition. The Engineers of Murder are only called upon to make the working drawings, and draw out the specifications of bloodshed. Tinkle a bell, touch a wire, and our enemy is dead. . . .[22]

By the end of the war, no one was better entitled to render a final verdict than William Tecumseh Sherman, who led his battle-toughened veterans on the march through Georgia and the Carolinas. He does so with pride, and without illusions.

[March 23, 1865] . . . I don't believe anything has tended more to break the pride of the South than my steady persistent progress. My army is dirty, ragged and saucy. I have promised them rest, clothing and food, but the railroads have not been completed as I expected and I fear we may be troubled thereby. I am just informed that the telegraph line is finished from the sea to this place, so our lines of communication will be shortened. Strange to say we are all in fine health and condition, only a little blackened by the pine smoke of our camp fires. I would like to march this army through

New York just as it appears today, with its wagons, pack mules, cattle, niggers and bummers, and I think they would make a more attractive show than your fair [i.e. Sanitary Fair].

. . . . .

[April 5, 1865] Officers and soldiers have in my foresight and knowledge a childlike confidence that is really most agreeable. Whilst wading through mud and water, and heaving at mired wagons the soldiers did not indulge a single growl, but always said and felt that the Old Man would bring them out all right; and no sooner had we reached the Cape Fear River at Fayetteville than a little squeaking tug came puffing up the river with news, and we had hardly spread out in the camps around Goldsboro than the locomotive and train came thundering along from the sea ninety-six miles distant, loaded with shoes and pants and clothing, as well as food. So remarkable and happy a coincidence, which of course I had arranged from Savannah, made the woods resound with a yell that must have reached Raleigh.

. . . . .

[April 9, 1865] The sun is warm, the leaves are all coming out, and flowers are in bloom, about as you will have it a month hence. The entire army has new clothing, and with soap and water have made a wonderful change in our appearance. The fellows who passed in review before me with smoke-black faces, dirty and ragged, many with feet bare or wrapped in cloth, now strut about as proud as young chicken cocks, with their clean faces and bright blue clothes. All are ready to plunge again into the labor and toil and uncertainty of war. . . .[23]

This, at war's end, was the citizens' Army of the North.

The Voice of Politics

AT THEIR BEST, democratic politics are a cohesive force. In their quest for votes, parties seek and find a basis for compromise of conflicting interests, and thus relieve the tensions that endanger the consensus regarding fundamentals that are necessary to democratic government. At their worst, democratic politics are a disruptive force, broadening existing fissures and opening new ones, thereby recklessly endangering national unity as parties and factions within parties grasp for power. Each group may be sincere—though few are wholly so—but it is the sincerity of the fanatic, that will rack and burn his opponent in the name of holy faith. During the Civil War, with notable exceptions, Northern politics and politicians were at their worst.

Not only were Republicans arrayed against Democrats but factions within each party waged their own battles with such ferocity that there were times when they appeared to be a greater danger to the Union than the Confederate Army. It was his struggle with these forces that tested Abraham Lincoln's political skill. He met the test superbly and, in doing so, proved himself one of the nation's truly great politicans. Though unable to knead the warring factions into a harmonious whole, he did hold together a sufficient body of them to do what all along he declared he must do—preserve the Union. He had loyal aides, notably William H. Seward, his Secretary of State, who at the war's beginning declared, "No party now, but all for country," and who was thereupon stigmatized by Republican Radicals as a traitor both to his party and to his country's welfare. But in the end it was Lincoln himself who bore the brunt of partisan attacks.

A frontal assault was mounted by the Peace Democrats, labeled Copperheads by outraged fellow citizens. Under the strain of Civil War, the Northern Democratic party disintegrated into factional groupings. The central party organization was under the control of the War Democrats who opposed emancipation and other policies of the Lincoln administration, but claimed to support the war effort. A second faction, Unionist Democrats, deserted their party to coalesce with the Republicans. Finally there were the Peace Democrats who branded the war a failure, demanded an armistice, berated the Lincoln administration for stamping out liberty, and called for a national convention where Northern and Southern delegates might negotiate for a new union of the states. An unsigned letter of July 8, 1862, to General George B. McClellan, himself a War Democrat, was undoubtedly written by a fervent admirer, but it also presents the pacifistic views of a Peace Democrat, even though these might be used to cloak the aims of an incipient military dictatorship.

A few of your friends have met together to interchange our views relative to the deplorable condition of our country and after deliberating in profound secrecy we have concluded to address to you a letter containing the results, the substance of which is this suggestion to you.

That you, after fully maturing your plans and preparations turn your army toward Washington, take possession of the city with all the public departments, assume the sole control of all our government and hold the same as Provisional President until an election can be had throughout the whole United States for all the officers of the General government, Congress &c. Declare all the acts of the present administration null and unconstitutional. . . . Guarantee to the South all their constitutional rights in consideration of their returning fealty, then hold this government in your military power until the dispairing [*sic*] people can, by their efforts restore harmony to our distracted country. A "Coup d'etat" in fact, than which no public movement would be more popular or more welcome to a people on the verge of ruin. Every state would rally to your support and every heart would swell with thankfulness for deliverance from this civil war.

. . . . .

Where is our country drifting to? Suppose the whole object of the North be consummated our ruined country is the result, and no reconciliation can ever be hoped for from the injured, incensed, down trodden people of the South.

We can see no salvation for our country except through this glorious ordeal. You can, sir, with your noble, unambitious views make yourself the savior of this Republic. . . .[1]

It is unlikely that there were many Copperheads in the Army, but in September 1862, a New York Herald *reporter did detect a spirit of unrest, caused by the Emancipation Proclamation, that he believed bordered on revolution. Unchecked, it would certainly strengthen and perhaps bring about the triumph of the Peace Democrats.*

A deep and earnest feeling pervades the army . . . in reference to the proclamation of the President. The army is dissatisfied and the air is thick with revolution. It has been not only thought of but talked of and the question now is where can the man be found. McClellan is idolised but he seems to have no political ambition. The sentiment throughout the whole army seems to be in favor of a change of dynasty. They are unwilling to submit to the control of the faction which has attempted to direct the Government and whose policy is enunciated in the recent proclamation. . . . God knows what will be the consequence, but at present matters look dark indeed, and there is large promise of a fearful revolution which will sweep before it not only the administration but popular government.[2]

A month later a Michigan Radical Republican saw Lincoln's policy of coalescing with Unionist Democrats as nothing better than surrender to the Copperheads—a surrender to be followed by a further democratically contrived dismemberment of the Union.

Don't shut your eyes to the damnable project of detaching the western states from the eastern. If the rebellion succeeds, that project will be espoused by the western democracy & I *fear they will carry it out*. The anti-tariff cry would rend the heavens & *free trade* down the Missi[ssippi] be the chorus. . . .

The Republicans are having a hard contest in this state with the combined forces of "Unionism and democracy," both which mean the same thing, *id est,* peace with the rebels *at any rate,* at any sacrifice.

My dear friend, *we must have victories* & that *soon*. Mr. Seward's policy is cruel & self-destructive. It is destroying the government. The spirit of the people is sinking under the Seward-McClellan do-nothing policy. Good God!—What are they thinking about to let this beautiful fall pass without fighting. . . .[3]

The election of 1862 was a disaster for the Republicans. They lost such key states as Ohio, Indiana, and Lincoln's own Illinois. Almost everywhere, their vote ebbed from the 1860 level. Although the victors were the War, rather than the Peace, Democrats, the latter were encouraged. In February 1863, a group of them met at Delmonico's restaurant in New York City to complete the organization of the Society for the Diffusion of Political Knowledge, a propaganda agency. As President of the Society, Samuel F. B. Morse, the inventor, in his inaugural address, attacked the war as the work of fanatics and defended the aims and motives of Peace Democrats.

. . . Nothing in these days of our country's trial has so saddened the hearts of patriots, and caused such universal misgiving touching the stability and even the existence of our cherished Government, as the constantly recurring evidences of a deep and wide-spread demoralization, pervading the public mind, to which the rostrum, the press, and I am sorry to add, the pulpit, in a lamentable degree, lend their powerful influence to strengthen and perpetuate. Fanaticism rules the hour. The *fanatic* is on the throne. I use the term fanatic in no loose sense. Fanaticism is a frenzy, a madness. It is not, as it pretends to be, a zeal springing from enlightened reason, founded on the rock of God's word, but a spirit of the pit, clothing itself in our day in the garb of the angel of light, the better to deceive the minds of the unthinking and the simple. Fanaticism has been well defined, "enthusiasm inflamed by hatred," and the truth of the portrait of the foul fiend is exhibited before us every day.

History, ever repeating itself, as time completes its cycles, has not yet closed its sad volume of disastrous hallucinations. It is preparing its pages and reddening its pen to record the story of the foulest tragedy of earth—the most frightful that is yet to deform the annals of the past.

Can patriotic men, persuaded of such an issue, be silent, be idle? There may be those who fold their arms and shut their eyes, and lull their apprehensions with baseless dreams of a future "visionary, impossible Union," a Union begotten of force and fear, not a Union begotten of peace and love; a Union to be created when the South shall be wiped out of existence, and its soil prepared for Northern colonization; when the Southern earth shall be "without form and void," and has become the desolate habitation for the advent of the new Northern man. But there are others who have awakened to the realities of the times. They can not but read the portentous signs of a coming destruction. . . .

The heresies of the Church must be grappled with by the untainted theologians of the land, for there are thousands of these who have not bowed the knee to the abolition Baal. The heresies of the state can be and must be reached in a constitutional way by the intellects of the country. If I have read the provisions of the Constitution aright, this meeting in its object and its mode of reaching that object, is wholly and completely constitutional.

. . . . .

We have been charged with disloyalty. Men use words very loosely in these times of excitement. What is disloyalty? It is unfaithfulness to the sovereign. Where is our sovereign? Will it be said that it resides in the powers that be, and these we are commanded not to resist? If there are any associated with us who propose to resist the powers that be, I have not been acquainted with them. There is one of the powers that be, and that too the very chief of these powers, which seems to be strangely left out of view in our political discussion in these eventful times. There are some, I understand, who believe the sovereign power to exist in the President; others [believe] that it rests in the national, executive, legislative, and judicial bodies collectively, and others [believe that it resides], in the States; and many if not most, have very indefinite and confused ideas of these powers that be. Each of these is a power, and there are many others, each of which, in the legitimate exercise in its proper order of its own delegated duties, is not to be resisted without blame. But it seems to be forgotten that there is a power in the State sovereign to each and all these powers, one to which all of them are subject. Can we overlook the great truth that the very foundation of our governmental system is based on the sovereignty of the people? Do I mistake or exaggerate when I say that presidents, and governors, and all the departments, whether of State or federal machinery, are all subordinate to the people?

. . . . .

The order, then, of classification of these powers is, first the people, then the State Government, and then the Federal Government. The people in their sovereign capacity and right have absolute power over and above all other powers. . . . Can any political power be conceived as more absolute than this? It is supreme over all the other powers. . . . And now to whom are we appealing in forming this Society? To the *supreme power*. We have nothing to do with any of the other powers, but to use them, so far as we may in their several subordinate stations, as means of reaching the sovereign; and we intend reaching his throne with our petition only through the well-known constitutional channels of access. We mean to use our rights of free discussion, and look for the answer to our appeal of the ballot-box.

Is this treason? Is this conspiracy? Is this resisting the powers that be? Is it disloyalty to appeal to the *sovereign*, or to exercise that portion of the sovereign power which of right belongs to us as part of the people? . . .[4]

The Republican Radicals, because they were powerful in Congress and had a large popular following, were a greater menace than Peace Democrats to Lincoln's policy of uniting all factions behind victory in war and the preservation of the Union.

Radical, when used to describe the radical Republican faction in Civil War politics, implies a literal acceptance of the Latin origin of the word "radix," meaning root. The Radicals were determined to go to what they regarded as the root of the sectional controversy to destroy slavery, and with it all related aspects of Southern society. Later the South could be rebuilt in the image of Northern institutions. Although not "leftists" in the twentieth-century connotation, The Civil War Radicals were in many respects the "wave of the future." They not only accepted, but on occasion anticipated changes in the social, economic, and political fabric of American society. They were the "activists" of the 1860's in contrast to the conservative supporters of Lincoln (and perhaps the President himself) who were too often willing to settle for the preservation of existing traditions and institutions. This was one source and touchstone of their popular support.

Though bound together by the conviction that if the war ended with slavery intact, it would not be worth the price of winning it, the Radicals were not a cohesive group. They included "old" abolitionists, doctrinaires (such as Charles Sumner), new industrialists eager for tariffs and other favorable legislation, agrarians who hated the slaveholder's alleged monopoly of Southern land, German liberals who supported the war as a fight against universal tyranny, and humanitarians genuinely interested in the Negro's welfare. Virtually all of these were sincere in their convictions, whatever these might be.

There were also Lincoln haters among the Radicals and unmitigated demagogues motivated chiefly, if not wholly, by a thirst for power. Senator Benjamin Wade of Ohio was a politician of this type. He was primarily concerned with the power struggle which swirled around the Lincoln administration and the army. In a characteristic speech delivered on the Senate floor, he cried for vengeance on Southern and Northern traitors alike. His definition of traitor was inclusive enough to include all who would temper justice for rebels with mercy.

. . . Mr. President, that man is not quite honest who . . . argues constitutional questions in this Senate, and invokes the Constitution in behalf of the rights of every man precisely as he would in times of peace where there were isolated cases of delinquency, and where it was safe to bring a man to trial. The man who says it, and would have you proceed with these traitors precisely as you would

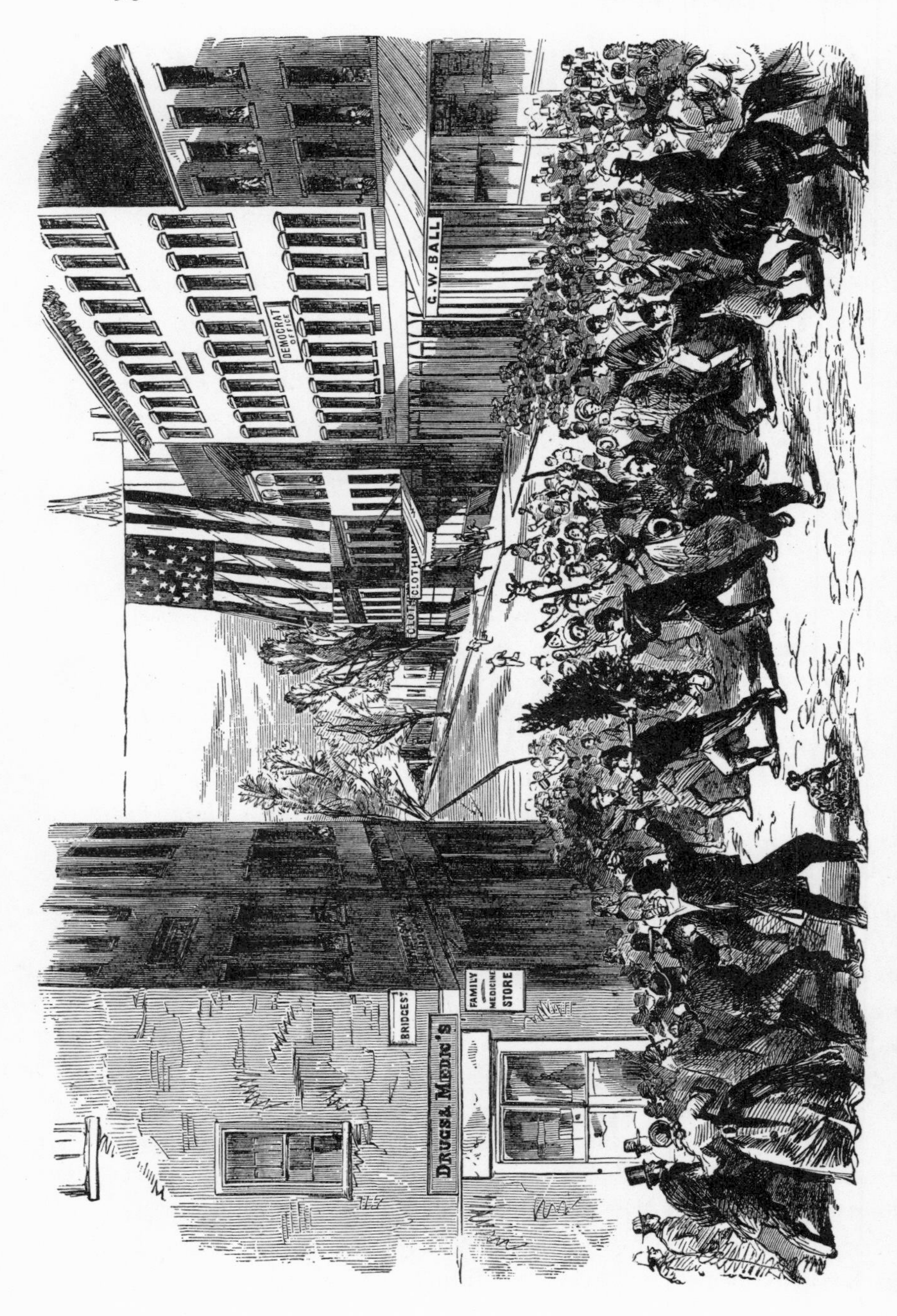

INDIGNITIES SHOWN A MASSACHUSETTS EDITOR FOR PUBLISHING EXPRESSIONS OF SYMPATHY WITH THE SOUTH

in time of peace is endeavoring to deceive the public. Can you prosecute a traitor south of Mason and Dixon's line? As the old saying is, you might as well try the devil in hell, and summon as jurors his chief angels. It is impracticable; it cannot be done. When they stand up here contending that men should be tried by all the constitutional guarantees that are thrown around them in peaceful times? I repeat what I said when I was up the other day, as no jurist has yet undertaken to define the limits to which a man might go in the honest defense of his life when assailed, so no statesman would undertake to limit the powers that the Government might use to preserve its life when assailed by traitors. I defy the gentleman to make an argument worthy of the name against that proposition.

Do you think that we will stand by, yielding to your argument, while you fetter our legs, and bind our arms with the Constitution of the United States that you may stab it to death? Is that your idea of the Constitution, that it is made to tie the hands of honest men from its defense, while traitors may stab it to the heart? That is the use you would make of the Constitution of the United States. Sir, I say again, I have no scruples about the Constitution of the United States as wielded against traitors in this time of violent revolution. You have seen that the ordinary course of the common law and of the Constitution cannot be followed. Shall the Constitution lie down and die? Must we give up all our glorious principles that were defended by it because traitors have assailed it in such a way that they have prevented its operation? Sir, folly like that would deserve the ignominous fate which would inevitably follow so foolish a course.

Mr. President, as I have said heretofore, it is a remarkable fact, that although thousands upon thousands of men have fallen victims to this rebellion on the field of battle, and many thousands more have been mangled and wounded, inflicting misery, poverty, and death upon millions of people, we are yet told on this floor that we should be tender-footed, that we cannot tie the hands of a miserable traitor from giving information to the enemy, and thus aiding them to carry on this accursed war. Is that the logic of the Senator? Sir, he will find but few adherents here; he will find less among the people, for they are entirely ahead of us in all that pertains to the vigorous prosecution of this war and a vigorous dealing with traitors according to their crimes. Why, sir, in every hole and corner of this city, nay, in almost every city of the United States, and in the country, too, you find these slippery, slimy, glib-tongued traitors who are ready on all occasions to give information of all the movements of your Army and of every other important fact to the enemy, so that they have it earlier than we. You would not expect that a man taken with arms in his hands, fighting against our armies, persecuting us to death, should go entirely without punishment; and yet he does the enemy infinitely less service than the man who, pretending to be loyal, worms himself into the knowledge of the most important secrets of your Executive, and then goes forth and gives it to your enemies, whereby thousands of your men may die in vain upon the field of battle, and all brought about by this slippery, slimy traitor. There are men who would get up afterwards in this Senate, and, with tears in their eyes, plead the cause of just such a wretch as that who, with all the evidence of guilt upon him was sent off for a little while to sojourn in one of our fortifications, and call it inquisitorial, tyrannical, devilish.

Sir, the man that makes use of these arguments need not tell me he is loyal. I tell you the danger to our institutions is not so great from traitors in the field with arms in their hands as it is from the nimble-tongued, slippery hypocrites who go forth apologizing for them, branding every energetic measure of the Administration as tyrannical and wrong, and endeavoring to deceive the people and stir them up to hostility against this wise, this just, this most moderate Administration. I do not believe the people are going to be deceived by it. I do not believe that your night meetings to reconstruct the Democratic party, your resolutions of censure accusing them of tyranny here and intimidation abroad—I do not believe all these things and all your machinations will be able to deceive an awakened people who understand all your arts and are determined to back a wise Administration in the course it shall pursue.[5]

Senator John Sherman, throughout a long political career, was a moderate man. Yet in a letter to his brother, written in 1862, he cautiously admonishes the General for "leniency to the rebels," and pleads the political advantage of enlisting under the Radical banner.

If we ever intend to compel the South to submit to the laws we must make friends of the blacks. . . . If we can't depend upon the loyalty of the white men of the South I would give the land to the blacks or colonise a new set. By the way the only criticism I notice of your management in Memphis is your leniency to the rebels—I enclose you an extract. I take it that most of their complaints are groundless—but you perceive from it the point upon which public opinion rests. The traitors South are enemies to be punished and not persons to be conciliated. . . . Le Vendee presents the historical parallel. I cannot but think that enough distinction is not made between those in the South who are friendly & those who are not. The former should be favored even if the motives of their loyalty are unworthy. Even if poor, ignorant & vicious they ought to be encouraged at the expense of the wealthy & educated Traitors. Such is not the only lesson of history—the dictate of policy but is the general popular sentiment. . . . You notice that Fremont, Butler, Mitchell, Turchin & Corcoran are popular while Buell, Thomas, McClellan & others are not. It is not for military merit, for most persons concede the inferiority in many respects of the officers first named, but it is because these officers agree with and act upon the popular idea that we must treat these rebels as bitter enemies to be subdued —conquered—by confiscation—by the employment of their slaves —by terror—energy—audacity—rather than by conciliation.[6]

Radicalism attracted businessmen with an eye to dollars, as well as politicians seeking votes. A month before the attack on Fort Sumter, Republicans were defending themselves against shafts of criticism aimed by Southern spokesmen deprecating their greed and lack of a gentleman's proper accouterment. In doing so they identify the Republican party with the dynamic influence of business enterprise that was being quickened by the Industrial Revolution. It is interesting to note the epithet carpetbagger predates the Reconstruction Period in American history.

Correspondents of southern papers, writing from Washington city at the time of the inauguration, and a few days after, attempt to depreciate the appearance and character of the great throngs of northern men by saying that they had a lean and hungry look, and were deficient in clothing, as they all carried carpetbags. One correspondent quotes a railway baggagemaster as saying that there was not more than one trunk for a hundred passengers. So far as regards baggage, this is true. The northern people are accustomed to travel about three times as much as southerners, and as time is valuable to them they cannot encumber themselves with heavy baggage. Southerners who were in the habit of going to Washington, under former administrations, to get positions, went resolved not to be refused, and therefore had to carry baggage enough to provide against all emergencies. We of the north are of a more thrifty and business-like turn. The carpetbag is an institution with us, and in the party which the Washingtonians regarded with so much contempt, according to these correspondents, were thousands of the most respectable merchants and other citizens of the north, men of means far beyond those who travelled with so much baggage to bore previous administrations. But were they ever so poor; what a miserable idea this is to be put forth in a republic. Here is the inauguration of a Chief Magistrate, and the masses of the common people are supposed, by these scribes, to have no interest in it. No one need be ashamed to belong to the carpetbag industry. The carpetbag is the emblem of the business man. It characterizes thousands who transact the vast commerce between the interior and the seaboard, carrying on operations which amount to millions of dollars, and building up fortunes and trade, palaces and cities, before which the region whence come the gentlemen with many trunks must shun comparison. Hitherto the interests of these men have widely separated them from politics. But the dawn of a new era brings with it consequences to them of no ordinary kind. It would be a good thing for Washington city if it could always have such a class of people visiting it by thousands. They would infuse into it new life.[7]

As the war progressed, the identification of some business interests with the Radical program became more pronounced. A New York correspondent, whose address was No. 17 Wall Street, New York City, wrote to the Secretary of the Treasury, Salmon P. Chase:

A number of gentlemen of good position and influence are on the point of forming an association here for the purpose of disseminating what they conceive to be sound political doctrine and knowledge.

It will favor the formation of a permanent National Banking System—a high protective Tariff—the abolishment of the present faulty elective Judiciary System—and will oppose most religiously any settlement or attempted settlement of our present difficulties by any Compromise whatever with slavery.

As soon as the Association has been fully organized and become operative, we hope to have the honor of forwarding you notice of the same, and of deserving your hearty approval and that of your friends. . . .[8]

Western agrarian and Eastern business interests ordinarily had little in common. They did, however, join in the demand for the destruction of the "slaveocracy." George W. Julian, an Indiana Congressman, presented the views of the agrarian radical.

. . . What shall be done with these immense estates, brought within our power by the acts of rebels? One of two policies, radically antagonistic, must be accepted. They must be allowed to fall into the hands of speculators, and become the basis of new and frightful monopolies, or they must be placed under the jurisdiction of the Government, in trust for the people. The alternative is now presented, and presses upon us for a speedy decision. Under the laws of Congress now in force, unchecked by counter legislation, these lands will be purchased and monopolized by men who care far more for their own mercenary gains than for the real progress and glory of our country. Instead of being parceled out into small homesteads, to be tilled by their own independent owners, they will be bought in large tracts, and thus not only deprive the great mass of landless laborers of the opportunity of acquiring homes, but place them at the mercy of the lords of the soil. The old order of things will be swept away, but a new order, scarcely less to be deplored will succeed. In place of the slaveholding landowner of the South, lording it over hundreds of slaves and thousands of acres, we shall have the grasping monopolist of the North, whose dominion over the freedmen and poor whites will be more galling than slavery itself, which in some degree tempers its despotism through the interest of the tyrant in the health and welfare of his victims. The maxim of the slaveholder that "capital should own labor" will be as frightfully exemplified under the system of wages slavery, the child of land monopoly, as under the system of chattel slavery, which has so long scourged the southern States. What we should demand is a policy that will guaranty homes to the loyal millions who need them, and thus guard their most precious rights and interests against the remorseless exactions of capital and the pitiless rapacity of avarice.

. . . . . .

Nothing can atone for the woes and sorrows of this war but the thorough reorganization of society in these revolted States. Now is the time to begin this work. We must not only cut up slavery, root and branch, but we must see to it that these teeming regions shall be studded over with small farms and tilled by free men. . . . Labor must be rendered honorable and gainful, by securing to the laborer the fruits of his toil. Instead of the spirit of Caste and the law of Hate which have so long blasted these regions, we must build up homogeneous communities, in which the interest of each will be recognized as the interest of all. Instead of an overshadowing aristocracy, founded on the monopoly of the soil, and its dominion over the poor, we must have no order of nobility but that of the laboring masses of the country, who fight its battles in war and constitute its glory and its strength in peace. Instead of large estates, widely scattered settlements, wasteful agriculture, popular ignorance, political and social degradation, the decay of literature, the decline of manufactures and the arts, contempt for honest labor, and a pampered aristocracy, we must have small farms, closely associated communities, thrifty tillage, free schools, social independence, a healthy literature, flourishing manufactures and mechanic arts, respect for honest labor, and equality of political rights. . . .[9]

Abolitionists, Republican politicians, businessmen with an eye to profit, and farm leaders with an eye to a new frontier of small farms for yeoman farmers, had a rational base for supporting the Radicals' demand that there must be no appeasement of the South, no welcome for the prodigal brother, but only punishment for the criminal. The majority of the Northerners did not share these interests and, on the eve of the war, if they lacked Lincoln's charity, they were equally without Ben Wade's rancor. The sentiments of many, however, changed as the war progressed with its burden of grief and anger. Bitterness and outrage supplanted relative tolerance. The new mood was nourished by news stories, eyewitness accounts, cartoons, congressional reports, political speeches, and even sermons devoted to lurid presentations of Southern atrocities. A sample is to be found in an address delivered by the Reverend Nathan Sidney Smith Beman, President of Rensselaer Polytechnic Institute.

. . . What have been the moral developments, I ask, of this war? Where do we see humanity opening its gushing heart, amid scenes adapted to close it with strong bands of steel? And where has barbarism outstripped its former self in deeds of unwonted infamy? Go to the battle-field, and there read a lesson never to be forgotten. Where do you find, and upon whom do you charge the most fiendish cruelty? Who has assailed the wounded soldier, that lay bleeding and helpless on the ground, with thrust after thrust with the bayonet? Who dug up the body of a brave officer, and cut off his head, and burned his flesh to ashes? Who have stripped dead men of their apparel, and left them naked on the field to be eaten up of dogs, or to decay there? Who have crammed dungeons rank with filth and feculence with prisoners and the wounded, and denied a dying man a cup of cold water even, in the last extremity? Who have boiled the flesh from dead men's bones, and then manufactured these bones into ornaments for themselves and their friends, and for sale in the markets? Who have been in the habit of shooting their captives made in war, for showing their faces at the windows of their prison-house,—and then been elevated to special honors for such foul deeds? But I need not enlarge this truly humilating catalogue. I ought to add here, that this is not a fancy sketch, got up for the occasion. I have drawn, not upon an excited imagination, but upon sober facts, for this dark picture. I have conned the details of recent history, and not the wild romance of war, for what I have now stated. These things, and much more of the like character, is [*sic*] confirmed by credible witnesses, and embodied in "The Report of the Joint Committee on the Conduct of the present war", made to the Senate of the United States, on the 30th of April last.

. . . . .

I close these horrid details by saying, that no human institution in civilized life ever bred such men as form the basis and superstructure of this rebellion—*or could do it—except SLAVERY*. And yet many among us love it and defend it. They look upon it as others do upon *rum,* as one of the great and good gifts of God. And too many who love the one, love the other also.

But this so-called divine institution [slavery] is doomed. It has all the sad marks of God's reprobation upon it. . . . We have flattered it by concessions, propped it up by compromises, bribed it by special gratuities, defended its life and honor by mob violence, made presidents by the mysterious magic of its name, and told the earth and the heavens of our determination to cling to this American idol, if we cut loose from everything else. During the present fearful struggle, the rebels have fought bravely to shield it from injury and keep it from death, and we, by many anomalous acts, have played the fool, for the same purpose. Our generals in the field who tried to make the traitor Breckinridge—*the slave-holder's candidate*—President, have been true to their political instincts, and waged war *slowly,* yea, *TENDERLY,* for fear of inflicting too severe a punishment upon the rebels by marring their idolized institution, and lest by overthrowing it altogether, they might exterminate forever the possibility of all similar insurrections. The institution must be spared as far as possible, and above all its *tender roots* must be left unharmed in the soil. Was ever national infatuation more absurd, or more extravagant? . . . Slavery, in our present agitations, is the all-pervading element. But the foundations of the system are breaking up. . . .[10]

The invitation to hate and destroy was also delivered in verse.

SONG OF THE SECESSION WARRIOR.

SLIGHTLY ALTERED FROM THE CHOCTAW.

I made a spur of a Yankee's jaw,
And in New-Orleans I shot his squaw—
Shot his child like a yelping cur.
He had no time to fondle on her,
  Hoo! hoo! hoo! for the rifled graves!
  Wah! wah! wah! for the blasted slaves!

I scraped his skull all naked and bare,
And here's his scalp with a tuft of hair!
His heart is in the buzzard's maw,
His bloody bones the wolf doth gnaw.
Hoo! hoo! hoo! for the Yankee graves!
Wah! wah! wah! for the blasted slaves!

With percussion-caps we filled each gun,
And put torpedoes where he'd run;
And with poisoned bullets and poisoned rum
Helped him along to kingdom come.
Hoo! hoo! hoo! for the Yankee graves!
Wah! wah! wah! for the blasted slaves!

KNICKERBOCKER.[11]

So Republican Radicals, Peace Democrats, and even War Democrats, from different motives, in different ways, and in varying degrees, opposed Lincoln's policies. Lincoln responded by rallying his own forces to fight a political war of survival at home, while the armies of the North battled the Confederacy.

The largest group supporting the President consisted of Conservative Republicans. Their conservatism lay in their moderate attitude towards the South and the Negro, and in their inclination to accept and preserve the status quo. They supported the war for the preservation of the Union and emancipation as a part of the war effort. They were not particularly concerned with the Negro after he was emancipated, and refused to envisage the rebellious states as conquered provinces. They opposed destroying the white planter's aristocracy, providing the latter would return to the Union and, after January 1, 1863, accept emancipation. Radical Republican politicians considered Seward as the Conservative leader. The rank and file who had voted Republican in 1860 sensed rightly that it was Lincoln.

Senator Edgar Cowan expressed the Conservative view while replying on the Senate floor to a demand for confiscation of the property of all rebels.

Mr. President, I do not agree to that opinion [i.e. the one expressed by Senator Howe], and I will give my reasons for it. . . .

Ninety-nine out of every hundred of these men with whom we are at war to-day are our brethren. Why? Will any gentleman, who has taken the pains to look into the history of rebellions, who knows anything of men or of mankind generally, undertake to assert and say that the masses of the people South are traitors and rebels as against the Government of the United States? If that were true, if that could be true, then our war is worthless. But, Mr. President, it is not true. This rebellion is the work of a few men, and its spread and its enlargement is the fault of the General Government of these United States, not the fault of the people of the southern States. . . . This rebellion sprung up just as all rebellions do. It is first in the hands of a few, bad, desperate men, who overawe the community, and seize, if they can, the insignia of power and establish a *de facto* government. . . . I say, Mr. President, that Mr. Buchanan put his hands in his breeches pockets and said [of himself] and the General Government, "we can do nothing, we cannot coerce a State," and all that kind of thing, and the little fire there kindled was allowed to burn and spread by his neglect and that of the General Government. . . . The masses of the people were obliged to submit and yield, however unwillingly, and under the circumstances it was all they could do; and Mr. President, I have not a doubt that if we could rescue them tomorrow from the tyranny of that government which is over them, they would come back gladly to their allegiance, never to leave it again. And our efforts are to be directed, and solely directed in my judgment, to suppressing that armed rebellion, seizing the men who fomented it, and punishing them by the law and with severity. Let everybody else be treated with kindness and conciliation. Let them be brought back, if possible in that way. . . . True . . . [the masses] are now angry and enraged. In war that is always the case; but their resentment against us can have no deep foundation because it is not based upon wrong unredressed, nor upon injuries which have not been avenged. It is merely the result of the collision; and if the collision were once ended it would cease to be. . . .[12]

Tens of thousands of Northern and border-state Democrats rejected both the Peace and the so-called War factions of their own party and rallied to Lincoln's support. They did not become Republicans;

most of them were even less interested than the Conservatives in the fate of the Negro, and they would not fight to free him or to reconstruct the social and economic state of the South. They were, however, fiercely loyal to the Union and determined to preserve it. Eventually they were to unite with Republicans in the National Union party, a coalition that reelected Lincoln in 1864. Andrew Johnson, senator, Military Governor of Tennessee, vice-president and, after Lincoln's assassination, President of the United States, was their most distinguished leader. In his vindictiveness against slave-holding "aristocrats" he was akin to the Radicals, but it was the anger of a white commoner against the governing class and did not stem from sympathy for the Negro or dislike of slavery. He was for the Union. He made his position, and that of most "Unionists," clear in a speech delivered in Cincinnati on June 19, 1861.

. . . I know that there has been much said about the North, much said about the South. I am proud, here to-day, to hear the sentiments and the language which have been uttered in reference to the North and the South, and the relations that exist between these two sections. (Applause.) I am glad to hear it said in such a place as this that the pending difficulties—I might say the existing war—which are now upon this country do not grow out of any animosity to the local institution of any section. (Applause.) I am glad to be assured that it grows out of a determination to maintain the glorious principles upon which the Government itself rests—the principles contained in the Constitution—and at the same time to rebuke and to bring back as far as may be practicable, within the pale of the Constitution, those individuals, or States even, who have taken it upon themselves to exercise a principle and doctrine at war with all government. . . . (Applause.)

I mean the doctrine of secession, which is neither more nor less than a heresy—a fundamental error—a political absurdity, coming in conflict with all organized Government, with every thing that tends to preserve law and order in the United States, or wherever else the odious and abominable doctrine may be attempted to be exercised. I look upon the doctrine of secession as coming in conflict with all organism, moral and social. I repeat, without regard to the peculiar institutions of the respective States composing this

Confederacy; without regard to any Government that may be found in the future or exists in the present, this odious doctrine of secession should be crushed out, destroyed, and totally annihilated. No government can stand, no religious, or moral, or social organization can stand, where this doctrine is tolerated. (Applause.) It is disintegration—universal dissolvement—making war upon every thing that has a tendency to promote and ameliorate the condition of the mass of mankind. (Applause.) Therefore I repeat, that this odious and abominable doctrine—you must pardon me for using a strong expression—I do not say it in a profane sense—but this doctrine I conceive to be, *hell-born* and *hell-bound,* and one which will carry everything in its train, unless it is arrested and crushed out from our midst. (Great Applause.) . . .[13]

In the mid-term elections of 1862, the Republicans were badly beaten. Governors and state legislatures were lost. They barely retained control of the national House of Representatives. Naturally the factions blamed one another. Thus Senator John Sherman speaks for the Radicals.

. . . What is the cause and what will be the effect of the recent elections [?] . . . No doubt many causes conspired to defeat the Union parties. The two I will name were the most influential, and yet the least will be said about them.

The first is, that the Republican organization was voluntarily abandoned by the President and his leading followers, and a no-Party Union was formed to run against an old, well-drilled party organization. This was simply ridiculous. It was as if you should disband your army organization because it was tyrannical, and substitute the temporary enthusiasm of masses to fight regular armies. Political as well as military organization is necessary to success. Ward meetings, committees, conventions, party cries are just as necessary in politics, as drills, reviews, &c., are in war, so the Republicans have found out. If they have the wisdom to throw overboard the old debris that joined them in the Union movement, they will succeed. If not, they are doomed.

The other prominent reason for defeat is, the people were dissatisfied at the conduct and results of the war. The slow movements on the Potomac and worse still in Kentucky dissatisfied and discouraged people. It was a little singular that the Democrats, some of whom opposed the war, should reap the benefit of this feeling, but such is the fate of parties. Lincoln was a Republican. He put and kept in these slow generals and we shall be punished for it by having an organized opposition limiting appropriations. No doubt the wanton and unnecessary use of power to arrest without trial and the ill-timed [Emancipation] proclamation contributed to the general result. . . .[14]

Only six weeks after the November elections, the North and Lincoln received another shattering blow—the disastrous defeat at Fredericksburg. This probably marked the nadir of the President's and the Northern armies' fortunes. Criticism of the administration's conduct of the war reached a crescendo of bitterness; factional politics began to take on a revolutionary aspect. In Illinois, Wisconsin, Indiana, and other states of the "northwest," discontent was so serious that the excitable Joseph Medill, publisher of the Chicago Tribune, *thought he could see the approach of complete disaster, unless the army were spurred on to victory by adopting the radical program.*

Public discontent is assuming alarming proportions in the West. Many think we are on the eve of an outbreak. The clousure [*sic*] of the Mississippi adds to the irritability of feeling. It is the fixed opinion of the people that no honest or serious effort has been made to open that river—that transportation monopolies and pro-slavery generals have plotted together to keep it shut—the former to be enabled to rob the farmer in conveying his produce to market by grievous charges, and the latter to play into the hands of their democratic rebel brethren. The first is believed by everybody and the second by the Republicans and not a few democrats. One thing is certain: either there must be "military success" or the Union is gone up, and that soon. A strife will then arise in the West on the issue of annexing the West to the Southern confederacy or keeping it with the east. Many will advocate the formation of a North Western Republic. The ultra Democrats have broken ground in favor of "reconstruction" with New England "left out in the cold" and a vast number of prejudiced men would favor it. Nothing but speedy, military success can prevent an explosion in the West that will leave nothing but a wreck of the old Union. That success can only be obtained in my judgment by freeing and arming the slaves, by carrying the war into the Cotton States and down the Mississippi river—leaving troops enough simply to guard Washington and the Potomac river—sending the rest to Charleston, Savanah [*sic*], Mobile, Pensacola and New Orleans and the cotton country where the blacks outnumber the rebels two or three to one, and lastly, to offer to every soldier a land warrant of 160 acres of confiscated rebel land, and to officers 320 and 640 acres. The army has lost its enterprise, its animosity, its locomotion, its combativeness. It is homesick, weary, discouraged, and disgusted. But let us possess the real estate of the Slave holders for the trouble of crushing them, and a new spirit would be breathed into it. Then the selfish interests of the individual would be united to the patriotic purpose of the war, and the two motives would propel him forward irresistably [*sic*].[15]

In the election of 1862, there had been coalitions on a local and informal basis between conservative Republicans and Democrats who supported Lincoln's conduct of the war. After the election reverses, Lincoln—rather than risk further defeat—resolved to make the coalition formal by fusing with those Democrats who supported him into a Unionist party. This infuriated the Radicals, but the President had, as usual, sensed the opinion of most of the people of the whole North and moved into a center position where he could rally maximum support. He could not eliminate factionalism so he harnessed as many factions as possible together in support of the single end of winning the war.

James G. Blaine of Maine was a staunch Republican; he was also one of the most astute politicians of his age. He realized the necessity of uniting with and supporting Unionist Democrats. In the summer of 1863, he wrote to Thurlow Weed, New York boss:

May I add one to the innumerable demands made upon your time & patience?—We are to have quite a contest with "Copperheadism" in this state—we have prepared for it by uniting all true

Union men in support of a gubernatorial candidate /Saml Cony/ [*sic*] always hither-to identified & quite prominently, with the Democratic organization—It would aid us vastly if we could have a speech or two at such points as Portland, Augusta & Bangor from such Democrats as Jas. T. Brady & D. S. Dickinson—

As Chmn of the Union State Committee I have written to these gentlemen earnestly inviting them to visit us some time in August—after the 12th—& address large conventions—

Can I have your aid in securing their presence? We would like to have Dickinson speak at half a dozen places if possible—He would have great influence here—We are prepared to pay liberally for all the services these gentlemen can render—

Were it not for the Draft we should have no contest—but that stirs up the Community very unpleasantly—

In this state we could have done better on the Volunteer system—with the Draft impending as an additional incitement to enter the service!—But it is too late to murmur now—[16]

Colonel Lucius Fairchild of Wisconsin, after losing an arm at Gettysburg, returned home to find himself a hero—and a potential vote getter. Although a Democrat, he now embraced the Unionist cause. His views express those of his party who rejected the Copperheads and positively supported the Lincoln administration. He spoke of himself as a War Democrat but he may more properly be classified as a Unionist Democrat.

You no doubt were much surprised when you heard of my accepting the nomination for Secy of State—I was myself—I refused it before breakfast, but in spite of that you see what a nomination it was, I did not refuse it because I had any intention of supporting the Dem. ticket for I never intended to do that but oppose it all in my power as I could do no other way and consider myself a good loyal citizen—I tell you the tendency of the leaders is to disloyalty and the effect of their continual fault-finding opposition to the govt is doing the rebels more good than can be counteracted by the good fighting of all our armies—

I disliked very much to be obliged to oppose our old friends but my duty makes me—No inducement on earth would make me go with them now. They are doing a world of harm. Very many old tried democrats will not go with them.

The War democrats are going to organize a party of their own, and they all recognize me as one of them, and say I did right in accepting it and they will support me— . . . It is not known whether they will nominate a ticket or not—Whether they do or not, they will labor hard to defeat the Copperheads. They are going to lay down a platform on which the party may live hereafter.

I hope you may see this as I do—and come out yourself as a war democrat in favor of giving the govt. an honest, earnest, support leaving all petty questions to be settled after the war is over, and peace gives us an opportunity to safely quarrel among ourselves—[17]

The gubernatorial contest in Ohio was one of the most critical elections of 1863. It pitted Clement L. Vallandigham (among the most able and articulate and certainly the most notorious of the Peace Democrats) against John Brough, the candidate of Unionist Democrats and Republicans. A correspondent of the Times *of London reported a political rally held at Carthage.*

The political meeting at Carthage [Ohio] reminded me of a Derby day at Epsom, only of a somewhat shabbier character, with a dash of an Italian masquerade and carnival frolic in it. The fair sex considerably outnumbered the lords of creation, and Young America mustered nearly as strong as the adult generation. There were huge triumphal cars, heavy boats and pontoons on wheels, drawn by four, five, or even ten pairs of good well-fed horses, with an endless flutter of flaunting flags, monstrous devices, a din of fife, trumpet and drum and the endless firing of light and heavy artillery. Pedestrians, horsemen, hack-carriages, long teams of draught horses, wandered about the trackless turf in every direction, with no apparent purpose, save only the enjoyment of the open air and the jolly company. It was a fair, a picnic, with cold fowls and veal pies emerging from capacious hampers, and corks knocked off the bottles of sparkling Catawba wine. To eat, drink and be merry was the great business of the political meeting. Here and there, indeed, in a corner under a canopy of some huge tree, Mr. Somebody from Indiana, or Mr. Nobody from Illinois, stumped away for very life, with a cluster of listless loafers around his extempore platform, pretending to listen, cheering occasionally, jeering more frequently; all this in a din of discordant music, the racking fire of great and small guns, and the shrill cries of apple women and vendors of fire-water. For the rest, there were children squalling, young people flirting, angry men swearing, drunken men reeling—all the varieties of a swarming, bustling crowd. . . .

Most of the cars were decked out for show and relied for effect no less on white, blue and red trappings than upon a show of lively and fresh female beauty. Cartloads of girls, as many as ninety in a single conveyance, were paraded round and round to the sound of merry music; school girls from ten to twelve years of age, young girls further advanced in their teens . . . all gaily dressed, their faces wreathed in smiles, beamed upon the delighted male multitude. Attired in motley colours, bare-headed, bare-necked, with hair streaming on their shoulders, begarlanded, some of them diademed, helmeted; here they were made to personify the 35 states; the Northern States in white or in their respective national colours; the Slave States in mourning sables. In other groups we were taught to bow to the "Goddess of Liberty," to the "Union," to "Columbia," to "Peace," to "Death." . . . Mixed with the beloved colours of the Union were mottoes and devices, among which I noted at the tail of a huge cart the two-headed Russian Eagle. . . . The largest car, with the heaviest freight of young damsels, professed to bring to muster "soldiers' sweethearts." Some of the devices were of a more sombre and truculent character. A huge piece of ordnance was paraded through the ground with the inscription "The Cannon our only Peacemaker"; another flag bore the inscription "Hell, hemp, or Canada for traitors." . . . Poor Vallandigham was to be seen here and there suspended on huge gallows in effigy. . . . One car exhibited the same unlucky Democratic candidate in the shape of a huge Guy [Fawkes], a colossal man of straw with a mask said to be an excellent likeness [of Vallandigham] . . . at which some zealous Republicans . . . kept hacking away with their sabres and poking with their bayonets.[18]

The picture is not one of democratic politics at its best. Nonetheless such rallies, or their cause, sufficed. Brough was elected, though Vallandigham was impressive in defeat. He polled almost 40 per cent of the vote. Two facts emerged. The North, at least as represented by Ohio, was by no means united. The Unionist Democratic-Republican coalition had saved Brough.

But large as the lesson was written, it went unread by Republican Radicals who continued to intrigue against the party chief. During the winter of 1863-64 they launched a move for the 1864 presidential nomination of Lincoln's Secretary of the Treasury, Salmon P. Chase. The boom failed to get off the ground and, as a consequence, when the National Union (Republican) Convention met in June, Lincoln's opponents were without a candidate. They grumbled and sulked. But in the end had no choice except to vote for the renomination of the President and for a Democrat, Andrew Johnson of Tennessee as his vice-presidential running mate. To add to Radical discomfort, Lincoln and Johnson were presented as National Union rather than Republican candidates.

The Radicals accepted Lincoln's nomination with ill grace. One of them, Horace Greeley, who frequently opposed Lincoln's moderate policies, expressed their bitterness in an editorial in the New York Tribune.

The Union National Convention yesterday presented, with entire unanimity, the name of ABRAHAM LINCOLN as a candiate for reelection to the Presidency of the United States. This nomination is in unquestionable accord with public sentiment and all its manifestations. A great majority of the Unionists believe and feel that Mr. Lincoln ought to be recognized and deferred to as President in every part of our country. They feel that rebellion in a republic adds perfidy to treason—that it is a repudiation of the most sacred voluntary engagements, as well as infidelity to country and to liberty. Hence they urge that the reestablishment of the National authority would be imperfect if the chief magistrate whose election was made the pretext for revolt were to be set aside, and the Rebels permitted to cover their retreat from their untenable position by a pretense that Lincoln's supercedure had obviated their chief objection to recognizing and obeying the National authority. Millions have doubt-

DON'T SWAP HORSES

less felt that to set Mr. Lincoln aside, and elect another President in his stead, would be plausibly accounted an admission that the Secessionists had some excuse for their treason.

We admit the force of this consideration; but it seems to us far outweighed by one that points to a different choice, and which we will here briefly indicate.

. . . . . .

That the President has made grave mistakes in the prosecution of our great struggle, all are aware; that he has *meant* to do wrong, no one really believes. . . . And now all the hates and spites and slights and disappointments of a four years' momentous struggle are to be conjured up against him; and against not him only, but against all who battle with him for the overthrow of the Rebellion.

We cannot but feel that it would have been wiser and safer to spike the most serviceable guns of our adversaries by nominating another for President, and thus dispelling all motive, save that of naked disloyalty, for further warfare upon this Administration. We believe the Rebellion would have lost something of its cohesion and venom from the hour in which it was known that a new President would surely be inaugurated on the 4th of March next; and that hostility in the loyal States to the National cause must have sensibly abated or been deprived of its readiest, most dangerous weapons from the moment that all were brought to realize that the President, having no more to expect or hope, could henceforth be impelled by no conceivable motive but a desire to serve and save his country, and thus win for himself an enviable and enduring fame.

All this is of the past. The will of the great majority of the Unionists has been heard, and it says, "Let us have Abraham Lincoln as our President for another term!" We bow to their decision, and ardently hope that the result may vindicate their sagacity and prove our apprehensions unfounded.[19]

Less than a month after his renomination, Lincoln added fuel to the smoldering party fires. The Wade-Davis Bill, embodying the Radical program for reconstruction of the Southern states, passed both houses of Congress. Although it was not as extreme as later measures were to be, it was based upon typically Radical assumptions. Lincoln killed it with a pocket veto, giving his reasons in a public statement to the people of the North. The statement was issued on July 7. Almost a month passed before the Radicals replied. When they did, it was a studied and bitter attack upon the President. He was accused of usurping congressional powers, defiance of the Supreme Court, defeat of the will of the people, and perversion of the Constitution. The "Manifesto" was published in Horace Greeley's New York Tribune *and closed with a direct appeal for popular support against Lincoln.*

. . . Such are the fruits of this rash and fatal act of the President—a blow at the friends of his Administration, at the rights of humanity, and at the principles of republican government.

The President has greatly presumed on the forbearance which the supporters of his Administration have so long practiced, in view of the arduous conflict in which we are engaged, and the reckless ferocity of our political opponents.

But he must understand that our support is of a cause and not of a man; that the authority of Congress is paramount and must be respected; that the whole body of the Union men of Congress will not submit to be impeached by him of rash and unconstitutional legislation; and if he wishes our support, he must confine himself to his executive duties—to obey and execute, not make the laws—to suppress by arms armed rebellion, and leave political reorganization to Congress.

If the supporters of the Government fail to insist on this, they become responsible for the usurpations which they fail to rebuke, and are justly liable to the indignation of the people, whose rights and security, committed to their keeping, they sacrifice.

Let them consider the remedy for these usurpations, and, having found it, fearlessly execute it. . . .[20]

The Wade-Davis Manifesto was not mere bombast. The Radicals, suppressed to the point of accepting Lincoln in June, renewed their quest for a new candidate and control of the Republican Party in August. Their scheme was to demand that the Baltimore convention which had renominated the President be reconvened at Cincinnati. There it would force Lincoln to resign as the National Union Party candidate and replace him with a man of their own choosing and persuasion. The August Plot never had a chance, since it failed to get the public support demanded in the Wade-Davis Manifesto. It did, however, have the support of many Radical politicians throughout the North. Probably its most significant center was New York City and its real ringleader John Austin Stevens, Jr., son of the president of the influential New York Bank of Commerce, and a close friend of Salmon P. Chase. Chase, however, was not the candidate most favored to replace Lincoln. Major General Benjamin Butler was the favorite of some Radicals for that honor. The following is a typical "call to the voters" circulated by those who were hatching the "August Conspiracy."

The undersigned, citizens of the State of Ohio, and unconditional supporters of the National Government, convinced,

That a Union of all loyal citizens of the United States upon the basis of a Common Patriotism is essential to the safety and honor of the Country in this crisis of its affairs, and

That none of the Candidates for the Presidency already presented can command the united confidence and support of all loyal and patriotic men,

Do Therefore respectfully invite their fellow-citizens of like views, in this and other states, to send delegates equal in number to their respective Congressional delegations to a CONVENTION to be held at CINCINNATI, on Wednesday, the 28th day of September next, for friendly consultation, and for the selection of Candidates for the Presidency and Vice-Presidency of the United States, in the confident hope of securing through their election the early return of Peace, by conquering the Rebellion, and of maintaining the Integrity of the American Union, the Honor of the Government, and the Rights and Liberties of the People.[21]

A letter written on August 27 by a J. K. Herbert from Cincinnati to General Butler was typical of the intrigue that was being carried on, and it represented the views of a potentially powerful group in the North.

This call [for a new session of the National Union Party convention] is being signed by nearly everybody here. Groesbeck & five Judges have given it the lead, and some of them are shoving it in person. Nothing ever hit this public so well, (so) I am told by such men as L. D. Campbell, who has been working with me here for 48 hours, and just now gone home.

I enclose you copies of editorials that I dictated to the *Gazette* and *Times*—they were in this morning's and evening's papers.

Knowing how much they wanted somebody to lean upon at the *Tribune* and *Post* offices in New York, I have at my own expense telegraphed these two documents to Jno. A. Stevens, Jr. this P.M., asking him to give them to the papers, & saying to him that "*every* body is signing here." Hon. L[ucius] D. C[hittenden] charges me to represent him in the meeting at Dudley Field's parlor on the 30th, as saying, "For God's sake, gentlemen, don't let up now—let us go through and we will carry everything by storm." Ben. Eggleston bids us privately God speed—can't lead just now. Judge Stanley Mathews, a Lincoln elector in this city, signs the call and circulates it for signatures.

I have sent it to B. Gratz Brown, Z. Charde [*sic*], Jno. Hickman, & others, with copies of the editorials enclosed.

Every man I have met says, "Give me Butler." A great many here think it would be wise to retain Johnson on the ticket as he is. Campbell is of those.

I try to get this in the mail to-night—go to New York tomorrow night [at] 10 o'clock, may write at length to-morrow. All goes charmingly—never was a more center shot at public desire & aim—the whole prayer here is for the East to "stand firm" and have the Con. even if they ratify Mr. L.'s nomination again.

I am much pleased with all I find west—the best men & two papers are committed here so that they cannot back out. . . .P.S. The *Com. Gaz.* & *Times* have all told me they preferred you to any other man for Pres.[22]

Plot begat plot. Conservative Republicans, gloomily sensing Lincoln's defeat in November, considered means of salvaging what they could—control of the party through discrediting the extreme Radicals. Henry J. Raymond grasped desperately at such a possibility. Raymond was chairman of the National Union Party. He was also prominent in the New York political faction led by Thurlow Weed, Secretary of State Seward's alter ego. He did not speak for Lincoln, but he may well have spoken for many Republican Conservative politicians and sensed the feeling of many war-weary Northerners. On August 21 he wrote to Simon Cameron:

I received your letter of the 11th some days since. I reciprocate fully your desire to act cordially in this canvas [*sic*] & indeed in all political matters for nothing but the most cordial and vigorous cooperation of all Union men can carry us through the impending crisis. I hear from every quarter the most discouraging accounts of the political future. Under ordinary circumstances & in time of peace I suppose it would be next to impossible to reelect any President who, in the absence of over-shadowing ability & prestige, should have to shoulder all the responsibilities, failures, short-comings & personal disappointments of a four years' administration. I had thought that in time of war the necessity of the country might lead the People to overlook all these drawbacks and keep Mr. Lincoln in power. But the indications just now are that these very *necessities* incline them to try a new man. I find everywhere a conviction that we need a change—that the war languishes under Mr. Lincoln and that he *cannot* or *will* not give us peace. . . . The country is tired & sick of the war & is longing for peace; at the same time I believe they would scorn & scout any peace that involved disunion; but the faintest hope of peace *with* union is hailed with infinite satisfaction. I fear that this desire for peace, aided by the impression or *suspicion* even that Mr. Lincoln does not seek or desire it, that he is fighting not for the Union but for the abolition of Slavery, & by the draft, the tax, the lack of victories, the discontent with the Cabinet and the other influences that are swelling the tide of hostility to the Administration will overbear it and give the control of Everything to the opposition. I agree with you that in that event we should speedily have recognition, disunion & ruin.

We *must* avoid & avert that result if it is *possible* to do so. I find great difficulty in raising the authorities at Washington to the necessity of active exertion in this matter, especially in the matter of *raising money*. With a disbursement of millions a day there ought to be not the slightest difficulty in raising whatever is needed for the proper expenses of a canvas [*sic*]—but I greatly fear we shall come short in this particular.

But more than this: It seems to me indispensable that *something* should be done at once important enough to arrest the attention of the whole country & turn the tide in Mr. Lincoln's favor. Great victories might do it—but we are not likely to get them. Now what would be the effect—on all parties—military & political—of a *direct proposition,* made in due form by Commissioners, from President Lincoln to Davis as the head of the rebel armies (the whole being military in its form) to *stop the war & disband both armies, on the basis of recognizing the supremacy of the Constitution,* all questions in dispute except the integrity of the Union to be referred to a Convention of all the States & both parties agreeing in advance to abide by its decision. I know the formidable objections that will at once occur to every mind to such a proposal; but let them not prevent a fair estimate of the advantages it holds out. In my judgment it would certainly be *rejected*—promptly & preemptorily. Probably the necessities of Davis's position at home might render this imperative. In that case we might reasonably expect from it a certain amount of disaffection among the Southern people—those of them who have been taught that the war is waged by us for abolition. . . .

It would also dispel utterly the impression which is damaging us at the North—that Mr. Lincoln is not waging the war *for the Union*, and would completely silence the clamor about peace which is now doing us so much damage. I cannot help thinking also that it would arrest all danger of resistance to the draft, facilitate the filling up of the ranks of the Army, reconcile public sentiment to the burdens of war and do a great deal towards uniting the North. And as a necessary consequence it would better our prospects & lighten our labors in the Presidential canvas [*sic*].

With the radical friends of the Administration it would possibly hurt us: but would it do so materially or sufficiently to offset its advantages in other quarters?

. . . If done at all it should be done at once—in advance of the Chicago Convention so as to take all the wind out of its sails & render it harmless. . . .[23]

While Republicans were engaged in plot and counterplot, the Democrats acted to pull their party together. Their national convention met in August and, on the twenty-ninth, nominated General McClellan. McClellan was a War Democrat. To appease the Peace Democrats a platform plank embodying their demands was adopted.

Resolved, That this Convention does explicitly declare, as the sense of the American people, that after four years of failure to restore the Union by the experiment of war, during which, under the pretence of military necessity, or war power higher than the Constitution, the Constitution itself has been disregarded in every part, and public liberty and private right alike trodden down, and the material prosperity of the country essentially impaired, justice, humanity, liberty, and the public welfare demand that immediate efforts be made for the cessation of hostilities, with a view to an ultimate convention of the States or other peaceable means, to the end that at the earliest practicable moment peace may be restored on the basis of the Federal Union of the States.[24]

So as August 1864 drew to a close, many observers, including Lincoln himself, questioned if the President's voice was that of the Nation. His own party was divided; the Democrats repudiated his ends, his methods, or both: the chairman of his own coalition foresaw his defeat. The war was going badly. Grant was seemingly bogged down in Virginia, despite unbelievable bloodletting; Sherman was wandering through the hills of Georgia. Mobile had not fallen.

That was August. September marked a change. On the second day of the month Sherman entered Atlanta. It was the military victory so long awaited by the people of the North. They began to close ranks. Even the Radicals, having failed to get support for their projected Cincinnati convention, straggled back, however reluctantly, to the support of the Lincoln-Johnson ticket. On September 18, one of them, Senator James W. Grimes of Iowa wrote:

. . . I hope you enjoyed yourself and gathered new strength for the next winter's campaign at the capital. . . . It is evident to my mind that the contest will be narrowed down to Lincoln and McClellan. Much as I disapprove of Mr. Lincoln's irresolute indecisive policy and much as I despise many of the corrupt scoundrels by whom he is surrounded, yet I shall not hesitate to vote for him & against McClellan's Chicago platform. It is the Chicago platform that will elect Lincoln. Few now want to vote for him. He is very far from being a popular man today. He will only be accepted because the *people* are so generously loyal to the government, and they are afraid to trust the men who concocted the Chicago platform & who, they believe, will surround McClellan should he be elected. One week before the Chicago convention more than one half of the republicans in the northwest wanted Lincoln defeated; one week after the convention none of them wanted him defeated by McClellan. . . .[25]

Grimes' no-alternative theme, though not explicitly stated, was implicit in an attack on the Democrats published in the Detroit Advertiser and Tribune, *a Radical newspaper.*

The American People are to-day being humiliated in the eyes of the world by the disgraceful anxiety of the Democratic leaders to get on their knees to the rebels and ask them to stop the war. These rebels began a war upon us to destroy constitutional government and erect on its ruins a Confederacy based on African slavery —they stole our money and disarmed the loyal States while drawing pay from the national Treasury—they took our forts by monstrous treachery—they have fought us with a barbarous hate, making drinking cups of the skulls of our dead heroes, and trinkets of their bones—in the appeal to arms we have retaken all their principal fortifications, overcome them in all the heavy battles of the war, recovered nearly two-thirds of the territory they originally claimed —we are twenty millions and they twelve millions—we are unbounded in resources, and with a larger reserve of fighting men, they are impoverished, and have put their last man in the field, and yet there are men among us who run up the white flag and go cringing before the rebels and usurpers for peace! And how do they meet us? Their ragged, half-starved bodies scoff at our pusillanimity, and deride us for want of pluck. Their President flings in our teeth the haughty ultimatum, "Withdraw your armies from every foot of our soil, and acknowledge our independence and you can have peace, but on no other terms!" And even yet, the Democratic leaders cringe at the feet of the rebels and implore terms! Is it any wonder the rebels are encouraged by such demonstrations and expect to succeed at last? Is it any wonder we are earning the contempt of foreign powers! We have boasted that we would maintain supremacy on this continent, and now we cower before three years of domestic rebellion. What has become of the National Spirit that it will tolerate these Copperhead cravens who are disgracing us? It is high time that the political poltroons were squelched, and the loyal masses had asserted their courage and dignity.[26]

Carl Schurz spoke for the liberals within the Radical movement. Schurz, German born, served as major general in the Union army. He had criticized Lincoln's conservatism on numerous occasions. But in the autumn of 1864 he called for unity behind the President, and in doing so proved himself one of the early prophets of Lincoln's greatness as it would be recognized by posterity.

. . . Now I must give you a little lecture. I do not share your opinion as to what we should not do in the present crisis. You would surely not have judged so if you had shared in the great struggles which are now over. You may have been surprised when I defend[ed] the present Administration in public. But I believe that a few words regarding my way of looking at matters will make things clear to you. Every crisis in human affairs has one principal question to which all minor questions must be subordinated. We are engaged in a war in which the existence of the Nation, indeed, in which everything is involved. A party has risen in this country that threatens to overthrow all the results of the war, and that at a moment at which the final outcome is hardly doubtful, if the policy introduced is firmly adhered to. There can be no doubt that the Government has made great mistakes; persons who are directing the fate of the country are certainly far from ideal statesmen, though not nearly as insignificant as their critics would represent them to be. But that is of minor importance. The most vital thing is that the policy of the party moves in the right direction, that is to say, that the slaveholder be vanquished and slavery abolished. Whether this policy moves in that direction skilfully or awkwardly, slowly or rapidly, is a matter of little consequence in comparison with the question whether a policy should be adopted that would move in another, a wrong and disastrous direction. Accordingly, it was easy for me to choose. I did not hesitate one moment. If Fremont and McClellan had been my bosom friends and the members of the present Administration had been my deadly enemies, I should nevertheless have supported the latter. . . . The signs of the times are now very favorable. The reelection of the President is almost certain unless some great military misfortune overwhelms us and that is not to be expected. The results of the election will determine the results of the war, and the worst will then be over. . . .

I wish to enlighten you on two other points. You are underrating the President. I grant that he lacks higher education and his manners are not in accord with European conceptions of the dignity of a chief magistrate. He is a well-developed child of nature and is not skilled in polite phrases and poses. But he is a man of profound feeling, correct and firm principles and incorruptible honesty. His motives are unquestionable, and he possesses to a remarkable degree the characteristic God-given trait of this people, sound common-sense. Should you read his official documents and his political letters, you would find this verified to a surprising extent. I know him from personal observation as well as anyone, and better than the majority. I am familiar with his motives. I have seen him heroically wage many a terrible struggle and work his way through many a desperate situation with strength born of loyalty to conviction. I have criticised him often and severely, and later I found that he was right. I also know his failings; they are those of a good man. That he has committed great errors in the endless embarrassments of his position, cannot be denied, but it can be explained. Possibly other persons, if in his position, would not have committed the same errors, but they would have committed others. Moreover, Lincoln's personality has a special importance in this crisis. Free from the aspirations of genius, he will never be dangerous to a liberal government. He personifies the people, and that is the secret of his popularity. His Administration is the most representative that the history of the world has ever seen. I will make a prophecy that may now sound peculiar. In fifty years, perhaps much sooner, Lincoln's name will be inscribed close to Washington's on this American Republic's roll of honor. And there it will remain for some time. The children of those who persecute him now, will bless him. . . .[27]

During the dark days of 1863, and most of 1864, the political voice of the North was that of politicians, editors, and an assortment of self-anointed spokesmen. On November 8, 1864, the voice that spoke was that of the people. It was not the voice of a mighty people speaking in thunderous unison, but the majority spoke loud enough to give Lincoln a mandate to prosecute the war to a victorious end.

The President received 55.09 per cent of the total vote cast, but a comparison with the 1860 returns shows that he lost strength in Maine, Michigan and Wisconsin, all Radical strongholds. The loss was probably caused by disgruntled Republicans staying at home or skipping the presidential candidates. In the whole North per se Lincoln's gains over his 1860 total were modest. The rest of his majority came from slaveholding border states and West Virginia, Kansas, and Nevada, which had not existed as states in 1860. The President had outwitted and outmaneuvered his opponents within and without his party. By resisting the extremists, and stubbornly clinging to the center, he had gotten the 1860 Constitutional Union vote, as well as that of Democratic Unionists, Republican Conservatives, and most of the Radicals. The result was not a landslide but it sufficed.

It did not, however, still the opposition. After the election, the violently partisan New York Express *expressed the views of the unreconciled.*

We are not among those who intend to ignore the great facts connected with Mr. Lincoln's reelection. We comprehended to what his election would lead four years ago, and all through August, September, and October, 1860, predicted that secession, disunion, and civil war, would be the consequences of that result, upon the Platform of Principles laid down and the nominees selected by the Convention held at Chicago in 1860. The *Express* did not then deceive its readers, nor the public, and will not do so now. Painful as is the confession of defeat, and the acknowledgement of the second victory of the Republican party, it is due to the truth to make it. Mr. Lincoln's success on the 8th of November 1864, means, then, the accomplishment of the following results:

1st The Prolongation of the War
2d The Abrogation of State Rights
3d The Continuation of Arbitrary Arrests
4th The Increase of Debt and Taxes
5th The continued Confiscation of Southern Property
6th The Abolition of Slavery in all the States
7th Continued War upon the Union as it was and the Constitution as it is
8th The support of the President in all Assumptions of Power
9th The exercise of Martial Law in States not in Rebellion
10th The presence of the Federal Military to control State Elections
11th The Abandonment of the Monroe Doctrine

12th The denial of justice in cases of false imprisonment and arrests

13th The administration of Test-Oaths, as in Maryland and Tennessee, by military officers of the Administration

14th The keeping up of the prices of goods in store; thousands having voted for Mr. Lincoln in order not to depreciate the value of property on hand. Prices, therefore, are to be kept up and increased.

These are some of the leading measures involved in the issues decided yesterday at the ballot-box. . . . If the majority of the people of these States, forgetting the great past, choose to be governed by military power, by the spirit of fanaticism, by combinations of the purse and the sword, by bringing the patronage of the Government into conflict with the freedom of elections, by the fear of doing right in the dread of some greater evil thereafter—if they love the character and rule of such a man as Abraham Lincoln, rather than the character and principles of a man like George B. McClellan—why then the minority must submit and hope for better men and better times hereafter. . . .[28]

Lincoln replied in his "Fourth Annual Message." He spoke with the confidence of a democratic statesman who has received a mandate from the people. It was the predominant voice of the North.

. . . The most reliable indication of public purpose in this country is derived through our popular elections. Judging by the recent canvass and its result, the purpose of the people within the loyal States to maintain the integrity of the Union was never more firm nor more nearly unanimous than now. The extraordinary calmness and good order with which the millions of voters met and mingled at the polls give strong assurance of this. Not only all those who supported the Union ticket, so called, but a great majority of the opposing party also may be fairly claimed to entertain and to be actuated by the same purpose. It is an unanswerable argument to this effect that no candidate for any office whatever, high or low, has ventured to seek votes on the avowal that he was for giving up the Union. There have been much impugning of motives and much heated controversy as to the proper means and best mode for advancing the Union cause, but on the distinct issue of Union or no Union the politicians have shown their instinctive knowledge that there is no diversity among the people. In affording the people the fair opportunity of showing one to another and to the world this firmness and unanimity of purpose, the election has been of vast value to the national cause.[29]

IV

The Negro's Place

"SEE OUR PRESENT CONDITION—THE COUNTRY ENGAGED IN WAR!—OUR WHITE MEN CUTTING ONE ANOTHER'S THROATS, NONE KNOWING HOW FAR IT WILL EXTEND; AND THEN CONSIDER WHAT WE KNOW TO BE THE TRUTH. BUT FOR YOUR RACE AMONG US THERE COULD NOT BE WAR, ALTHOUGH MANY MEN ENGAGED ON EITHER SIDE DO NOT CARE FOR YOU ONE WAY OR THE OTHER."

It was Abraham Lincoln speaking to a deputation of Negroes. As he so often did, he expressed simply and briefly the feeling of most of the people of the North. Later historians, in the throes of revisionism, might point to other aspects of sectionalism and modify the oversimplification that the Civil War was over slavery, but Lincoln's declaration that, "But for your race among us there could not be war," remains true. That "many men engaged on either side do not care for you one way or the other" was also true. In the North that meant most men. Northerners were opposed to the extension of slavery; in most cases, they refused to aid in the enforcement of the fugitive slave law; they wept over poor old Uncle Tom. But Uncle Tom was meek; he knew his place. The place of the Negro in the opinion of virtually all whites of the North was that of an inferior, to live his private life apart from his betters and be content to work as a servant or at unskilled labor. With few exceptions Negroes were segregated in the schools. In Indiana and Illinois, statutes forbade colored immigrants to take up residence. Not even the lowest house of prostitution would permit a Negro to visit the cheapest of its white bawds.

In 1862, Edward Dicey, an English journalist, visited the United States. His observations do not give a complete picture of Negro status in the North. Some Negro families were better off than those he portrays. But these were an exception. Other visitors from abroad were in substantial agreement with Dicey.

. . . The position of the Negro in the Free States was a subject which I was anxious to investigate. To an Englishman, it is a new sensation, almost the only new sensation in America, to enter for the first time an hotel where one is surrounded by negro servants. I recollect well the first evening that I dined in the New World. It was at the Everett House in New York, one the best hotels. . . .

I was seated waiting for my soup, in that calm state of enjoyment which every well-organized human being must feel after a long sea-voyage in sitting at a table which does not rock, when the folding-doors leading from the kitchen to the dining-hall were flung open, and a troop of negro waiters marched in together, two abreast, paced up the rooms in step, bearing the soup tureens aloft, solemnly parted to the right and left, deposited their burdens, and then took each his appointed station, in order to lift up the lids of the tureens at one end and the same moment on a given signal. This was my first experience of negrodom. Trivial as the incident may seem, there was in it a love of stage effect, a sort of dramatic talent, which belonged to a far other race than that Anglo-Saxon one of ours. So, throughout my stay in America, I could never look upon a negro face without a strange attraction. The coloured people form so marked a contrast to everything and everybody you see around you. . . . Negroes, like gipsies, are all very well as isolated figures in the social landscape, but they are out of place as a perpetual background. Still, with all of this, I have often wondered at how very little the Americans I met with seemed to know about the negroes who lived amongst them. I tried frequently to obtain information from persons interested in the negro question, as to the prospects and position of the free negroes, but without much success. The truth is, the negroes, slave or free, are a race apart, in both North and South.

Everywhere and at all seasons the coloured people fo[illegible]a-rate community. In the public streets you hardly ever see a [illegible] person in company with a white, except in the capacity of se[illegible]

FISH OUT OF WATER

Boston, indeed, is the only town I visited where I ever observed black men and women walking about frequently with white people. I never by any chance, in the Free States, saw a coloured man dining at a public table, or mixing socially in any manner with white men, or dressed as a man well to do in the world, or occupying any position, however humble, in which he was placed in authority over white persons. On board the river steamboats, the commonest and homeliest of working men has a right to dine, and does dine, at the public meals; but, for coloured passengers, there is always a separate table. At the great hotels there is, as with us, a servant's table, but the coloured servants are not allowed to dine in common with the white. At the inns, in the barbers' shops, on board the steamers, and in most hotels, the servants are more often than not coloured people. . . . White servants will not associate with black on terms of equality. . . . I hardly ever remember seeing a black employed as shopman, or placed in any post of responsibility. As a rule, the blacks you meet in the Free States are shabbily if not squalidly dressed; and, as far as I could learn, the instances of black men having money by trade in the North, are very few in number.

. . . . .

The free negro has not a fair chance throughout the North. The legislation of the country is as unfavourable to the status of free blacks, as the social sentiment of the people. . . .[1]

Few Americans of the time found anything reprehensible in what Dicey saw. A Quaker's plea for justice for the Negro, published in Philadelphia in February of 1863, reveals, more starkly than Dicey's report, the prejudice and ill-treatment accorded Northern blacks.

Several petitions have been presented in the legislature of this State, praying that an addition be made to the Constitution, or that a law may be enacted prohibiting the immigration of any mulatto or coloured person in Pennsylvania, imposing banishment on any free colored person coming into the State after the passage of such law or enactment, and the repudiation of any slave found within its limits. These petitions have been referred, in the House, to the judiciary committee, to report thereon. Although nearly all of them appear to have been got up within one county (Berks), and there is reason to believe that such a measure will not receive the sanction of the legislature, yet it is well to bear in mind, that in the fluctuations of party policy, there are often those entrusted with the power of altering and making laws, who are not governed by the unalterable principles of right; and that though a majority of the citizens may be opposed to such a wrong, yet there are very many strongly prejudiced against the coloured race, and in an evil hour their voices may prevail.

Several of the free States have given sorrowful evidence of the will, on the part of large portions of their citizens, to yield to this inveterate prejudice, and so to shape their legislation, as to exclude this afflicted people, to keep those of them already within their jurisdiction in a state of degradation, and without the enjoyment of many of what we consider our dearest rights. . . .

Similar petitions, and petitions to remove all coloured persons out of the State, were presented last year to the legislature of Ohio, which being referred to the "Standing Committee on Federal Relations," that committee, after premising that "they have given the subject their most serious consideration, with a desire to give practical effect to the wishes of many of the citizens of the Commonwealth from almost every section, and proceeding from all classes and parties," makes the following statement, which, humiliating as is the acknowledgment, we believe may also be truly said respecting the feelings and views of very many within our own State.

"The negro race is looked upon by the people of Ohio, as a class to be kept by themselves; to be debarred of social intercourse with the whites; to be deprived of all advantages which they cannot enjoy in common with their own class. They have always been deprived of the elective franchise in this State, and no party among our citizens has ever contemplated that they should be given that right of citizenship; and for aught that appears to the contrary, the coloured man in Ohio will not, in all future time that he may remain an inhabitant of the State, attain any material improvement in the social or political rights over that he now enjoys."

. . . . .

We cannot shut our eyes to the evidences frequently given, that the same intolerant spirit which is thus shown to pervade so large a class in each of the States we have referred to, is rife among great numbers of the citizens of this State also, and that it is ever and anon urging them to take measures to have the door shut against every poor black seeking to find a home upon our soil, and to subject those already residing among us to greater indignities and hardships.

It is a striking exhibit of man's inconsistency, that so many are loud in their protestations against the sin of slavery, and in attributing the dreadful war, under which the country is suffering, to the vile passions developed and cherished by that unchristian system, while they show themselves to be indulging in the same spirit and feelings towards the poor blacks, which urge the slaveholder to maintain his course; by seeking to brand them as an inferior race; refusing to accord them their rights as fellow-men, and using their power to debar them of the opportunity to raise themselves from the low condition into which they have been sunk by the long-continued tyranny of the imperious whites. If the dreadful crimes of the slave system at the South, and the participation in it by connivance, at the North, have brought upon the Nation this dire rebellion and all its attendant evils, how can we expect that the just punishment of a righteous and offended creator will be shortened or mitigated, if the same blinding and malignant spirit is allowed to keep up in our midst continued persecution of this portion of his children, and to assert its influence in our legislative halls, by urging the adoption of measures cruelly unjust towards the poor blacks, and inimical to the true interests of the whole State. . . .[2]

There can be no doubt that Lincoln detested slavery. At no time in his career did he waver from the conviction that it was morally wrong and socially unjust. In 1864, in reply to "Loyal Colored People of Baltimore," he told them: "I can now only say, as I have often before said, it always has been a sentiment with me that all mankind should be free. So far as able, within my sphere, I have always acted as I believed to be right and just; and I have done all I could for the good of mankind generally." In the same year he wrote in a letter to Albert G. Hodges: "I am naturally anti-slavery. If slavery is not wrong, nothing is wrong. I cannot remember when I did not so think and feel."

But in spite of his conviction, attested to by word and action, that slavery was evil, Lincoln's compassion for the Negro was short of that which he felt for Southern white men, even those among them who were slaveholders and rebels. He would, as circumstances permitted, free slaves and give Negroes justice. But he regarded them as apart, and preferred to be rid of them, for their own well-being and happiness as well as for that of the whites. He told them so in measured words when a deputation called upon him at the White House.

. . . You and we are different races. We have between us a broader difference than exists between almost any other two races. Whether it is right or wrong I need not discuss, but this physical difference is a great disadvantage to us both, as I think your race suffer very greatly, many of them by living among us, while ours suffer from your presence. In a word we suffer on each side. If this is admitted, it affords a reason at least why we should be separated. You here are freemen I suppose.

A VOICE: Yes, sir.

The President—Perhaps you have long been free, or all your lives. Your race are suffering, in my judgment, the greatest wrong inflicted on any people. But even when you cease to be slaves, you are yet far removed from being placed on an equality with the white race. You are cut off from many of the advantages which the other race enjoy. The aspiration of men is to enjoy equality with the best when free, but on this broad continent, not a single man of your race is made the equal of a single man of ours. Go where you are treated the best, and the ban is still upon you.

I do not propose to discuss this, but to present it as a fact with which we have to deal. I cannot alter it if I would. It is a fact about which we all think and feel alike, I and you. We look to our condition, owing to the existence of the two races on this continent. I need not recount to you the effects upon white men, growing out of the institution of Slavery. I believe in its general evil effects on the white race. See our present condition—the country engaged in war! —our white men cutting one another's throats, none knowing how far it will extend; and then consider what we know to be the truth.

But for your race among us there could not be war, although many men engaged on either side do not care for you one way or the other. Nevertheless, I repeat, without the institution of Slavery and the colored race as a basis, the war could not have an existence.

It is better for us both, therefore, to be separated. I know that there are free men among you, who even if they could better their condition are not as much inclined to go out of the country as those, who being slaves could obtain their freedom on this condition. I suppose one of the principal difficulties in the way of colonization is that the free colored men cannot see that his comfort would be advanced by it. You may believe you can live in Washington or elsewhere in the United States the remainder of your life [as easily], perhaps more so than you can in any foreign country, and hence you may come to the conclusion that you have nothing to do with the idea of going to a foreign country. This is (I speak in no unkind sense) an extremely selfish view of the case.

. . . . .

There is much to encourage you. For the sake of your race you should sacrifice something of your present comfort for the purpose of being as grand in that respect as the white people. It is a cheering thought throughout life that something can be done to ameliorate the condition of those who have been subject to the hard usage of the world. It is difficult to make a man miserable while he feels he is worthy of himself, and claims kindred to the great God who made him. In the American Revolutionary War sacrifices were made by men engaged in it; but they were cheered by the future. Gen. Washington himself endured greater physical hardships than if he had remained a British subject. Yet he was a happy man, because he was engaged in benefiting his race—something for the children of his neighbors, having none of his own.

The colony of Liberia has been in existence a long time. In a certain sense it is a success. The old President of Liberia, Roberts, has just been with me—the first time I ever saw him. He says they have within the bounds of that colony between 300,000 and 400,000 people, or more than in some of our old States, such as Rhode Island or Delaware, or in some of our newer States, and less than in some of our larger ones. They are not all American colonists, or their descendants. Something less than 12,000 have been sent thither from this country. Many of the original settlers have died, yet, like people elsewhere, their offspring outnumber those deceased.

The question is if the colored people are persuaded to go anywhere, why not there? One reason for an unwillingness to do so is that some of you would rather remain within reach of the country of your nativity. I do not know how much attachment you may have toward our race. It does not strike me that you have the greatest reason to love them. But still you are attached to them at all events.

The place I am thinking about having for a colony is in Central America. It is nearer to us than Liberia—not much more than one-fourth as far as Liberia, and within seven days' run by steamers. Unlike Liberia it is on a great line of travel—it is a highway. The country is a very excellent one for any people, and with great natural resources and advantages, and especially because of the similarity of climate with your native land—thus being suited to your physical condition.

The particular place I have in view is to be a great highway from the Atlantic or Caribbean Sea to the Pacific Ocean, and this particular place has all the advantages for a colony. On both sides there are harbors among the finest in the world. Again, there is evidence of very rich coal mines. A certain amount of coal is valuable in any country, and there may be more than enough for the wants of the country. Why I attach so much importance to coal is, it will afford an opportunity to the inhabitants for immediate employment till they get ready to settle permanently in their homes.

. . . . .

The practical thing I want to ascertain is whether I can get a number of able-bodied men, with their wives and children, who are willing to go, when I present evidence of encouragement and protection. Could I get a hundred tolerably intelligent men, with their wives and children, to "cut their own fodder," so to speak? Can I have fifty? If I could find twenty-five able-bodied men, with a mixture of women and children, good things in the family relation, I think I could make a successful commencement.[3]

Lincoln spoke out for the migration of the Negro because it would benefit the white man in America, and perhaps, incidentally, the black race. Joseph Parrish Thompson, pastor of the Broadway Taber-

nacle in New York City, did so for another reason: because American freedmen might regenerate Africa.

. . . We have chosen to bring the question of African capacity and destiny into our own bosom, till it has distracted our councils, destroyed our trade, and driven us to war as the only refuge from anarchy and the terrorism of a slaveocracy. When we have thoroughly subdued this rebellion, we must carry the war literally into Africa, and teach her people how to fight against slavery with the cotton gin, and from behind cotton bales of their own making.

Africa has been happily styled "the continent of the future."

. . . . .

There is . . . nothing in history, in the characteristics of the race, in physical geography, or in climate, to forbid the development in Africa of a civilization, which, though having a continental type, will be second to none on the face of the globe. The providence of God most clearly indicates that the time has come for enlightened, liberal, systematic, earnest measures for civilizing Africa. During the past ten years, geographical research, the instinct of curiosity, the love of adventure, the enterprise of commerce, political ambition, and missionary zeal—all these various and powerful motives have prompted the exploration of the African continent; and as a result of this, we have an amount of knowledge touching Africa, its physical geography, its resources, its population, its commercial advantages, which enables us to map out that continent with a proximate accuracy, and to form definite plans for its development.

. . . . .

The frequent use of the prejudice against color and race as an argument for colonization, . . . has caused the black man, however unreasonably, to regard the Colonization Society as his masked enemy, and has brought it into collision with the growing antislavery sentiment of the times. No doubt these mistakes will be corrected in the future and Liberia will yet win a worthy place among civilized nations. But the Providence of God is now appealing to the representatives of the African race in this country to go forth for the redemption of the land of their fathers, and thus also for the redemption of their brethren in bonds; to go not as exiles under a ban, but as pioneers in an army of civilization—not as refugees from

UNCLE CLEM: "Say, Massa Jim, is I wan of them onfortunate niggers as you was reading about?" YOUNG GENTLEMAN: "Yes, Uncle Clem, you are one of them." UNCLE CLEM: "Well, it's a great pity about me.—I'se berry badly off, I is."

oppression, but as missionaries of social reform, equipped with industrial arts, with liberal education, with Christian faith; and this call of Providence, coming in part through the inviting reports from Africa, and in part through the demand for skilled labor upon African cotton, in part also through that indefinable spontaneous feeling in many minds that preludes a great movement—this call of Providence has stirred the hearts of men of African descent, not to escape from petty annoyances here, but to attempt a noble work beyond the sea for the home of their ancestors, and for freedom and humanity in coming generations. . . .[4]

Overseas colonization of free Negroes was a futile answer to the racial dilemma. During the Civil War, two small expeditions left Baltimore for Liberia (1862); another, with Bernard Kock as promoter, removed four hundred Negroes to a Caribbean island and failed miserably as a colonizing venture. But at least colonization was a tolerant view and attempted a constructive solution of the Negro's problems. Most Northerners were less charitable. And as the war progressed with its rising casualties, anger at the Negro increased. He could at least fight—mix his blood in death, although not in life, with that of his white neighbors. Thus, Governor Israel Washburn of Maine, in a letter to Vice-President Hannibal Hamlin, warned of discontent in the North if "Sambo" did not join in the battle.

Why have our rulers so little regard for the true & brave white men of the north? Will they continue to sacrifice them? Why will they refuse to save them by employing black men—our armies hereafter must be recruited from the South & not the North. It is right, expedient, necessary. The men cannot be raised North, at least, so long as the present policy remains—disloyalty is growing rampant even in New England—traitors no longer fear the govt.—only union men. Why are our leaders unwilling that Sambo should save white boys?[5]

They said it in verse, too. Verse that not only demanded that the Negro fight, but revealed a deeply ingrained contempt for him.

Some tell us 'tis a burning shame
To make the naggers fight,
And that the thrade of being kilt
Belongs but to the white;
But as for me, upon my soul,
So liberal are we here,
I'll let Sambo be murdered instead of myself
On every day in the year.
  On every day in the year, boys,
  And in every hour of the day,
  The right to be kilt I'll divide with him,
  And divil a word I'll say.

In battle's wild commotion,
I shouldn't at all object
If Sambo's body should stop a ball
That was coming for me direct;
And the prod of a Southern bayonet—
So generous are we here—
I'll resign, and let Sambo take it,
On every day of the year.
  So hear we all, boys, darlins,
  Don't think I'm tippin' you chaff,
  The right to be kilt we'll divide with him,
  And give him the largest half.[6]

The demand was made on a more rational level by an abolitionist, Elizur Wright, who scarcely two weeks after the outbreak of hostilities accurately assessed the future role of the Negro in the War.

The war at its foundation is all about the black man. Between magnanimity and contempt we northerners may be willing to fight it out for him. But events are not ruled by men, and before the war is through the black man is almost certain to be fighting for himself on one side or the other . . . have you duly weighed the probability in his fighting against the federal govt.? . . . Is it less than a "military necessity" to forestall the possibility of this, by exercising the war power of annihilating property, in its application to slave property—compensation to be made of course, but *only* to proprietors who are loyal to the government . . . an early proclamation to this effect, would by its moral force more than half finish the war, and would be easily pardoned by the most pro-slavery at the North on the score of necessity.[7]

There was, however, dissent over the Negro soldier, as in most other matters. There were Northerners, although certainly a minority, who would not even grant the Negro the dignity of dying in his own cause. A white gentleman might fight for him, but should not be asked to fight with him.

The enlistment of Negro troops began on South Carolina's Sea

Islands in April 1862. In the words of Charles Carleton Coffin, "There was strong prejudice in the army against employing Negroes. The New Jersey troops in the department of the South were bitterly hostile. Colonel [Thomas G.] Stevenson, of Massachusetts, a gallant officer, having imprudently given utterance to his feelings upon the subject, was arrested by General [David] Hunter, which caused a great deal of excitement in the army, and which attracted the attention of the country to the whole subject."

The day after the colonel's arrest an argument took place that not only illuminates both sides of the question, but also reveals the depth of feeling that separated the protagonists. It happened in the cabin of a steamer. "Several ladies, one or two chaplains, fifteen or twenty officers, four newspaper correspondents and several civilians" were present. The narrator is apparently one of the newspaper men and he undoubtedly exaggerates his own or a colleague's triumph over the unhappy officer. He also implies the spectators were on his side. The latter, however, appear to have been content to smile and remain uncommitted.

A young captain in the Tenth New Jersey opened the conversation.

"I wish," said he, "that every negro was compelled to take off his hat to a white man. I consider him an inferior being."

"You differ from General Washington, who took off his hat and saluted a negro," said one of the correspondents.

"General Washington could afford to do it," said the captain, a little staggered.

"Are we to understand that in this age a captain cannot afford to equal a negro in politeness?" was the provoking question of the correspondent.

"Do you want to be buried with a nigger, and have your bones touch his in the grave?"

"As to that I have no feeling whatever. I do not suppose that it will make much difference to the bones of either party."

"Well, when I die I want twenty niggers packed all around me," shouted the captain, excitedly, turning to the crowd to see the effect of his sarcasm.

"I presume, sir, you can be accommodated if you can get the consent of the twenty negroes."

The captain saw that he was losing his argument by losing his temper, and in calmer tones said: "I want to see the negro kept in his proper place. I am perfectly willing he should use the shovel, but it is an outrage upon the white man—an insult to have him carry a musket."

"I would just as soon see a negro shot as to get shot myself. I am perfectly willing that all the negroes should help put down the Rebellion," said the correspondent.

"I am not willing to have them act as soldiers. Put them in the ditches, where they belong. They are an inferior race."

A second correspondent broke in. "Who are you, sir?" said he; "you who condemn the government? You forget that you as a soldier have nothing to say about the orders of the President or the laws of Congress. You say that the negro is an inferior being; what do you say of Frederick Douglass, who has raised himself from slavery to a high position? Your straps were placed on your shoulders, not because you had done anything to merit them, but because you had friends to intercede for you—using their political influence—or because you had money, and could purchase your commission. You hate the negro, and you want to keep him in slavery, and you allow your prejudice to carry you to the verge of disloyalty to the government which pays you for unworthily wearing your shoulder-straps."

The captain and the entire company listened in silence while another correspondent took up the question.

"Gentlemen, you denounce the negro; you say that he is an inferior being. You forget that we white men claim to stand on the highest plane of civilization—that we are of a race which for a thousand years has been in the front rank—that the negro has been bruised, crushed, trodden down—denied all knowledge, all right, everything; that we have compelled him to labor for us, and we have eaten the fruit of his labors. Can we expect him to be our equal in acquisition of knowledge? Where is your sense of fair play? Are you afraid that the negro will push you from your position? Are you afraid that if you allow him to aid in putting down the Rebellion, that he too will become a free man, and have aspirations like your own, and in time express toward you the same *chivalric* sentiments which you express toward him? How much do you love your country if you thus make conditions of loyalty?"

The captain made no reply. The whole company was silent. There were smiles from the ladies. The captain went out upon the deck, evidently regretting that the conversation had fallen upon so exciting a topic. . . .[8]

But once the barrier was broken, the Negro troops earned respect as soldiers. A white officer in a Massachusetts Negro regiment described not only the training of the colored troops but the change of attitude towards them.

The attention of the country at large was first seriously directed to the consideration of this new element in the army when Governor John A. Andrew obtained an order from Edwin M. Stanton, Secretary of War, authorizing him to organize persons of African descent into separate corps for the volunteer military service. As a consequence, a line of recruiting depots, running from Boston to St. Louis in the West, and to Fortress Monroe in the South, was established and maintained to the close of the war. Two infantry regiments, the Fifty-fourth and Fifty-fifth, and one cavalry, the Fifth, were raised, and the ranks kept at the maximum number; a good piece of work, involving an immense amount of labor, which was mainly done by two citizens of Medford—George L. Stearns and Richard P. Hallowell.

Public opinion in the North was either avowedly hostile to this scheme or entirely sceptical as to its value. In Philadelphia, recruiting was attended with some little danger, and with so much annoyance that the place of rendezvous was kept secret and the squads were marched under cover of darkness to the depot. In Ohio it was considered a good joke to get the "darkies on to Massachusetts"—a joke that was bitterly repented when Ohio at a later day tried in vain to get those same "darkies" credited to her quota. In Boston there were contemptuous remarks by individuals from both extremes of society; by certain members of a prominent club, who later on hissed the Fifty-fourth Regiment from their windows as it marched on its way to the front; and by a Boston journal whose editors disgraced their columns with reflections too vulgar for repetition. There was, too, much good-natured laughing and harmless joking among other classes. Before long, however, the prevailing undertone of thought became thoroughly respectful and kind, while the pecuniary aid given was limited only by the amount asked for.

The colored man from the free States as a soldier may be conveniently and fairly tested by the record of our Massachusetts regiments, for the reason, as we shall see later, that those regiments contained every known variety of citizen of African descent, and were recruited from every class and condition of colored society. That the Massachusetts regiments were not composed of picked men, except as to physique, is conclusively shown by the statistics. . . .

. . . Colonel Robert Gould Shaw was not a sentimentalist. He imposed the strict discipline of the Second Regiment, from which he came, upon the Fifty-fourth. The men of a slave regiment required, and in the case of the First South Carolina received, treatment very different from that required by mixed regiments like the Fifty-fourth and Fifty-fifth. In a slave regiment the harsher forms of punishment were, or ought to have been, unknown, so that every suggestion of slavery might be avoided. This was Colonel T. W. Higginson's enlightened method—the method of kindness, and it was successful. Colonel Shaw's method was the method of coercion, and it too was successful. The unruly members of the Fifty-fourth and Fifty-fifth were stood on barrels, bucked, gagged and, if need be, shot; in fact, treated as white soldiers were in all well-disciplined regiments. The squads of recruits which arrived at Readville for the Fifty-fifth could hardly at first sight have been called picked men. They were poor and ragged. Upon arrival they were marched to the neighboring pond, disrobed, washed and uniformed. Their old clothes were burnt. The transformation was quite wonderful. The recruit was very much pleased with the uniform. He straightened up, grew inches taller, lifted, not shuffled, his feet, began at once to try, and to try hard, to take the position of the soldier, the facings and other preliminary drill, so that his ambition to carry "one of those muskets" might be gratified. When finally he was entrusted with the responsible duties of a guard, there was nothing quite so magnificent and, let me add, quite so reliable, as the colored volunteer. The effect of camp discipline on his character was very marked. His officers were gentlemen who understood the correct orthography and pronunciation of the word "negro." For the first time in his life he found himself respected, and entrusted with duties, for the proper performance of which he would be held to a strict accountability. Crossing the camp lines by connivance of the guard was almost unknown. "Running guard" was an experiment too dangerous to try. The niceties of guard-mounting and guard-duty, the absolute steadiness essential to a successful dress-parade, were all appreciated and faithfully observed. The cleanliness of the barracks and camp grounds at Readville was a delight. Not a scrap of loose floating paper or stuff of any kind was permitted. The muskets, the accoutrements, were kept clean and polished. Every one was interested, every one did his best. The Sunday morning inspections discovered a degree of perfection that received much praise from several regular as well as veteran volunteer officers. It is not extravagant to say that thousands of strangers who visited the camp were instantly converted by what they saw. The aptitude of the colored volunteer to learn the manual of arms, to execute readily the orders for company and regimental movements, and his apparent inability to march out of time at once arrested the attention of every officer. His power of imitation was great, his memory for such movements was good, and his ear for time or cadence perfect. You may call the imitative power a sign of inferiority, or what you will. We have now to do with the negro as a soldier, and as such it may be accurately said that the average colored soldier adapts himself more readily to the discipline of a camp, and acquires what is called the drill, in much less time than the average white soldier. These characteristics stand out clear and are undisputed by those who have had experience in both kinds of regiments. Treated kindly and respectfully, the average colored citizen is the most inoffensive of persons. He prefers to get out of rather than in your way. Innately he is a gentleman. Instinctively he touches his hat when passing. The requirements of military discipline were very favorable for the full development of these traits, so much so that in the matter of etiquette and polite manners one felt that he was in command of a regiment of a thousand men—each man a possible Lord Chesterfield.[9]

The confidence the Negro troops earned in training was justified by their conduct in action.

It was during Grant's summer campaign against Petersburg in 1864 that the colored regiments showed to greatest advantage as a fighting force. As the Federals poured across the James River towards their objective—Petersburg—the southern gateway to the Confederate capital, Major General Benjamin F. Butler's Army of the James made a coordinate advance. As part of this movement, Major General William F. Smith's Eighteenth Army Corps plunged southward from the Appomattox River. It ran into heavy Confederate resistance. Under General Smith, Brigadier General Edward Hinks led the Third Division, which counted in its musters large numbers of Negro troops. These Negro volunteers fought a brilliant and ferocious action on June 15. General Hinks reported it in detail:

At about 1 A.M. of the 15th instant I had moved Duncan's brigade, consisting of the Fourth, Fifth and Sixth and Twenty-second Regiments U.S. Colored Infantry; Holman's (Provisional) brigade, consisting of the First U.S. Colored Infantry and one wing of the Fifth Massachusetts Cavalry (dismounted); Angel's battery and Choate's (colored) battery, from the several positions which they previously occupied, to the immediate vicinity of Broadway, and at 2 A.M. reported in person to Maj. Gen. W. F. Smith at Broadway. In accordance with his orders I concentrated my command in the immediate vicinity of Cope's house, below Broadway, on the road from City Point to Petersburg, at about daylight, with directions to take my place in column immediately following Kautz's cavalry.

The field return of the day exhibits the following effective force of the division present for duty: Duncan's brigade, officers and men, 2,200; Holman's brigade, officers and men, 1,300; Angel's battery, officers and men, 136; Choate's (colored) battery, officers and men, 111; aggregate, 3,747.

. . . . .

In the gallant and soldierly deportment of the troops engaged on the 15th instant under varying circumstances; the celerity with which they moved to the charge; the steadiness and coolness exhibited by them under heavy and long continued fire; the impetuosity with which they sprang to the assault; the patient endurance of wounds, we have a sufficient proof that colored men, when properly officered, instructed, and drilled, will make most excellent infantry of the line, and may be used as such soldiers to great advantage.

Our losses were quite heavy of officers and men, as shown in the

BATTLE OF
MILLIKEN'S BEND

inclosed summary of casualties, marked A. Among the wounded were Col. H. S. Russell and Maj. Z. B. Adams, of the Fifth Massachusetts Cavalry, who fell while gallantly leading their regiment in the charge at Baylor's farm, and Lieut. Col. Nathan Goff, Jr., of the Twenty-second U.S. Colored Troops, who fell in the movement upon the enemy's works. . . .[10]

Emancipation was also controversial. The Republican platform of 1860 made no threat to attack slavery in the States where it already existed; Lincoln underlined this policy in his first inaugural address. Northern opinion supported him. Abolitionists were unpopular. Moreover, though most Northerners disapproved of slavery, such disapproval was tempered by indifference. George William Curtis wrote in August 1861:

. . . There is very little moral mixture in the "anti-slavery" feeling of this country. A great deal is abstract philanthropy; part is hatred of slave-holders; a great part is jealousy for white labor; very little is consciousness of wrong done, and with the wish to right it. How we hate those whom we have injured. I, too, "tremble when I reflect that God is just." . . .[11]

If antislavery feeling in the North lacked moral fervor it was bolstered by other forces. One of these was economic. As early as the autumn of 1861, Sinclair Tousey, a self-made entrepreneur, presented the dollars-and-cents argument for emancipation.

. . . Having thus established the position that Emancipation will crush out the insurrection, I will now consider its effects on the whites of both sections, South as well as North. I assume that there is a certain amount of labor to be done in the Southern States, and that the freed negroes, from experience and acclimation, are the best qualified persons to perform that labor, and would be employed to to do it under a system of wages (instead of the lash), prices being regulated by the laws of demand and supply. These negroes being thus paid for their work would consume more of the products of white men employed in the mechanic arts; more especially those products not absolutely necessary to life, as cheap ornaments, and those thousands of fancy articles that an uneducated people are so fond of, and which they always buy so freely in proportion to their means. But it may be said, this system of wages would enhance the cost of the products grown by the labor of these people, and this increased cost would have to be borne by the consumers of these products.

If this were true, it would be owing to the fact, that these black people free would get more for their labor than black people in bondage; and if this were so, then it would follow, that the freeing of these people would have the effect of *"levelling up"* the price of labor to a point where the poor white men of those regions could afford to do it, a condition of things not heretofore existing in any slave State, the rule there being, that the planter, who owns both capital and labor, can afford to do work cheaper than the poor white, who merely owns his labor, which he wishes to sell, and can find no market for, because he cannot work as cheap as the black slave of the capitalist. Hence it is, that there are so many of the "poor white trash" scattered all over the South. Emancipation, according to this reasoning (originated by the opponents of Emancipation), would benefit the poor white most decidedly. The increased demand by the freed blacks for the products of the whites, both South and North, would add greatly to the demand for the labor of these whites, and thus Emancipation would benefit them pecuniarily, to say nothing of its removing the degradation now attached to labor in consequence of Slavery. Where there are no slaves, laboring men are respectable and respected. Where Slavery exists, the laborer is neither. The New England States illustrate the one condition, and the South the other. But, say some, if you emancipate the negroes they will not work; the stimulus of wages is not sufficient to induce them to labor. Well, grant that they will not. Suppose they choose to drag out a miserable, hand-to-mouth existence, as the poor whites of the South now do, and earn barely enough under the pressure of starvation to support life?

What then? If they refuse to work as regularly and efficiently as heretofore, will not *their refusal make a demand for the labor of the poor whites of both sections, and thus materially help to draw off from the great cities of the North the surplus labor, now vainly seeking employment, and thus greatly benefit those laborers?* Such neglect to work by the freed negroes would have none other than a beneficial effect on the poor whites, by giving them the work that the free blacks refuse to do but if the freed blacks go on and work industriously for wages, then their increased ability to consume would of necessity make an increased demand for the products of white men, now employed in the manufactures consumed by the blacks. Thus Emancipation, like all GOOD DEEDS, would bring its own reward. . . .[12]

Wendell Phillips, probably the greatest of the antislavery orators, presented broader and more persuasive reasons for emancipating the slave.

. . . I would claim of Congress—in the exact language of Adams, of the "*Government*"—a solemn act abolishing slavery throughout the Union, securing compensation to loyal slaveholders. As the Constitution forbids the States to make and allow nobles, I would now, by equal authority, forbid them to make slaves or allow slaveholders.

This has been the usual course at such times. Nations, convulsed and broken by two powerful elements or institutions, have used the first amount of assured power—the first moment that they clearly saw and fully appreciated the evil—to cut up the dangerous tree by the roots. So France expelled the Jesuits, and the Middle Ages the Templars. So England, in her great rebellion, abolished Nobility and the Established Church; and the French Revolution did the same, and finally gave to each child an equal share in his deceased father's lands. For the same purpose, England, in 1745, abolished clanship in Scotland, the root of the Stuart faction; and we, in '76, nobles and all tenure of estates savoring of privileged classes. Such a measure supplies the South just what she needs—capital. That sum which the North gives the loyal slaveholder, not as acknowledging his property in the slave, but a measure of conciliation—perhaps an acknowledgment of its share of the guilt—will call mills, ships, agriculture into being. The free negro will redeem to use lands never touched, whose fertility laughs Illinois to scorn, and finds no rival but Egypt. And remember, besides, as Montesquieu says, "The yield of land depends less on its fertility than on the freedom of its inhabitants." Such a measure binds the negro to us by the indissoluble tie of gratitude—the loyal slaveholder by strong self-interest—our bonds are all his property—the other whites, by prosperity, they are lifted in the scale of civilization and activity, educated and enriched. Our institutions are then homogeneous. We grapple the Union together with hooks of steel—make it as lasting as the granite that underlies the continent.

People may say this is a strange language for me—a Disunionist. Well, I was a Disunionist, sincerely, for twenty years. I did hate the Union, when Union meant lies in the pulpit and mobs in the street, when Union meant making white men hypocrites and black men slaves. (Cheers.) I did prefer purity to peace—I acknowledge it. The child of six generations of Puritans, knowing well the value of union, I did prefer disunion to being the accomplice of tyrants. But now, when I see what the Union must mean in order to last—when I see that you can not have union without meaning justice—and when I see twenty millions of people, with a current as swift and as inevitable as Niagara, determined that this Union shall mean justice, why should I object to it? I endeavored honestly, and am not ashamed of it, to take nineteen States out of this Union, and consecrate them to liberty, and twenty millions of people answer me back, "We like your motto, only we mean to keep thirty-four States under it." Do you suppose I am not Yankee enough to buy Union when I can have it at a fair price? I know the value of union. . . .[13]

This view was not universally accepted. Samuel Sullivan ["Sunset"] Cox, Democratic congressman from Ohio, spoke for many in a speech prepared for delivery in Congress in June 1862. He entitled his address "Emancipation and Its Results—Is Ohio to be Africanized?"

. . . Labor will then [after Emancipation] go down to a song. It will be degraded by such association. Our soldiers, when they return, one hundred thousand strong, to their Ohio homes, will find these negroes, or the best of them, filling their places, felling timber, plowing ground, gathering crops, &c. How their martial laurels will brighten when they discover the result of their services! Labor that now ranges from one to two dollars per day, will fall to one half. Already in this District [of Columbia] the Government is hiring out the fugitives at from two to eight dollars per month, while white men are begging for work. Nor is the labor of most of these negroes desirable. No system of labor is so unless it be steady. They will get their week's wages, and then idle the next week away. Many will become a charge and nuisance upon the public charity and county poor tax. . . . If they are distributed into the country, they may work for a little time and for small wages, and work well for a time; but when work grows irksome, and they "become too lazy to play," they will steal. Corn and chickens disappear in their vicinage, with the facility of shirts from the hedges where Falstaff marched his tatterdemallions [*sic*].

And for this result *directly* to northern labor, what compensation is there to the southern half of our country by their removal? Herein lies the indirect effect of their immigration upon northern labor. By this emancipation, the labor system of the South is destroyed. The cotton, which brought us $200,000,000 per annum, a good part of which came to Ohio to purchase pork, corn, flour, beef, machinery &c., where is it? Gone. What of the cotton fabric, almost as common as bread among the laboring classes? With four millions of indolent negroes its production is destroyed, and the ten millions of artisans in the world who depend on it for employment, and the hundred millions who depend on it for clothing will find the fabric advanced a hundred per cent. So with sugar, and other productions of slave labor. For all these results, labor will curse the jostling elements which thus disturb the markets of the world. Another indirect effect upon the labor of the North, and especially of Ohio, is that the markets of the South will be closed, not by blockade, but forever. Our prices of corn, wheat, pork, beef &c., will be reduced by a contracted market. The surplus in Ohio, the past year was, of grain 25,000,000 bushels; of hogs 1,000,000; of cattle 300,000, exports from the State, or more than $50,000,000 worth; while other articles of export were worth $50,000,000 more. This production is above that which Ohio can use. If our market is restricted, who suffers? The farmer. . . .[14]

Two months later John Sherman, also from Ohio and a United States Senator, expressed a different opinion—one undoubtedly shared by a majority of the people of the North. In a letter to his brother, General William T. Sherman, he wrote:

. . . You can form no conception at the change of opinion here as to the Negro Question. Men of all parties who now appreciate the magnitude of the contest and who are determined to preserve the unity of the government at all hazards, agree that we must seek the aid and make it the interests of the negroes to help us. Nothing but our party divisions and our natural prejudice of caste has kept us from using them as *allies* in the war, to be used for all purposes in which they can advance the cause of the country. Obedience and protection must go together. When rebels take up arms, not only refuse obedience but resist our force, they have no right to ask protection in any way. And especially that protection should not extend to a local right inconsistent with the general spirit of our laws and the existence of which has been from the beginning the chief element of discord in the country. I am prepared for one to meet the broad issue of universal emancipation. . . .[15]

Lincoln agreed with Sherman that slavery was "inconsistent with the general spirit of our laws" and that it was an "element of discord in our nation," but he did not justify emancipation on this basis. From the beginning of the war he had stated that freeing the slaves was contingent upon its effect on preserving the Union. When the Proclamation was finally issued it freed, or would free, only those in areas still in rebellion. When it was declared in effect, it excluded those areas within slave states that were not in rebellion by reason of occupation by Northern armies. Some nine months after it had been declared in force, he was still defending it purely on grounds of its contribution to saving the Union. His letter, written August 26, 1863, incidentally reveals that at this date there was still sufficient antiemancipation sentiment in the North to require an answer.

. . . You dislike the emancipation proclamation; and perhaps would have it retracted. You say it is unconstitutional. I think differently. I think the Constitution invests its Commander-in-Chief with the law of war in time of war. The most that can be said—if so much—is that slaves are property. Is there—has there ever been —any question that by the law of war, property, both of enemies and friends, may be taken when needed? And is it not needed whenever taking it, helps us, or hurts the enemy? Armies the world over, destroy enemies' property when they cannot use it; and even destroy their own to keep it from the enemy. Civilized belligerents do all in their power to help themselves, or hurt the enemy, except a few things regarded as barbarous or cruel. Among the exceptions are the massacre of vanquished foes, and noncombatants, male and female.

But the proclamation, as law, either is valid, or [it] is not valid. If it is not valid, it needs no retraction. If it is valid, it cannot be retracted, any more than the dead can be brought to life. Some of you profess to think its retraction would operate favorably for the Union. Why better *after* the retraction than *before* the issue? There was more than a year and a half of trial to suppress the rebellion before the proclamation [was] issued, the last one hundred days of which passed under an explicit notice that it was coming, unless averted by those in revolt, returning to their allegiance. The war has certainly progressed as favorably for us, since the issue of the proclamation as before. [I know, as fully as one can know the opinion of others, that some of the commanders of our armies in the field, who have given us our most important successes, believe the emancipation policy and the use of colored troops constitute the heaviest blow yet dealt to the rebellion, and that at least one of those important successes could not have been achieved when it was but for the aid of black soldiers. Among the commanders holding these views are some who have never had any affinity with what is called abolitionism, or with Republican party politics, but who hold them purely as military opinions. I submit these opinions as being entitled to some weight against the objections often urged that emancipation and arming the blacks are unwise as military measures, and were not adopted as such in good faith.]* You say you will not fight to free negroes. Some of them seem willing to fight for you; but, no matter. Fight you, then, exclusively to save the Union. I issued the proclamation on purpose to aid you in saving the Union. Whenever you shall have conquered all resistance to the Union, if I shall urge you to continue

*"The portion inclosed in brackets was inserted after the original letter had been mailed." But Lincoln requested, in a separate letter, that it be added.

fighting, it will be an apt time, then, for you to declare you will not fight to free negroes.

I thought that in your struggle for the Union, to whatever extent the negroes should cease helping the enemy, to that extent it weakened the enemy in his resistance to you. Do you think differently? I thought that whatever negroes can be got to do as soldiers, leaves just so much less for white soldiers to do in saving the Union. Does it appear otherwise to you? But negroes, like other people, act upon motives. Why should they do anything for us, if we will do nothing for them? If they stake their lives for us, they must be prompted by the strongest motive—even the promise of freedom. And the promise being made, must be kept. . . .[16]

Whatever the sentiments and arguments pro and con, emancipation became a part of the national policy and, in consequence, a war aim on January 1, 1863. But this is not to say that Northern feeling towards the Negro had altered. Even the abolitionist William Lloyd Garrison, in what he probably regarded as a eulogy to the freed Negro, was patronizing. The qualities praised are docility, faithfulness. Did Garrison regard docility as a virtue in white men? Was he himself docile? To whom was the Negro to be faithful—himself, or the white man who gave him orders?

We were told, all along, that if our principles should be reduced to practice, and our measures carried out, there would be the most terrible consequences both to the master and to the slave; that society would be overturned, and every part of the South red with blood and conflagration. What has been the result? The work of emancipation is going on, not in a peaceful state of society, but in the midst of civil war, the worst time in which to try such an experiment—civil war upon a colossal scale. Yet as the slaves emerge from the house of bondage, how docile and peaceable is their conduct! They are behaving not only as well as we said they would, but transcending even our anticipations and prophecies. (Applause.) Wherever they have been tried, whether merely in digging ditches, trenches and rifle pits, or whether "armed and equipped as the law directs for military duty," they have discharged their responsibilties in the most faithful manner. In my judgment, it stamps them as a remarkable people; so remarkable, that I really have in my mind great doubts whether any other people upon the face of the earth could go through the same sufferings and degradation, and come out with so much credit to themselves. (Applause.) . . .[17]

Most Northerners were even less well disposed than Garrison towards the Negro. They regarded him, free or slave, as a pariah, an inferior to be kept in his place. When he was not rendering service to his betters, that place was apart.

After Lee's surrender to Grant (in fact the day before Booth shot Lincoln) an incident occurred in Philadelphia that was characteristic of the Negro's past bondage, his present status, and his future struggle. A "Freedom Rider" appeared—not in Alabama or Mississippi but in Pennsylvania.

Rev. J. W. Allston, pastor of the colored Episcopal Church in this city, yesterday afternoon got upon the platform of a Lombard street car, to ride downtown. The driver objected, and the incident drew a crowd. In that vicinity are generally to be found numerous Irish people and negroes engaged in sunning themselves. Mr. Allston declined to get off the car. The conductor did not venture to eject him. Several Irishmen came up to the vehicle, insisting that he "should be kicked off," while a number of colored people, possessing the necessary means to carry the case to trial, insisted that the preacher should stand his ground, and bring the case to an issue. While the argument was in progress five cars severally came along, and strung out behind the first one. The conductor declined to proceed, Mr. Allston declined to alight, and there was gradually collected a considerable crowd of people. At this juncture the conductor stepped off the car, walked down Twelfth street to Ald. Morrow's office, one square distant. He there took out a warrant against Mr. Allston on a charge of assault and battery and inciting to riot. Alderman Morrow's constable walked up to the car and removed the divine, who was then ordered to enter bail to answer at Court, which he did.[18]

Negro Quarters—Army of the James

The same day that this incident occurred, Horace Greeley wrote in his personal correspondence: "We are a pro-slavery people to-day, in the great city of Philadelphia, which gave Lincoln nearly 10,000 majority in '60 and again in '64, a black Union soldier is not allowed to ride in the street cars; I tried to pilot through a most respectable colored clergyman, but was obliged to give it up. . . ."

Following the Allston affair, the railway company put special cars on its lines for Negro passengers, but these were boycotted; within three weeks after the experiment began, the average daily number of Negro passengers decreased to seven or eight. The conductors reported Negroes as saying, "if we can't ride with the white people, we prefer to walk."

But whatever the whites wanted, whatever their convictions, whatever their actions, the Negro was part of their war. Before the last shots were fired no less than 178,895 Negro troops served in the Union army. Lincoln finally came to speak of the colored soldiers as "very important, if not indispensable." The Negro was also a part of society. Let him have the last word.

The abolitionist Frederick Douglass was probably the best known Negro of his time. He was a brilliant orator who spoke for his people over a span of four decades. In 1862 he protested against the project to colonize the Negroes outside the United States. In doing so, he presented the claim of his race to be Americans.

It is one of the strangest and most humiliating triumphs of human selfishness and prejudice over human reason, that it leads men to look upon emancipation as an experiment, instead of being, as it is, the natural order of human relations. Slavery, and not Freedom, is the experiment; and to witness its horrible failure we have to open our eyes, not merely upon the blasted soil of Virginia and other Slave States, but upon a whole land brought to the verge of ruin.

We are asked if we would turn the slaves all loose. I answer, Yes. Why not? They are not wolves nor tigers, but men. They are endowed with reason—can decide upon questions of right and wrong, good and evil, benefits and injuries—and are therefore subjects of government precisely as other men are.

But would you have them stay here? Why should they not? What better is here than there? What class of people can show a better title to the land on which they live—than the colored people of the South? They have watered the soil with their tears and enriched it with their blood, and tilled it with their hard hands during two centuries; they have leveled its forests, raked out the obstructions to the plow and hoe, reclaimed the swamps, and produced whatever has made it a goodly land to dwell in, and it would be a shame and a crime little inferior in enormity to Slavery itself if these natural owners of the Southern and Gulf States should be driven away from their country to make room for others—even if others could be obtained to fill their places.

But unjust and revolting to every right-minded and humane man as is this talk of the expatriation of the slaves, the offense is not more shocking than it is unwise. For a nation to drive away its laboring population is to commit political suicide. It is like cutting off one's right hand in order to work the better and to produce the more. To say that Negroes shall not live in the Southern States is like saying that the lands of the South shall be no longer cultivated. The cry has all along been, we must have negroes to work in the South, for white men cannot stand the hot sun and the fell diseases of the rice swamp and the sugar plantation. Even the leaders of the rebellion made it one of their grievances that they could not get more negroes, though from motives of policy they have now dropped this plank from their platform. No one doubts that the Gulf States mean to have more slaves from Africa just so soon as they shall get well settled in their independence. Again, why not allow the colored people of the South to remain where they are? Will they occupy more room in freedom than slavery? If you could bear them as objects of your injustice, can they be more offensive as objects of your justice and your humanity? Why send them away? Who wants to take their places in the cotton field, in the rice swamp, and sugar fields, which they have tilled for ages? The whole scheme of colonization would be too absurd for discussion, but that the madness of the moment has drowned the voice of common sense as well as common justice.

There is a measure now before Congress duly reported from one of its Committees proposing, first, to make the Negroes leave the land of their birth, and secondly to pay the expense of their enforced removal. If such a measure can become a law, the nation is more deeply wicked than any Abolitionist has hitherto ventured to believe. It is a most mischievous and scandalous proposition, unworthy of any man not dead to the claims of every sentiment of honor and humanity. I predict that if it passes it will become like the Fugitive Slave law—it will lie dead upon the statute book—having no other effect than to alarm the freed men of the South and disgrace the Congress by which it is passed.

Once free the slaves, and at once the motives which now require their expatriation will become too weak to breathe. In the single little State of Maryland, with climate and soil which invite the white laborer to its borders, there are at this moment nearly one hundred thousand free colored people. Now, notwithstanding that Maryland is a Slave State, and thus possesses a strong motive for getting rid of their free colored people, the better to hold her slaves—and notwithstanding the circumstances of climate and soil—that Slave State only a year or two ago voted down by a large majority of their [*sic*] people the inhuman and barbarous proposition concerning her free colored population.

The number of colored people now on this continent and in the adjacent islands cannot fall far below twenty millions. An attempt to remove them would be as vain as to bail out the ocean. The whole naval power of the United States could not remove the natural increase of our part of this population. Every fact in our circumstances here marks us as a permanent element of the American people. Mark the readiness with which we adapt ourselves to your civilization. You can take no step in any direction where the black man is not at your back or side.—Go to California and dig gold: the black man is there. Go to war with Mexico, and let your armies penetrate the very heart of the country, and the black man is there. Go down into the coast of North and South Carolina, and the black man is there, and there as your friend, to give you more important and more trustworthy information than you can find among all the loyal poor white trash you can scare up in that region. The Negro is sometimes compared with the Indian, and it is predicted that, like the Indian, he will die out before the onward progress of the Anglo-Saxon race. I have not the least apprehension at this point. In features and complexion, the Negro is more unlike the European than is his Mongolian brother. But the interior resemblance is greater than the exterior difference. The Indian wraps himself in gloom, and proudly glories in isolation—he retreats before the onward march of civilization. The humming of the honey bees warns him away from his hunting grounds. He sees the plowshare of civilization tossing up the bones of his venerated fathers, and he dies of a broken heart. Not so with the Negro. There is a vitality about him that seems alike invincible to hardship and cruelty. Work him, whip him, sell him, torment him, and he still lives, and clings to American civilization. . . . [19]

V

The War and Northern Economy

AT THE BEGINNING of the war, economic statistics favored the North. The ratio of its advantage in wealth was 4.5 to 1, in railway mileage 2.5 to 1, in real and personal property (exclusive of slaves) 6 to 1, in manufacturing 10 to 1. In 1860, Massachusetts alone manufactured goods that were 60 per cent more valuable than those produced in the entire Confederacy. But statistics do not win wars. The economic potential must be realized. The successes and shortcomings in the effort to achieve this potential are an important aspect of the North at war.

It was not a total mobilization in the modern meaning of the term. There was no system of priorities, or rationing; there was no draft of economic manpower. The Lincoln administration was woefully inefficient during the early years; the War Department had little system or order. Speculation, inflation, a shortage of funds in the Treasury, and contractors' dishonesty hampered the Union's slow, cumbersome adjustment to war needs. Laissez-faire traditions were a further drag.

Yet progress was made. Wartime financing surmounted the money problems; under Stanton, the War Department from January 1862 on was much more efficient than under Cameron; if corruption did not disappear, it diminished. The war did not bring about the birth of the industrial revolution in America, but in some ways—although not in all ways—it did hasten its growth. Mechanization increased in both industry and agriculture. Of major importance was the federal government's operation of its own plants for the production of small arms and other products. Although it did not manufacture a major part of all the ordnance and other supplies that were used by the army, the government in its armories, laboratories, and workshops did establish a standard of quality which had its effect upon all that was accepted for military use.

Finally, in spite of speculation and an element of "shoddy" running through wartime prosperity, there was a solid basis for the Northern economy that made it a vital factor in the eventual victory. Production increased; uncertainty about the future often led to a healthy caution; cash sales, rather than a risky credit, predominated. Consolidation, mergers, realignment in banking and industry occurred. At times these latter developed into monopolistic combinations, but they provided a certain stability in uncertain times.

At the outbreak of the war, shot and shell, cannon, small arms, uniforms, and shoes were needed by the army. And in a country still predominantly agricultural, an increase in farm produce was vital. Only three weeks after the bombardment of Fort Sumter the American Agriculturist, *the leading farm journal of the North, pleaded for increased food production, and assured its readers that they would be helping themselves, as well as the war effort, if they would raise just "one bushel more."*

There is now every encouragement to cultivators, to increase the products of their fields to the last bushel, the present season, whether those products be wheat, corn, barley, oats, beans, peas, potatoes, carrots, turnips, orchard fruits, or garden vegetables. This does not necessarily imply the planting or sowing of more ground; though every acre that can possibly be tilled well, that is, so as to yield a fair profit, should be under cultivation this year. The winter grains are, of course, already growing, yet the filling up of bare spots with spring varieties, the clearing out of obstructed drains or dead furrows, and the application of some kind of manure as a top-dressing, may materially increase the yield. For the crops yet to be put in, a thorough preparation of the ground, a selection of good seed, with the application of the last shovelful of manure from the barnyard, poultry yard, etc., will all tell in cash next Autumn. Nothing makes our severe labors in the field less irksome, than to *feel* that we are putting in a crop so *well* that it can scarcely fail to give good returns. The satisfaction will be still greater, if we have reasonable prospects of realizing good prices for the resulting crop.

. . . . .

Again, as we write, the sounds of martial music, and the gathering hosts of armed men that almost momentarily pass our window, betoken an impending war of no small magnitude. Of that war, its causes, and its aims, this is not the place to speak. So much is certain, that if continued, it will transfer a vast multitude from the producing to the consuming classes. As one result, those who are not called from their homes to the service of their country, will find more work upon their hands, which, with the increased demands upon their fields, will require greater skill and effort.

The foreign demand will alone greatly stimulate the market for agricultural products, and enhance prices, thus affording means for liquidating debts incurred for land, and for implements, and other liabilities, perhaps unwisely contracted in the past. Let, then, every cultivator of the soil take hold with increased energy and confidence, and spare no effort of hands and brain to secure at least "one bushel more," either by tilling better than ever before, or by increasing the area under cultivation, or by both of these means.[1]

By September the Agriculturalist *was able to report a modest increase in the wheat crop. It also assured its readers that despite low prices, depreciation of the currency, and taxes, the prospects of a healthy profit were still good.*

. . . From a careful survey of the numerous reports from all parts of our own wheat growing States, we conclude that, taken as a whole, the crop now gathered will be above an average one. This will afford a supply for home use, and a moderate surplus for export, —not enough to overstock the market, or keep prices very low.

The war caused a depreciation in the Southern State Stocks, so largely used as bank securities at the West, and this, of course, depreciated the bank bills. The depreciation went so far as to nearly destroy the bank issues in all the States west of Indiana, except Iowa, and the result was, that for several months there was no money afloat, either to pay debts or to buy grain. Latterly, large amounts of gold have been forwarded from the East, which is beginning to find its way into the Western country. The constant demand for breadstuffs for Eastern consumption, and for export, will tend to greatly increase the circulation of gold and specie-paying bank bills among the masses at the West. The immense sums now being expended *at home* by our General Government, are beginning to set money afloat. The Treasury Notes, of which a million dollars a day are now provided for, and are being issued, will, during the continuance of the war, add greatly to the sound circulating currency of the country, and money will soon be plentiful, at least among those who produce the necessities of life, breadstuffs, and meat. People must eat, and there are *about* as many mouths to be fed in war as in peace. Those who have crops to sell will therefore find a market for them; and as for breadstuffs, the foreign demand and the abundance of money, will keep the prices up to a paying figure, at least.

. . . . .

There is some anxiety in regard to the system of direct taxation established, but this is needless. The amount to be raised annually, averages less than two dollars for each inhabitant of the Free States. It will fall heaviest upon those best able to meet it; and very few persons would hesitate to voluntarily subscribe this amount to support and maintain a free government, to the influence of which we are so largely indebted for the prosperity we have enjoyed.

To the cultivators of the soil the present state of the country presents the strongest incentives to exertion. Their products will be in demand, however much all other commodities may be depreciated. He who fails, through fear, or sluggishness, to put in every acre of wheat possible, and to increase the products of his acres to the highest point, fails in his duty to himself, to his family, and to his country. There is every motive to increased exertion, and to a careful study of the best methods of cultivation. If all other incentives fail, the certain prospect of full returns for the products of the soil, will surely stimulate to active and *well directed* labor.[2]

Women and machines played an important part in increased agricultural production. "The Volunteer's Wife" (see p. 42) had prom-

ised that "Ruth can drive the Oxen . . . I can use the hoe." The promise was kept. Young women went into the fields to gather in the harvest and received relatively high wages. In 1864, at South Merrimack, New Hampshire, young women were making two dollars per day and board for reaping. Frequently, however, it was not a hoe but a mowing machine to which the farm wife put her hand.

. . . At the present time so perfect is machinery that men seem to be of less necessity. Of all the labors of the field, mowing was formerly deemed to be the most arduous, and the strongest men were required for it. We have seen, within the past few weeks, a stout matron whose sons are in the army, with her team cutting hay at seventy-five cents per acre, and she cut seven acres with ease in a day, riding leisurely upon her cutter. This circumstance is indicative of the great revolution which machinery is making in production. War occupations, even on a most gigantic scale, do not seem to check the supply of food. That food is not produced, however, in much greater ratio per acre, while its value [is less] compared with what the farmer is required to purchase—necessary groceries and clothing require a far greater number of bushels of grain than formerly, and interchange is not readily effected.[3]

The progress of mechanization was dealt with by the Cincinnati Gazette *in 1862.*

A hundred thousand agricultural laborers are gone; how are we to meet the deficiency? We have met it chiefly by labor-saving machinery. A few years since, McCormick came to Cincinnati to manufacture his reapers. The idea then was, that they were suitable only for the large prairie wheat-fields. It was the only agricultural machine we had, and it was met, as usual, by doubt and hesitation. Soon after, this machine and others appeared at the World's Fair [in England], and it was pronounced a great success. Since then we have reapers, mowers, separators, sowers, drills &c., making a great aggregate of agricultural machinery, which does the work of more than three-fold the number of men, who (without machinery) would have been required to do it. Indeed, without this machinery, the wheat, oats, and hay of Ohio, in 1862, could not have been got in safely. Besides, this machinery, which was at first only intended for large farms, now operates on the smallest; and on the large tracts steam is successfully employed, multiplying tenfold the labor-saving power. At Dayton, Springfield, Lancaster, Canton and Cleveland, large factories are engaged in turning out agricultural machines; so that we have the benefit both of the making and the use of agricultural machinery. The mode in which the harvest of 1862 has been principally got in is this. One farmer in the neighborhood buys a machine, whether reaper or separator, and goes round doing the work of his neighbors at so many cents per bushel. It is thus that machinery has done the work of thousands of men, who have thus been spared for the war. . . .[4]

The ultimate influence of mechanization on the American farm was discussed the following year in the American Agriculturist.

Dealers in agricultural implements report that the demand for labor saving machines during the present season has been altogether unprecedented. The manufactories of mowers and reapers, horse rakes and pitchforks, etc., although worked to their utmost capacity, have been unable to fully meet the orders. This has of course resulted in a large degree from the scarcity of laborers caused by the transferring of so many men to the field where other harvests than those of agriculture are being reaped. But it is also due, in some measure, to the influence of the agricultural press, which has for years been educating the farming community to the practicability of substituting animal and mechanical power for hand labor. This fact is one of the compensations of the war, and no slight one either. Its influence will be felt long after peace shall have called the absent laborers to their homes. It is, in fact, an emancipation of thousands of men from the necessity of severe toil; an emancipation which furnished no elements for political agitation, but which is none the less noteworthy. No man will willingly return to the old routine of muscle work, after having once enjoyed the comparative ease in haying time, bestowed by a good mower. One effect of this release of so many laborers will be to allow the cultivation of a much larger area of land. The Great West already owes much to the successful introduction of mechanical contrivances into agriculture, and its

IMPORTANT IMPROVEMENTS FOR FARMERS.

This Machine is as Perfect a Mower as any Single Mower now offered for 1865.

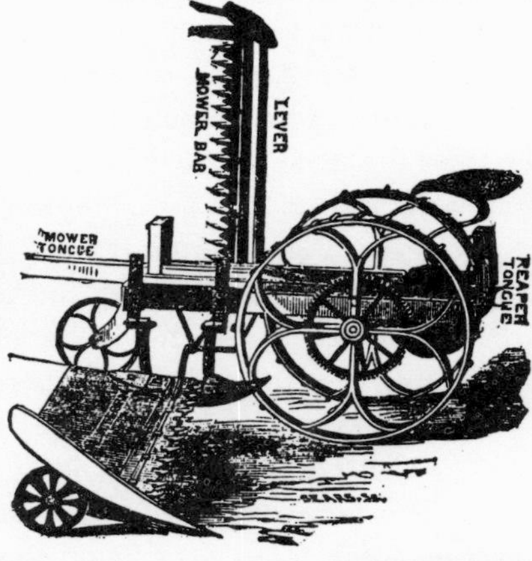

It is the most perfect Reaper and has a Self Rake which gave universal satisfaction in over 2,500 cases last year.

We admit many good Machines were made before, but the combination so that **singly they should be both excellent,** having **Forward Cut** in Mowing and Bar **off the ground,** and the Reaper with **Rear Cut** and **Side delivery** and **Self Raking,** and then an arrangement by which the Machine might WEAR OUT BOTH SIDES OF ALL COGS AND MACHINERY, were points none had attained. We **Warrant the 2 in 1 to do all this,** MAKING IT WORTH DOUBLE PRICE, and yet we can afford it the SAME as the best first class Machines. Cash price, $175 for No. 1 Mower; $200 for Mower No. 2; $240 for Mower with Hand-Rake; but the **best** of all, the cheapest of all, and embracing all, is the **Self Raker, only $265.**

SMALLEY'S CORN PLOW AND CULTIVATOR

on wheels. Driver's Seat, does the work of Harrow, Shovel Plow, Cultivator, Stubble plowing, and Drill. With two horses and a boy all this work can be done and ride comfortably *twice as fast and much better than formerly.* Cheapest Implement, considering its uses and durability, ever made. Ride when you plow corn, &c., henceforth. Cash Price, with 7 Steel Cultivator Teeth and four Cast Plows, $68. Improved by using Steel Plows, polish in any soil, $72.

ADDRESS AND ORDER IMMEDIATELY, for Agents who sold 16 last year order now 100 to 200.

J. W. BAIN, Prest. American Agricultural Works,
17 Courtlandt-st., New York City.

All kinds of Implements and Machinery at Manufacturers' prices. Self-Acting Gas Machines for from 10 to 300 Burners Warranted entirely satisfactory.—Preserve this advertisement.

fertile prairies will ere long receive still larger accessions from this cause. The influence of this change will also be widely felt in the number of young men willing to follow the profession of farming, now that so much of exhausting labor is relieved. The work of the farmer will take rank above mere manual labor, which will always hold a lower place than the exercise of skill. Although this may appear of little account in any particular neighborhood, in the aggregate, the results will be of great importance. Agriculture needs the brain work of many a man whose muscles are not strong enough to handle the scythe, and not a few such will be added to the ranks by the general introduction of farming by machinery.[5]

West of the Mississippi River, too, farmers lived under the clouds of war. They followed its progress, weighed victories against defeats, and speculated on its outcome. They also found in war a stimulus to the "pursuits and arts of peace." In 1863 the Davenport, Iowa, Daily Gazette *reports on this silver lining.*

It is gratifying to note that while popular attention is so much directed to the all important questions of the war, its progress, victories and probable results, the pursuits and arts of peace are not only receiving ordinary consideration but are enlisting in their service more of enterprise, industry and skill than ever before. Certainly this is true, at least, in relation to the agricultural interests of the loyal States; and in none more true than in Iowa. At no former period in the history of our State has there been so much of intelligent effort directed to secure a speedy development of our agricultural resources as now. A new energy seems to have been infused into the farmers of Iowa, and they press on in their labors with a praiseworthy emulation that gives hopeful assurance of a harvest of rich success. The old style dependence on the cultivation of one or two staples to the exclusion of all else is being abandoned. Our farmers have learned by dear experience that a few acres devoted to flax, sorghum, &c., is at least as profitable and far more certain of affording a return than a much larger tract of wheat alone. They are learning too, that of all States in the Union Iowa is especially adapted to the raising of good beef and fine wool. And so we are entering on an era of truly progressive farming. Wherever the traveler in Iowa goes, he sees a diversified agriculture in progress, or being introduced, that presents a pleasing contrast to the thriftless raising of wheat and corn that a few years since seemed to be the sole thought of Iowa farmers. Now, well kept pastures, weedless fields of corn and sorghum, droves of cattle, flocks of sheep, sugar mills and spinning wheels will be seen, where ere [*sic*]-while broad acres of shriveled or rusted grain, reapers and fanning mills were alone visible. The dawn of Iowa's greatness as an agricultural State is breaking; its morning brightness and noon-day glory will come in due time.[6]

Horses were a problem. They could not be produced by machinery, and horses and mules were the tanks, trucks, and jeeps of the fighting forces in the 1860's. The need was met but the price was high. General in Chief Henry Wager Halleck reported in December 1863 that horses were being used up so badly in the army that a remount for the whole service was being required every two months. He predicted that 435,000 horses would be needed in 1864 because of want of skill in their use, and often "culpable neglect" of the animals. Stock breeders were saying that if the evil went unchecked the breed would be permanently injured. In 1866, a year after the war, there were 6 per cent fewer horses (including the Southern States) than in 1860. Mules were fully 30 per cent less than in 1860. Vermont had 69,071 horses in 1860, and 49,222 in 1866. Recuperation in New England was slower than in the West. In his report of January 1, 1864, the Commissioner of Agriculture cited some pertinent facts:

By comparing the census returns of farm stock in 1850 and 1860 it will be seen that horses increased 47 per cent. in that decade. The same rate of increase would have given 18⅘ per cent. for the increase from 1860 to 1864, and the rate of increase should have been proportionally greater for the loyal States. But instead of that rate of increase, which would have added 789,438 to the horses of these States, there is a decrease of 150,000. There should have been, therefore, at least 939,438 horses more than we now have. Such a deficit will require a supply that will not be equal to the demand for years to come. . . .[7]

In Illinois, the farmers' problems were not confined to those of production. Chicago banks attempted to unload on them bank notes secured by Southern stocks.

The Currency War in Chicago.—We alluded to this in our last, but as the war is still raging and growing hotter, and it is one in which the people of the country are deeply interested, the occasion calls for something more on the subject. It is well that our people should understand it fully, that they may be prepared to stand from under when the crash comes.

The state of the case, as we understand it, is about this. There are some 25 or 30 Banks of this State whose circulation is mostly secured by Southern stocks, which are now almost worthless in the market. Up to a month or two ago, before stocks had fallen to the present low figure, the bills of most of these banks were comparatively well secured, and they were readily taken in all business transactions. Gradually, however, as stocks kept falling, the country became distrustful of this currency, and kept sending it to Chicago, until at present most of it (to the amount of say $1,700,000) has accumulated in that city. Foreseeing this, Dunham, of the Merchants Loan and Trust Company, at an early day, commenced throwing it out, while most of the other bankers in Chicago, having their coffers full of it, refused to do so, their determination obviously being to get their "decks clear" of it before dashing it. This they sought to accomplish by sending it into the country to buy produce; but notwithstanding the large sums sent out in this way, the money would come back upon them faster than they could shove it. Thus their coffers were still full, until a week or two ago, they found it necessary to take other steps to aid in giving it credit in the country, and for this purpose they got up a circular signed by most of the prominent bankers and business men in Chicago, agreeing to take this currency, (which for the sake of distinctness, has been felicitously christened "stumptail"), at par "during the war." The manoeuvre, however, promises but limited success. The country is distrustful as ever and prefers to hold on to their produce rather than exchange it for stumptail.

Their distrust is heightened by the course of the dealers in stumptail themselves. Professing not to discriminate, yet if a grain dealer from Ottawa sells a boat load of grain to a Chicago dealer, he is paid, say 40 cts. a bushel in stumptail, or 37 cts. in good Illinois currency; or, if he takes all stumptail and wants it exchanged for "preferred" Illinois currency, they will charge from six to eight per cent. We even know of instances where Ottawa dealers have sent off this currency to Chicago houses on the "stumptail circular," and have been allowed but 80 cents on the dollar for it! They will have a fine time in getting up confidence in the country by pursuing a course like this.

But the upshot of the matter is this. We have been looking over the list of stumptail banks and their securities, and, by a little figuring, find that, at present prices of stocks, their bills are worth ranging from 50 to 60 cents on the dollar—none over 60, the average being little over 50. There are $1,700,000 of this currency in Chicago. On it there must be a loss of $850,000. Who shall lose it? Shall the wealthy Chicago bankers, who have been turning it over and over for months, and making more than all they'll lose out of it by enormous charges for exchange, &c., &c.; or shall it be the farmers—the produce raisers of the country?

"But," say the bankers, "the currency is needed. Drive it out, and we have nothing left to move our crops." The plea, in lawyer phrase, is bad. It is true, we have in this State at present six millions less of currency than we had last December; but it is also true that the Eastern States stand ready to furnish us with all the currency we need to move our crops.—New York is not only full of good currency, but of gold. They want our wheat and corn, and are ready and willing to pay gold for it; and if our farmers insist on taking that and nothing else, they will get it. True, they must take a cent or two less on the bushel; but would it not be better to take even a third less, than to swap their grain for stumptail, which may in three months be as worthless as the old Continental scrip? We shall have no good money until we drive this stumptail out, and the farmers are the only men that can do it.

Why, look here! Exchange on New York sells in Chicago at 10 @ 13½%. For preferred Illinois currency you can buy it at 4 @ 5; for gold at about ½%. Who loses these 12%? Not the banker, of course; nor the merchant, for he must make it up by additional charges on his goods. It comes out of the producer. Yet many a farmer imagines because he is getting a cent or two more for his grain in "stumptail," and can buy goods with it at par, he is doing better than if he dealt in gold and silver!

We conclude, therefore, by commending, as we did in our last, the determination of our bankers to set their faces against the attempt of a party in Chicago to foist this "stump-tail," upon the country, and by expressing the hope that the producers of this county will in this matter fully back our bankers up. The agreement in Chicago to take this "stumptail" is a hollow delusion. It is already broken, as we have shown. Besides, what does an agreement between five hundred men amount to, when, by a single one breaking it, the whole thing is nullified?[8]

But the farmers, surmounting all difficulties, responded to the challenge. The army was fed, clothed, and mounted. There was food for the civilian population and a surplus of wheat for export. This latter was large enough to lead later historians to conclude that "King Wheat" had proved mightier than "King Cotton" as a factor in war diplomacy.

Industrial production was more complex than farming. Exposed to the evils of chicanery, speculation, and bureaucratic bungling, its progress was checkered.

At the beginning of the war, the immediate problem was to equip the army. The War Department was ill prepared for the strain thrust upon it. To begin with, there was a lack of money. Quartermaster General Meigs wrote to a deputy quartermaster general:

Your letter of the 14th in regard to estimates and requisitions is received.

It has been impossible for the Treasury to fill them all, for the reason that it does not contain the money, and to ask that all be sent at once, and to urge, as you suggest, to send a part, only aggravates the impatience of contractors, is to prevent the Treasury making any remittances.

The condition on which alone you purchased Skinner's cloth, and on which alone that and the English blankets could be obtained, was cash payment. I know that injustice is done to well-deserving contractors, who had the right to expect cash. I have asked for the remittance; I cannot make it, as I am not the banks, the capitalists, the people, nor the Secretary of the Treasury.

Many other injustices are the result of this war, and great as this is, it is one of the least; so long as there are found merchants, manufacturers, or capitalists who will take the risk of supplying this department with clothing or other indispensable stores for the defense of the country, we must continue to exert ourselves to obtain them.

I will make every proper exertion to remit money, but I cannot add to the cares and toils of the Secretary of the Treasury by personal solicitations for money, which he tells me he has not been able to procure, and I must make this distinction in urging particular claims which every man or corporation or nation has to make in order to carry on operations indispensable to the life of a nation, costing, however, more than its daily income.[9]

Invention contributed to the economic strength of the North. Nonetheless, it created problems. Old-line officers, confused by the rush for contracts to supply the latest arms, resisted change. Lieutenant Colonel James W. Ripley, who headed the Ordnance Department, wrote on June 11, 1861:

A great evil now specially prevalent in regard to arms for the military service is the vast variety of the new inventions, each having of course, its advocates, insisting upon the superiority of his favorite arm over all others and urging its adoption by the Government.

The influence thus exercised has already introduced into the service many kinds and calibers of arms, some, in my opinion, unfit for use as military weapons, and none as good as the U.S. musket, producing confusion in the manufacture, the issue, and the use of ammunition, and very injurious to the efficiency of the troops. This evil can only be stopped by positively refusing to answer any requisitions for or propositions to sell new and untried arms, and steadily adhering to the rule of uniformity of arms for all troops of the same kind, such as cavalry, artillery, infantry. The U.S. muskets as now made have no superior arms in the world. I say this with confidence, from my entire familiarity with the manufacture of these arms, and from the fact that the celebrated Enfield rifle of England is the result of a long visit and minute examination and close study of the arms made at Springfield Armory and of the machinery and tools and mode of conducting operations there, by three British officers, who were selected by their Government for the special service. They had the machinery for the Enfield Armory made in the vicinity of Springfield from U.S. patterns, and they engaged the services of several of the armory mechanics, one to take the general charge of the Enfield works as master-armorer, and others to take charge of the stocking, forging and other principal departments of manufacture. It is, in my opinion, decidedly objectionable to enter into contracts for any other arms than those of the regular U.S. patterns. . . .[10]

On July 1, 1862, a report was submitted to the Secretary of War by a commission authorized to "audit and adjust all contracts, orders, and claims on the War Department in respect to ordnance, arms and ammunitions." It speaks for itself.

. . . It may be stated, generally, that we have found the system under which have been issued the numerous orders or contracts for ordnance and ordnance stores that have been referred to us strongly marked with improvidence. The amount of these orders or contracts has been ascertained to be largely in excess of the public wants, and the prices fixed by many of them beyond necessity or reason.

The unexampled demand for arms consequent upon the sudden breaking out of the present gigantic rebellion, and the extraordinary circumstances under which the Government arsenals were drained of their best weapons before a blow was struck, afford some explanation of the excess of price referred to; yet, it must be confessed, not by any means a full and satisfactory one. It is to be traced, in a large degree, to a neglect of those common precautions which prudent men of business exercise in the conduct of their private affairs, some of which, too, had been specially provided for and required by the acts of Congress.

First, as to foreign arms, it was of course absolutely necessary to resort to these in equipping, within a few months, more than half a million of men, and it was impossible, in all the workshops of Europe, to have had arms manufactured as rapidly as our public

SHAPING THE BARREL.
POLISHING MACHINE.
ROLLING THE BARREL.
FINISHING.
TESTING THE BAYONETS
STRAIGHTENING THE BARRELS
POLISHING BAYONETS.
TURNING THE STOCK.
PLANING MACHINE.
PUTTING THE MUSKET TOGETHER
BORING MACHINE
RIFLING MACHINE
MANUFACTURING MUSKETS,
U.S. ARMORY,
SPRINGFIELD MASS.

necessities required. Under such circumstances prices naturally rose, and inferior (often second-hand) arms had to some extent to be purchased.

But these difficulties were greatly aggravated by the lack of system which prevailed. The States and the General Government entered the market together as rival purchasers, and thus the members of the same national family bid directly against each other. The folly of this is the more remarkable when it is remembered that these arms bought by the States were, in fact, for the use of the General Government, and will, no doubt, in the end be paid for by it. The General Government itself employed, directly or indirectly, numerous agents not acting in unison, and often becoming, therefore, competitors of each other. A few of these made purchases directly for the Government; the greater number sprang up in the shape of "middlemen," to whom, though not dealers in arms or skilled in their value, contracts were awarded upon their own terms, only to be sublet to the actual importers. Under a system so ill considered, extravagance was unavoidable. It was greatly increased by many of these contracts being loosely worded and imperfectly guarded, while some were granted at prices much beyond even the highest rates which could be fairly considered as engendered by the system itself.

. . . . .

It has been impossible for us to protect the Government against lamentable losses in these loose and irregular transactions. In regard to a considerable portion of these foreign arms, Government inspection was permitted in Europe before shipment, but so utterly inadequate and so incompetent was the force assigned to this duty that it became a mere empty form, devoid of all utility and protection. Of this and other negligences and imprudences the practical result has been that a large proportion of our troops were armed with guns of a very inferior quality; that tens of thousands of the refuse arms of Europe are at this moment in our arsenals, and thousands more still to arrive, not one of which will outlast a single campaign, while most of them will never be issued at all, being entirely unfit to be placed in the hands of civilized troops. Add to this that in many cases these unserviceable arms were paid for at rates which, under a system of vigilance and obedience to law, would have procured improved rifles of the first class.

As regards orders or contracts for domestic arms, though the abuses in this branch are less glaring . . . yet the system here also has been essentially faulty, and the loss to the Government thence resulting very large. . . .

These contracts are chiefly for the Springfield rifle musket. The quality of this weapon—the best infantry arm in the world—has been carefully and sufficiently guarded.

But, first, the orders were greatly in excess of what the Ordnance Office estimated to be the wants of the service. One million one hundred and sixty-four thousand Springfield muskets had been contracted for, while the Chief of Ordnance reports to this commission that half a million is the number actually needed for a year to come, beyond what the Springfield Arsenal can supply.

. . . . .

Secondly, The price—in every instance $20 per gun, including appendages—is, the commission now believe, higher by several dollars than it need or ought to have been, at least when the contract was for a greater number than 25,000.

It is true that the vast and unnecessary number of Springfield muskets contracted for, especially at such high rates, has very sensibly increased to the manufacturer the cost of the arms by causing an unexampled demand for materials (particularly of suitable iron for gun barrels, an article of which the present supply is limited) and for skilled labor; and in the early part of our investigations this consideration, together with the want of accurate and reliable information on the subject, so far weighed with us that we confirmed the first four contracts for 50,000 guns each, made with experienced manufacturers, at the price of $20, which had been fixed by the Ordnance Office. But as we proceeded in our investigations, and as additional evidence came before us, we became satisfied that, for any amount over 25,000, $16 per gun would afford a fair profit to the manufacturer. . . .

Thirdly. The neglect to obey the law . . . which provide[s] that all contracts for army supplies shall, except in cases of emergency requiring and admitting of "immediate delivery," be preceded by public advertisement inviting proposals, has been prolific in evil results. Indeed, it is to the persistent disregard of this law . . . that speculators and "middlemen" are indebted for the saturnalia of success they have enjoyed since the commencement of the war.

. . . . .

But an enforcement of the law in regard to advertising would effect more than a mere reduction in price. It would cut up by the roots an abuse which during the present war has threatened, in this branch of the administration, serious injury, alike to the interests of the service and to the public morals. Contracts based on private proposals favor, and indeed necessarily lead to, the creation of a class of "middlemen," most of them mere speculators and adventurers, to whom, instead of to the manufacturers themselves, orders for supplying the wants of the Government have often been directly or indirectly granted. . . . The class of men referred to are generally rapacious and unscrupulous, and thrust themselves between those whose interest it is to deal, and who ought in every case to deal, directly with each other—the government in need of arms and the manufacturer producing them. Having thus, through unavowed instrumentalities, obtained their contracts, many of them at once put them on the market for sale. A large manufacturer, who has failed to get a contract for muskets, assures us that within a few days past such contracts to the amount of 200,000 guns have been offered to him by these traders in Government patronage. . . .[11]

The War Department's efforts to supply the army were further complicated by business interests that felt the Northern economy would be better served and the people, "so nobly pouring out their blood and treasure," more justly treated if war profits were kept at home instead of going to European manufacturers.

Having learned that Colonel Thomas was sent in the last steamer to Europe for the purpose of purchasing clothes, &c., for the Army, and that Mr. Smith accompanied him to advise and assist in making contracts for these goods, and that the Government had sent letters of credit for a very large amount to be used in Europe for these purchases, and feeling assured that this step will have a most disastrous effect upon all interests and classes of the people of this country as well as upon the Government itself, the undersigned, a committee of the Board of Trade of the city of Boston, most respectfully, but most earnestly, request your attention to the facts they now lay before you, and that the orders to the agent of the Government for the purchase of clothing in Europe may be annulled.

In the first place, they would urge the rescinding of this measure on account of its effect upon the financial operations of the Government and the community. The arrangement entered into by the honorable Secretary of the Treasury with the associated banks of New York, Philadelphia, and Boston, to the extent of $100,000,000 already, and prospectively for a much larger amount, has thus far been carried out faithfully by the Government and the banks to the great benefit of the country. But it must be obvious that a serious check, if not an entire stop, will be put to this arrangement if the specie thus freely paid out shall be sent to Europe, as it must be if this measure of importing goods should be pursued instead of circulating among our own people and returning in the natural course of business to the source whence it emanated; and not only so, but should a panic arise from the fear that the country is to be drained of specie (and that will be the inevitable consequence of this movement, if continued) the people will stop investing in Government securities and most disastrous consequences will follow.

. . . . .

In the second place they would urge the rescinding of this measure on the ground of justice—justice to the people who are so nobly pouring out their blood and treasure for the maintenance of the Government and the institutions of the country. The government has made no appeal to the people in vain either for men or money; hardships, privations, and sacrifices have been cheerfully borne, but should it not be entirely reciprocal? And where it is possible should not the interests of the people be protected? The first question, therefore, to be asked in this connection is, is it absolutely necessary to go abroad to procure these supplies? We answer most confidently that, in our judgment, it is by no means necessary. The large order sent to Europe some time ago by the Department for blankets seemed to be a proper and necessary precaution to insure the soldiers an ample supply, as the sudden call for so many blankets and clothing of various kinds found the woolen machinery in part otherwise occupied, and it could not be changed at once and put upon coarse blankets and heavy cloths, hence there might be more uncertainty as to an ample supply of the heavy blankets for soldiers and horses. To that measure there was no objection; necessity required it, wisdom justified it, and patriotism applauded it. But the present case is very different. Our woolen mills have incurred great expense in altering their machinery so as to execute the orders of the Government. Many of them are running night and day, and now that the difficulties caused by the dry summer and the delay occasioned by the change in machinery are over they are undoubtedly producing at a rate which will be sufficient by the 1st of December to give complete suits to all the men now in the field, supposing the number to be 400,000, and to repeat this every six weeks thereafter. . . .[12]

The Quartermaster General disagreed, and in doing so revealed the plight of the soldiers during the early months of the war. Apparently, some of the people "so nobly pouring out their blood" needed overcoats more than dividends.

The within communication from the Board of Trade of Boston has been handed to this office with a request to transmit it to the Secretary of War.

The matter has been discussed with the Secretary, and I am of [the] opinion that the order to inspect and purchase an extra quantity of cloth was a wise one and ought not to be revoked. While the public, not truly advised as to the orders of the Government and

HO! FOR RICHMOND!

ARTICLES FOR SOLDIERS

AT

Richmond, Wilmington, Charleston, Savannah, and other Places should be sent by

THE HARNDEN EXPRESS,

No. 65 Broadway.

excited by reports such as have been published in certain newspapers that the Government had sent out a credit of £5,000,000, or $25,000,000, and in other papers that $60,000,000 had been sent out, may misjudge it, the fact is that it is proposed only to spend $800,000 in these purchases, and to purchase and ship only for instant and pressing wants of the service.

Governors daily complain that recruiting will stop unless clothing is sent in abundance and immediately to the various recruiting camps of regiments.

With every exertion, this department has not been able to obtain clothing to supply these demands, and they have been so urgent that troops before the enemy have been compelled to do picket duty in the late cold nights without overcoats, or even coats, wearing only the thin summer flannel blouses.

The want of clothing more than the want of money discourages enlistments. This department would gladly pay cash and provide clothing, but it has not been able to satisfy the demands for either one or the other, and as promptly as the service demands.

The financial question is in the hands of the capitalists, the merchants and the Treasury Department.

Should the Board of Trade be right in its opinion, and the domestic manufactories be able to supply regulation cloth enough before cloth can be imported from Europe, it will be gladly purchased at any reasonable price and made up into clothing.

Could 150,000 suits of clothing, overcoats, coats, and pantaloons be placed to-day in depot, it would scarce supply the calls now before me. They would certainly leave no surplus.[13]

In 1862, the Secretary of the Navy recommended to Congress that government-owned and -operated workshops be established to supplement private enterprise in the construction of "ironclads" for the navy.

The progress of events renders it certain that iron will hereafter enter largely into the structure of vessels for marine service, although it will never entirely supercede wood. Our country produces the material in abundance, and we have no occasion to seek it from abroad. While our forests are disappearing, inexhaustible resources in iron are being developed. That it is for the interest of the government to be prepared to meet some change in the material and structure of our naval vessels need not be repeated. It must provide the necessary yards and establishments for each, and have them properly located, in which to build its ships-of-war, and at least one of them should be specially adapted to iron. No private establishment can undertake such heavy work as the government requires for its armor and steam purposes. Possessing advantages that no other nation enjoys, we should avail ourselves of them. . . .

In the construction of the iron and iron-clad vessels which the department has now in progress every effort has been made to have them promptly completed. It is believed that nearly every rolling-mill has been engaged that is able to do the work; and yet these vessels are several months behind the time within which they were to have been completed. The department is convinced that the contractors have done their best; and yet it is with great difficulty these comparatively small vessels and the moderate sized iron required can be procured for them as soon as wanted, so much does the demand exceed the capabilities of the mills to supply. These facts demonstrate the necessity for public works where vessels of great magnitude are to be constructed. Had the government been prepared for this heavy work, much of the delay which has embarrassed naval operations might have been avoided. Private establishments would have been relieved, and enabled to furnish a larger quantity within the scope of their own manufacture. . . .[14]

A hundred years or more have passed; welfare capitalism has successfully challenged the laissez-faire state; yet the outraged response in 1862 to Secretary Welles' proposal has a familiar ring.

The Secretary of the Navy, in his recent report to Congress on the condition of affairs under his supervision, urges, among other matters, the establishment of national foundries and forges, wherein a heavier class of wrought and cast-iron can be made than it is possible, in his opinion, to do in our private shops. We cannot see the utility of such a measure. It is true that at present the rolling mills and foundries of the country are urged to their utmost capacity in order to meet the demands made upon them for plating, &c.; but this is owing to the limited time allowed to the proprietors to fulfill their contracts, as also to the imperative needs of the country. To build and fit out a fleet of from forty to fifty iron-clad vessels and batteries might well tax the energies of any nation unburthened by war and with all its departments of government in prosperous condition. How much more difficult is it, then, to do so when its force is paralyzed, and its energies are benumbed by the rampant treason and insubordination which is detected on every side! If it were a paramount object, in founding such national establishments, to secure a better and more thorough class of workmen than could otherwise be obtained, we could most heartily co-operate with the Secretary and second his efforts in all possible ways. Such is not the case. No better workmen can be found in this country, or in any other, than those which throng our private foundries; it is immaterial whether they be native or foreign. If they are exotic, they have been attracted hither by the superior wages they receive, as well as by the increased social and political privileges they enjoy.

To establish national workshops is to offer a premium for all sorts of incapables, who may have political influence; and it is now, or has been until very recently, as difficult to obtain employment in Government yards as if there was no especial hurry or urgency. We have this statement from good mechanics who have sought for work and not found it, owing wholly to their being unacquainted with "some influential man in their district," or their entire ignorance of all kinds of political machinery. Not only can these facts be established, but it is also true that, at a period when the Government required the services of engineers of experience to fill acting appointments on the transport, dispatch, and iron-clad vessels and batteries which it is constructing, this same political shibboleth presented itself and became a grievous stumbling block in the way of men who really desired to serve their country. This error has been practiced to the injury of the acting navy appointments.

National workshops would not obviate the difficulty alluded to, by any means. How vast or how great would the Secretary have this or these establishments? Or how large a sum would he be willing to recommend Congress to appropriate for the purpose? How long would it take to build such a national workshop or shops, and how many subsidies would have to be provided for friends of the contractors? What length of time would elapse before the shops were stocked with tools, and what eminent firms would receive the whole contracts for supplying them? What ante-diluvian systems and what crablike progression would be inaugurated in spite of the mechanical world outside of these festering Government yards? It is not chimerical, in view of former experience in these matters, to assert that favoritism would be the rule, and that manifest injustice to a deserving class of men would be practiced.

It is hinted that the private establishments cannot turn out sufficient work to answer the demand, as also that they cannot make as large a class of forgings or castings as might be desirable. These are singular assertions in view of the facts. At this writing, all the foundries in the country are busy on the heaviest kind of work—shafts, cylinders, boilers, all of the first class in respect to dimensions, are going forward on every hand. What Government could do more? There are steam hammers and foundry floors that will, in respect to the former, fabricate armor plates or shafts that no ship in the navy could carry; and as to the latter, there are pits where such slight things as condensers weighing thirty-five or forty tuns can be constructed. If there is any special need for more massive products or better material than are now furnished, we are much in error.

But there is yet another point which would, we think, act materially against the successful operation of national workshops. And this is the contract system which the government observes toward private establishments, and is properly insisted upon to guard against fraud and delay. How can there be any guarantee to the public, in a time like the present, that their interests are consulted as far as possible, equal to that now afforded by the spectacle of the private workshops in the various States in full blast night and day? Not only this, but heavy forfeits are insisted upon from the contractors . . . in case of noncompliance with the provisions of their pledge. How can a government exact forfeit from itself?

We repeat that, in our opinion, the country has no need of national shops at this or any subsequent period, further than those which are necessary to complete repairs upon ships already in service; and we doubt very much whether these could not be better accomplished in private shops. . . .[15]

Transportation also presented problems. That of moving iron ore is an example.

The shipments [of iron ore] for 1861 were small compared with the previous year, or the present . . . [because] of the common derangement which existed in consequence of the attempted secession of a number of the States, and the civil war which it brought and is still upon us. . . . The shipments [of] the year just closed, would have been at least 50,000 more gross tons if the tonnage could have been had to move it. But with the Mississippi River closed, its demand to move the Western produce to the seaboard via the lakes, occupied so much of it at such high rates, that it was impossible to obtain sufficient [tonnage], at reasonable rates, to satisfy the popular demand. As it was, almost fabulous rates were paid—as high as five dollars per ton—to get a portion of this amount into market. Had the popular demand been fully supplied it would have required an amount but little less than 200,000 tons [of iron ore]. . . .[16]

The steamboat was a significant technological innovation in the Civil War. The logistics and, to no small degree, the strategy of warfare in the Mississippi Valley were based upon its service on the rivers. The riverboats were a decisive factor in the North's victory.

Yet here again we must compare the potential of this development with the reality. It is another instance of the Laocoön-like struggling of the Northern military administration with the economic problems involved in adapting resources to the war effort. A report from the Quartermaster's Department, Office of Transportation, at St. Louis, described the gross inefficiency in acquiring and using steamboat transportation; the difficulties of chartering, the maze of contracts that were made to transport supplies, the waste of government funds, the demurrage of vessels for unessential purposes, and the delays in unloading.

I have examined with care the letter of the Quartermaster-General to you of May 23, with the inclosed copies of letters from Colonel Swords and Captains Schmidt, Jenkins, and Ferry. The reasons assigned for the extraordinary expense of transportation on the Ohio are, I have no doubt, in the main correct, and many of the suggestions for an improvement are, I think, good. The radical objections to the proposed convention of steam-boat owners to fix rates are, that you cannot, as in the case of railroads, get at any tangible permanent body with which to negotiate. The interests are as numerous and varying as the boats, here to-day and remote to-morrow. Again, expenses and dangers vary with the season of the year, the kind of service from or to which the boats are taken, the time engaged, whether employed in the transportation of freight or troops, and many other causes, owing to which it is almost impossible to fix upon any satisfactory rules, or to form a just judgment, even when an officer has had much experience and uses every effort to do justice. I fully concur with Colonel Swords in the opinion that the best and cheapest way of doing Government transportation is by the 100 pounds or by the piece, under general contracts. Had this been adopted on the Ohio I have no doubt, from my own experience, that it would have saved a very large sum of money and great labor and annoyance to the Quartermaster's Department. When, by your order, I took charge of transportation at this point [St. Louis] in the winter of 1861-'62, the charter system was the sole mode of doing Government transportation. Convinced that this plan was wrong in principle, with your approval I at once discharged every boat, and soon after made contracts by the piece or 100 pounds, and have never since that time chartered boats for general transportation, though we have transported hundreds of thousands of men, and hundred of thousands of tons of freight. When I have chartered or impressed boats it has, with rare exceptions, only been done on the requisitions of superior officers, or in great emergencies admitting of no delay, and requiring the instant movement of large bodies of troops, as in the transfer of General Pope's army from New Madrid up the Tennessee, General Grant's army from Memphis to the Yazoo, or the like, and when time was deemed of too great importance to admit of negotiation, or when negotiations would only end in evident extortion. The result of the change was a great and marked improvement in every respect. We have secured unprecedently low rates, not half what has been paid for mercantile transportation during the same period. . . . All our troubles and complaints have arisen from the emergencies which I have mentioned, when nearly every transport was required (and most of them to lie idle for months at a time). I have no doubt but that the cost of Government transportation on the Ohio and its tributaries has been much greater than was necessary—perhaps even 40 per cent. . . . I have no doubt . . . that this increased expense has often arisen from the improper interference of line officers, and . . . from a lack of cordial co-operation of quartermasters. To my own knowledge, boats costing from $200 to $300 per day have been frequently most unnecessarily detained for many days on unloading. In other cases they have been kept nominally for other purposes but really only to accommodate officers with quarters. In other cases they have been used in numbers, and for weeks and months, for storage, when a small sum properly expended would have built sheds or warehouses, ample for all purposes.[17]

The railroads, too, had their problems. The American Railroad Journal *pointed them out in 1863 in an article which is, in spite of the troubles described, optimistic.*

. . . The derangement of business on the Pennsylvania and Maryland railroads has been great. We particularly regret the interruption of traffic on the Pennsylvania Railroad. This splendidly equipped road has been actively and profitably engaged in carrying the accumulated products of the West, its two great channels of the Mississippi River and the Baltimore and Ohio Railroad, having been closed. We trust it will again, and shortly, resume its business. Prices are seriously affected, and for shares of the former, no takers could be found in Philadelphia on Tuesday morning. All the lines running North and West in connection with those of Pennsylvania sympathized with the sufferers. Under this state of things the Erie and Central with their lines of connection westward and southward have suddenly found their capacity strained to the utmost, to meet the demands of fugitive Pennsylvanians and alarmed merchants; the Express companies having their centres of operation in this State have also been fully employed in transporting valuables in their compact forms. Ten millions of dollars in specie were received in this city in a single night this week from Philadelphia, and there is no doubt the deposits of diamonds, plate and other precious commodities sent hither for safety from Washington, Baltimore and Philadelphia are more than fifty millions of dollars. It is incumbent on the Fathers of the City that this property shall be carefully protected. Such things as contributions are sometimes levied by invaders, and it would be a disgrace and shame to New York, if its harbor should be entered by an enemy's cruiser, and a forced loan be exacted as an indemnity against violence. We indulge the hope that a change of measures and of men will relieve us from these difficulties; all of which could have readily been guarded against by even a moderate share of sagacity. In the mean time the great Northern and Western railroads continue to transact an enormous business. We continue to note the coupons and dividends coming due from these companies, which will all of them be paid with their usual promptness. The war has brought up all these properties, the holders of which have so far been remunerated proportionably [*sic*] for their losses elsewhere. To every cloud even the darkest, there is a silver lining. . . .[18]

Notwithstanding difficulties, the railroads responded immediately to the burden placed upon them by war and, in doing so, shared in wartime prosperity. The American Railroad Journal *of January 10, 1863, after reviewing the state of the Northern economy, and summarizing factors contributing to it, emphasized the role of the railroads.*

. . . The result, or present condition of commercial affairs is so far, much more favorable than the most sanguine ventured to predict, or even hope. The great test of national prosperity, or soundness—an abundance of all the necessaries of life, and an active employment for our population, was never better fulfilled than during the past year. A part of this prosperity may be artificial, growing out of the vast expenditures for the war, but there can be no doubt that with a continuance of peace, the internal commerce of the country would have been vastly greater than it has been, and that the increased stimulus imparted to it by the war has, by no means, equalled what has been lost to it by the isolation of the South.

Several causes have contributed to produce the state of things that exists. The industries of the Free States have been wholly uninterrupted and undisturbed by the war. The harvests in these have been most bountiful for two years past, at the same time that those in Europe have been very bad, creating an immense demand upon this country to supply the deficit abroad. Our vast system of public works had been fully completed previous to the breaking out of the rebellion, giving a commercial value to the products of the interior most remote from markets. The enlargement of the Erie Canal, completed in 1860, was a most opportune event, as without its greatly increased capacity it would have been impossible to convey to tide-water one-half of the produce that reached it during the year. The value of this enlargement cannot be over-estimated, as the freight received through the canal was also almost the only basis upon which the nation had to rely in the payment of its imports, and to make good its foreign balances after cotton had disappeared from our exports. But for the enormous exports of grain in 1861 and 1862, a commercial revulsion would have been inevitable, prostrating, perhaps, the credit of the nation as well as that of the commercial community. Instead of such revulsion, the balance of trade was so largely in our favor in 1861, that we imported over $50,000,000 in gold over the amount exported, while the product of our mines for that year could not have been less than $60,000,000. We have exported gold, largely, in 1862, but not more than the yield of our mines, leaving in the country, at least, $100,000,000 more than when the war commenced.

We have stated so much in general terms in order to show the basis upon which our commercial prosperity rests, and as a necessary explanation of the enormous advance that has taken place in every kind of railroad property, as well as in a very long list of public securities. There are now in the Loyal States 23,140 miles of railroad, costing $966,442,219. The market value of this vast investment, in 1861, was excessively depressed, owing mainly to our political troubles which threatened, for a time, to leave us without government, or social order. Confidence gradually revived, and the immense increase in the traffic of our roads turned attention to their securities. It was not, however, till after the commencement of 1862, that any extraordinary advance took place. On the first day of January of that year, New York Central sold at 80; Erie Common at 32; Preferred at 54; Hudson River at 38; Harlem Common at 12½; Preferred at 31; Michigan Central at 49; Michigan Southern Common at 19; Preferred at 39; Galena and Chicago at 65; Cleveland and Toledo at 35; Chicago and Rock Island at 51, and Chicago, Burlington and Quincy at 58. These were among the most well known and best sustained stocks on the list. The advance in several of these have exceeded one hundred per cent. In others not named it has been vastly greater, so that in the whole list of shares dealt in at the New York Stock Exchange, the advance in their aggregate market value has considerably exceeded one hundred per cent; in other words, has doubled—an advance due not to any considerable extent to extrinsic causes, as the prices at which they are now selling cannot be regarded as beyond their values. Their traffic during the year must have increased fully one quarter, while the condition of the roads has been greatly improved. . . .[19]

In spite of difficulties, the North's war economy did not, from the standpoint of military logistics, fail. Perhaps it was through sheer weight, but in the end it did break through. Statistics are apt to be dull, but significant and often exciting facts are frequently revealed by columns and strings of numbers. Such is the case of the Annual Report of Secretary of War Stanton to President Johnson, November 14, 1866. Figures reveal the mountains of materials that were produced, transported, and utilized. Incidentally, the number of items related to horses or horse-drawn vehicles serve as a reminder that it was a horse-drawn war.

From January 1, 1861 to June 30, 1866, the Ordnance Department provided 7,892 cannon, 11,787 artillery carriages, 4,022,130 small-arms, 2,362,546 complete sets of accouterments for infantry and cavalry, 539,544 complete sets of cavalry horse equipments, 28,164 sets of horse artillery harness, 1,022,176,474 cartridges for small-arms, 1,220,555,435 percussion-caps, 2,862,177 rounds of fixed artillery ammunition, 14,507,682 cannon primers and fuses, 12,875,294 pounds of artillery projectiles, 26,440,054 pounds of gunpowder, 6,395,152 pounds of niter, and 90,416,295 pounds of lead. In addition to these there were immense quantities of parts provided for repairing and making good articles damaged, lost, or destroyed in the service. . . .[20]

An article, published in 1863, indicated the extent to which the Northern economy (and prosperity) had become associated with war-related activities.

. . . Seldom, if ever, has the business of Massachusetts been *more active* or *profitable* than during the past year. The war has brought into activity many mechanical employments for which there is little occasion in time of peace; for example, as the manufacture of arms and ordnance, camp and garrison equipage, saddlery and artillery harness, and military clothing and accoutrements. It has, also, greatly stimulated the manufacture of boots and shoes, and of woolen goods; while the subsistence of the army has furnished a constant and remunerative market for breadstuffs and provisions. There is hardly a branch of domestic industry which has not been actively employed. The cotton manufacture alone has been interrupted by the loss of the raw material, and has given less occupation to labor than usual; but there was never a time since this branch of industry established itself in New England, when the profits realized from it have been so considerable. . . . The necessity of transporting great bodies of troops from point to point along our seaboard, and of furnishing them subsistence, has called into the service of the government a vast fleet of transports, for the hire of which owners have received rates of compensation greatly exceeding the ordinary profits of commerce. Every steam vessel, capable of navigating either the ocean or harbors and rivers, has been thus employed, and many more, previously regarded as worn out, and no longer seaworthy, having been flimsily repaired, and made to pass through a hasty or corrupt inspection, have gone out laden with valuable property, or invaluable lives, to be wrecked or rescued, as the chances of the weather, or as skillful seamanship might determine. The shipyards, both public and private, have been worked to their utmost capacity, in the construction of iron-clad gunboats and other vessels of war; while machine shops, rolling mills, and foundries have been equally busy in building their engines, rolling their armor plates, and casting their guns. . . . The wants of the army have come in to make good the loss of the Southern market . . . and the government has been a liberal and sure, if not a ready paymaster. Labor has been in great demand, wages have risen, and

MORRIS'
Concentrated Lemonade.

This Article
presents in a CRYSTALIZED, CONCENTRATED form,

PURE LEMONADE.

Its **Portability** recommends it for **Travellers** and **Soldiers**, and its **Economy** for **Family use**. For

INVALIDS

suffering with **Fever** in any form, or with **Great Thirst** it is **constantly prescribed** by **Physicians**, as it is the most **grateful** and **refreshing** of **drinks**.

THE U. S. SANITARY COMMISSION

have used it in very large quantities for the **SOLDIERS IN HOSPITALS** for two years past, and it is highly recommended by them as a Preventive and

CURE for SCURVY

in the **Army** and **Navy**. It is an **indispensable** article in every **SOLDIER'S KNAPSACK.**

FOR EXCURSIONS AND PICNICS,

or **PARTIES**; for **Hotels**, **Restaurants**, and for making **Punches**, nothing can equal it; being both

CONVENIENT and ECONOMICAL.

The Editors of the AMERICAN AGRICULTURIST recommend it highly.

Prepared with special care, with **Pure, White Sugar**, it is always ready for **Immediate use**, by simply dissolving in water.

One tablespoonful of the powder makes a large glass of

PURE LEMONADE,

Warranted to contain nothing but the **Lemon** and **Sugar**.
For sale by all Druggists and Grocers.
Put up in cases of 2 dozen each.

WM. H. MORRIS, Wholesale Agent,
151 Nassau-Street, New-York.

LODI POUDRETTE.

THE LODI MANUFACTURING CO., with an experience of 24 years, again offer a uniform article of **Poudrette**, prepared from the **night soil** of the City of New York.

The experience of thousands of customers attests to the fact that it is the **cheapest** and the **very** best fertilizer in market. It is particularly adapted for Tobacco, Corn, Potatoes, and Garden truck. A pamphlet containing directions for use, &c., may be had free by addressing a letter to the

LODI MANUFACTURING CO.,
66 Courtlandt-st., New-York.

Pioneer Sorgo Machinery.

COOK'S EVAPORATOR.

8,000 in use. All Warranted.

None Returned.

First Premiums at 35 State Fairs.

"Simple affair. Operates admirably. The best apparatus."
—*American Agriculturist.*

"Of all the Evaporators we have seen, the most satisfactory results are from Cook's."—*Prairie Farmer.*

"The only one which attained general success last year."—*Ohio Farmer.*

"Six years' thorough trial demonstrates that it is without a rival either in the economy of its use, or the excellence of its work."—*Genesee Farmer.*

We manufacture a Pan for Brick Arch on the same principle at about half the price of the Evaporator.
SORGO HAND BOOK SENT FREE.
BLYMYER, BATES & DAY,
Manufacturers of Evaporators, Cane Mills, &c.
Mansfield, Ohio.

THE VICTOR CANE MILL.

New Style Vertical Mill.

Triumphant at State Fairs.

"Our attention was arrested by the performances of a New Sorgo Mill, shown by the inventor, Mr. Clark, of the Clark Sorgo Machine Company, of Cincinnati. Every effort was made to choke the mill, by crowding it to excess with cane, bagasse, *limbs of trees*, nearly the size of a man's wrist, etc.; but its motion was as steady and inexorable as the wheel of fate. The striking feature in the mill is the rejection of the scraper, or 'Dumb Return,' by which a saving of at least one third of the power was effected. There is not a key in the whole mill; so that it can be taken to pieces and set up again in a few minutes. The lower journals rest in oil-tight boxes, and the oiling arrangement is perfect. Spring scrapers clean the back rolls, and a perforated plate or bridge prevents the bagasse from 'mopping up' the juice as it leaves the mill. Nearly two thousand mills have been put out by the Clark Sorgo Machine Co. during the last season. Such is the popularity with which the new mill has been received. It merits the attention of every Sorgo cultivator."—*Indianapolis Journal.* (At the Indiana State Fair.)

Our Mills embrace no less than 11 different patents, which cover about every excellence attainable in a mill. Send for Sorgo Hand Book.

CLARK SORGO MACHINE CO.,
Manufacturers of Cane Mills, Sawing Machines, &c., &c.
116 Main-st., Cincinnati, Ohio.

the trade is again in a high state of prosperity. Wealth has flowed into the State in no stinted measure, despite of war and heavy taxes. In every department of labor the government has been, directly or indirectly, the chief employer and paymaster. Vast contracts have been undertaken and executed with the use of no other credit than such as is based on government vouchers and certificates of indebtedness.[21]

Northern industry not only managed to meet the demands of the military; it expanded on more than a few fronts. In spite of the loss of the Southern market, the demands for goods increased to such an extent that the producer could "name his own price." As with agriculture, invention played an important part in the prosperity of wartime industry.

It is very natural that many persons at the outbreak of the war should have prophesied business stagnation and general inactivity of industrial enterprises. "When war wages its wide desolation," said these modern prophets, "the country will be ruined and not one stone left upon another of all that commercial and manufacturing greatness which is our pride and boast." If the reader is curious to see how far these visions have been correct he has only to look at the published list of patent claims. . . . There are no less than 218 patents, reissues, designs, &c., all of which bear date May the 3d and 10th, showing them to be of recent origin. . . . It shows convincingly that war, instead of being an evil to the general manufacturing interests, lends increased impetus to all branches of it. Save in the cotton manufacture (which languishes for want of material), there is hardly one other that is not busier than it has been in years gone by. Iron is in such demand that the producers of it command their own price, paper is the same, woolen goods are the same, wearing apparel of every sort is costly, and this is in spite of all that inventors are doing to reduce the price by making more of it in less time than was formerly required. The progress of invention during the war has been steadily increasing, and it is difficult to foretell what the consequences would have been to the nation had not the people lent their inventive skill in the hour of trial. Without the *Monitor* we should have been overwhelmed by the *Merrimack;* without the shot and shell of Stafford, Parrott, Sawyer, Shenkl, James,

Hotchkiss, and others, we should have suffered many a defeat; without Sharps' rifle, the Burnside breech-loader, the Spencer repeating-rifle, &c., the efficiency of our armies would have been seriously impaired; and we might continue the list indefinitely.

It is not alone in the manufacture of munitions of war that this inventive activity has been so strikingly manifested, but in all the various avenues of traffic and trade, on the farm and in the warehouse, the fact remains the same. There are machines now for every conceivable and inconceivable purpose, but these, so far from supplying the demand, actually increase it. The sewing machine is a case in point. Let no man cease his exertions to lessen the severity of labor because some other enterprising person has been in the field before him. When this war is ended the sun will not shine upon a land so blest in all that constitutes true prosperity; it is apparent that those who have new and useful machinery, processes, or materials wherewith to aid manufacturers, will not lose their reward.[22]

There was, of course, an ugly side of the wartime economy. Shortages of consumer goods, currency, price inflation, and speculation were born of or, already in existence, nourished by war.

Interruption of the normal trade with the South, and the fear that commercial relations with the Far East might be disrupted, led to price rises and scarcity of consumer goods. Substitutes began to appear. Sorghum and maple sugar were widely used for "sweetening," and there were experiments in extracting sugar from beets. Chicory seed supplemented coffee. Farmers in southern Illinois tried to raise cotton. More tobacco was planted in Wisconsin and New England. Paper was made from poplar wood and one mill reported that it produced a strong "brown paper" from cattails. A few of the shortages and what might be done about them were discussed in the Philadelphia Public Ledger, *November 4, 1862.*

CHICORY SEED.

THE GREAT SUBSTITUTE FOR COFFEE.

A supply of the genuine article just received by the Subscriber, and will be mailed post-paid to any address, upon receipt of the price affixed. Packets containing 1 ounce, 15 cents, 8 ounces, 60 cents, 1 pound $1.00.

Directions for culture accompany each package.

B. K. BLISS, Springfield, Mass.

In a time of civil war the natural course of trade is interrupted and . . . it becomes necessary to resort to temporary substitutes, or so to economise the use of materials as to be able to keep the price of manufactured articles within limits which will not be a denial to the public of their use. . . .

Cotton waste largely enters into the manufacture of paper, but the high price of cotton, and the cutting off of its production at the South, have diminished the manufacture of cotton fabrics, and as a consequence the amount of "waste" which the cotton mills furnished. In addition to this the wants of our military hospitals have encroached upon the other sources of supply—cotton rags, which are now converted into lint for the soldiers' wounds. These causes have lessened the usual sources of supply to the paper mills and the effect is seen in the increased, and increasing price of paper, which is operating very severely upon newspaper publishers, and raising the price of newspapers. It becomes a duty, under these circumstances, that every housekeeper should save every cotton rag about the house rather than destroy it as worthless, as so many do. They can be sold for a price which pays well for the small trouble of putting them into a bag each day and sending them to the paper dealers, or purchasers of rags for the paper mills. . . .

Turpentine, used so generally in the arts, has advanced . . . and a great many substitutes have been resorted to instead. . . . Why could not a supply be furnished from the pitch-pine forests of Pennsylvania, New York and even New Jersey? The pines which grow in this vicinity are not as rich in resinous substances as those of North Carolina, and, therefore, in ordinary times, the manufacture of turpentine could not be carried on profitably here in competition with the turpentine manufacture of the South, but the price of the article has so enormously increased within the last eighteen months, that, with the absence of competition, the lessened production from the pines of this region might be amply compensated for by the greatly increased price of turpentine. . . .

In regard to India rubber there is greater difficulty in finding substitutes for its use, or means of supply from sources not generally used. South America and the East Indies furnish the caoutchouc which enters so largely into manufacturing operations and domestic uses. But the common milk weed or silk weed exudes a juice from its stems, when cut, which seems to have many of the properties obtained from the India rubber tree, and we have been informed by a manufacturer of India rubber goods that it will yield a gum of the same qualities, but that the plant cannot be procured in sufficient quantities to be depended upon. If the fact was well established that the plant would yield a gum identically like India rubber, it probably would not be very difficult to get a sufficient supply to at least keep the price of India rubber within moderate bounds. . . .[23]

The Treasury's lack of money with which to meet the expenses of war was met in part by the issuance of legal-tender notes. This greenback (or paper money) policy evoked bitter attack. A constituent wrote to Senator John Sherman of Ohio.

I am much obliged for the copy of Sec Chase's Financial Report for 1863, which I received on Saturday Evening 23rd inst.

I have given it some examination not as much as I intend however. This I can say, from the examination given, that the whole paper money system, set in operation by his Financial Policy, appears to me as a "*Great Southern Sea Bubble.*" It . . . reminds me of the story of the Hottentot who said "this world could not stand without it had something to stand on." Well what does it stand on? "*Why on a great Turtle's shell back!*" And what supports the Turtle? "*Why I have not thought of that,*" said the Hottentot. So it is with Sec Chaces [*sic*] Financial Policy—It all rests upon "*Lamp black and Rags.*" But what does this rest upon? Why he hasent thought of that! *First* comes the expences of a great war paid for by "*Lamp black & Rags*" in the shape of Treasury Notes, or "*Legal Tenders.*" These in turn are taken up by "*Lamp black & Rags*" in the shape of Bonds—The Bonds form a basis for the issue of *bank notes* to be redeemed by "*Legal Tenders,*" when paid out a second time by the Government! So the thing runs—Treasury Notes for *Bank* Notes, and vice a versa, *Bank* Notes for *Treasury* Notes. It seems to me about as *practicable* a scheme as it would be to start *perpetual* motion by *mechanical power,* or for a man to lift himself 30 feet high by the seat of his breeches. It is one great cheat—one grand swindle! The Government needs men and means! The Constitution points out the way by which they can be obtained. The mode which it furnishes authority for, is *"loans, taxes, duties, imposts and excises."* Any other mode is unauthorized, and *"Legal Tender,"* which lies at the bottom of Chase's Financial Policy, *confiscates* the excess of assets, in the shape of credit and debt, of every *Loyal Person* in the country, to the last *dollar* he may have, and gives him *promises* in its place that may turn out mere *worthless rags.* So far as I am personally concerned, I find my most valuable means for the support of myself and family are *depreciated* by this policy in *two* years, all the income arising for *six.* It being equivalent to a direct annual tax of *3 times* the whole amount of my income. A government tax of ½ of the income would be *severe taxation,* but a law which takes *3 times* your income is as unjust as *Hell itself.* That is the operation of "Legal Tender" upon me, and of which I complain. Lay your Excise Tax; and while I would like to have whiskey and tobacco bear all that can be got out of them, still dont conclude that Tobacco Chewers and drunkards can be taxed enough to pay the expences of this war. You have levied ¢ 3½ per ton on coal, put it up to ¢ 25 or ¢ 50.—Put cotton to 10 cts per lb. and allow no drawbacks for exportation. Make a tax law after this style, and their [*sic*] need be no *occasion* to create such a debt as *will never be paid.*[24]

But the greenbacks had their friends. William E. Dodge was a respected New York business leader. Near the end of the war, in a lecture delivered at Baltimore, he presented the case for the defense.

. . . Many have criticised very severely the result to which the Government came, in contemplating the judicious measures to be pursued, in order to secure the necessary amount of means to carry on this war. When the Government decided to issue a national currency, and to make that currency the representative of coin, by making it a legal tender for past and future debts, it was entirely a new and untried experiment. Many doubted its expediency; many denounced the measure, and bespoke for it nothing but ultimate ruin. They contended that the only safety for the Government was to adhere strictly to a specie basis; that they were bound to employ the currency of the country, rather than to issue a currency of their own, and give to it the character of a legal tender; that they were bound to sell the bonds of the Government, necessary to the continuance of the war, in the open market, thus keeping down prices, so that the debt of the Government should not become enormous by the enhanced prices which must result from an increased issue of currency.

Now, if you go back to 1861, and the early part of 1862, you will recollect the depression that was almost as extensive as the country. There was a great want of public confidence; there was a great doubt as to the ability of the Government to continue the war, and it was not until after the amount of Government currency thrown into the volume of circulation, had begun to be felt in the increase of business, the advance of prices, and the demand for various articles—it was not until this took place, that the deep, dark cloud that had rested over the finances of the country began to give way. The enormous purchases necessary to carry on this tremendous war, made it absolutely necessary that the Government should issue an amount of circulating medium sufficient to float . . . the bonds that were necessary to be sold in the open market. They saw perfectly well, that in the increase of circulation, in the impetus that would be given to all kinds of business, that the articles necessary to carry on the war would be enhanced in price, and that the debt would necessarily be swollen; but the alternative was, whether they would issue such an amount of currency as would keep up the business of the country, or whether, with a currency barely sufficient to do the business on a peace basis, they would undertake to sell their bonds in this market, or in the European markets, at such prices as they could obtain in specie—thus keeping every interest in the country depressed. They saw at once . . . if the great manufacturing, commercial and agricultural interests of the country were depressed —it would be utterly impossible to maintain the war; and the alternative, desperate as it was, became absolutely necessary, and the result fully vindicates the wisdom of the Government. . . .[25]

Good or bad, currency inflation plus shortages produced price inflation. The worker, whose wages failed to keep pace with the advance in food, rent, and clothing, suffered most.

Two years ago, the man who received $1.50 per day, could satisfy his wants with that sum just as well, if not better, than he can now with $3.00 per day. Nearly every article of consumption has doubled, and if wages are not permitted to keep pace with the cost of necessaries, the producer is daily robbed of one half his earnings. Let us look at it: we say two years since, and even later, the difference we submit between that time and the present, can be verified by every house-wife:—

1861,			1863,
	Beef,	8 to 10c.	15 to 18c.
	Lamb,	8 to 10	14 to 23
	Mutton,	6 to 8	13 to 15
	Coffee,	10 to 16	30 to 50
	Tea,	35 to 100	100 to 2.50
	Sugar,	5 to 10	12 to 20
	Rice,	4 to 5	10 to 12
	Muslins,	6 to 12	25 to 50

The only articles of provision, perhaps, that approximate to former prices, are pork and flour, but even these family staples are much higher. Fuel, coal 33½ and wood 20 per cent. advance. Rents will soon range from 15 to 20 per cent. higher; for the poor must remember, as tenants, they will be forced to pay the landlord's increased taxes. Clothing, for male and female, has also gone up in proportion; and many articles heretofore used by the families of workingmen, are now wholly beyond their means.

It will be found, also, that workingmen are subjected to other ills by the fictitious value placed upon the necessaries of life. Flour has become classified into several brands, which plainly indicate impurity in one or more of them, and means something more than the mere color of the wheat; hence, the purchaser of second or third quality is apt to eat his share of worms and other insects, or nauseate his stomach with musty, sour bread. Should he patronize the small loaves of the baker, he will most likely share the same fate. In the article of coffee, the ingenuity of avarice has been taxed to multiply the different modes of adulteration. The vegetable and chemical trash mixed up with a small portion of the pure article, with a "patent" brand, is enough to weaken the digestive organs of an ostrich. Tea undergoes the same fraudulent process, and our lady readers cannot be too careful in the selection of the article. These adulterations, in many cases, must result in shattered health, if not premature death, unless overcome by the elasticity and vigor of the strongest constitutions. . . .[26]

War increased the opportunities for speculation. Harper's Monthly *described "Wall Street in War Time."*

"The battle of Bull Run," said a late eminent financier, . . . "the battle of Bull Run makes the fortune of every man in Wall Street who is not a natural idiot."

He foresaw a long war, great expenditures, and consequently, taxes being almost unknown, vast issues of paper-money, with their inevitable results, namely, active speculation, an advance in the price of all articles exchangeable for money, and . . . he went to work and bought 75,000 shares of stock on the spot.

. . . . .

Paper-money brought every one into Wall Street, and interested every family in the ups and downs of stocks. It circulated like fertilizing dew throughout the land, generating enterprise, facilitating industry, developing internal trade; the railways found their business increase beyond their most sanguine expectations; dividend-paying roads had extra profits to divide; embarrassed enterprises cleared off their debts, and became lucrative to their owners; every body wanted to own railway property. Within a few weeks after the first issue of legal tenders, stocks began to rise, and rose steadily, with slight interruptions, till April, 1864, when Mr. Chase, by selling his surplus gold for legal tenders, created an unexpected money panic, and the whole fabric of stock speculation toppled to the earth, overwhelming in the ruin thousands of unlucky operators.

It is keeping within bounds to say that $250,000,000—in paper-money—was realized as profits by the operators in stocks between 1862 and 1864. The difference between the aggregate price of the railroad and miscellaneous shares and bonds dealt in on our Stock Exchange at mid-summer, 1862, and the price of the same securities on 1st August, 1864, is more than that sum. Many popular shares rose 300 per cent.

This profit was divided among many thousands of people. In 1863, and in the first quarter of 1864, every body seemed to be speculating in stocks. Nothing else was talked of at clubs, in the streets, at the theatres, in drawing-rooms. Ladies privately pledged their diamonds as margin with brokers, and astonished their husbands with the display of their gains. Clergymen staked their salary, and some of them realized in a few months more than they could have made by a lifetime of preaching. One man, who had nothing in the world but a horse, sent him to a broker's stable, and persuaded the broker to buy him a hundred shares; he drew from the broker, a few months after, a balance of $300,000.

. . . . .

The labors and profits of the brokers were enormous. One house checked more than once for $4,000,000 in a day. A day's commissions, in the case of a leading firm, were not infrequently $5,000. Nearly all the leading members of the board lost their voices from constant bawling, and talked in the evening as though they were in the last stage of bronchitis; clerks seldom left their offices before 11 or 12 P.M., a liberal dinner at Delmonico's being allowed by their employers as a stimulus to exertion. The day was not long enough for the gamblers.

At half past 8 A.M. they began to collect in William Street, and by half past 10 the police could hardly keep the thoroughfare open. All day long the crowd ebbed and flowed between the boards and the street, shouting, screaming, swearing, quarreling, tussling, and not a few of them cheating and lying. A man-milliner from up-town, of short stature but prodigious lungs, was always a leading personage in the crowd: his bids rose like muffled thunder from under other men's coat-tails. The little rogue made $100,000, and went off to Europe with it. . . . When evening fell the throng adjourned to the Fifth Avenue Hotel, and the rooms adjacent, which were hired for the purpose. There night was made hideous by discordant bids and offers. . . . The Fifth Avenue Board, on an exciting night, was probably the nearest approach to Pandemonium we can hope to witness on this earth.[27]

A brief case study in speculation was published in the New York World *of January 31, 1863. Alexander Turney Stewart came to the United States from Ireland about 1820. Beginning with a small retail store, he became one of the merchant princes of New York City.*

In 1864 his net income was $5,000,000. On this he paid a federal income tax of $250,000. The World's *story is undoubtedly biased, perhaps unfair, but it does reveal the methods of the speculators and the criticism engendered by speculation.*

Mr. A. T. Stewart of this city has refused to sell cotton goods at any price, and . . . has been engaged in buying up all the goods he could purchase . . . empty stores have been taken, warehouses rented and filled to the rafters with goods, and, this done, . . . he closed sales and waits for coming events. It is well known that Mr. Stewart's connection with the government is such that he has early information of changes to take place, of movements to be made, and the signs of the times are within his vision. He has had the monopoly of one kind of goods for which the sale has been great, and the past year has been to him probably the most successful year he has ever known . . . and when he holds up and refuses to sell a class of goods men begin to open their eyes. If we have a battle and do not win, cotton goods will run up like gold.[28]

The first American oil well was brought in at Titusville, Pennsylvania, in 1859. It touched off a speculative boom that continued throughout the Civil War. Quick wartime profits went into it.

Nothing in the history of this country, if we except the furor that followed the opening of the gold fields in California, has caused so much excitement in business circles as the rapid development of the petroleum oil interests. There are oil stock exchanges, oil stock journals, and all the other appliances of regular commercial and financial operations. Oil cities even have sprung into existence, and speculation is running up to fever heat; hundreds of Joint Stock Companies have been organized, and a still larger number are now rapidly organizing. Thousands of persons are being allured to invest their money in the stocks of these companies under the stimulus of promises of large dividends.

. . . . .

According to a carefully prepared table now before us there are more than three hundred and fifty organized companies now in existence, with published capitals, ranging from $50,000 to

$10,000,000, and one company proposing to consolidate several others with it, a capital of $15,000,000. . . .[29]

There was another side of the oil speculation story, one of failure and blasted hopes.

Immediately upon leaving Irvine, the banks of the river began to show the decaying monuments of many small fortunes ruined. Four years ago, when the first oil excitement arose, labor attempted to emancipate itself from capital. . . . Poor men with a few dollars in hand, and a few more borrowed, banded in small parties, resolved to sink oil wells on their own account, and reap for themselves the splendid gains that generally fall to the rich man's share. These laborers took leases on small fragments of river front, agreeing to pay an eighth, a sixth, a quarter, or even half of all the oil found, to the land proprietors, as "royalty"; and proceeded without order, system or forethought to sink their wells. With appliances of the rudest kind they set to work. . . .

Had the oil been found in great abundance near the surface, shallow wells would have been sufficient. . . . But good wells lie from 100 to 600 feet deep—both too great for the rude appliances. . . . Consequently these banded laborers soon expended all their means, and were compelled to give up their works. . . .

The low price of oil four years ago—when, indeed, it was worth less than the barrels that contained it—helped the other causes of failure. Now, through the whole oil region, abandoned derricks stand rotting slowly down, warning many and attracting more. They warn labor to keep its own sphere. They attract capital, with the erroneous suggestion that some indications of oil must have existed where so much work was done. . . .[30]

Although not to be classed on the seamy side of the war with shortages, inflation, profiteering, and speculation, invention, too, brought suffering to some. As it has throughout history, machinery took away men's jobs, and as they have throughout history, the displaced, however futilely, fought back.

About two thousand men have been employed in this city, in handling the immense quantity of grain that arrives here from the West. These men are called "strikers," "shovelers," and "trimmers." During the last season, there were introduced into the harbor two "grain elevators," which readily performed the work of many men, and did it much more rapidly. This season, five more elevators have appeared, so that altogether the machines in use will perform about two-thirds the work required. The men have heretofore formed a Protective Union, and have resolved not to work in connection with the elevators, or for any man who employs them. They contend that the great dust which the elevators raise is injurious to life, and furthermore that the manner which the ships are loaded often causes the cargoes to shift, the ships to roll and ultimately to sink and be lost.

. . . . .

The grain shovelers met in very large numbers at Tammany Hall last evening—including, of course the "trimmers" and "strikers," who are equally interested in moving the grain. The meeting was addressed by several gentlemen—among others Mr. B. D. Allen, who has been 30 years in the business, and Mr. W. B. Barber. The first speakers elicited the utmost enthusiasm. They denounced the owners of the elevators as capitalists and speculators, who were robbing the honest laborer of his due. They held forth the idea that if the grain shovelers would only hold out, they would ultimately compel the withdrawal of the elevators, and the performance of all the work by hand. They disclaimed any idea of raising a mob, or of interfering with any who choose to work. . . . While their resolve to adhere to their determination was expressed with all the force which a thousand throats without laryngial defect could give, they at the same time manifested a determination to do everything peacefully and legally.[31]

Though the ugly side was a significant part of the Northern wartime economy, it was outweighed by the fair side. Greed was tempered by industry; ineptitude by determination. On the whole it was the soldiers who paid the price of war. The home front prospered; and some business enterprise laid the foundation for the expanding financial-industrialism of the next half century. Textiles, which faced the greatest hazards by reason of cotton shortages, had their problems but survived and even increased their profits.

The war has developed some remarkable changes in the textile industries of the country. In anticipation of the rebellion, it was prophesied that the loss of cotton would utterly ruin the manufacturers of cotton goods; but, so far from this gloomy prediction being realized, the first two years of the war have yielded larger profits to manufacturers than any former period in the history of the cotton trade. Manufacturers held large stocks of both raw material and goods, on each of which they realized an immense advance, giving them in one year a larger aggregate gain than they had realized in four ordinary years. This enabled the large corporations to pay handsome dividends to their stockholders, and yet reserve an ample fund for meeting any difficulties that might occur before the supply of cotton was restored. Before the close of 1863 the surplus of cotton goods was completely exhausted, and the market had to depend for its supply entirely upon the current production. Here came the crisis when the loss of cotton began to make itself most felt, and the prices of cotton and of goods were to be regulated strictly by supply and demand. The result of this new position of affairs has been that during the whole of the present year cotton fabrics have been growing steadily scarcer, until there is not at present in the hands of wholesale merchants probably more than ten per cent of the stock of ordinary times, whilst the goods most in demand are engaged under contract for some weeks in advance of production. This of course places manufacturers in a position for making their own prices, and so insures to them a fair profit; but at the same time they are experiencing the heavy drawback of having over one-half their machinery kept idle, and consequently depreciating in value. An increase in the receipts of cotton has enabled manufacturers to start up a small additional number of looms during this year, which, however, has been found very difficult, owing to the extreme scarcity of skilled operatives. . . . It is clear, therefore, that our great cotton industry, with its $160,000,000 of capital, has not yet got through the difficulties in which it became involved by the rebellion. There are, however, satisfactory indications that the trade will prove able to meet its embarrassments without serious damage.

The woolen manufacture has perhaps profited more by the war than any other branch of industry. Fabricants have realized large profits through the steady advance on raw material, their stock of wool having increased in value between the period of buying and working it from twenty to fifty per cent. The scarcity of cotton goods has resulted in an increased demand for woolen fabrics, which by creating a comparative scarcity has enabled producers to realize high prices for their goods. The very large demand for army woolens, creating an additional consumption of about 25,000,000 pounds of wool, has also proved on the whole very profitable to manufacturers.

Some of the large woolen manufacturing corporations have paid immense dividends during the last two years, and yet reserved sufficient to replenish or largely extend their machinery. . . .

This prosperity of our textile industries, under the pressure of an exhaustive war, affords conspicuous evidence of the strength and industrial resource of the nation, and shows that with all our losses the substantial interests of the country are yet acquiring strength, and laying a basis for commercial expansion on the return of peace.[32]

The production of iron was probably the most important industrial growth in the North during the war. The Merchants' Magazine and Commercial Review *of December 1863 reported its progress.*

During the year 1862, prices in irons of all kinds were marked by a continually upward movement. This movement had none of the feverish excitement which characterized those of tin and copper. It slowly followed, indeed, the advance in gold, but it derived its chief impetus from the progress of the demand, arising from government consumption, and from the general revival of trade. It was, therefore, for the times, healthily and steadily moved forward through the season, unchecked by the temporary events or contingencies of the year. The restriction of exportations hither, on English account, induced by the uncertainty of American politics, and the fluctuations of gold and exchange, tended greatly to the benefit of the American iron master, and gave him a fair start for that race of competition with England which must ensue in future years. These circumstances yielded to him a control of the home markets at a time of immense demand, and at prices the most liberally profitable. They secured to him an accumulation of capital to fall back upon in less prosperous times.

The trade of the year was done mostly for cash; credit, indeed, was seldom asked for. During the summer months, the Pennsylvania trade, at a meeting, resolved thereafter to shorten the time on cash bills to ten days, and on time bills to four months, from date of invoices. . . .

The high prices of the past year have stimulated to the utmost the production of all kinds of iron. Old furnaces, rolling-mills and forges are put, or being put, into a condition for the most active operation;

new ones are projected in various parts of the country, and many are near completion. The home supplies of iron will, in the course of a year or so, equal any demand.

. . . . .

The supplies of American bar and rail-road irons will be greatly enhanced during the next few years. Like that of pig irons, the production has been stimulated by high prices, and mills have been started in various parts of Pennsylvania, and in New York and New Jersey. Their make, when the rolls are all in motion, will, with the older mills, be nearly adequate to supply the whole demand of our Eastern markets. The cheapness of producers' costs—because of proper location, contiguous to coal and ore beds, and the markets of New York and the Eastern and Western cities—may enable them to compete successfully with the English irons, and perhaps, indeed to a large extent, drive them out of our markets. . . .[33]

The response of Northern manufacturers to the demands of the war for iron was graphically illustrated by the expansion of plant facilities in Pittsburgh. Production, however, was still primitive in technique and Lilliputian in size compared to the postwar era. Steel production was negligible.

Quite a number of new rolling mills have been put up by Pittsburgh manufacturers during the past year. Messrs. Lyon & Shorb of the Sligo Works have put up a mill two hundred in length by one hundred and four feet in width, capable of turning out armor plates of the largest size; the firm has also erected a sheet mill ninety feet long by eighty feet wide. The Messrs. McKnight, of the Birmingham Works, have erected a new sheet iron and armor-plate mill, the buildings of which are sixty by eighty feet. The plate mill has a capacity of fifty tuns per week, and is constructed with a view to the rolling of sheet iron, for the production of which it has a capacity of one thousand tuns a year. The Messrs. Jones and Laughlin, of the American Works, have erected a building two hundred by one hundred and twenty-five feet, within which is constructed two sheet mills, and a twelve-inch train for bar, and three thirty-eight inch trains for small iron and hoops, three heating furnaces and two annealing furnaces. The capacity of these mills is thirty tuns per day. Messrs. Reese,

Graff & Dull have built a forge, a plate mill and a sheet mill occupying a building two hundred and five by one hundred and five feet. The plate mill is constructed for rolling armor plates for naval uses, ten feet long and from one to one-and-a-half inches thick, weighing from one thousand and six hundred pounds to a tun each. The plate mill has a capacity of one hundred tuns, the sheet mills a capacity of fifteen tuns, and the forge of two hundred and ten tuns a week. They have also erected a hoop mill of two trains with a capacity of eighty tuns per week. . . .[34]

In January 1865, only a few months before the end of the war, R. G. Dun and Company sent to its subscribers an analysis of business conditions. It revealed the North as having achieved a general prosperity based on an integration of all segments of the economy.

In our annual review of the condition of the Mercantile, Manufacturing and Trading interests of the country, we are warranted in congratulating subscribers and friends upon the general[ly] existent healthy state of affairs. Our record, during the past year, shows only 510 failures, with liabilities amounting to $8,579,700, which, by comparison, exhibits a remarkably healthy state of the trading community. The number of liabilities of failures for the past eight years are as follows:

	NUMBER	LIABILITIES
Total Northern States 1857 . .	4,257 . . .	$265,818,000
Total Northern States 1858 . .	3,113 . . .	73,608,747
Total Northern States 1859 . .	2,950 . . .	51,314,000
Total Northern States 1860 . .	2,733 . . .	61,739,474
Total Northern States 1861 . .	5,935 . . .	178,682,170
Total Northern States 1862 . .	1,652 . . .	23,049,300
Total Northern States 1863 . .	495 . . .	7,899,000
Total Northern States 1864 . .	510 . . .	8,579,700

In submitting these figures, we call attention to the fact of a large diminution in the amount of annual failures since the rebellion broke out. This we attribute mainly to that rigid caution which has [been] obtained in our business community in dispensing credits, and to the increased value of stocks on hand.

The immense and general prosperity of all branches of agriculture has augmented the wealth of the trading classes, and the scarcity of labor, suitable to the requirements of the mechanical interests, has tended to increase wages, and enhanced receipts of the operating classes. These, the principal consuming interests, on account of their vast number, and constituting, as they do, the material wealth of the country, have created an unusually large expenditure through the channel of the retail trade, and yielded returns that enabled this class of merchants to meet their obligations promptly to the jobber. The latter has, therefore, been prompt with the importer and commission merchant. Hence, the natural conclusion must be that each, acting in harmony with the other, has produced a more satisfactory result than could have been anticipated by even the most sanguine. . . .[35]

VI

Social Strains and Stresses

IN GENERAL, war unites a people. Cracks and fissures, that are present to some degree in any living society, temporarily close. But others open. Some of these are the results of existing conflicts and tensions; others are war-born. In the American Civil War, among the deepest of these latter, was the conflict waged in the North against the war itself. This opposition was frequently heightened by a hatred of the draft—sometimes mortal in its intensity. It is impossible to justly generalize on how much of this was principle and how much determination to stay out of the battle; certainly there was an interaction. Whatever their motivation, the extremists in the antiwar agitation were the Peace Democrats, variously known as Copperheads, Knights of the Golden Circle, and Butternuts. Their activities ranged from public protest and draft evasion to violence and murder. As a consequence, in some communities neighbor was turned against neighbor, sometimes with reason, sometimes as a result of morbid suspicion. Such a community was Middletown, Indiana, in the winter of 1862-63, when, following the bloody defeat at Fredericksburg, Northern morale was nearing its lowest ebb.

Two or three days ago Lieut. Hancock, of our 19th regiment, went down to Owen County to reclaim some deserters who were hiding there, taking with him a little guard of three men. . . . They passed on through Spencer, the county seat, without discovering their men, but pretty late in the evening found one . . . at a little town called Freedom.—Taking him in charge, they went on about four miles to a village called Middletown, where there was another deserter . . .

whom they intended to take that night. It was about one o'clock, possibly later, when they entered the street of the straggling little town, but late as it was Lieut. Hancock noticed a light burning in a school house they were approaching. He asked . . . the prisoner, what it meant—"Why," said he, "it is a meeting." "What sort of a meeting can be held at this time of night?" "The Knights of the Golden Circle," was the reply. The prisoner than stated that the purpose of the order was to protect deserters, and that he had frequently been assured of the protection of its members. Thinking it likely that in an assembly of this character a deserter would probably be found, Lieut. Hancock ordered a couple of the guards to go in, and they went in. A sentinel was standing inside the door with a gun. He had been on guard outside, but at so late an hour he had probably thought that there was no danger of interruption and had gone in to hear the speeches. There were some forty or fifty persons present, as well as the soldiers could judge, and they were listening to Mr. Thomas Landrum read a New York paper. Mr. Lindsay C. Abril presided, or appeared to be the presiding officer. As the audience noticed the soldiers they rose up in alarm, but Mr. Landrum not seeing them kept on. Some one asked what they wanted, and Sergeant Lundy answered that he had come to hunt for a deserter, and he meant to do it. This announcement cleared the house. Landrum rolled up his paper and sank out of sight. Abril followed the crowd out, and coming up to Hancock, whom he knew as an old neighbor, and Democratic supporter in past times, asked for some whisky. He was answered that the party had none. He then told Hancock that he "had better be getting away as there was danger." Hancock showed him a revolver ready cocked and said "I have a party of a hundred cavalry back there in the woods, and if there is any trouble made here it will be a bad job for those who make it."—At this the party broke in most admired disorder and scattered off in all directions.—There was not a soul visible in a half minute afterwards. . . . What sort of meeting it must have been with an armed sentry at the door, sitting at one o'clock in the morning, and thrown into the panic of terror by the announcement that the soldiers of their own name, blood, and birth were within sight, anybody can guess.[1]

Some three months later, the Indianapolis Daily Journal *described a "Butternut Mass Meeting": ". . . The first arrivals to the meeting were in wagons and on horseback. . . . One wagon was decorated with Butternut bushes." They also came by rail. Extra cars were put on regular trains coming into Indianapolis from various points: Madison, Terre Haute, Lafayette, Peru, Cincinnati and Bellefontaine, Ohio. Some of these cars were coaches, others were freight cars, but in all about 119 extra cars were in service. They did not come in a spirit of brotherly love, nor were they greeted with Christian charity.*

. . . It was a large meeting, and it contained a most offensively visible element of as mean treason as ever went unpunished. . . . There were probably ten thousand persons present, certainly not more.

. . . . .

While the great body of the meeting was orderly . . . there was a considerable section of it eager for a row, and well armed to make a row a serious affair. The number of revolvers seen, fired and captured during the day is almost incredible. At the Police Court about forty were taken from persons arrested for "carrying concealed weapons." On the Lafayette train, as it was returning in the evening, pistols were fired in such numbers as to resemble the "fire at will" practice of a regiment. It was a perfect fusillade till the weapons were emptied, and that they had to be emptied at all is an ugly proof that they were brought here for no pacific purpose. On the Terre Haute train fully five hundred shots were fired. This occured just west of the Soldiers' Home, and the bullets flew over, around and into the Home as thickly as if it were a Union hospital in range of rebel rifles. They rattled on the roof, fell on the floor and whizzed through the trees, and the adjoining buildings received a liberal share of the same storm. It may have been accidental, but the bullets *didn't get into the pistols accidentally*. The soldiers, used as they were to being shot at, were no little surprised at this unexpected volley. From one of them we learn the facts we have stated. On the Cincinnati train, also, a great many shots were fired, and in a part of the city where lives might have been lost by it. So, too, on the Peru train. These little exhibitions of "Copperhead" sentiments were not lost on the military authorities. A gun was placed on the track of the Central road near New Jersey street, before the excursion train left, to stop it if any such dangerous demonstrations were made. The train came up loaded, inside and out, but halted before it reached the gun, and backed down to Virginia Avenue. There an infantry party surrounded it, and a policeman boarded it and demanded the surrender of all pistols on it. They were handed over to the number of nearly *two hundred.* The Peru and Cincinnati trains were also intercepted and nearly two hundred revolvers taken from each one. Altogether about *one thousand pistols* were thus taken from persons attending the meeting. Undoubtedly the owners were K.G.C.'s, with whom a large portion of the Democratic party have no sympathy.

. . . . .

Since the above was written we learn that about *fifteen hundred* revolvers have been taken, with a large number of knives. One knife two feet long was found and taken out of the stove in one of the cars of the Cincinnati train. On one woman no less than seven revolvers were found. . . . A large number of pistols were thrown out of the windows of the cars, when it was found that their possession was likely to prove troublesome, and many were found by boys on the track, or in the creek which borders the other side of the track. . . .

The firing from the cars, which forced the military to search for weapons, was more serious than we at first supposed. From the Cincinnati train a number of shots struck the dwelling houses on New Jersey, East, and Noble streets, and several persons narrowly escaped death. One ball passed between the head of a woman sitting in her front yard, and the head of her little baby whom she was holding in her arms, just grazing the temple of the child. We also heard that a man was wounded by one of the shots from the Bellefontaine cars, but we could not learn the truth of the report last night. . . . The whole number of pistols taken, it was thought by the military last night, would reach *fifteen hundred or two thousand.*[2]

In 1864, a full-fledged Copperhead-soldier riot occurred in Charleston, Illinois. If such violence was not common in the North, neither was the Charleston incident unique.

CHARLESTON, MARCH 28, 9 P.M.

This afternoon a dreadful affair took place in our town, the most shocking in its details, that has ever occurred in our part of the State. Early in the morning squads of Copperheads came in [*sic*] town from various directions, and, as the sequel will show, armed and determined upon summary vengeance upon our soldiers. During the day premonitions of the coming trouble were too evident. Some of the soldiers, about to return to their regiments, were somewhat excited by liquor, and consequently rather boisterous, but not belligerent—were more disposed for fun than fight. About 4 o'clock, a soldier, Oliver Sallee, stepped up to Nelson Wells, who has been regarded as the leader of the Copperheads in this county, and placing his hand good-naturedly against him, playfully asked him if there were any Butternuts in town? Wells replied, "Yes, G-d, d--n you, I am one!" and drawing his revolver shot at Sallee, but missed him. In an instant Sallee, was shot from another direction, and fell, but raising himself up, he fired at Wells, the ball taking effect in his vitals. He (Wells) went as far as Chambers and McCrory's store, and passing in, fell dead.

The Copperheads were gathered behind Judge Edwards' office, loading their firearms, and then would step out and fire from the corner at the soldiers indiscriminately, with guns and revolvers. . . . The Copperheads were seen to hurry to their wagons, hitched at the Square, and gather therefrom several guns, which were concealed under the straw. They were freely used and with terrible effect. Thomas Jeffries was the next to fall, receiving an ugly wound in the neck. Wm. Gilman was shot by B. F. Dukes, the ball striking a rib on his left side and glanced off. . . . Colonel M(itchell) received several shots through his cloths [*sic*]. . . . Dr. York, Surgeon of the 54th Illinois, while passing through the Court House, was approached by someone from behind, who took deliberate aim and shot him dead. . . . A soldier, Alfred Swim, Co. G 54th Illinois, was shot, and taken to Drs. Allen & Van Meter's office, where he soon died. . . . Wm. G. Hart, Deputy Provost Marshal, was shot in several places—in the head and vitals; his wounds are probably mortal. James Goodrich, Co. C 54th Illinois, received a shocking wound; being shot in the bowels; his wound we fear, will prove mortal.

Unarmed as our boys were, Col. Mitchell soon rallied all he could, citizens and soldiers, and improvising such arms as could be had, gathered at the south-west corner of the Square, as the Copperheads retreated down the street running therefrom. Dispatches were sent to Mattoon for soldiers and 300 were soon on the way. The Copperheads halted somewhere near Mrs. Dickson's and remained for some time, then turned and went off . . . in a northerly direction, cutting the telegraph wire as they went. . . .

How many there were of the Copperheads, we do not know, . . . We think there may have been from 100 to 150, and all mounted. Who their leaders were, we do not know precisely. J. H. O'Hair, Sheriff of this County, was seen to fire three times at the soldiers. . . . Others of less prominence were equally war-like.

Immediately after the soldiers arrived, squads, mounted upon all the horses that could be found, were started out in every direction in pursuit—Col. Brooks in charge of one, Lieut. Horner another, &c. Up to this writing, 9 P.M., some twelve persons have been captured, and the pursuit still kept up after more. . . .[3]

In some areas discord was intensified. Thus the conflict between labor and capital, that had been quickening with increased immigration from Europe, needed only a lag between wages and prices to serve as a further catalyst. The war created such a lag. During the last months of 1863, there was a more or less spontaneous demand for wage increases, accompanied by strikes and demonstrations. An uneasy middle-class response to this movement appeared in a Philadelphia newspaper.

. . . In many parts of the country, laboring men and mechanics are demanding higher wages. In New York this demand is more general than in any other city. In Boston the principal movement is among the employees of the National Government. In Washington, it is of the same nature. The persons employed in the navy yard and the Government works near Boston demand more money for their labor, while in the public printing office and at the treasury extension in Washington, a demand is made for more money and less labor. The printers and masons ask that their wages shall be increased, and the hours of labor decreased. In New York the movement is general. The drivers on the street railways, the machinists and lithographers, the workmen on the iron-clad vessels now being built, the shipwrights and longshoremen, are all engaged in combinations to effect an advance in their wages. . . .

The most suggestive and interesting feature of the labor movement in New York is what is called the strike among the working-women. . . . The hardship is especially seen in those branches of women's employment devoted to the making of clothing. For making a whole suit of boy's clothing, a woman is paid sixty-eight cents; and to do this she must work fourteen hours. A "baster" on cavalry pantaloons can make thirty-two cents a day; twenty cents is paid for making a linen coat, two of which can be made in a day; cap-makers receive thirty-five cents a dozen; vest-makers fifty cents apiece. By sewing books, women can earn seventy-five cents a day, but this is the highest sum we see in the list we are quoting. . . .

The condition of the laboring man is better in America than in any other part of the world. . . . The laboring man with us must have his morning newspaper, a weekly journal for the family, one of the magazines, and a few histories and volumes of reference for his children. He must have his holiday, his evenings for the prayer-meeting or the play. He sees a career in which the sons of other laboring men have become eminent, and so, instead of taking his boy with half-formed bones and sinews to earn his daily bread, he keeps him at school and undergoes privation that his tastes and habits may be gratified. This is the daily bread of the American laborer, and it is proper that he should earn money enough to gain it. Before the war all these things might have been obtained for less money than it is now necessary to pay. The war, which has stimulated business and trade, has reduced the value of money, as all wars invariably do. Taxation, the conscription, perhaps; the difference in values, the increase in the price of many necessary articles of life, consume that portion of the laboring man's income that formerly went towards giving him some of the luxuries of life. Many a laboring man is fortunate if he can live at all. . . .[4]

A more violent reaction came from the Pennsylvania coalfields. Charles Albright, in a letter to President Lincoln, described resistance by miners to the draft, and equated it with demands—accom-

panied by violence—for higher wages. Martial law, backed by several thousand soldiers, would not only end defiance of the draft, it would also send those workers not shot as traitors back to the pits —presumably at the old wages.

It is perhaps proper that you should fully understand the condition of society about the coal mines in the Lehigh region. At the risk of trespassing upon your time I will undertake the explanation.

Since the commencement of the draft a large majority of the coal operatives have been law-defying, opposing the National Government in every possible way, and making unsafe the lives and property of Union men.

They are so numerous that they have the whole community in terror of them. They dictate the prices for their work, and if their employers don't accede they destroy and burn coal breakers, houses, and prevent those disposed from working. They resist the draft, and are organized into societies for this purpose. The life of no Union man is secure among them, and the murder of such a citizen is almost a nightly occurrence.

The civil authorities make no effort to arrest this state of things. They say they are powerless and that to attempt the arrest and punishment of these traitors and miscreants, without having the ability to do it successfully and effectually, would only add fuel to the flames. Besides all this our "civil authorities" here seem to have too much sympathy for these very men, and they know it and are not slow to take advantage of it. They have closed up several large collieries and threaten that all must suspend work until the National Government suspends the operations of the draft against them. These men are mostly Irish and call themselves "Buckshots."

They have caused the high price of coal more than any other thing. Many of them with the work they do make from one hundred to two hundred dollars per month.

Committees of these men have waited upon operators and have told them that they must stop work; that they intend to end the war by cutting off the supply of coal and thus embarrass the Government and create coal riots in the large cities. This is a part of the rebel programme. If they can have their own way a few weeks longer they will work serious mischief, set afoot a most damaging fire in the rear, and very successfully "embarrass" the Government.

The question becomes a serious one, and the remedy to be applied should be immediate. What is to be done?

A military force of several thousand men should be sent to the coal regions, martial law declared, and summary justice dealt out to these traitors. Protection should be afforded to those willing to work, and those who will not work should be sent to work on military fortifications during the continuance of the war. It will not be safe to have them about. Nothing but thorough work will answer.

As the case now stands the national laws and authorities are defied and powerless. The Government, as in the case of New York, must take hold of this matter; the same element is at work here, while the injury to be inflicted may be as serious. I most earnestly beg of you to give the subject your careful thought. I understand a committee of coal men will call upon you and make a more full explanation of the whole matter. . . .[5]

Militant opposition to labor was general throughout the North. In Detroit, this led to the formation of the Employers' General Association of Michigan. There were also auxiliary associations "composed of owners and managing agents of some particular line or branch of manufacturing or mechanical business." The preamble and constitution of the General Association appeared in the Detroit Advertiser and Tribune.

Whereas, We the undersigned citizens of ____________________ and interested as owners, or managing agents, in manufacturing or mechanical business, find the following state of things to exist in relation to our various pursuits, that is to say: The working-men have, for a long time, been associated together in thorough organizations, known as "Trade Unions." And however laudable the motives may have been, in which these "Unions" originated, they have at length, come to assume a dangerous attitude, and to act a disorganizing and ruinous part. For example: They assume to dictate to employers, and the employed, the rates of wages to be demanded and paid; what men may be employed, and what number of apprentices; who shall be discharged, and who retained; when, and on what terms our establishments and businesses may be operated and carried on, or stopped, always vigilant to take advantage of the shifting condition of business and work on hand, and having, apparently, little or no regard to the justice or proprieties of the case, and enforcing their demands, as against the employers, by "strikes," and, as against working-men by both contributions and threats.

As a natural result of this system of general and persistent interference, our business is thrown into a condition of much uncertainty. Its essential relations are seriously deranged. Business-like calculations and arrangements, especially such as involve prices for work and time of completion and delivery, are thus rendered quite impracticable: We cannot enter into contracts for work of importance, or proceed with it with any degree of safety, either to ourselves or patrons.

That is not all. These "Unions" prescribe a uniform rate of wages for each workman of any particular trade. For instance: They decree that each moulder shall be paid a given sum per day; each finisher another sum; each blacksmith another; each common laborer another, and so on with every class.

The pernicious consequences, resulting to labor as well as to employers, from these uniform rates, are such as should be expected. Discriminations in favor of skill and efficiency, are, in great measure, excluded. The bungler and laggard is placed on the same footing as the skillful and efficient. Merit receives no recognition, or reward; indeed it is ignored. As a natural result, the motive for exertion is taken away. The man of skill and natural energy, sinks down into the habits of the bungler and inefficient. Original gifts being deprived of a principal incentive, remain underdeveloped. In this way, skill and merit are depressed, and labor is reduced both in quality and amount. . . .

. . . . .

To the general end here stated, each Auxiliary is empowered to fix, grade, and regulate, from time to time, the *maximum* rates of wages to be allowed and paid to the different classes of employees in its particular branch of business; and, also, the *minimum* prices to be charged for different kinds of articles and work; and, likewise, to do all such other things, as shall be judged best for accomplishing the objects aimed at. . . .[6]

The Unionists' reply to the Employers' General Association was published in the Detroit Free Press.

In the *Advertiser and Tribune* of July 25th is an article announcing to the public that the employers of this city, had formed themselves into an "association," for the purpose of protecting the manufacturing interests in this locality. . . . This spokesman of the employer's [*sic*] begins by enlisting public sympathy in their behalf, by an unwarrantable attack on the mechanics and Unions, charging the members thereof with trying to subvert the public interests to their own private gain, stigmatizing them as being the tools of designing leaders, thus hoping to make themselves appear in the light of martyrs at the hands of their employers [*sic*], and thereby cover the real design of their "association," which appears, judging by this article, to bring down the working classes to a condition little above the level of Russian serfs. . . .

Are these associated employers as honest in dealing with their employees as they would make themselves appear in public print? They assume the right to determine what reward working men shall receive for the work they do. It is granted that when they would exclusively dictate to us the amount—the "maximum,"—we shall receive for our labor, they wrong us; and we cannot and will not agree to such terms. Our labor [*sic*] should be free to seek the best market; but this it is proposed to destroy—he is threatened: "If you leave my employ you can't work in this town." This course has been pursued; and further, certain employers have followed men after leaving their employ, and caused such men to be discharged from good situations, merely to gratify a malignant spirit of revenge; and it is but fair to infer that what has been done by private individuals, would be carried out more fully by this "Association." Another evil connected with these capitalistic associations, is, that those now in operation, in several of the Eastern cities, will not hire men or women (factory girls), unless the applicant can produce a certificate stating that the bearer is at liberty to seek employment elsewhere, they having no further need for his or her services; thus virtually forcing on poor men and helpless women, the English convict ticket of leave system.

. . . . . .

We are rather under many obligations to this Employers Association for their avowals; for every act of oppression on their part will only bind us closer together, and while we are always ready to meet employers, to settle any difficulty that may arise between our respective associations, we expect to be met as men, and not with haughty arrogance so commonly assumed by employers when treating with their hands.[7]

The growing bitterness of labor was also voiced by Benjamin Lewis, presiding officer of the Utica, New York, local of the International Typographical Union.

. . . Much has been said and written about the "dignity of labor"; and certainly I am not one of those that would cavil at the title or detract from the "dignity." I believe in the "dignity of labor"—that "labor" which creates the wealth of nations, though it comparatively seldom enjoys it. But I for one protest against the use to which that term is often applied, and the purposes it is often made to serve. Is it not true—and has not our own experience proved it to be true—that those who in words most magnify labor, are the very ones who in deeds have the least sympathy with it? How many there are, who believe that the "dignity of labor" is a very fine doctrine to preach, but a very poor doctrine to practice. To such labor is indeed very "dignified," while it crouches to their cupidity, or allows itself to be made the stepping-stone of their ambition. With them, the "dignity of labor" is the "dignity" of a blind instrument, and not the "dignity" of intelligent manhood. In their ideas, the laboring man is associated with the spade and pickaxe he grasps in his hands; the blacksmith is one with his hammer and anvil; the carpenter is one with his plane and saw; the pressman is one with the press he runs; and the compositor is one with the stick and rule he holds in his hand. To them, the *man* is nothing more—sometimes I have thought he was less—than a little elongation, a sort of extra-handle to the instrument of his calling. . . .[8]

At least in some lines of trade, such as that of the hat finishers, war-related changes affected the security of journeymen workers.

Especially at the war's end, a flood of new employees or "green hands" threatened the established craftsmen. The bleak future was discussed by an English hat finisher who was employed in American shops during the Civil War.

Before the commencement of the war, a man in the trade, with economy and ordinary prudence, if employed even two-thirds of his time, might have saved money, as he could have supported a moderate family with six dollars a week. That time in the United States like a dream of the past, is gone, and I fear never to return. From the open nature of both the hat trade and many other branches of skilled industry in America, a few years will thoroughly overstock them with hands, the immediate consequence of which will be a corresponding depreciation in the value of labour. In the meantime from the loose system of apprenticeship which prevails, journeymen are being turned out as if by steam. I think the time is not far distant on this continent when the exclusive system of European guilds will be introduced into the various branches of skilled industry. As long as trades offer inducements to young men to join them, few will be content to spend their lives in the drudgery of the fields, or in what is looked upon as the meaner occupations of civilized life. The working-classes in America will be more impatient under a severe commercial pressure than any other people, when their Government ceases to spend a thousand millions of dollars annually, as they are doing while I am writing. They will find that four years of feverish prosperity have swelled their ranks and narrowed the field of their labour at the same time. This will not only be the case; but when the whole trade of the nation is made to collapse like an empty bladder, and the overstocked labour-market supplemented by return [*sic*] volunteers who have escaped death in the field or by disease, the struggle to live in many cases will be one of life and death.

One of the worst features in the hat trade in America for the journeyman, is the constant liability to be moved about from one establishment to another. When an employer finds his business begin to slacken, he immediately discharges a number of his men. This uncertainty prevails, throughout the whole trade. It is therefore a matter of indifference where a man removes to; he is never safe from being shuttle-cocked from one place to another. I have known twenty men shopped who were all on the road again in less than a fortnight. No fault can be found with the employers for thus sending the journeymen about their business when it may suit their taste or convenience, inasmuch as the men are in the habit of playing the same game when their end of the beam is up. . . .[9]

The workers were not the only ones to suffer from high prices. With inflation, a lag in new building, and a total lack of rent controls, one of the major social problems in the cities was high rents. The upward spiral of housing costs threatened middle-class renters with loss of status in New York City.

One of the time-honored customs of our city requires both landlord and tenant to "declare their intentions" on the 1st of February in relation to the rental year commencing the 1st of May. The house-owners have made their declaration, and, to the horror of pater familias, struggling to keep himself and babies from the contamination of a "low-neighborhood," his landlord demands an increase of rent fully averaging 25 per cent. above the rates of last year. The intentions of the tenant becomes, therefore, the question of vital importance in the family circle; they agitate the breakfast table and disturb the serenity of the bedroom confab; they penetrate even to the nursery. Especially is this the case in the middle stratum of humanity, where the entire social economy now turns upon this all-absorbing matter—the rate of the yearly rental. The salaried man, whose annual income is a fixed quantity, looks despairingly toward Brooklyn or to the shores of New Jersey, and presents to himself the alternative of emigration or a boarding-house. And it is upon this class that the rise in rents is about to press most heavily. By means of trade associations, combinations, strikes &c., mechanics and craftmen have brought about a rate of increased remuneration for their labor proportionate to the increased cost of living, but no regular or commensurate rise in the salaries of clerks, Government employees and others receiving fixed wages, has taken place, and to them the rent question is of absorbing interest. Even emigration offers but little relief to the harried clerk, for the rush to Brooklyn and Williamsburgh, Hoboken, and Jersey City, is so great, that rents which are, of course, dependent on demand, have risen more than fifty per cent. in all accessible suburbs of New York. . . .

With the great increase in the population of the city since the war, there has been but little increase in the number of dwelling houses. During the years 1861 and 1862 building was almost suspended, property owners not caring to improve their lots while all was uncertainty and peril. In 1863 and 1864 labor and material became so costly that the holders of real estate decided to wait for cheaper times. Nearly all the houses erected since the war have been built by men of means for their own use, and have done but little to remove the pressure of a largely increased population.

The number of merchants who have come here to reside from St. Louis, Louisville, New Orleans, Baltimore, and other Southern and Western cities, is large, and has created a brisk demand for first-class houses. Many West Indians, Mexicans, and South Americans, are residing in this city, temporarily attracted by the advantages of doubling a gold income by converting it into currency, thereby enabling them to enjoy the luxuries of the metropolis at a cheap rate. Among this class, there is a great demand for furnished houses and so desirable is this class of houses now, that we have heard of one in a fashionable locality renting as high as $2,000 per month. For a good furnished house the figures vary from $2,500 to $15,000, and even $20,000 per annum. In the more desirable portions of Fourteenth and Twenty-third streets, in Madison-avenue and parts of Fifth-avenue, houses are readily rented for the coming year at the rate of $2,000 to $5,000, the price [*sic*] in former times, for the same houses, being from $1,000 to $3,000. In Union square the average rent demanded for the coming year is $3,000, and the tenants are principally boarding-house keepers, to whom this once fashionable locality is now abandoned. But the rents demanded for these particular localities have very little effect on social economy generally. It is the high prices charged for medium houses decently located that creates all the commotion in the family circle. . . . Upon the class who rented these houses the high rents fall as a heavy burden. Their social pride must be sustained. Mrs. Grundy must be consulted. It is impossible for them to move to a cheaper house in the city. It is equally impossible to rent part of a house, because that would be living in a tenement house, of which they have a

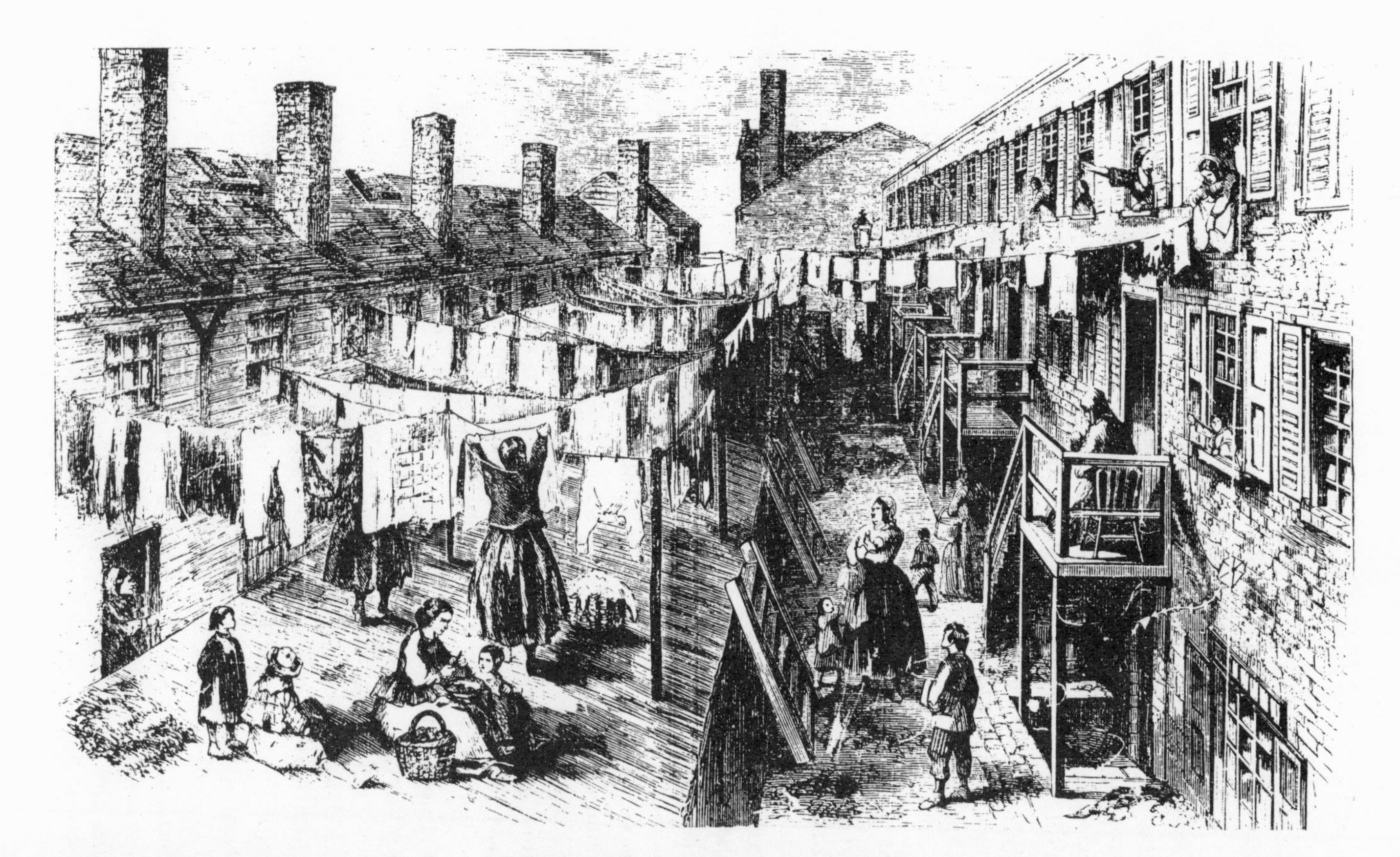

Unsanitary Conditions in Rivington Place

horror. They must either give up housekeeping and go to a boarding-house, or leave the city in search of cheap rent. . . .[10]

The suffering of the middle class was slight, however, compared to that of the underprivileged masses compelled to live in tenements. In a report of 1865, New York City's Council of Hygiene and Public Health flashed a beam of light into the dark recesses of the slums. Three-fifths of the tenements described in the Association's report were occupied by foreign-born tenants. Waste-water and slops were thrown into nearby gutters. Toilets were merely trenches, sunk a foot or two into the ground. In the words of the report: "In some of the apartments of the tenant-houses the rags that cover the floor in lieu of a carpet reek with filth. They have become a receptacle for street-mud, food of all kinds, saliva, urine and faeces. . . . The bed clothing is often little better."

. . . That the evils and abuses of the system continue undiminished, is seen on every hand. Not only does filth, over-crowding, lack of privacy and domesticity, lack of ventilation and lighting, and absence of supervision and of sanitary regulation, still characterize the greater number of them; but they are built to a greater height in stories, there are more rear tenant-houses erected back to back with other buildings, correspondingly situated on parallel streets; the courts and alleys are more greedily encroached upon and narrowed into unventilated, unlighted, damp, and well-like holes between the many-storied front and rear tenements; and more fever-breeding wynds and *culs-de-sac* are created as the demand for the humble homes of the laboring poor increases.

. . . . .

It is not our purpose to present unnecessary details upon this subject, but simply to state what nuisances are to be regarded as injurious to public health and to individual welfare in our city. They may be enumerated as follows: (1) filthy streets; (2) neglected garbage and domestic refuse; (3) obstructed and faulty sewers and drains; (4) neglected privies and stables; (5) cattle pens and large stables in the more populous districts; (6) neglected and filthy markets; (7) slaughter-houses and hide and fat depots in close proximity to populous streets; (8) droves of cattle and swine in crowded streets; (9) swill-milk stables and their products; (10) bone-boiling, fat-melting, and their accompaniments within the city limits; (11) the sulphuretted, ammoniacal, and carburetted gases and offensive exhalations that are needlessly liberated and widely diffused in gas manufacture and purification; (12) the accumulations of dumping-grounds and manure-yards in vicinity of populous streets; (13) the present management of refuse and junk materials in the city; (14) the unreasonable overcrowding of the city railway cars, and the absence of all sanitary authority, permitting the unguarded transit and public exposure of persons with small-pox and other loathsome maladies in the public conveyances and otherwise in the streets; (15) the neglect of dead animals in the streets and gutters of the city.

. . . . .

The 173 slaughter houses in this city are too offensive to health and decency to be longer permitted in their present localities. These establishments are now thrust into the midst of the most crowded districts, and it is to be observed that a loathsome train of dependent nuisances is found grouped in the same neighborhoods. We need not comment upon the offensive and debasing influence of the scenes and processes of the slaughter-pen. . . .[11]

Revealing a sharp departure from the romantic and sentimental trend of the times in literature, Rebecca Harding Davis's short story dealing with human degradation in the Ohio Valley iron mills was a landmark of realism. The slums she described were as appalling as those of New York City. She also reveals the failure of the clergy to reach the workers of the North. "Life in the Iron-Mills" appeared during the first month of the war.

. . . Shall I go over the history of the hours of that night? how [*sic*] the man wandered from one to another of his old haunts, with a half-consciousness of bidding them farewell—lanes and alleys and backyards where the mill-hands lodged—noting, with a new eagerness, the filth and drunkenness, the pig-pens, the ash-heaps covered with potato-skins, the bloated, pimpled women at the doors—with a new disgust, a new sense of sudden triumph, and, under all, a new, vague dread, unknown before, smothered down, kept under, but still there? It left him but once during the night, when, for the second time in his life, he entered a church. It was a sombre Gothic pile, where the stained light lost itself in far-retreating arches; built to meet the requirements and sympathies of a far other class than Wolfe's. Yet it touched, moved him uncontrollably. The distances, the shadows, the still, marble figures, the mass of silent kneeling worshippers, the mysterious music, thrilled, lifted his soul with a wonderful pain. Wolfe forgot himself, forgot the new life he was going to live, the mean terror gnawing underneath. The voice of the speaker strengthened the charm; it was clear, feeling, full, strong. An old man, who had lived much, suffered much; whose brain was keenly alive, dominant; whose heart was summer-warm with charity. He taught it to-night. He held up Humanity in its grand total; showed the great world-cancer to his people. Who could show it better? He was a Christian reformer; he had studied the age thoroughly; his outlook at man had been free, world-wide, over all time. His faith stood sublime upon the Rock of Ages; his fiery zeal guided vast schemes by which the gospel was to be preached to all nations. How did he preach it to-night? In burning, light-laden words he painted the incarnate Life, Love, the universal Man: words that became reality in the lives of these people—that lived again in beautiful words and actions, trifling, but heroic. Sin, as he defied it, was a real foe to them; their trials, temptations, were his. His words passed far over the furnace-tender's grasp, toned to suit another class of culture; they sounded in his ears a very pleasant song in an unknown tongue. He meant to cure this world-cancer with a steady eye that had never glared with hunger, and a hand that neither poverty nor strychnine-whiskey had taught to shake. In this morbid, distorted heart of the Welsh puddler he had failed.

Wolfe rose at last, and turned from the church down the street. He looked up; the night had come on foggy, damp; the golden mists had vanished, and the sky lay dull and ash-colored. He wandered again aimlessly down the street, idly wondering what had become of the cloud-sea of crimson and scarlet. The trial-day of this man's life was over, and he had lost the victory. What followed was mere drifting circumstance. . . .[12]

But everyone did not suffer from the war. Fortunes were made and frequently spent in gross and ostentatious revelry. The New York

Herald *gave a political as well as social connotation to the "Age of Shoddy."*

. . . All our theatres are open except Mrs. John Wood's, which will open on Thursday, and they are all crowded nightly. The kind of entertainment given seems to be of little account. Provided the prices are high and the place fashionable nothing more is required. All the hotels are as crowded as the theatres; and it is noticeable that the most costly accommodations, in both hotels and theatres, are the first and most eagerly taken. Our merchants report the same phenomenon in their stores: the richest silks, laces and jewelry are the soonest sold. At least five hundred new turnouts may be seen any fine afternoon in the Park; and neither Rotten Row, London, nor the Bois de Boulogne, Paris, can show a more splendid sight. Before the golden days of the Indian summer are over these five hundred new equipages will be increased to a thousand. Not to keep a carriage, not to wear diamonds, not to be attired in a robe which cost a small fortune, is now equivalent to being a nobody. This war has entirely changed the American character. The lavish profusion in which the old Southern cotton aristocracy used to indulge is completely eclipsed by the dash, parade and magnificence of the new Northern shoddy aristocracy of this period. Ideas of cheapness and economy are thrown to the winds. The individual who makes the most money—no matter how—and spends the most money—no matter for what—is considered the greatest man. To be extravagant is to be fashionable. These facts sufficiently account for the immense and brilliant audiences at the opera and the theatres; and until the final crash comes such audiences will undoubtedly continue.

The world has seen its iron age, its silver age, its golden age and its brazen age. This is the age of shoddy. The new brownstone palaces on Fifth Avenue, the new equipages at the Park, the new diamonds which dazzle unaccustomed eyes, the new silks and satins which rustle over loudly, as if to demand attention, the new people who live in the palaces and ride in the carriages and wear the diamonds and silks—all are shoddy. From the devil's dust they sprang and unto devil's dust they shall return. They live in shoddy houses. They ride in shoddy carriages, drawn by shoddy horses, and driven by shoddy coachmen who wear shoddy liveries. They lie upon shoddy beds, which have just come from the upholsterer's and still smell of shoddy varnish. They wear shoddy clothes purchased from shoddy merchants, who have erected mammoth stores, which appear to be marble, but are really shoddy. They set or follow the shoddy fashions, and fondly imagine themselves *a la mode de* Paris, when they are only *a la mode de* shoddy. Their professions and occupations are pure shoddy. They are shoddy brokers in Wall street, or shoddy manufacturers of shoddy goods, or shoddy contractors for shoddy articles for a shoddy government. Six days in a week they are shoddy business men. On the seventh day they are shoddy Christians. They ride luxuriously to a shoddy church, where a shoddy clergyman reads to them from a shoddy Bible and preaches a shoddy sermon written upon gilt-edged paper; and, during the appropriate passages, this shoddy successor to the old Apostles wipes his weak eyes with a shoddy lace handkerchief as he mildly pleads with his hearers, who are sleeping soundly upon their shoddy cushions, and begs of them to believe that the Saviour was crucified with intolerable torments in order that the shoddy aristocracy might be gently wafted upon the wings of shoddy angels to a shoddy heaven. Nor are their politics less shoddy than their religion. They belong to the shoddy party, which is always loyal to shoddy, and they vote the shoddy ticket, and support the shoddy administration which is conducting this shoddy war, not for the obsolete idea of the restoration of the Union, but for the profit and perpetuation of a shoddy dynasty. Oh, for some Junius, with a pen as keen as shoddy steel and words that burn like shoddy "Greek fire," to write the history of this shoddy age, and prophecy that downfall of shoddy which is to come! Already shrewd Daniels scent a storm in the Babylonish air; but still the days are golden and King Shoddy marches on triumphantly. Let us, then, enjoy the present, the Park, the theatres and the opera, and leave the future to take care of itself. That is the sum of shoddy wisdom, and we shall not question such high authority.[13]

In 1864, an article in Harper's Monthly *commented further on the antics of the new rich.*

The old proverb says: "That which comes easy goes easy." The suddenly enriched contractors, speculators, and stock-jobbers illus-

"At Home. Small and Early." Refreshments

trate its truth. They are spending money with a profusion never before witnessed in our country, at no time remarkable for its frugality. Our great houses are not big enough for them; they pull them down and build greater. They, like the proud and wanton Caligula, construct stables of marble at a fabulous cost, in which their horses are stabled (some, doubtless, to be fed on gilded oats), with a luxury never hitherto indulged in by the most opulent of our fellow-citizens. . . .

These Sybarites of "shoddy" buy finer furniture than was ever bought before, and dress in costlier cloths and silks than have been hitherto imported. No foreign luxury, even at the present enormous prices, is too dear for their exorbitant desires and swollen pockets. The importations of the country have arisen to the large amount of thirty millions of dollars a month, chiefly to satisfy the increased appetite for luxurious expense.

The ordinary sources of expenditure seem to have been exhausted, and these ingenious prodigals have invented new ones. The men button their waistcoats with diamonds of the first water, and the women powder their hair with gold and silver dust.

As excess overflowing the natural channels of enjoyment, is always sure to take an irregular and perverted course for the indulgence of its unchecked vagaries, it is not surprising to find the boundless extravagance of the times assuming forms at variance with propriety and taste. Parties, provoked to excessive folly and wild extravagance by an imperial court willing to enervate the people by debauchery that they may become too languid for resistance to tyranny, has, among other forms of dissipations, invented a grotesque kind of fancy ball. In this the guests represent things instead of persons. For example, one presents herself as a kitchen, with her person hung all over with pots and kettles, wearing a saucepan for a helmet, like Sancho Panza, brandishing a shovel and tongs, and playing the part of a kitchen wench with probably a dish-clout hanging to her tail. Another of a more sentimental turn is a flower garden, festooned with roses and bearing a spade and rake. A third is a pack of playing-cards, bedizened all over with clubs, diamonds, and hearts, and so on with every possible transformation of the human spiritual being (supposed to be rational) into the senseless, material thing.

This absurdity has been imported by our wealthy New Yorkers, together with other Parisian extravagances. Last winter, during which high carnival was held by our *nouveaux riches*, a dame . . . got up one of these grotesque fancy balls. She herself appeared on the occasion as music, and bore upon her head an illuminated lyre supplied with genuine gas, from a reservoir and fixtures concealed somewhere under her clothes. "We don't feel this war," they say. . . .

. . . Unfortunately, our people are so imitative that when one simpleton, provided he be rich, leads the way, all follow. Every man and woman thinks he must do as his wealthy neighbor does. . . . The shops of the dry-goods man, the jeweler, the dealer in carpets and cabinet-ware, and the gilded establishments of the restaurateur were never so crowded. The tradesman hardly shows any but his most expensive wares, which his greedy customer snatches up without solicitation. Thus camel's-hair shawls, at fifteen hundred dollars or more, go off briskly at the price; rivers of diamonds (*rivière de diamants*) flow unchecked by any regard for cost. Aubusson tapestry carpets of fabulous expense are bought unhesitatingly and recklessly trod upon, and dinners are eaten and wine drunk at Delmonico's and *Maison Dorée* at a price *per* head in a single sitting, which would support a soldier and his family for a good portion of the year. . . .[14]

To the tensions between employer and worker, the hardship and misery growing out of poor housing, and the disgust engendered by the "Age of Shoddy" must be added antagonism between East and West. Some of its causes were of long standing: creditor versus debtor; the restless speculative frontier arrayed against the stable and conservative East; industrial and commercial interests in conflict with agricultural ones. The war brought new sources of friction. The West complained that the East was getting too many government installations and war contracts; the East resented the draining to the West of their workers; both sides regarded their troops as better than the other's. Basically, it was a power struggle between sectional economic interests, but it had emotional overtones.

In 1862 the Chicago Times *reported the call for a mass meeting to be held at Dixon, Illinois.*

A mass meeting has been called at Dixon, Ill[inois]., to be held December 1, of the farmers, manufacturers and mechanics of Lee and adjoining counties, for the purpose of "taking measures to promote and protect the industrial interests and to give expression to their views and wishes on the subject of our national finances and currency."

These are stated to be the objects of the meeting. . . . There is not a word respecting the African in the call. But interests directly affecting the individuals who assemble are to be considered. It is a western meeting to deliberate upon western interests. If the farmers of Lee and adjoining counties have ascertained that in the new tax law a heavy burden is laid upon their shoulders while New England farmers are but slightly taxed, we apprehend that they will take measures to reduce the inequality. If western manufacturers find that the peculiar manufactures in which they are interested are carefully hunted up and oppressively taxed while the cotton lords of New England are protected in both the tax and tariff laws, we think they will be very likely to inquire the wherefore. The Dixon meeting is a movement in the right direction. Irrespective of all party feeling, there should be an earnest looking after their own interests by western men. New England in making the negro squeal, has diverted the attention of the West from the dive she was making into Western pockets. . . .[15]

During the war it was frequently suggested in the West that it should reconstruct a Union with the South and "leave New England out in the cold." This was never seriously considered by the majority of Westerners, but it did send chills down the spines of Eastern politicians and businessmen. Amory Dwight Mayo attacked attempts to "sow dissension" and tried to reassure both sections.

One of the most detestable manifestations of the last four years of war has been the persistent attempt of large numbers of treasonable and disaffected men to sow dissension between the Free States east and west of the Alleghanies. In the Middle States more than one man with an honorable name and position has been found shameless enough to arraign New England as the cause of all our woes, and propose compromise with treason on the basis of her expulsion from a "reconstructed Union." It would have been well if the efforts of demagogues farther West had been as soon appreciated and as thoroughly scorned as were those machinations of the people of the East. Our Western traitors, found a better soil in the Southern and foreign-born masses inhabiting vast districts of our new country; while the natural pride of a great and rapidly-growing section of the Union offered a weak side for their approach. These men, in the earlier period of our conflict, succeeded in imposing upon a considerable portion of the Western press and people a mass of falsehood and prejudice which has slowly been dispelled, though at one time it threatened the most serious results.

This mischievous influence took the form of appeal to the pride of the Western people; and from stump and "sanctum," in all its States was heard the charge that the government at Washington was in the power of the East, which was represented as a grim "old fogy," intent only on its money-bags, holding in leash the youthful hero who burned to exterminate rebellion, or to present the olive-branch according to the locality addressed; for this depreciation was timed to estrange both loyal and disloyal men, and thus lay the foundation for the separation of the new Free States from the old, and their union with the South. Unfortunately, too many patriotic men were deceived by this artful plot; and for a season the bitterest denunciation of the government and "the East," as its "old man of the sea," raged through the columns of Union journals, and made association even with loyal circles often a perpetual conflict for an Eastern man.

It cannot be denied that there was much in the slow march of events in the first two years of the war—in the painful efforts of the government to fully comprehend the awful magnitude of the struggle, in the succession of military disasters in Virginia, in the greed of commercial gamblers in the great Atlantic cities, and the frequent disparagement of the new States by conceited functionaries in the old—to foster this wretched jealousy. It never came from the heart of the Western people. It was the result of treasonable manipulation of their great earnestness and inexperience in revolution by the foes of the country. The West, of course, felt the imminence of the danger to the Union before the East. Disunion to her was provincialism—her reduction from a leading power in the great republic to the tail of the South or the satellite of the North. She feared to wait the slow motions of executive power, or the dull movements of pedantic generals, while her pathways to the Atlantic and Pacific were cut off, and a ferocious enemy menacing her borders. Just then came in this miscreant clique to poison her mind and fill her heart with blind rage against her mother and other self.

But, happily, that danger is rapidly declining. The great common sense of the Western people pointed to the one solution through the sword; and the West, under the lead of her Sherman, Rosecrans, and Grant, has bounded along her path of glory, every step a victory till success has made her generous and appreciative, and experience, shown her what manner of men they were who were proclaimed her friends. All the elements of immediate military success were in her hands—a population better adapted for war, and richer in able-bodied men than any on earth; the sting of imperious material and social necessity; the conformation of the country over which they were to march to reach the foe. Every attempt to raise a storm against the East has been drowned in the shout of a new victory over the South, till blatant treason has subsided to snarling copperheadism, and loyal men and Union journals have learned to distrust a policy that could only feed the hopes of rebels, and divide the hearts of patriots. . . .[16]

There were other tensions of prewar origin which continued into the war years. For three decades preceding the war, one social reform movement after another swept across the North. When the fighting began, most of these reform crusades subsided, but they were not completely extinguished. Temperance advocates, faced with a discouraging future, nevertheless continued to speak out. One of them was John Marsh, whose executive committee report was read at the twenty-eighth anniversary meeting of the American Temperance Union, May 12, 1864.

When one nation is at war with another, or with a different portion of its own subjects for life, it pauses not to inquire after progress; nor is it ever discouraged for want of success; nor does it fold its hands in indolence and yield up the conflict in despair. LIFE, LIFE! ONWARD, ONWARD! VICTORY, VICTORY! is the watchword. Enemies there may be within as well as without. This is part of the battle. Sacrifices must be made, of course, and the object is worth it. Months and years may be consumed. Better is endless strife than submission for an hour. . . . Of one false impression and general complaint . . . your Committee, in their Report, feel bound to take early notice. That is, that the temperance cause is dead, and the conflict is ended, because it is felt to be a vain one. . . .

That the war would cause a great increase of intemperance, was at its outbreak the universal expectation. The unnatural excitement everywhere its attendant, the feverish state of the public mind, the enlistment and gathering of troops, the marching and countermarching, the fatigues, the *ennui* of camp life, the sickness and wounds and desolations of hospitals, the universal medical use by surgeons, through false principles of philosophy in the medical bureau, and the exultants of victory, all secured extraordinary use of the intoxicating cup. . . . It would have been strange had it been otherwise. But it argues no defect in our principles or death of our cause.

Your Committee have endeavored to be observant of the signs of the times and to meet the wants of the hour. The system of flooding the army with temperance tracts specially prepared for the soldier, commenced before our last Anniversary, has been persevered in until more than a million and a half of these monitors have been sent forth. Three hundred and sixty-seven Regiments have in the past year been each supplied with a thousand by as many Sabbath schools contributing and selecting their Regiment. These tracts have met the soldier in his encampment and his marches, in the hour of frivolity and temptation, and while sick and confined in hospitals, have warned him of danger, reminded him of home and his obligations to loved ones, and elevated him to thoughts of a better habitation than earth can afford. Chaplains and officers have spoken gratefully of their influence in restraining, guiding and saving. Hundreds and thousands have been induced to sign the Pledge, and resolve that if they must be hurled into eternity, they will die sober and not drunken. . . .

At Camp Convalescent, in Virginia, where a large number of tracts have been sent, a spirited temperance weekly meeting has been held, a pledge roll with more than 4,000 names for total abstinence has been hung in festoons round the hall. Our publications have attracted the attention of that noble institution, the Christian Commission, and they are now regularly sending monthly 3,500 of our Journals into the army, for the sick and wounded in hospitals, and frequently call for supplies of our tracts, at one time for 20,000, at another for 50,000, for distribution; a cooperation to us peculiarly pleasant. While remembering the army and public bodies we have not been unmindful of our Home population. Finding a readiness in Sabbath schools to do good, we made a proposal to them in January last to become tract distributors in their own neighborhoods; and we offered to furnish every school with 2,000 pages of good tracts, in twenty varieties, for Home Circulation, postage paid, for two dollars. To this offer 189 schools have responded, and in four months we have thus sent abroad 74,508 tracts. . . . The Youth's Temperance Advocate is receiving better patronage than at any former period, and has a monthly circulation of some 20,000.

. . . . .

Among the embarrassments of the hour there are not a few tokens of good. If the war has given increase to drunkenness, it has also shown intoxicating liquor to be the nation's greatest foe, by endangering and bringing certain ruin upon the nation's arm of defence. It has justified the most rigorous measures for the suppression of the liquor traffic, and rendered contemptible all complaints of prohibitory law as unconstitutional and an interference with the liquor dealer's rights. . . .[17]

Although it was not a reform activity, anti-Catholic nativism had created many stresses in American life, especially in the 1850's when it reached its climax in politics. After 1860, it was eclipsed by other issues, but it was there, nonetheless, and continued in various guises during the war. One of these was an attack upon alleged plotting by the Papacy and European Catholic leaders against the federal union and the Lincoln government.

The British Minister and the President of the United States cannot be ignorant of the nature of the struggle which the French Revolution of 1789 inaugurated. It is hardly necessary to mention to those acquainted with history, that the restoration of the Bourbons to the throne of France was followed by the so-called Holy Alliance, the secret object of which was the suppression of revolution—the perpetuation of *absolutism* and the *Roman Faith* everywhere. . . . Is it necessary to allude to the momentous fact that here commences a struggle with republicanism, constitutionalism, and protestantism, on the part of these powers, which is only just on the point of culminating? . . . In pursuance of this plan, several newspapers were started in this country—the *Boston Pilot* and afterwards the *Freeman's Journal.* . . . The first thing the *Boston Pilot* did was to commence an attack on Puritanism. Well was it understood that in this principle our free institutions originated; could that be disintegrated, the way was prepared for the overthrow of these institutions. In leveling their artillery against Puritanism, they expected to obtain the sympathy of episcopalians, as well as the irreligious and indifferent of all classes of the North. . . .

Availing themselves of the incompatibility of Northern and Southern institutions—of the elements of an oligarchy which there existed—they determined to intensify and perpetuate this antagonism. Already had Northern free institutions shown their superiority over slavery in developing the commercial and industrial resources of the North, and in giving to New York City the ascendancy over her Southern rival—Charleston. . . . We do not say that Calhounism had its origin in Austrian machinations; by no means; that was a product of Southern soil—of Southern ambition—an ambition growing out of an entire discordance between a slaveocracy and a democracy. But when nullification chameleonlike, changed its color, and commenced a systematic attack on Puritanism, by presenting an organized resistance to the abolitionism in the North, we do say, that the Austro-American influence lent its aid to intensify this resistance, and appropriate it to its own ends and purposes. . . . The Irish emigrants of the North were in direct sympathy with Rome, and formed the bulk of the democratic party; Austrian agents seized upon the sympathy, and arrayed it against Puritanism, and put it in connection with the slaveocracy of the South, which was also hostile to Puritanism; from this source, therefore, the slaveocracy received its inspirations.

. . . . .

A new step was now taken towards consolidating the Roman hierarchy on our soil.

The country was laid out into dioceses, bishops and archbishops appointed, and the first council of these bishops assembled at Baltimore with closed doors! With the erection of the hierarchy, the next step was for the bishops to get control of the church property in their respective dioceses, and then make this property hereditary in their office by act of Legislature; thereby constructing an episcopal aristocracy, with immense lands, tenements, and revenues—which are inalienable, always increasing, but never diminishing—transmitted from bishop to bishop, a spiritual aristocracy more terrible than any other with which the nations have been cursed! We say these bishops are demagogues in disguise,—dukes in the habiliments of the church, with vast domains,—their dioceses being in fact duchies, and their people destined to become *subjects,* forming a Northern oligarchy akin to the Southern, and affiliating with it. The council of bishops is antagonistic to Congress, and stands as the executor of the canon law, which is opposed to and subversive of our civil law on our soil.

. . . . .

Is it difficult to comprehend the machinery at work here? The Austrian minister in close communication with the secession leaders and representatives at Washington, and with Archbishop Hughes, who, with the provincial bishops *commanding* in their respective dioceses supported by an Irish military of 150,000 men, in ambush behind the democratic party, with occasional manipulations of republican leaders, compose an organized force in the northern States, with numerous other agencies at work,—all controlled and guided by foreign potentates, and designed to be used in the direction mentioned. Their grand purpose being to get possession of England and the United States, and then remove protestantism. The details of their movements, will, of course, depend upon circumstances; but their main object is to centralize and *imperialize* the government; and they are endeavoring to effect this through the disintegration of the States of the Union—not merely the Southern from the Northern, but the Western from the Eastern. This, however, is only for the purpose of weakening the elements of opposition; and then, if they should succeed, they will reconstruct the government; in which case the principles of republicanism, protestantism and civil liberty will be ignored; and then, when thus centralized and made one gigantic machine, with an army of half a million of men, they will hurl it against England.

For this purpose, the affiliated societies of the "Knights of the Golden Circle," and the Butternut organizations running through the Northwestern States, are designed to be used, while the Irish military organization . . . known among themselves as the Fenian Brotherhood, in connection with the Emmet Monument Association, will operate upon New England, New York, less through the Western States—more in the armies of the Union. It will be somewhat startling to the public, probably, to be told that the greater number of these Fenians are in the Army of the Potomac, not for the purpose of securing the permanency of this Union, but for that of embarrassing the action of the administration, and, in the meantime, making soldiers of themselves, that they may be better prepared to fight England. . . .[18]

One of the saddest of the war strains was that of caring for refugees. The Civil War, too, had its displaced persons.

. . . The contending armies surging to and fro over extensive regions of country . . . desolated them completely, seizing not only garnered but growing crops, cattle, horses, and mules, and destroying ruthlessly dwellings, barns, and fences, often applying the torch to those edifices which shot and shell had spared. From these desolated regions, often infested with guerrillas, whose murderous malignity spared neither age nor sex, fled their wretched inhabitants, mostly women and children, homeless and penniless, nearly naked and often starving, wearied, sick, and dying, seeking shelter and sustenance within the Union lines, at Nashville, Vicksburg, and Memphis. Military necessity forbade their remaining in these advanced posts of the Union armies; and rendering them what assistance could be spared in the way of food, the Government shipped them to Cairo, Louisville, St. Louis, Cincinnati, and other points. Here they were landed, sick, helpless, and friendless. . . .[19]

The river towns were not prepared to care for the refugees. Nor were they always sympathetic. On April 4, 1864, George F. Davis of Cincinnati wrote to Ohio Senator John Sherman.

The large influx of poor whites from "The Southern Border States," coming as they do from homes made desolate by the ravages of war, and in need of everything, has made it necessary to organize for their relief. . . . We find the work one of increasing magnitude, and presenting difficulties that we cannot surmount. The Refugees are mostly women, children, and old men. They are brought on Gov[ernmen]t Transports and left on the Levee at Cairo and other points, dependent on the *charities* of the people whose sympathies are exercised by coming in contact with them. They are mostly the families of those who have relatives in the Union Army, and who are driven out because of their sympathy for the Federal Government. They have a right to the fostering care of the nation, and should not be thus humbled. We can only assist them temporarily, for they are already upon us by thousands. . . . It is not right for the Government to cast these people upon the *Northern* Border States, for while it will afford the Southern States the opportunity to get rid of their pauper population, they will all become such unless taken care of. . . . The Contrabands are much more easily managed for they will work and can in a measure be made to do so if they refuse. . . . The Southern people ought to look with shame upon these specimens of their white population. . . . We cannot make a white woman work, and if today we should erect a "Refugees' Home" it would be permanently filled in a few days with as worthless a class of people as you can imagine. . . . [There must be some plan put into operation] "to give these people the proper relief, and to guard the States on the Border from being overrun with these people."[20]

Limited aid did come to these unfortunates from local benevolent agencies, and especially from the United States Union Commission. A special agent of the Refugee Relief Commission of Ohio described some of these efforts:

From the inclosed [*sic*] slip of paper I infer you have misunderstood my application for aid to White Refugees. With you, I agree *money* is not the best form of aid. I petitioned for seed, ploughs, sewing machines, washtubs &c., to be bought by the appropriation and given to the destitute. I approve of your giving them the use of the lands, but there they have no seed nor ploughs. . . . I mail with this a printed petition for each member and in all 4000 all over the country to draw out a popular expression. . . . This commission here is preparing documents for the whole country. . . .[21]

Finally, another minority group, the Society of Friends, felt the stresses of war as a harrowing experience. Quakers' attitudes on the war issues, their problems of conscience, and related themes were treated in an article which appeared in a Quaker periodical.

We have heretofore abstained from much remark on the civil war, which is now sorrowfully distracting our country, but it is in vain to ignore the fact that this subject is uppermost in the minds of the mass of the people, and that Friends are not only deeply interested in it, but in too many instances are carried away by the prevailing spirit of the communities around them. The feeling of the necessity of subordination to government is so deeply imbedded in the very foundations of society, that all good citizens are ready to sustain the powers that be, as far as their conscientious restraints will allow. This sentiment, which is so nearly universal, even in monarchical countries, acquires increased force in a Republic, from the participation of the people, as well in the choice of their rulers, as in the law-making power. The government of Pennsylvania originally rested mainly on moral power; and though, with the growth of population, and the ingrafting of varied elements on the original stock, the peace principle has been replaced by a government of physical force, that force has been of a mild and restraining, rather than an aggressive or even a violent character; the soldier has been rather a supernumerary in society, and, even in the execution of the militia laws, provision has been made for respecting the conscientious scruples of those who felt restrained from aiding the government by the power of the sword. Now, however, many of those who are convinced of the benign principles of peace, as taught in the New Testament, find their faith sorely tried. The central power of the government is attacked; a great and prosperous nation is threatened with anarchy and total dismemberment, and the President, chosen by the people to administer the laws, calls upon all to unite in sustaining his authority by force of arms. His appeal has been responded to with spontaneous alacrity; the terrible passions of hatred and revenge are fearfully awakened; war has become the occupation of the nation; and love of country, the hatred of slavery, and even the desire for permanent peace, are appealed to on its behalf.

That many of the young and ardent in our own religious Society should have been drawn into the whirlpool of popular enthusiasm, is not to be wondered at. The apparent connection of this contest with the anti-slavery movement, in which Friends have taken such a lively interest, has induced the desire, on the part of some, to have a war prosecuted with vigor, which seems to them to promise, as one of its results, the long-desired enfranchisement of the colored race. But happy as such a consummation would be, if accomplished by wise and moderate means, we must not forget that the ground of our Christian profession is equally at variance with war as with oppression, and that they are twin offspring of the uncontrolled and corrupted passions of the human heart. Neither can claim justification in that benign religion which breathes peace on earth and good will to all men; both are in direct violation of the plainest precepts of our holy pattern, and contrary to the whole spirit of the dispensation which He came to introduce among men. War is, in its very nature, incapable of settling differences on principles of justice and equity. Physical force is the arbiter which it substitutes for those moral and intellectual agencies on which men instinctively rely, in times of peace, for the adjustment of questions in dispute. In war, the strongest and most skillful party is most likely to be victorious, no matter what the merits of the controversy may be; and even after the physical contest is terminated, the original cause of dispute must generally be settled by treaty. We are aware that those Christian professors who advocate warlike measures are apt to claim providential interference on behalf of the cause which they espouse; a belief in that Providence in the affairs of men which we all instinctively adopt, forbids us to deny the merciful regard for erring and finite man, continually extended by the Creator and Sustainer of the universe; but that this is necessarily exhibited in the triumph of the right, is contrary to all teachings of history, or our present experience. The thousands of slaves annually brought from the coast of Africa are prisoners of war, cruelly wrested from one barbarous tribe in the interior by the superior prowess of another. The tyrannical and oppressive rule of all the great despots of the earth rests wholly on the sword. Man's finite judgment is confounded whenever he attempts to reconcile the course of events in this world of ours, with the truest ideas of right and wrong he can arrive at; the problems of our time sufficiently illustrate the total incapacity of the profoundest intellects to reach those great issues which lie buried in the future of this once peaceful land.

In reiterating these oft-repeated views of the inconsistency of war with enlightened reason and Christian principle, we are aware they will be met by the plea of necessity. . . . But is it ever necessary to do wrong? Does any plea of apparent necessity require the stifling of conscience—the smothering of those tender emotions implanted by the Creator, and designed to be nourished into a growth of purity and happiness for this life, and that which is to come? But even supposing the necessity of resisting wrong and outrage by force, this does not justify those, to whom the rich legacy has descended, of a purer morality and a higher standard of Christian attainment than that which generally prevails. It is the peculiar mission of the Society of Friends to hold up the principles of peace, setting the example of returning good for evil, and owning, before all men, the brotherhood of the human race, their common obligations to the Author of their being, and to each other. These principles never shine so brightly as when contrasted with the spirit of strife and contention; and those who are favored with strength to maintain them, in such times as these, will be a blessing to the nation at large, by cultivating the arts of peace, exercising the ministrations of humanity and Christian kindness to all alike, and preserving much that is good from the destruction that follows in the train of war. . . .[22]

VII

Ways of Life

THE WAR profoundly influenced all aspects of Northern society. Newspapers were full of war news, mass meetings were held, and war-related activities churned the waters of daily life. Yet in city, town, and country, the main currents of activity flowed on in the old, well-worn channels. The ways of life, then, present a picture characterized by contrast.

First, there was the surge of patriotism, the breathless pride in the citizen-soldiers who had rallied to the flag. On the Fourth of July, 1861, in Lafayette, Indiana, there was almost a spirit of carnival.

The eighty-fifth anniversary of American Independence was celebrated in this city yesterday with a degree of enthusiasm unparalleled in the memory of the oldest inhabitant. Before the hour indicated in the published programme for the commencement of the patriotic exercises, the public square and all its approaches presented a dense mass of human beings.

The most careless observer could not fail to be struck with the undue proportion of females in the throng,—a fact no wise remarkable when we reflect that the Battle Ground county has nearly one thousand fighting men in the field. But as the eye surveyed the vast multitude the towering forms of stalwart men gave ample assurance that the reserve guard of the Grand Army would be equal to any emergency which may yet arise, and that sooner or later this wicked rebellion must yield to the irresistible power of numbers. . . . A more enthusiastic, and at the same time more orderly demonstration was never witnessed in this city. The published programme was carried out spiritedly and to the letter. Col. Brown, at the head of his gallant command, joined in the parade, and his regiment was everywhere hailed with the waiving of handerkerchiefs and the plaudits of the multitude. Capt. Cassell, with the Zouaves, won encomiums of which the lamented Ellsworth might have been proud, and the Star City Cavalry, under Dr. Worrall, and the Chauncey Home Guard completed a military pageant worthy of the day and of the occasion. The firemen, although but few in number made a handsome appearance. Dr. A. M. Moore, Chief Marshal of the day, and his efficient aides, deserve honorable mention for the admirable manner in which they conducted the exercises. There was no confusion,—everything on the programme, from the rope walking to the oration, passed off decently and in order. Altogether it was a day to be remembered; and whatever may be the future of our unhappy country, the 4th of July, 1861, will be golden with memories to those who participated in the varied enjoyments of the Star City celebration.[1]

After the bloody Second Battle of Bull Run, in the late summer of 1862, the carnival spirit of the early days of the war was gone. Then the people of Boston (and of other communities also), shocked into hectic activity by the emergency calls for medical supplies, tried within a few days to make up the deficiencies which complacency and a lack of farsighted planning had brought about.

The man does not live who has seen Boston stirred to its very depths as it was yesterday. The winds had been blowing for a week, and there had been an unusual moving of the waters; but yesterday there came a perfect tornado, and such a storm of public feeling as it waked up Boston never knew before.

. . . . .

From seeing the friends and acquaintances I went out to observe the more general indications of the public mind, and found every body I met with an excited face on. In the cars and on the street, in the stores, and at the hotels, every one was insisting that we had not, that the Government had not, appreciated the magnitude of the work to be done, and every one appeared like a man who, coming

THE UNITED STATES HOSPITAL AT GEORGETOWN, D.C., FORMERLY THE UNION HOTEL

suddenly to realize the immense importance of something, wonders that it has not always seemed to him as great as it does just then.

In the afternoon, at two o'clock, I found that all the stores were closing up, and every one was either devoting himself to getting up and keeping up the excitement, or yielding to and being carried along by it. Meetings every afternoon. A large decorated platform in front of the Old South Church was filled constantly, and the crowds in front made passing difficult; and the Common heard a great deal of eloquence, and saw a great deal of enthusiasm during the past week.

Sunday came, and the great heart of Boston was full. The most appalling rumors of our losses in killed and wounded were in circulation, coupled with the calls for lint-bandages and sick supplies. Whether true or not, it was circulated, and had its influence, that after the first call for surgeons and supplies was responded to but slowly, a message came calling "for God's sake" to send on shirts, and bandages, and surgeons. Then reports went around that seventeen thousand of the wounded had been already brought into Washington, and the call seemed no ordinary appeal to human sympathy and patriotism. Gov. Andrew sent notice around to all the churches of the city. Many of them suspended immediately with a short and fervent prayer; service for the afternoon was abandoned, and the churches were opened for the receival of the contributions for the wounded. All the church-going population of the city thus heard the appeal and never were human sympathies more promptly or liberally responsive to the call of suffering than yesterday in Boston. . . .

The call had been made, and the congregations separated, each one wending his way diligently to his home, and thinking of every thing he might contribute. Many a mother, whose family could poorly spare it, contributed towels, table-cloths, sheets and shirts, and the more competent poured in their full proportions, sometimes in bales, of whatever could be of value in the emergency.

All these supplies were gathered together in various parts of the city, but the principal depot was at Tremont Temple, where the crowd of people bringing bundles and baskets, and the teams bringing in empty boxes for packing, and the express wagons loading up the packages which were ready for transportation, created a scene of activity which is very unusual of a Sunday in the quiet city.

The cars upon the horse railroad were stopped and not allowed to pass, and the sidewalk was roped to prevent the travel, and give the contributors an opportunity to bring their gifts into the treasury.

On entering the Temple hundreds of women and girls were seen busily and quietly at work, some tearing into strips old garments or sheets, while others were stitching together the pieces and rolling them up. Others were preparing lint, and there were many who had done this work at home, and sent in their lint and bandages all made and ready to be packed. Outside the Temple there was started a subscription-paper, on which all sorts of amounts, ranging from ten cents to two hundred dollars, were subscribed, and the whole amount thus put down was five thousand two hundred dollars.

There was a lack of boxes, and many merchants opened their stores, and after sending out what empty boxes could be found, poured out upon the floor the contents of those which were full, and sent the cases to the Temple.

Wines and liquors of every description and in surprising quantities were sent in, and one merchant contributed a whole wagon-load of packages of Bay rum. Such quantities were sent in that no lack of stimulating materials will occur for a long time. One merchant sent in enough material for three thousand pounds of lint, and I believe that an almost fabulous amount of bandages will have been prepared—enough to wind the whole army in cotton cloth if it should be necessary.

Many were engaged in nailing up the boxes as fast as they were packed, which were then put upon the express wagons and taken to the Worcester depot.

At five o'clock last evening, nine long freight-cars went out, and Mayor Wightman and several of the city police accompanied the train. Twenty-six surgeons, in answer to the call, went to Washington immediately.

Supplies continue to come in to-day from the surrounding towns, and they will be forwarded as they arrive. The excitement has not subsided to-day.[2]

Small towns in the West, as well as Eastern cities, did their bit in civilian volunteer activities. In particular, the churches were often the centers of war-related projects. Bellefontaine, Ohio, was one of these communities (the same Bellefontaine that in 1863 had sent Butternuts to an antiwar rally in Indianapolis).

Editor of the Republican:—As you frequently, through the Republican, request your readers to give you the news and local items of the different townships, and as no one else feels disposed to give an item, or any proceedings of the citizens of our township (Miami), I will undertake it myself.

On the Sabbath day preceding the day on which our Good President and Noble Governor proclaimed that the people should meet in their different churches and render thanks to Almighty God for his many blessings so kindly bestowed upon us, it was announced by the pastor of the M. E. Church of Quincy, that there would be services on said day in said Church, and that a collection would be taken up to relieve the necessities of the families of Soldiers, &c., accordingly a goodly congregation convened and after an appropriate discourse for the time and occasion, and a powerful appeal to the hearts and purses of the audience, and which appeared to have had its desired effect, for on taking up the collection, we had just $128.65. It was then given out that there would be services again in the evening, when there would be another collection taken up. In the evening the church was crowded with a well behaved and attentive congregation, when they were addressed by Rev. Wm. M. Galbraith, Presbyterian minister from Degraff. A more appropriate discourse from a very appropriate text (Deut. 8th ch. 10th verse) could hardly be gotten up for such an occasion, followed by another eloquent appeal from our worthy pastor, after which another collection was taken up, which swelled our day's collection to $150.15, and when I inform you that this collection was made in the west end of Miami (and with few exceptions, by the loyal citizens of the west end, for the east end, neither participated in our exercise, nor contributed to the above fund) you must come to the conclusion that that motto which we so frequently hear quoted "charity begins at home" is hardly applicable to the citizens of Miami, and if the eastern end of our township will do as well as we have done, we will then challenge any township in the county to do as well, in proportion to population, and if we are beaten we will acknowledge the corn, and try it again.

We meet again on to-morrow for the purpose of procuring wood, meat, flour, &c., of which our farmers have abundance and to spare, and which on former occasions they have contributed freely, and of which I have not the least doubt they will do again to-morrow, and for the same laudable purpose viz.: the aid and comfort of Soldiers' families. . . . Quincy.[3]

To offset the irreligious and allegedly corrupt influences of life in the army camps, the Northern churches, through the New York Bible Society, made an attempt to sustain Christianity and even spread its influence among the soldiers by a mass distribution of Testaments.

The war excitement naturally colored the past year's operations of the Society. The special distribution made necessary by it bears a large proportion to the Society's entire distribution; and though we have not been insensible, in the effort to meet new and unexpected demands, of the necessity of maintaining our settled channels of Gospel distribution, we have necessarily yielded to the immediate and pressing call made on the Society and its agents. . . .

Two public meetings (one on Sabbath evening, May 19 [1861], the other on Sabbath evening, November 24), held at Irving Hall [New York City], at which eloquent gentlemen made stirring addresses, served to apprise the Christian community of the manner in which the Society met its new obligations. . . .

This Society exists to meet cases of destitution of the Scriptures due to whatever cause, and it immediately became sensible of the new demand addressed to it. From the 19th of April [1861], when the first Bible was given to the New York Seventh Regiment, to the present time, it has not willingly suffered a single defender of his country, whether at sea or on shore, to leave New York unfortified with the shield of God's blessed word.

In this distribution, embracing the supply of the volunteer and regular land forces and the naval service, we have used already some 85,568 volumes, costing $12,042.67, principally the nonpareil New Testament, neatly bound in cloth with gilt edges, costing about fifteen cents a volume; varied in some cases, generally of cavalry, with the edition adding the Psalms. It was deemed desirable to make the book presented inviting in appearance, that it might be esteemed as a gift; compact in size, so as not to occupy too much space; and yet at a cost not to waste the Society's means.

These books have been distributed among over 100,000 men, comprising 139 regiments and batteries, holding every grade of rank from the general officer to the drummer boy. Of these regiments and batteries, 87 were from this city [New York], including seven of the three months' men, and 16 distinctively German or French; 23 were from other parts of the State, and 28 were from New England; 19 from Massachusetts alone.

Books have been furnished in the English, German, French, Italian, Spanish, Danish, Swedish, and Portuguese languages. . . .

The distribution has been effected, when possible, by personal grant of the agent to individuals at their quarters; often, in the case of regiments from abroad, to the men while at dinner at the Park barracks; standing in line awaiting the order to march; paraded in from the City Hall to receive their colors; or even on the march down Broadway, as in one notable case where a captain was seen at the head of his men, a Bible in one hand, his sword in the other; and in another, of an officer with his red-covered Testament strapped across his breast on the outside of his uniform. . . .

. . . Great encouragement and satisfaction are found in the general avidity for Bibles which our agents have met in their labors. Where the character of the regiment has been distinctively Romanist, the books have been civilly declined save in individual cases, which have been furnished with caution. It is a notorious fact that many of the troops sent from this city were of a class little likely to pay much respect to the ministers of God, and little subject or accustomed to influences which would make the Word a welcome gift. But among such we have yet to see any general unwillingness to take the Bible, and have, on the contrary, met an almost universal willingness to receive it, the officers facilitating and encouraging our efforts.* . . .

The soldier as he dons his uniform is born into a new life. His mind is open to new influences; and the American soldier is alert to learn all that appertains to his new situation and circumstances. If he finds the Bible furnished as part of the equipment which is to fit him for the performance of his new duties, we may reasonably hope that he will strive to discover wherein consists its usefulness.

Nor must we fail to remember that the men to whom we may furnish the Bible, with all the moral support due to the sanction of their offices to our distribution, are largely those who are beyond our ordinary reach. And we believe that in making this distribution, we yield to considerations of prudent patriotism, as well as endeavor to follow the promptings of piety and philanthropy. If the teachings of the Bible and the love of God it inculcates can be diffused into and through the hearts of our soldiers, not only shall they become mighty in battle, but we shall have the assurance that their might will never be used save against their country's foes. Six

---

* The distribution to the Excelsior Brigade was made an impressive ceremony. The men were drawn up in line, addressed by General Sickles and their chaplains; prayer was offered; and then to appropriate music from the regimental bands, our Testaments were distributed, a Bible being presented to the General.

hundred thousand men, thinking and working together, exert an enormous influence. It is ours to see to it to the extent of our means and opportunity, that that influence shall be for good.[4]

The United States Christian Commission for the Army and Navy was one of the most vigorous of the nondenominational but religion-rooted organizations formed to serve the volunteer army. It was closely allied to, and indeed developed from, the Young Men's Christian Association.

. . . At a convention of delegates from Young Men's Christian Associations, held in the city of New York, Nov. 16th, 1861, the following persons were appointed as a United States Christian Commission:

Rev. Rollin H. Neale, D. D., Boston; Geo. H. Stuart, Esq., Philadelphia; Charles Demond, Esq., Boston; John P. Crozer, Esq., Philadelphia; Rev. Bishop E. S. Janes, D. D., New York; Rev. M. L. R. P. Thompson, D. D., Cincinnati; Hon. Benj. F. Mannierre, New York; Col. Clinton B. Fisk, St. Louis; Rev. Benj. C. Cutler, D. D., Brooklyn; John V. Farwell, Esq., Chicago; Mitchell H. Miller, Esq., Washington; John D. Hill, M. D., Buffalo.

The object of the Commission was to promote the spiritual and temporal welfare of the officers and men of the United States army and navy, in co-operation with chaplains and others. . . .

The headquarters were established at New York. . . .

During the year, B. F. Mannierre and Rev. Dr. Cutler resigned, and their places were filled by the appointment of Jay Cooke, Esq., of Philadelphia, and Rev. Jas. Eells, D. D., of Brooklyn, New York, on the commission. . . . The design of the Commission has been to arouse the Christian Associations and the Christian men and women of the loyal States to such action toward the men in our army and navy, as would be pleasing to the Master; to obtain and direct volunteer labors, and to collect stores and money with which to supply whatever was needed, reading matter, and articles necessary for health not furnished by Government or other agencies, and to give the officers and men of our army and navy the best Christian ministries for both body and soul possible in their circumstances.

To carry out this design, Christian men, ministers, merchants, lawyers, surgeons and others, have offered their services freely, in numbers ample to distribute all the stores and publications contributed, and all the Commission has had means to purchase.

Our Chairman, Geo. H. Stuart, a merchant of Philadelphia, has given the Commission office room and room for storage; the services of clerks, porters &c., and his own time and labors, free of all charge. . . . The Government, various Generals, and other officers in command, the Surgeon-General, Medical Directors and Surgeons in charge, have kindly aided us by passes, stores, ambulances, transportation, and opportunities of labor.

All railroads applied to, have given free passes to our delegates, and telegraph companies, free transmission of our messages. The American Bible Society has freely given us Testaments for distribution; the Tract and Publication Societies and Boards have generously contributed publications, and the people have given stores—not enough to save the necessity of buying many things to meet emergencies and special demands, yet very liberally.

. . . Stores have all gone directly to [the soldiers] . . . from the hands of our own delegates, or of those known by them to be worthy of all confidence. The money expended in arousing the people at home to cooperate with the Commission, has been very little indeed. . . . An amazing feature in this work, is the interest it has excited wherever it has become known. Meetings under the auspices of the various Associations and Committees, have been thronged from first to last, and full of interest. Stores have come in unsought, and contributions have been liberal and cheerful. . . .

Steadily the labor at headquarters in Philadelphia has increased. Relief has been sought, and by division of work and systematic arrangement, found. Much that was done at first in the central office, has been turned over to the agencies at Washington, Baltimore, and elsewhere.

. . . . .

The commission has had two general divisions of labor, the one at a distance from, the other at the seat of war. The work in camps and hospitals at a distance from the scenes of conflict, has been under the charge of Young Men's Christian Associations, in such places as have loyal associations in them willing to undertake it, and of Army Committees formed for the purpose in other places.

The work at the seat of the war has been done by the Commission, aided by the Associations and Committees near the scenes of conflict.

. . . . .

Delegates are fitted out at our headquarters in Philadelphia, each with his commission with railroad passes indorsed on it, his memorandum-book to take notes in and instructions to guide him, his haversack, stored with food for body and soul to those needing it, his blanket and strap, to be his bed at night, in a strait, and if going to the battle-field, his bucket and cup, and lantern and candle, enable him to give drink to the famishing, by night as well as by day.

Supplies of stores and publications are sent forward for them to the rooms of our committees or agents nearest the field of their work; and for the battle-field, a trunk for each company of three, five, or six delegates . . . packed with choicest and best articles, for instant use for the suffering on the field, is taken with them as personal baggage, to make sure they have them the moment they get there.

They are divided into companies, and each company has its captain appointed, and they are each supplied with a metallic badge, neatly engraven—CHRISTIAN COMMISSION, to be pinned upon the breast of his coat, and worn to distinguish him in any company.

. . . Forewarned of a coming battle, stores are sent in advance. These trunks are kept on hand ready packed, and stores are kept packed . . . in boxes and barrels, marked "Stores for the next battle." And when forewarned of a battle approaching, they are sent to the most convenient place in the vicinity of it.

Our delegates are instructed to report themselves in all possible cases to the proper authorities, whether officers, surgeons, or chaplains . . . for instruction and direction, and in every case to respect the established regulations.

Three hundred and fifty-six delegates have been sent, and three thousand six hundred and ninety-one boxes, &c., of stores and publications have been distributed by them in person.

These delegates have aided in the relief of many thousands of the wounded on the field, and in their removal to comfortable hospitals. They have washed and dressed them, taken off their bloody, filthy garments, and put on those that were clean and comfortable; cooked and given them food; prepared and given them drink by the way. They have prayerfully pointed the dying to Jesus, and when dead given them Christian burial; in some instances digging the grave with their own hands. They have written and mailed letters for them to their friends, have met their yearnings for sympathy, attended to dying requests, and in many other ways comforted, instructed, cheered, and benefited them.

They have preached the Gospel in camps and hospitals, from man to man, tent to tent, to little groups and vast assemblies, in temporary chapels and under the broad canopy of the heavens, and afforded Christian ministries in all the many forms needed by our brave men.

Men of all sections of our country, and of all segments of our army, have been alike and impartially cared for by our delegates. They do not ask what State a suffering soldier is from, or what regiment he belongs to, before giving him relief.

. . . . .

Stores and publications, amounting in value to one hundred and forty-two thousand one hundred and fifty dollars, have been distributed to soldiers in hospitals and camps.

. . . . .

Aid has been given in the formation of libraries, and in securing newspapers and the larger periodicals for reading-rooms in some of the United States General Hospitals. . . .[5]

One of the most effective, and certainly the best known, of the unofficial, voluntary civilian organizations, was the United States Sanitary Commission. As a pressure group, it was partially responsible for bringing about, through an act of Congress, a reorganization of the Medical Department of the Army, and the appointment of Dr. William A. Hammond as Surgeon General. It has been called "a great machine running side by side with the Medical Bureau wherever it went." In 1864, the New York Evening Post *described its activities.*

Almost everybody, now-a-days, is a stock-holder in the United States Sanitary Commission; and being so, feels desirous to know how the capital, of which he or she furnished a part, is used. Those who helped to collect a million in New York, and six hundred thousand dollars in Brooklyn, not to speak of the other sums gathered in Boston and elsewhere during the past winter, are curious to know if these dollars are really benefitting our wounded brethren, and whether the relief and comfort given is in proportion to the liberality of the public. This desire is reasonable, and we have taken some pains to secure, from authentic and independent sources, the information required to satisfy it. The particulars which we print below are the substance of reports made to us by several gentlemen, not officially connected with the Sanitary Commission, who have visited Washington, Belle Plain and Fredericksburgh [*sic*], and have seen there what is done by the Commission.

It is known that there is at Washington a Central Depot of the Sanitary Commission. At this place there was, before Grant crossed the Rapidan, a corps of fifty trained and skilled men, used to the care of the wounded, experienced in cooking, handling the wounded, and in all the services which position in the field suggests for making the helpless comfortable. This is the field-corps—its members are paid, and are under military discipline. They form a nucleus around which is gathered a larger corps of volunteer attendants and agents, ladies and gentlemen who serve at their own expense, and who come only at the call of the Commission. At the Central Depot, of course, large supplies of suitable clothing and food are stored. Two items, thirty thousand woollen [*sic*] shirts, and a ton of condensed milk, will give the reader some idea of the extent of these stores; while the following items, picked hastily and at random from an inventory now before us, will show the great variety of articles needed: hay for bedding, oakum for wounds, stockings, shirts, drawers, trowsers, chip hats, pillows for the head and for stumps of limbs, slings of various sizes, paper, envelopes, pencils, sponges, ring-pads for wounds, towels, brooms, buckets, bed-pans, crutches, drinking cups, matches, tobacco, pipes, liquors of different kinds, oranges and lemons, spoons, soft bread, oatmeal, cornstarch, farina, dishes of different kinds, tents, bedticks, shoes, slippers, beefsteak, blackberry cordial, canned fruits and vegetables, dried fruits, pickled onions and cabbage, lanterns, candles, soap, canes, fans. We have selected from the long list only a part of the articles—such part as is most suggestive of the various wants of the helpless and maimed sufferers. . . .[6]

At times, the Northern towns and cities located close to army camps (such as Springfield, Illinois) resented and feared the effects of the war in a very tangible way. Rowdy elements among the troops invaded the peace and quiet of the town or countryside and aroused fears about the future of society, when such hooligans should return to it after the war.

Some dozen or more soldiers from Camp Yates were in the City yesterday afternoon, drunk, swaggering in the streets and bullying the citizens. Some of them we recognized as having been in the calaboose before. Now, if their captain will continue to allow these men to leave the camp and disturb the peace of the city, we hope the police will endeavor to put a stop to the practice. Heretofore, when a soldier raised a muss and got into the calaboose, it has been customary to deliver him up on the demand of his captain. Let it be understood that this will not be allowed any more, but that the civil authorities will exercise full jurisdiction over these offenders, and punish them as they do others, and we will have fewer breaches of order and of law. We are getting tired of these disorderly soldiers. There are but few of them, but they create a good deal of trouble.[7]

Perhaps to a greater degree than in cities and towns, the rural population, during the first distracting year of war, tried to cling to accustomed ways of life. But the war did intervene, so that things were not quite as they had been before. When they survived, the most typical of rural diversions, the agricultural fairs, were altered in 1861. The executive committee of the Illinois State Agricultural Society decided that, at their annual exhibition for that year (held in Chicago), they would give gold medals to the best firearms and materiel of war exhibited, along with prizes for garden vegetables and fruits. The effort to make the Crawford County, Ohio, fair bigger and better than it had been in peacetime was valiant, but the results were disappointing.

AUGUST 16, 1861.

It is hoped that the farmers and town people of Crawford will not neglect to make preparations for the next Fair to be held in Bucyrus, on the 18th, 19th and 20th of September next. The increased number of improved horses and cattle, the orchards laden with the best of fruit, and the fields that have already harvested an abundant yield of grain, added to the advance of arts and manufactures, place it within the means of our citizens to get up a most interesting agricultural and mechanical show. We know that the cry of "hard times" is not altogether unfounded, and that we are passing through an exciting era of our national history, but our wealth and happiness, and advance in intelligence and social condition, depends in a great measure upon ourselves and we know of no better way to encourage effect in these respects, than by showing what we have already accomplished, through the agency of our County Fair. But for many of the attractive features of the fair, the Society must depend upon the skill, industry and kindness of the ladies. Our citizens will recollect the deficiency last season in the departments, more especially depending upon the ladies for their attractiveness, and we trust the ladies of our town and county, who possess as much capability as any in the State, will see that these departments are properly adorned with their handiwork, and make it the most interesting part of the exhibition.

AUGUST 23, 1861.

We understand that great preparations are being made for our coming County Fair.

This is as it should be. If our country be in trouble, the growth of crops and stock, and the labor of our intelligent artizans, still continues, and our County Fair promises to be more attractive than usual, instead of less so.

Every one *can* do something to make our Fair more attractive, and if every one *will* do so, there will be no better Fair held this year throughout the Union.

Every class of ingenuity is this year encouraged with a comprehensiveness beyond precedent. From the riving out of a couple of hundred shingles, the preparation of an ox yoke, of half a dozen hickory brooms, and of a good farm basket, up to the preparation by expensive machinery of reapers, mowers and ornamental house work.

Those possessing articles of curiosity or the productions of their own refined taste, are respectfully requested to exhibit them (See rule 11)

IN THE FAIR

The taste of the ladies, the industry of the laborer, the enterprise of the ambitious, the liberality of the capitalists, the judgment and interest of all are appealed to, and present indications seem to show that the appeal will be met with unexampled success.

MUSICIANS—Have you noticed the liberal premiums offered to encourage your talent, taste and refining exercises?

MILITARY COMPANIES—Are you preparing for such a display as will do credit not only to your township, but to your intelligence and patriotism as individuals?

MILITARY BANDS—Are you preparing to arouse the already active patriotism of all, by the "spirit stirring drum, and ear piercing fife?"

OUR FIRE COMPANIES—We know you are on hand, and preparing to maintain the honor of our town against all competitors.

PLOUGHMEN—Who are going to carry off the liberal premiums awarded here? We hope in our hearts that some poor portionless boy, will bear away the banner. We hope too that he will not do this without a warm and honorable strife, with those who are neither poor nor portionless.

LADIES—Without you we can do but little. We depend upon your taste, skill, judgment and energy to adorn our halls, and we know that the productions of your handiwork will be there, for when were you ever backward in any laudable undertaking?

LET ALL BE ON HAND—If our surrounding counties stop their Fairs, we cordially invite them to ours, and Little Crawford will loom out as greatly as usual.

SEPTEMBER 27, 1861.

The Fair last week was in one particular a success, and in another, a failure. Financially, it was a success, as the attendance was almost as large as usual, and the receipts sufficiently large to pay the current expenses—a result unlooked for this year. But the exhibition was a failure. A number of those who have heretofore taken an interest in the institution, were opposed to holding a Fair this season, and after it had been decided to hold it, instead of assisting to make it what it should be, threw cold water upon the enterprise, from as many pipes as they could control. The impression got abroad that it was doomed to be a failure, and of course it was. The exhibition of stock was very light, the mechanical department was almost nothing. Floral Hall was ditto, and the exhibition of Fruits and Vegetables very slim.

We regret this exceedingly. The Agricultural Society have done a good work in stimulating the farmers and mechanics of the county, and it should be kept up and improved every year. With as progressive farmers as any in the State, with the richest soil, and the finest stock, there is no reason why the Annual Fair should not be superior to anything of the kind in Northern Ohio. All that is necessary to make it so, is for the farmers and mechanics to take hold of it and say that it shall be good, and it will be. Grounds should be purchased and permanently fitted up, and the institution put into proper trim at once. We hope our enterprising citizens will not allow the Society to languish and finally die out. It is too powerful an instrument for good to be lost. We shall refer to this subject again.[8]

Even though the impact of the war was pervasive, and sooner or later felt everywhere, in many respects, and for most people, life went on much as usual. Thus, in 1864, when the struggle was in its fourth year, an English visitor in Boston found no trace of it worth recording. Instead, he was impressed with solidity and stability. To him, wartime Boston was a place where one of its leading citizens could live the life of a "model English gentleman."

. . . The general features of the city are not in any way particularly remarkable. It is not a Paris, nor a London; but there is a good old English stability about the red-brick buildings, a wealthy comfort in the private mansions, a luxurious display in the windows of the stores, and a pleasant undulation in the ground on which the city stands, that compensate for the lack of a Tuilleries or a St. Paul's, and, to my mind, make Boston a very delightful city. But, after all, I suspect its chief feature of recommendation in my eyes was its similarity to an English town; and if there had only been a little smoke in the atmosphere, and none of those beautiful Virginian creepers twining up the faces of the private houses, I could have imagined myself at home again in one of our quiet, old-fashioned cities. . . .

The next day I was introduced by my two fellow-passengers from England, whom I met here by arrangement, to a well-known Boston man, Mr. Loring. He made his fortune at the Bar, where he attained a very high position, and has now retired to live at ease upon the earnings of his early labours. Nothing could exceed the civility with which he treated me, a perfect stranger to him, simply upon the introduction of my companions, who carried a letter to him from an English friend. He took us to all the chief objects of interest in the city: to the Court House, the Museum, the Public Library, and the Law Court; then to his club, an extremely comfortable establishment . . . and, finally he invited us to spend a day with him at his country seat on the sea-shore, about twenty miles from Boston, which we did; and a very pleasant day it was. The train soon ran us down to Salem, a fashionable watering-place of the Bostonians, and at the next station, where we dismounted, we found in waiting for us a handsome carriage and pair, sent by our host to take us up to his house. The gate leading to his property was close by, and thence we had a most lovely drive through a prettily wooded glen, resembling those sweet dells that abound in the Scottish Highlands, and at the end of it we emerged upon a low rocky promontory, running out into the bay of Salem, on the margin of which stood one of the prettiest summer residences conceivable. There our host received us, and after an introduction to his family, we started with him to survey his grounds. They were very tastefully laid out. Nature had done the greater portion of the work for him; what artificial additions he had made were in excellent harmony with the original. A few skilful arrangements of loose boulder stones, a wild creeper dexterously trained, a natural cavern ingeniously taken advantage of, sufficed to enhance the beauty of this leaf from Nature's book, and afford a specimen of landscape gardening which I have rarely seen equalled. His farm was as neat as his garden. His cattle of good breed, some of them fine Alderneys. His pigs, to my surprise, Suffolk. . . . His stables, not less neat and wholesome. . . . His barn and yards perfect models of what farm premises should be.

. . . Here was the model English gentleman reproduced in all his ease and luxury, surrounded by the comforts of an elegant house, a large circle of friends and visitors, carriages and horses for the pretty drives in the neighborhood, yachts and sailing boats for the bay, and spending his leisure hours of relaxation from the cares of public life in just the sort of model farming which pleases the pride and pilfers the pockets of the genuine squire in Old England. . . .[9]

There were draft riots in New York City. But the riots were bred in the slums and its victims were mostly the unfortunate creatures of the slums. As in Boston, New York's well-to-do lived securely. Nor did the war interfere unduly with pleasant summer vacations in nearby country homes.

. . . There is a large class of prosperous merchants, bankers, professional men and wealthy citizens who have the tastes and means to command such enjoyments and luxuries as the country affords; who need the change in scenes, associations, employments and objects of interest, for themselves and their households, and who enjoy with keen relish, the seclusion, the comparative freedom from restraint, the pure, sweet air, the broad, open sunshine, and the numerous other rural advantages which are essentially denied them in their city homes.

In former years this class of people resorted almost exclusively to the sea-side, and to a few popular mineral springs, taking in, perhaps, Niagara in their transit, and rarely venturing into the wild and unexplored region of Lake George. They returned to town in the early days of September, with many a backward, longing look at the attractions and delights from which they reluctantly tore themselves away, and settled down again to the weary tread-mill of business. But for some years past this class has largely increased in number, and instead of confining themselves to their former resorts, they now seek the upper country, and prolong their stay in the glorious days of Autumn. Many of them have provided permanent summer homes, among the hills and on the lake or river shores. They have bought, and built, and planted, until they have identified themselves with the chosen spot, and as their trees have taken root in the fertile soil, so have their affections taken root in the beautiful country. They hasten gladly to these rural scenes with the opening of Summer, and they leave them with great regret when the exigencies of business require their presence in the city,—when . . . the passenger birds fly Southward. This class of our population is provided for. Their ample means assure them a free choice of summer resorts, and adequate command of all the appliances of pleasant country living.[10]

If a gentleman, or his wife, preferred fashionable resorts to a quiet summer home—and if he could afford it—war did not prevent him from indulging his taste.

Although it reached the apex of its reputation later, Newport, Rhode Island, during the war, was already a summer focal point for wealth and society. As described in the New York Evening Post, *it appears to have been untouched by war. Apparently not even the band leaders felt it appropriate to play national airs, and the* Post's *correspondent complained, not on the grounds that such songs might be more fitting, but because the musicians were not skillful enough for opera music.*

. . . Newport is just now in the very height of the season in point of numbers, fashion, and gayety. The hotels are all crowded to their utmost capacity, although in the early part of the season it was predicted that some of them would be compelled to close on account of the scarcity of guests and the improbability of their increasing. . . . The Ocean House is the favorite hotel, being much larger and far better located than any of the others. It is also admirably well kept, and the company is made up of quiet, orderly, refined people, who come to enjoy the surf-bathing and cool breezes for which the place is so justly celebrated.

Every evening an excellent band is stationed in the large hall, and the music contributes very greatly to the pleasure of the guests. It is a somewhat singular fact, and one which I regret to feel bound to mention, that the leader has so far, since I have been here, omitted playing our national airs. . . . It may not be improper further to suggest that all leaders of orchestras and bands seem to think it essential to their reputation as scientific artists that they should play nothing but elaborate music. This would be all well enough if the listeners were artists or amateurs, but the truth is that two-thirds of those who usually make up an audience at a concert make no profession of a knowledge of music, and will generally be far better pleased with simple familiar airs than with elaborate scientific "opera" music.

The rides about Newport are far more pleasant and agreeable than any of the other popular summer resorts that I have any knowledge of. In this respect, as well as in point of climate, Saratoga is no comparison to it. Bellevue avenue, running about three miles south from the Ocean House to the sea, is lined on both sides with beautiful cottages situated from five to fifteen rods back from the line of the street, and surrounded with grounds highly ornamented with shrubbery and trees. On this avenue the most wealthy visitors have secured locations for summer residences—some truly splendid, among which may be mentioned those of "M. Barreda, Peruvian Minister," Gardner Brewer, merchant prince of Boston, and August Belmont, late Minister to the Hague and now the Chairman of the National Democratic Committee.

On Bellevue avenue every pleasant afternoon there is a magnificent display of vehicles of every description. Just now the rage seems to be for "four-in-hand" teams, of which there are about a half dozen here, and more expected. So far as style is concerned, it is generally conceded that the "turn-out" of L. W. Jerome, the wealthy Wall street banker, is superior to all others, though there are one or two that overmatch his in point of speed and value. . . . The equipage that throws all others in the shade, and causes them to "pale their ineffectual fires," is that of the aforementioned chairman of the Democratic National Committee. It consists of a low barouche drawn by four elegant and fiery "thorough-breds," with postilions mounted on the left or "near" horse of each pair. Two footmen in extreme livery are suspended from a high seat on the back of the carriage, technically called the "rumble." The barouche is lined with rich satin damask, and the outside trimmings are of heavy gilt. The postilions are dressed in buckskin breeches and high top boots, with black silk velvet jackets and caps highly ornamented with gold lace. The men are peculiarly well formed, having been selected and trained in Europe with especial reference to their "build" and the extra size of their "calves." Their livery is imported at a cost of about $1,000 a suit, and the cost of the whole affair may be conjectured when I state that the horses are valued at $25,000, the carriage at $5,000, and the harness and other trappings at $3,000. When the royal *cortege* makes its appearance on the avenue with the democratic prince in full costume, all other vehicles instinctively give way, as though the occupant was indeed a "crowned head." The stables of his democratic majesty are said to contain some forty horses. . . .[11]

If surf bathing, carriage rides, and band music were not to the taste of Northerners seeking recreation, other avenues were open. Some sports prospered. Baseball increased in popularity during the latter years of the war; so did fishing. Horse racing flourished. Although inaccessible to most New Yorkers, the Fashion Course on Long Island often attracted as many as ten thousand spectators to the trotting races.

As we all along predicted, the first of the great races between the famous black gelding, General Butler, and the celebrated stallion, George M. Patchen, drew an immense multitude to the Fashion Course. We do not remember ever to have seen as many people congregated at one time in that grand place of resort. It is well that the builders of the great stand knew how to make a substantial structure, for, had they not done so, it must have tottered to its foundation and come down in ruins on Wednesday, under pressure of the masses who swarmed all over it. The like was never seen! . . . At the same time, the new stand was fully occupied; and those portions of each devoted to the especial accommodation of the ladies, were thronged to their utmost capacity with beauty and fashion. Besides this, all the apartments of the Club House, affording a sight of the course, were also filled with ladies. . . . In the inside circle, that is, the great body of the grounds, the throng of vehicles was such as we never saw before. Almost as far as the eye could reach, there was a black mass of carriages and horses, with pedestrians wending in and out among them. There were some very elegant and gay turnouts, belonging to gentlemen of the city, and horsed with pairs of good trotters. . . . Now, as the black gelding Butler and the bay stallion George M. Patchen, are taken to be two of the best trotting horses that this country, which really originated the breed, has ever produced, it is no wonder that their six matches for $30,000, at one and two-mile heats, in harness, to wagon and under saddle, produced a deal of excitement among the lovers, owners, breeders, dealers and employers of the trotting horse. These are legion; everybody that owns a trotter up to ten miles an hour upon the road, fondly hopes to see the day when he will fly along in 2m. 40s., and feels a sort of personal interest and concernment in the fine trots.

. . . . .

The refreshment tables under the main stand were under the management of Mr. Thomas Johnson, who conducted everything as well as could be. The crowd was immense, and sometimes remarkably obstrepulous [*sic*]. Several times there was a fracas, and while fighting they would rush out on to the stretch, where some were severely handled. The pickpockets were too numerous, too bold, and too intimately organized to be tolerated on future occasions. . . . This class of persons must not be allowed to drive the people away from the scenes of sport and recreation. . . .[12]

Prizefights generally were illegal. Nonetheless, if they were willing to make the effort, sportsmen could occasionally see one. Just ten days after the bloody battle of Chancellorsville, with Lee gathering his forces for the northward sweep that was to culminate at Gettysburg six weeks later, less than a hundred miles away from the site of that epochal battle, the "Great Prize Fight" was fought at Charlestown, Maryland, a village on the railroad line between Philadelphia and Baltimore. The spirit was one of carnival; war was present only in the persons of the gladiators. As such wars go it was epic—sixty-one rounds with bare fists.

. . . In order to be in time, and to have an opportunity to look about them before the hour of action arrived, many left this city on Sunday evening and by the morning trains on Monday. It was not, however, until the evening trains from New York reached Philadelphia that a good conception could be had of the multitude bound to the scene of the fight. In and about the principal hotels, there was a crowd like that which assembles on the eve of a great political convention. Charlestown, in Maryland, was known to be the chosen place, and the night trains took on the major part of those who intended to be present. At about two in the morning, a halt was come to at a solitary sort of station, where two or three scattering frame tenements were the only buildings in sight. These were already mostly occupied, and some hundreds passed the balance of the night in a sort of *bivouac* under the rail fences. Fires were built, stories were told, jokes ran round like quicksilver, and, in anticipation of the commencement of operations early in the morning, the crowd was very jolly. At dawn of day, a move was made down toward the river, where the site chosen for the ring had been discovered by parties of scouts who had gone out for the purpose in the darkness. It was upon a little level spot, quite close to the river, and on the pitch of a slope of green turf. Those who had provided a snack for breakfast, now took it with the keen appetite and relish a night passed in the open air creates. The morning was misty, thickly overcast, and threatening rain. The ring was pitched under the superintendence of Kit Burns and Coburn's brother, Jim, and when all was in readiness, the couple of thousands, or thereabouts, already present, began to look for the arrival of the men. But hours wore away, and the latter did not come. The best of feeling seemed to prevail, but not unaccompanied with some impatient expressions at the tardiness of the principals and their seconds. If there had been any efforts made by the neighboring authorities to put in a stay of proceedings, they might have done it now. Once or twice there was a cry that the men were coming, and the scattered crowd rushed tumultuously to the ropes to secure good positions. These were false alarms. . . . A cold wind sprang up from the bay, and the waves began to tumble in upon the shingly beach, ominous enough of a coming storm. . . .

We marvelled much at the long delay; but soon after the arrival of the train from the South, the immense concourse of people packed up close to the ropes, and it was plain that the moment of action was nearly come. Meantime, however, stages had been erected for the better accommodation of many, and country carts drawn up and devoted to the same purpose. The farmers' wives in the surrounding houses had also reaped a harvest by selling coffee, pancakes and fried pork, to the hungry multitude; and an enterprising individual, who had the foresight to provide an extempore bar, by means of a barrel of whisky, two bottles and one glass, drove a roaring trade.

At last, Ned Price sprang briskly into the ring, and, calling the company to order, made one of those neat speeches which fully entitle him to succeed Harry Holt in the title of "Cicero of the Ring." It was terse, to the purpose and remarkable for good sense, as well as for excellent delivery. He said that he had been appointed referee, and, though it was against his inclination, he had agreed to act. The best man must win. No quibble would be allowed to decide it; and, before proceedings commenced, everybody must get back ten feet from the ropes of the inner ring. Persuaded no less by his determination than by his eloquence, the crowd forthwith got back from the inner ropes.

McCool first appeared, having for his seconds Australian Kelly and Johnny Roche, with Tom Chaffers for bottle holder and Harry Hill for Umpire. He was received with a loud cheer. But it was not like the thundering hurrah which greeted Coburn on his arrival. Jim Cusick and Hen. [*sic*] Winkle attended the latter, with Frank McIntire for bottle holder and Captain Norton for Umpire. The toss for choice of corners was won by McCool. Up to this time the odds of ten to eight had been laid upon Coburn; but now, as if inspired by the confident bearing of McCool, and also by his manifest great size in comparison with that of Coburn, the friends of the western man offered 90 to 100 and laid it several times. It was soon followed by a bet of 100 even. Joe now walked across the ring towards his formidable looking opponent and offered to lay $500 even on himself. This was taken, and McCool soon after offering to bet $200 more, that was also wagered by the principals. They were stripped. Joe looked well enough to eye and his muscular development showed to great advantage. But it was understood that he had not been altogether well internally for a few days and he had a plaster on his abdomen. He stands nearly five feet ten, and has that upright sort of bearing which is said to have made *Louis le Grand* look like a tall man. But now, compared to McCool, he looked little. The latter is six feet one, and his weight was 180 lb. He had not, however, the muscular developement of Coburn, . . . About three thousand people were now present, for the last train had brought up a strong division from Washington and Baltimore.

THE FIGHT

Round 1 McCool's position was bad. His left arm was stuck out like a hedge-stake, and his right not held so as to cover the body and guard the head. Coburn, with his hands well up, and lightly poised upon feet that never kept the same place or position for more than an instant at a time, sparred with that elegance and readiness which distinguishes his style in the boxing school. McCool led off out of distance, and before he could recover, Coburn planted left and right, drawing first blood from the top of the cheek bone. They now closed, and after a trifling attempt to fib his man McCool threw him, but not heavily.

. . . . .

Round 61 Coburn hit his man right and left in the middle of the head, and was going at him again, when poor Mac fell on his face.

Five times more the game fellow came up, but it was only to be hit and sent down, without the power of making any return. Kelly then threw up the sponge, and Coburn was the winner in one hour and ten minutes.[13]

Unless they were farmers, most Americans did not own country homes. Nor did they spend their vacations at Newport or attend harness races and prizefights. They were at work. Life for the majority, in its daily routine, was not greatly altered. Wartime descriptions of Lewiston, Maine, and the countryside surrounding Chester, New Hampshire, could be descriptions of New England at peace.

Lewiston was a mill town. During the first three years of the war its population increased by 1,333. Robert Ferguson, an English clergyman and popularizing historian, visited it.

From Portland I proceeded to a place called Lewiston—a rising seat of manufactures. Here, I was informed by one of my fellow passengers on board the *Persia*, a New England engineer, are some of the finest and newest cotton mills of the United States. The power is supplied by the Androscoggin river, which here makes a picturesque fall of fifty feet. . . .

"What a place for churches!" was my first thought when I awoke in the morning, and heard bells ringing all around slowly and solemnly as if for service, while from the distance came a grand, deep note as if from some old cathedral. But I remembered in a moment what I had heard of the great bell at the Androscoggin Mill, which is said to be the same size and weight as that of St. Paul's, weighing 11,000 pounds, and then I knew that these were factory bells, which seemed to say in their grave and solemn tones, "*laborare est orare.*" . . .

The workers had, on the whole, much the same appearance as in England, for the days when the factory girls carried parasols and wrote poetry, as we used to read of their doing at Lowell, have long since been at an end. A great part of them live in boarding houses belonging to the company, and subject to strict regulations. The houses close at ten at night, and no one is admitted after that hour without reasonable excuse. Any irregularity of conduct on the part of any of the inmates is to be instantly reported by the mistress to the manager. Sunday is to be observed with strict decorum; all the inmates to be vaccinated, etc. Wholesome as these regulations are, I doubt whether our English operatives would be found very ready to submit to so much discipline.

These mills are all owned by joint-stock companies, and have, as I was informed, been kept at work all through the cotton famine. One of them had just declared a dividend of fourteen per cent., which is enough to make the mouths of English mill-owners water. I apprehend, however, that this result has been owing rather to the rise in gold than the profits in manufacturing.

Lewiston, as I was informed, is the only place in the State of Maine where the law against the sale of intoxicating drinks is at present strictly carried out. . . .[14]

Life in rural New England, the psychology of its people, and their adjustments to wartime demands were described in a letter written in 1864 to the editor of The Country Gentleman.

. . . Chester, N[ew] H[ampshire] . . . is on the height of land between the Atlantic Ocean at Boar's Head in Hampton, and the Merrimac river at Manchester, twelve miles from the latter place, twenty-five from the Ocean and fifty from Boston. To a man who was not born to it, all this region looks hard and unproductive. There are no broad prairies, no rich bottom lands—only rocky hills, and between them small tracts of swamp land. Although the country has been settled a hundred and thirty years, a great portion of it is covered with wood and timber. The best land is usually upon the high swells, and the fields which have been cleared of stones and well cultivated, are excellent for fruit and hay, yet still require hard work for any cultivated crop. Fields that have been under the plow for a hundred years continue to furnish a good crop of stones at each new plowing, and if you presume to set your plow two inches deeper than your father set his, a double crop of stones and labor is your sure reward. Yet this is a country blessed, in all that makes life desirable, far above the average of even our own favored nation, infinitely above England or France, usually esteemed the foremost nations of the world. Here are illustrated what we profess to prize as above all price, the republican ideas of independence and equality. Education and property are fairly distributed, and if none are very rich, none are in want of the comforts of life. I to-day heard a well-informed citizen remark that even now, in the midst of war, it would be difficult for a person inclined to be charitable to find in this town a person who is fairly the object of charity. A half-dozen insane, or idiotic, or foreign paupers, are supported on what we call a "poor farm," and the rest of the population are able to take care of themselves.

A stranger here always inquires, how do the people live? What do they raise?

We may answer the last question by saying they raise men. This little town, of about 1,300 people, which cast just 278 votes for Governor in 1863, has sent as soldiers to the war, 130 men, and is now two ahead of all the calls upon it. Two citizens or natives of Chester have been Governors of the State; two Chief Justices; two Senators in Congress; one Attorney General, and so on through a long list, showing, perhaps, that our boasted equality gives this deserving town somewhat more than a mathematical proportion of the honors.

How the people live in these small New England towns is no easy question to answer. Indeed, it cannot be answered, except in detail. In general, they do not live by farming, they do not live by manufacturing; they do not live on the interest of their money, for they have none; yet they live, and live well and happily and independently. If we look at an individual we know how he and his family are supported, for here in the country we know all our neighbors' affairs. Here is what we call a farmer: He has one or two hundred acres of land, most of it wood-land and rough pasture. He keeps perhaps twenty head of cattle, one horse, a few sheep, three or four swine and some poultry. He labors daily with his hands, performing most of the hard work on his farm, plowing with oxen, his boys helping him when necessary. He plants say three or four acres of corn and potatoes, sows as many with oats, or rye, or barley; raises all his vegetables, pork, butter and corn, and sells a little, but not much of each. The growth of his stock is worth one or two hundred dollars a year. He has an orchard which gives him apples worth as much more. He cuts every year some timber and wood for market. His children all attend school half or two-thirds the year, for education is what everybody prizes as the road to respectability, if not to fortune. The wife works, but she does not like to see her daughters work, but prefers to have them attend school and to learn music. The daughters do not go out to service; they regard that as degrading. They sometimes go into the mills at Manchester, where they are well paid and live respectably, and save money, if they have a mind so to do. Or they became teachers, for somehow New England girls take a much finer polish than the boys, and all the country knows that if female teachers are wanted, New England girls best supply the want. The boys "work out" when they are eighteen or twenty, having no such pride about service as the girls have, and either earn money with which to go to college or buy land at the West. The father and mother stick by the old farm, neither poor nor rich, usually comforted by seeing their children prosperous, though usually not more than one son remains with them, and so the generations go. When the farmer dies, he leaves to the son who has remained at home, but little except the farm, but his life has been well spent, his family well cared for through a good education, and nobody suffers because his estate is small. . . .

This is a great country for apples, and although the climate is severe, the Baldwin thrives wonderfully on these hill-sides, and peaches have usually flourished better on the hills than on more level lands in a warmer climate. The frost holds off two or three weeks later on the hill than on the plains, so that the Isabella grape in a majority of seasons will ripen tolerably well in the open air.

I have alluded to manufacturing as a source of profit. Although there is no water power nearer than Manchester of any account, there is always some branch of home industry which helps the females of the family to supply their own wants.

For many years all the women in the neighborhood were engaged in making palm leaf hats, taking the raw material of the traders, who paid them in goods or money for their labor, which they performed at home. Now the same material in the nicer form is manufactured into the kind of hats known as Bogota, which most of your readers vainly imagine to be imported from some unknown country. I have one for which I last year paid 50 cents in this village, very much like yours, Messrs. Editors, for which you paid six times as much. Of late the manufacture of shoes has to some extent afforded employment to persons of both sexes. . . .[15]

Chicago was a lustier, less-inhibited reflection of Boston or New York. There, too, there were "elegant residences" and rows of houses of "the meanest kind." There, too, growth and improvement were not interrupted by war. Between 1860 and 1865, the population increased from 109,260 to 196,000.

. . . Just now Chicago is in a transition state. It is rapidly passing from a condition of bottomless mud to Nicolson pavement; and from the era of wooden shanties to permanent and costly buildings. It is now undergoing a change, and is gradually expanding outward and upward and is hardening into brick and marble. This hardening process, commencing only a few years back, has extended away in every direction until the march of improvement has driven the flimsy wooden structures well into the suburbs.

[In] the West Division . . . the list [of "elegant private residences"] is headed with the residence of Peter Schuttler, because it is the most costly structure of the kind, not merely in Chicago, but, with few exceptions, in the United States. It is located on the corner of Adams and Aberdeen Streets . . . and with grounds occupies one quarter of the entire square. It is Norman in style, is built of brick, and cost $200,000. Its grounds are spacious and enclosed with a light iron fence; and these grounds, so far as their area will permit, are handsomely laid out with winding walks and shrubbery, and planted with a great variety of shade and flowering vegetation. The house is lavishly supplied with porticos, balconies, vestibules, cornices, and towers. But this excess of decoration on the exterior is even surpassed by that within. The doors are of fabulous richness, the frescoes are in marvelous profusion; in short all the interior decorations are of the most palatial character.

. . . . .

The North Division contains the houses of the oldest residents, and is the seat of the real aristocracy of the city. On Rush, North Dearborn, Erie, Ontario, Huron, and Pine Streets, are some of the finest residences of the city. . . . Many of these residences are, like the houses of Cambridge, Mass., surrounded by spacious and beautiful grounds filled with a profusion of stately shade trees. . . .

So far as lavish display is concerned, the South Side in some portions has no rival in Chicago, and perhaps not outside New York. In richness of exterior Wabash and Michigan avenues already rival in their location and marble fronts and expensive ornamentation the finest streets in the world. . . . These lofty fronts, coming squarely to the sidewalks, have a glittering, heartless appearance, that stamps them as apt representatives of fashion. They have display, richness, a sort of stern unpitying grandeur but no warmth, no geniality.

. . . . .

There are miles of wooden houses of the meanest kind that must be removed, and their place supplied by substantial brick or stone, and there are leagues of wretched, bottomless streets that must be filled, graded, and paved.

. . . . .

Tasteless imitations and abortions . . . make up the bulk of our public and private buildings. . . . [There is also need for] planting of shade trees along our walks, and the filling with plants the squares owned by the city and intended for parks. . . . A thing which would add vastly to the beauty of Chicago, would be the filling up of the unsightly vacancy now existing between Michigan avenue and the railroad piers that cross an inward sweep of the lake. Once filled, this would form one of the finest esplanades in the world. . . .[16]

In 1862, Edward Dicey, an English journalist, visited the United States. Among other places he went to Racine, Wisconsin, where he stayed long enough to perceptively describe the wartime ways of life in a small city.

. . . The amusements of Racine [Wisconsin] are about as limited as if it stood in our midland counties. Judging from the posters of ancient date which hung upon the walls, a passing circus, an itinerant exhibition of Ethiopian minstrels, and an occasional concert, were all the entertainments afforded to the inhabitants. Some of the street advertisements would have been novelties to English townsfolk. A Mrs. Francis Lord Bond was to lecture on Sunday evenings on spiritualism; a fancy fair was to be held for the Catholic convent of St. Ignatius, and a German *choralverein* was to meet weekly for the performance of sacred music. Then, even in this remote and far away corner of the States, there were the war advertisements. The Mayor announced that a great battle was expected daily before Corinth, and requested his townspeople to provide stores beforehand for the relief of the wounded. The Ladies' Aid Committee informed the female public of Racine that there would be a sewing meeting every Friday in the Town Hall, where all ladies were requested to come, and sew bandages for the Union soldiers; every lady to bring her own sewing-machine. Then, too, there was the requisition of the Governor, calling for recruits to fill up the gaps in the ranks of the Wisconsin regiments, who were cut to pieces on the field of Shiloh.

Of course, a town of the importance of Racine must have a press. In more prosperous days there were three dailies published there; but times were bad, and the dailies had collapsed into weeklies. These were the *Advocate*, the *Press*, the *Democrat*; and a German paper, the *Volksblatt*. As a sample of a Western country newspaper, let me take a copy I picked up of the *Racine Advocate*. It is of the regular unwieldy English four page size, and costs six shillings annually, or five halfpence a single number, and is headed with a poetical declaration of faith, that

"Pledged but to truth, to liberty and law,
No favours win us, and no fears shall awe."

The advertisements, which occupy two of the four pages, are chiefly of patent medicines, business-cards, and foreclosure sales. The local news, as in all American country papers, is extremely meagre, and there are no law reports or accounts of country meetings. The politics of the paper are staunch Republican and antislavery, and the leading articles are well written, and all on questions of public not local politics, such as the Confiscation Bill, General Hunter's Proclamation, and Federal Taxation. . . . There were letters from the war, copied out of New York papers, and lists of the killed and wounded in the Wisconsin regiments; but fully one page of the paper was occupied by short tales and poems. When I say that their headings were, "How the Bachelor was Won," "A Girl's Wardrobe," "Gone Before," and "Katie Lee," the reader will have no difficulty in realizing to himself what the description of intellectual varieties afforded by the *Advocate* consisted of. . . .

Society in Racine is still in a primitive stage. Dinner-parties are unknown, and balls are events of great rarity; but tea-parties, to which you are invited on the morning of the day, are of constant occurrence. Probably there is as much scandal and gossip here as in an Old World country-town; but there are not, as yet, the social divisions which exist with us. If you inquire the names of the owners of the handsomest houses in Racine, you will find that one, perhaps, began life as a stable-boy, another was a waiter a few years ago in an hotel of the town, and a third was a brick-layer in early life. On the other hand, some of the poorest people in the place are persons who were of good family and good education in the Old World. A short time ago, the two least reputable members of the community were an ex-member of a fashionable London club and a quondam English nobleman. This very mixture of all classes which you find throughout the West gives a freedom, and also an originality, to the society in small towns, which you would not find under similar circumstances in England. . . .[17]

The westward movement was one of the most significant aspects of nineteenth-century America. War did not interrupt the rush to cheap and, after the passage of the Homestead Act in 1862, free land. A wartime observer reported a people "on the move." Although troops were among them, and caused crowding on the trains, most of the travelers were not going to the battlefronts.

When the war commenced many feared the destruction of railroads in the North, and the interruption of trade and travel from

INTERIOR OF A RAILWAY CAR

rebel raids; but these were few and far between. The increase of travel became so great that companies could scarcely furnish carriages to convey passengers and the numerous troops hastening to the fields of conflict in the South. Whole families, even of the poorest of people travelled extensively; in fact the Americans are a travelling people, few living where they were born; and the most [*sic*] travel in search of better locations, so that railroads and steamboats are often crowded, and the vast prairies often dotted by the white tents and moving waggons of thousands of emigrants, going farther west with their numerous herds, in search of richer lands, larger farms, and better homes. . . .[18]

War has its horrors, but though some of the more reprehensible techniques of advertising were employed during the Civil War, they were not spawned by the war. Nor were they, as yet, all pervading.

Perhaps in the 1860's they constituted but a shadow—a threat of things to come—rather than a present way of life.

An English clergyman reported on—and recoiled from—the wave of the future.

. . . The whole of this beautiful district [Mount Washington, New Hampshire] is very curiously disfigured by the manner in which the rocks are covered with advertisements. The great advertisers in America scorn to confine themselves to newspapers—they stamp their advertisements on the face of nature; so that not only he who runs may read, but must read whether he likes or not. Every prominent rock, not only in the White Mountain district but along the beautiful banks of the Hudson and in every place where travelers must congregate, is carefully painted in large letters with the name of some specific or other—the most persistently obtrusive being the "plantation bitters," and "sozodont," a preparation for the teeth. If you stand by the Profile Mountain to gaze on the wonderful old stone face, your eye is arrested by "Drake's Plantation Bitters," —if you pause by Echo Lake to listen, you are met by invitations to "Try the Sozodont," And echo replies, "O, don't," wrote a wag underneath.

Hardens and invigorates the Gums.

The greatest hit in the advertising line was made by the proprietors of the former on the occasion of Independence Day in Boston, when, as usual, there was a grand display of fireworks, and all Boston was there to see. The final tableau had just died away in darkness, when, in a moment, before the spectators had time to turn away their eyes, another shower of many-coloured lights lighted up the sky, and in all the glory of fire leaped out the words

DRAKE'S PLANTATION BITTERS!

and not in vain are all these ingenious devices if we may trust the statement put forth by the proprietors of this article that there were sold during the past year 179 miles of bottles. . . .

They have too sometimes a very quaint way of calling attention to their advertisements. Thus I saw at St. Louis the walls placarded in very large letters with the words

"AS PURE AS A SOUL WITHOUT SIN."

Drawing near with natural curiosity to know what that could be which laid claim to such a title, I read in very small letters below—THE UNFERMENTED BREAD. . . .[19]

The tide of materialism flowed strong during the first six decades of the nineteenth century, but it did not submerge other aspects of American life. During those years, the great preacher was better known than the great industrialist, and the town minister or judge at least as highly respected as its leading merchant or banker. The creative arts were still provincial and imitative; outside New England, the middle states, and Ohio, universities and colleges were for the most part unimportant institutions. The public school system was in some ways inadequate. But all were respected. Consequently when war came, music, literature, art, letters, and education were an important part of the Northern way of life. All felt the impact of war. Activity was impeded or stimulated here, quality was coarsened or refined there, but on the whole, as in its material aspects, the intellectual life of the North at war flowed in customary channels.

After having been in Europe during the first months of the war, John Sullivan Dwight returned to his duties as music critic in Boston. His joy at being home, together with his love of music, and perhaps a slight twinge of conscience at having been in Europe when patriotic devotion was being poured out for the Union, led him to consider the impact of war upon the cultural life he knew so well.

It is hard to realize that we are in the midst of civil war—that we are fighting the fight, perhaps the final one, of Civilization against a treacherous and arrogant pro-Slavery rebellion, with all its backward and Barbarian proclivities, when we can come together in peace and comfort, just as in the unsuspecting days, to meet the familiar music-loving faces, and listen to a concert of the Mendelssohn Quintette Club. Nothing perhaps in Boston could show so little change to one who went away not dreaming of what the year was to bring forth for us politically, as that quiet scene in Chickering's Hall, on Wednesday evening. There they were, the constant old habitués, the faithful ones, whose presence has been identified with the Quintette concerts from the beginning and throughout their twelve years' history—at least enough of them there were to make it seem the same sphere and the same life, until one began to look for others who were not there. There was the usual greeting and looking round for mutual recognition and congratulation on the return of a new season of quiet intellectual pleasures. . . .

And why should it not be so? Why shall not the inspiring thoughts, the beautiful spirit language, the harmonizing influences of Mendelssohn and Beethoven, claim their full share of attention, be enjoyed and felt as well now as in more peaceful times? Is music a plaything, or a soul's necessity? The real music-lover will not hesitate about the answer. The times of course demand much of sterner work; the best things in the long run must sometimes be postponed to what is best (that is, necessary) for the time being. But whatever stern work is required of us, whatever rough necessities of war are forced upon us peaceful and peace-loving people, we cannot forget that peaceful things are all the while the real end of life, and we must carry on a settled *life* of some sort, in times of war as well as of peace. Our fight is for Civilization; and we do well therefore to keep up all the civilizing elements and influences, and let all the sweet flowers blow, and wholesome fruits ripen, that we can, amid the storm. We must shelter all the seeds and nurseries of Civilization, of true culture and humanity, all the more jealously while the storm rages and while we are compelled to take up the weapons which hopeful Christian progress would fain have laid down forever and forgotten as entirely as the extinct monster races of the early geological periods. Called to fight for peaceful arts and influences, we must, at the same time, cherish and increase them where we can. True to the sterner duty, let us not forget the other also.

And so it naturally works. We are a human, a peace-loving, Christian people. We have found fine Arts, as well as sciences and industries, good for our souls, good for us socially—useful, indispensable—nay attributes and glories of a Free state as distinctive from a state of Slavery. We have not loved music from sheer idleness; it has been earnest breath of life to us. And so we contrive to make room for it even now, and allow the hot chambers of our straightened anxious life a little of its wholesome ventilation even in these dark days of the nation's trial. The traveller returning from abroad, therefore, was not surprised, in setting foot again in dear old Boston, and taking up a newspaper, to find a column full of opera and concert advertisements. We have accepted the crisis; we have chosen our part; we are in to the last drop of life blood, to the last dollar of our means, for the principles of freedom and humanity on which all our peaceful institutions rest. Having settled so much and taken up the war in earnest, we know that God will give us victory, will save his own good cause; and so we can dismiss the paralyzing doubts and fears, which did beset us with the first vague omens of the strife; we can thank God for a clear and hopeful *crisis,* in place of the suppressed poison, which by creeping "compromises" was silently and surely taking possession of the very vitals of our whole glorious system; and, while meeting the exigencies of the crisis in a manly way, we can still provide for a little genial life in our homes, and keep the sacred fires of Art and Education burning. Moreover, he is a poor worker who cannot play also. Mistrust the earnestness of that man, who cannot relax into genial social ways. It were a poor economy for the war, to think of nothing else; to hug to ourselves only that one anxious thought. For the strength and health of the whole body politic we need diversions and enjoyments. These were hardly possible in the first anxious and alarming days; no one could afford music then, for who knew what he could afford? No mind was free for any thought but one. But now our course is settled, and we sink back to some extent into the old wholesome settled ways of life. We must renounce much, make many sacrifices, bear many griefs, but we should not deserve success, nor be in half so fair a way to win it, if we refused God's sunshine. We need Art and Music all the more, now that the existence of all this is threatened. Let us keep these good angels on our side. Therefore it is nothing strange, nothing derogatory to the right temper of the times, that we can still raise an audience for the Quintette Club.[20]

Such doubts as Dwight had were not generally shared. In late August 1864, an article in the New York Musical World and Review *seemed to imply that war actually is a stimulant to composers, and reviewed the progress of music in the North during the American Civil War.*

Although the deadly struggle between two opposing foes, which is commonly called war, seems to exclude the idea of a reign of harmony, of a cultivation of music, history teaches us that the greatest works musical art can claim as its own were written in wartimes, and were enthusiastically espoused and propagated by the amateurs in Europe. Most of Beethoven's symphonies and his *Fidelio* were composed when Europe was convulsed by the Napoleonic wars, and when the Viennese especially, amongst whom the great composer resided, were more than once threatened to witness the horrors of war and the ravages of an invading foe. . . .

We need, however, not look to the past or to foreign countries to prove the truth of the old maxim, that there is an unavoidable link between society, artist, and art: the past three years in our own country have sufficiently illustrated the justice of this remark.

When the war first broke out, the profession, with few exceptions, thought there was an end of their services. Instead of this, their labors have increased, and although their remuneration by the public, shamefully enough has not always kept pace with the high prices of living, yet the teachers have done exceedingly well in all parts of the country. . . .

If we look upon the amount of music heard in these years of trial, we will find at once that it has certainly not diminished. Was the last season not as brilliant as ever? If the opera ever paid, it was last winter. Mr. [Max] Maretzek had never a better *ensemble* at his disposal than during the past season. And he together with the Germans under Mr. [Karl] Anschutz, gave us as good a *repertoire* as can be heard anywhere. As to mere instrumental music we simply point to the crowded attendance at our Philharmonic concerts, here as well as in Brooklyn, also to the great attraction offered by the Soirées for Chamber Music, given by Messrs. [Daniel] Mason and [Theodore] Thomas. The music performed by them last winter was

The Brooklyn Academy of Music: Opening Concert, January 15, 1861

as chaste and refined as can possibly be heard in the most artistic circles in Europe, yet we understand that the appeal made to the amateurs of this city was as heartily responded to as ever, in spite of the "war-times."

The same life and activity greets us in the Publishing Trade. Of course, the war caused a great many pieces and songs to be written, which alone would form in size quite a respectable catalogue. . . . A new market has been opened to our publishers by the enormously high prices which our importers of foreign *engraved* music must necessarily charge, in order to cover their expenses. Here is certainly a new and rich field for our publishers and if they know their best interests, which are not to appeal exclusively to the taste of the masses, they will soon find the means to cultivate that field to their best advantage. What is wanted in this country is the edition of some standard works, not only of a few pieces by the great authors, but, if possible, of their entire catalogue, at least of piano music. . . . Musically the war has done us no harm; on the contrary, besides other advantages, it has stirred up the energy and ambition of our home talents . . . and has, thus far, proved to be a more civilizing agent than anything else.[21]

A description of New York City's Broadway in 1864 shows the world of entertainment in full swing. Opera, concert, drama, minstrel show, circus, and a "feast of reason and the flow of the soul"—from which nude dancing girls had been banished—flourished. The hero of one play was a dragoon officer; otherwise there seems to have been no evidence that the nation was in the third year of one of the bloodiest wars of history.

The theatres in New York are in no way behind those in London in an artistic point of view, and much more airy, cleanly [*sic*] and comfortable. The most fashionable is Wallack's Theatre, and the best Niblo's Gardens. The opera is generally very much patronized; then there is a small French theatre, admirably conducted, and well worth a visit. There is also the Olympic, elegant in itself, well ventilated and commodious, but slightly deficient in talent.

The performances at the Academy of Music and the concerts at Irving Hall are of the first order, and the company very select. The Winter Gardens (as they are called), for theatricals, are well worth a visit. Fox's Theatre, in the Old Bowery, must not be forgotten; and there are one or two more of different degrees of merit in that locality. Again, in Brooklyn they boast of an opera-house. . . .

In black minstrels there is no deficiency, there being no less than three companies amusing the Yankees in the Broadway—Bryant's (the best), Wood's and Christy's. They are all clever, and amused me immensely. There is a very fair circus in the Broadway, and Van Amburgh's collection of wild beasts—a menagerie of the first order. . . .

The Americans are great lovers of relics and mementoes of departed heroes. Their desire to procure antiquities from Europe is well known. Who has not heard of the enterprising Yankee who wanted to purchase Shakspere's [*sic*] house at Stratford, and transport it bodily to his own favoured country?

. . . . .

With respect to the theatres, Wallack's is perhaps one of the most worthy of notice. I was so highly pleased with a visit to this Thespian temple, that I cannot pass it by without notice. The piece, entitled "Rosedale, of the Rifle Volunteer Ball," was the best I had seen for years. The play is full of interesting scenes and adventurous plot. The hero, a little child, is stolen by the gipsies, and, after hair-breadth escapes and countless perils, is rescued by a dragoon officer. The parts were well enacted, and the "upholstery of the stage" was worthy of Charles Kean himself. The theatre is large and elegantly decorated, and the ventilation is well managed.

Then in the Broadway is "The American"—a place of amusement to which ladies are not admitted. Here, in addition to the "feast of reason and the flow of soul," the creature comforts of smoking and drinking abound *ad libitum.* I would recommend the fastidious not to come here, for the very frequenters of the place are obliged to keep the windows constantly open, to enable them to breathe something more invigorating than smoke. Ten years ago, girls danced here in a state of nudity; but the authorities have now effectually put down such exhibitions.

Barnum, the prince of showmen and humbugs, is ever worth a visit of 25 cents. To see the West Indian fish and the snakes is alone worth the money. The latter are the largest in the world. They are fed once a month. We must not forget to mention the interesting couple, a giant and giantess, and the Lilliputian mannikin, whose weight is only 18 pounds. Moreover, we have a theatrical performance and a waxwork exhibition. A whale and hippopotamus are among the most conspicuous curiosities.

. . . . .

It is when the city has donned her winter garments of snow that she looks the fairest. All is bustle and excitement. The sleighs, driven with speed over the white street, filled with charming fur-muffled ladies, are a pretty sight. . . .

The ladies flock in great numbers to the Fifth Avenue Pond and Central Park to skate. Here you see all the fashion and the beauty of the city, watching or taking part in the healthy sports. In the Central Park (which is free for admission) from 20,000 to 50,000 persons may be seen. The Fifth Avenue Pond is situated between 58th and 59th Streets, and is more select, by reason of the charges, which are 5 dollars for gentlemen and 2 dollars for ladies. . . .[22]

Mrs. Julia A. Layton, herself an artist as well as an art critic, did feel that the war not only was a present influence but that out of it might develop a truly American art, free from the spirit of colonialism that had theretofore permeated the work of American artists. Her frenetic appeal for patriotism in art was published at the beginning of the war.

Little or nothing is now being done in the studios; many of our artists have shouldered the musket and gone off to the wars; yet it needs no prophet's ken to foresee that American art will arise from out of this political chaos rejuvenated and soar aloft on the extended wing of the American eagle. This same old eagle, by the way, has had too long a rest, and it is high time he addressed himself to a *coup d'oeil* of the most glorious country the sun ever shone upon.

It is not often in the *mêlée*, in the strife, that art is perfected; it is rather after the turbulent spirit has subsided and the waves of commotion have sobbed themselves into placid rest, that we may expect to realize the beneficial effects of this wholesome electric shock upon national art.

. . . . .

Yet these are perilous times for our artist confrères. In hours like these, when even moneyed men feel poor, when nothing is ordered, nothing bought, there must necessarily be suffering in the studio; and the most we can do is to open our galleries for the exhibition of their works, our pages to speak a genial word of encouragement and hope, and our hearts to a liberal outflow of fraternal sympathy—for art and literature go hand in hand. . . . American Artists: BE NATIONAL! Rest not satisfied with the rendition of the art of other nations, but depend upon your own identity for immortality. This is the duty you owe the past, the present and the future: it is the duty you owe yourselves and the goddess whom you worship. . . .

But have we no National Art? Go to the Governor's Room, City Hall; see the revered shades of the 'Heroes of the Revolution,' our

'Statesmen' and 'Warriors'; are they not worthily limned? In the historical *genre* we rank first among nations of the earth, young as we are in history. See the works of Trumbull, Vanderlyn, Weimar, the venerable Sully, yet living; the elder Jarvis, Catlin, Waldo and Jewett; Inman, Jarvis, Elliott, Huntington, Hicks, Morse, Gray, Mooney, Page, Kellogg and a host of others. And in sculpture, are we so far behind other nations that it can be said we have none? Is not the very presence of *Le Pere de la Patrie* in our council-hall a sufficient answer?

The public has a penchant for the landscape *genre*. None need be told that Church is great—that he is national. Has he not given us his 'Niagara' and his 'Heart of the Andes,' and is he not treating us this summer with his refrigerating 'Iceberg?' How those dazzling mountains of ice freeze into the very soul, awing us with the mystic revelations of another sphere! . . .

And have *we* no domestic nationality to evolve? Have we no *poesy of home*, whose episodes shall warm the heart and thrill the nation? These are serious questions; questions it is the duty of every conscientious parent, every loyal son and loving daughter to answer. Nationally we have been too rash, toppling down the sacred chimneys of our ancestors, in which the swallows have built their nests for centuries, to erect a shrine to innovation which we mistook for improvement. We have not sufficiently taught the youth of our land to respect the mighty shades of those who have gone before those dauntless pioneers of our national prosperity. . . . 'Home, sweet home,' is rapidly becoming a myth! Yet, thank God, it is not *too late* to retrieve our mighty, our *national* error! . . .

Why should *genre*-painting not succeed with us? Have we not as venerable sires, as glorious types of manhood, as dignified matrons, as noble youth, as beautiful maidens, and as lovely infants as other nations? Then, why should there be a dearth of the *depeinture* of the poesy of American homes? Why go to Europe for models when we have them at our own threshold? Our forefathers made sacrifices in subduing and settling this goodly soil, and it is for their children to perpetuate their spirit by fostering American Art. Let the public set the example of patronizing *genre*-paintings of the American brush, and we will give them a national art to be proud of. We have artists of merit silently struggling in our midst to evolve great thoughts. Americans! will you leave them and their families *to starve;* or worse than that, to *prostitute our nationality for bread?* ART-PATRONS! would you evince your patriotism? lay your gold on the shrine of your country by placing it in the hand of the struggling American artist. ARTISTS! yield not up the sacred heirloom committed to your charge for a mess of pottage; remember that your eloquent brushes are recording the history of a nation.

It is high time we came out boldly, and declared the INDEPENDENCE OF AMERICAN ART![23]

Actually, although it was not of the sort Mrs. Layton pleaded for, young American artists of the Pre-Raphaelite school, profoundly affected by the war and in protest against what James Jackson Jarvis called "a certain barrenness of thought and feeling" among the academic painters, did revolt during the 1860's.

What ought our artists to do for us? What they have done for us, so far, is to supply us with an expensive and grandiose sort of furniture. . . . Their work is bought as furniture, and treated as such by the purchaser. Our "stylish" houses are plentifully supplied with this as with other varieties of movable objects, the walls being covered with gilt frames and what they contain, as the floors are with chairs, each of a different and fanciful pattern.

. . . . .

It is our object to show that this sad condition of things is, in a great measure, the fault of the artists themselves. That they, or most of them, encourage the false system by painting pictures expressly designed to attract ignorant buyers. . . .

. . . . .

Have you ever thought what need there is of faithful recording? Do you know how little there is of it? The thinking man must suffer every day from the realizing sense he has of noble things to which the world's notice has never been called, noble things which speedily pass away, and which it is soon too late to seize. It is a rare thing, one of the rarest things, to find any account of anything fairly and completely given, the narrator telling the whole story, dwelling on the essential and not on the unimportant facts, putting the whole into the white light of truth, and not disguising it with the red and blue spectrum of his own theories and prejudices. Take the instance of our war. Our boasted free press has not done its duty by us. Have men been sent as "correspondents" to the seat of the war who have had power and will to seize the vital truth of great events and preserve it? Very seldom. . . .

Therefore the recorder has a useful and important purpose to perform. It is a truth not perfectly recognized, the power and beauty there is in the real, over the so-called ideal which uninventive people set up as a caricature of it. For instance, to keep to our war, now and then there appears in one of our illustrated papers a large wood-cut of some incident of the battle-field, bearing evidence of having been drawn from the real thing and drawn faithfully. . . . We remember such a picture in the "New York Illustrated News" representing the attempt of the rebel infantry to cross certain Chickahominy bridges checked by the fire of United States light batteries guarding the rear of the retreating army. In the foreground, on the height where the artist stood, were ranged the guns, the quiet unhurried cannoniers going on with their steady work, caissons and limbers drawn up in a regular line behind them, the whole as unalarmed and business-like as a drill and target practice at West Point. [A] quarter of a mile away was the principal bridge, beyond it the dense masses of the pursuing enemy, but evidently pausing. And around and beyond the bridge and all along the rebel front the shells were bursting. You could see how for hours the steady rain would go on, unchanging and inevitable, and your memory went back to the great slaughter on Malvern Hill, and your heart swelled with gratitude to the brave men who were fighting, in spite of heartless and worthless leadership, so gallantly for their country.

This was vigorous and it was good Art;—all because it was a true record of an interesting event. Get it, and compare it with the fancy sketches called "a bayonet charge," or "Stuart's cavalry on a raid," selected from English or American periodicals. These things are lifeless, tame, cold,—no one could make anything out of such subjects but a transcendant genius, and he would not be apt to try. . . .

As with events, so with beautiful things which pass away, or to which we have not access. Mr. Ruskin has urged it again and again upon young artists to paint the precious Gothic sculpture which is vanishing at the touch of vandal "restorers." . . .

Now in this country we have no such relics of the past. But we have those precious things which, coming once a year for a few days, are seen by but few, and noticed by fewer still. Who, reading Thoreau, has not realized that there was a world of which he knew very little?

. . . . .

Who has painted Thoreau's favorite plant, the "Poke Berry"? Who has painted a cherry tree in full bearing, or a branch of it, the red jewels set along the green ridge of each full leafed branch? . . .

It is the business of our artists to go out into the woods and fields and paint all the beautiful things there, one by one, and that with such accuracy that we can feel assured, after seeing one or two, that their report is worthy of credit. . . .[24]

Literature was influenced more by the war than were other aspects of the intellectual and artistic life of the North. There was a substantial body of "war literature." Nonetheless, war neither monopolized literary output, nor checked the currents already flowing. The war also was compatible with the prosperity of the book trade. Almost exactly three years after the firing on Fort Sumter, the American Literary Gazette and Publishers' Circular *reported on sales.*

The results of the recent trade sales in this city and in New York indicate a most flourishing condition of the trade. It may to some seem difficult to account for the prosperous state of the trade while the country is engaged in a civil strife which one would suppose would have the effect of draining and absorbing, or of diverting its resources, as well as of restricting the domestic market. But, instead of a depression of the book business, we have a greatly increased activity. The war has of itself added a new and imposing department to our literature, consisting of military treatises of all kinds, original and re-published, relating to all branches of the army and navy service. Besides this, we have official military reports, biographical publications, histories of the war, journals of officers, narratives of tourists, war-novels, and war-poems, political treatises and pamphlets without number. These issues are becoming almost innumerable, and their effect has been literally to add a new and vast department to our lists. Moreover, the very restlessness and the cravings of the times may lead the public to seek enjoyment in books. But, whatever the solution may be, the fact is so, that the book-trade has never before appeared to be so prosperous. At the trade sales in this city, the sales were larger and the prices were better than for many years before. . . .[25]

Dime books reflected the healthy state of American morals and the deplorable state of American taste, rather than patriotism or the stresses and strains of war. And they thrived like the green bay tree.

. . . These works are issued by Messrs. Beadle & Co. of New York, in virtue of an enterprise started in the year 1859. They already amount to several hundred separate publications, and circulate to the extent of many hundred thousands. This need hardly be stated to anyone who is in the way of casting his eye on the counter of any railway book-stall or newsdealer's shop. But the statistical statement, from authority, may excite some interest—that, up to April 1st, an aggregate of five millions of Beadle's Dime Books had been put in circulation, of which half at least were novels, nearly a third songs, and the remainder handbooks, biographies, &c. . . . The sales of single novels by popular authors often amount to nearly forty thousand in two or three months.

. . . . .

Why these works are popular is a problem quite as much for the moralist and the student of national character as for the critic. It is a satisfaction that, being so, they are without exception, so far as we can judge, unobjectionable morally, whatever fault be found with their literary style and composition. They do not even obscurely pander to vice, or excite the passions. And it is a striking fact, to be learned from Messrs. Beadle & Co's. account of sales, that the best books on their list are those for which there is the greatest demand. . . .

The success of Messrs. Beadle & Co's. undertaking has led other publishers in New York and Boston to engage in similar enterprises. As yet none of them so far as we are aware, has reached any great magnitude.[26]

Libraries had their difficulties but they were the customary ones rather than war-born. The Philadelphia Mercantile Library reported normal problems and achievements.

During the past year the prosperity which has attended the affairs of this institution so long and so uninterruptedly, has been again continued. Our very large list of stockholders and subscribers has suffered no such diminution as would have been expected from the events of the era. Our reading rooms are more frequented than they were wont to be, and the books, tables, files and other advantages of the Library, are more and more in use. . . .

For several years past, the Board has directed its attention to the improvement of such departments of the Library as have been found to be most deficient. In this manner the departments of Fine Arts and Medicine have received large additions, so that they are now superior to what they were. In the former, the board has placed a selection of bound music books, including the works of the great composers, and it is intended to enlarge this gradually, so as eventually to establish in this institution a thoroughly good musical collection for the use of members. . . . The Board is the more induced to this step, because it is not aware of the existence in this city of any extended collection of music to which the general public has access, a deficiency of some consequence in a city the size of ours.

In former years the Library has received such large additions in the departments of travel, religion, biography, history, and novels that most of the others have suffered in comparison. Natural History, which in the Academy of Natural Sciences fills a library of some twenty-five thousand volumes, exclusively devoted to it, comprises less than two thousand in ours. Law . . . can claim but two cases with us and those indifferently supplied. Foreign languages . . . fill . . . three cases only. There is not in all Philadelphia a good collection of scientific books, and ours, we are sorry to say, is hardly worth mentioning, despite the persistent efforts of the Board to increase our supply in that department. Nor have we any commercial collection worthy of the name. . . .

In seeking, as has been done for several years past, to give a greater breadth to its literary character, the Board has been pleased to find the public taste has thoroughly responded to the effort, and that all the additions which have been made to the hitherto restricted departments, have brought forward persons to read and use them. . . .

[To fill out our departments] we shall have to import from Europe to a much greater extent than ever before, as many of the works needed are foreign, and can be obtained cheapest in this way. This we have been doing for several years past, preferring to send out special orders for select lists of books, and thus be able to govern our purchases to suit the policy of the Board. We have selected diligently among the domestic book-sellers and shall continue to do so, having been able, in this way, to obtain large additions during the year. For a portion of the past year, our importations of foreign books were impeded by the great rise in sterling exchange, and after waiting for a change in this, the Board at length concluded a special arrangement with our London agent on favorable terms. . . .

That we stand very much in need of . . . [a new] building hardly admits of argument. The Board has felt it continually, and the increase in the number of visitors to our rooms has become so great as to force the matter on the attention of everybody. . . . In order to satisfy the demands of the present stockholders and subscribers, the novel department, for instance, must be enlarged to three or four times its present capacity. Much attention as we devote to this class we find it impossible to keep pace with the demands upon us. . . .[27]

There was a notable lack of "bookburning"—libraries continued to subscribe to Copperhead newspapers and stocked some pro-Southern volumes on their shelves.

The great Harvard librarian, John Langdon Sibley, showed an awereness of the war and of a library's most useful "war service." Although a doctrinaire Radical in his own beliefs, he sensed the value to posterity of preserving the complete *record of the war.*

One of the greatest favors to the future historian and philosopher would be to collect all the books, pamphlets, maps, files of newspapers, engravings, photographs, caricatures, ephemeral publications of every kind, even to printed notices, circulars, handbills, posters, letter envelopes, and place them beyond the reach of destruction, that as a collection they may reflect the sentiments and feelings which otherwise will in a great measure pass into oblivion with the occasions which gave them birth. If I could, I would appeal to every inhabitant of the continent to send me everything which could be obtained, in order that every phase of mind in every section of the country, North, South, East, West, for the Union and against the Union, for secession and against secession, might be represented on our shelves in all the variety of reasoning and imagination, virtue and vice, justice and injustice, fiction and fact, freedom and oppression, kindness and cruelty, truth and caricature, that can be found. I would say, send me collections, if possible, but if not, send to me a single pamphlet, book or picture, if you have one to spare.[28]

In spite of the Philadelphia Mercantile Library's need to import books from Europe, the North's domestic output was not negligible. Among works published during the third year of the war were George Ticknor's The Life of William Hickling Prescott, *John W. Draper's* History of the Intellectual Development of Europe, *Louis Agassiz's* Methods of Study in Natural History, *Longfellow's* Tales of a Wayside Inn, *and Bayard Taylor's* Hannah Thurston. *Under the heading* "Literature and Literary Progress in 1863," The American Annual Cyclopaedia *reported:*

In no period of the past history of the United States has the literary activity of the country been so manifest as in the year 1863. While the price of paper has more than doubled, and the cost of printing and binding been greatly enhanced, and at the same time the scarcity of skilled labor has rendered production difficult, the number of newspapers, periodicals, and magazines, has greatly increased, and the circulation of those previously established been much enlarged, and the number of new books issued surpasses that of any previous year. A tolerably complete catalogue of the books of the year enumerates 2,050 distinct publications, a considerable number of them extending to two or more volumes. The number of reprints has not been large. Aside from translations, and books on which a large amount of editorial labor has been bestowed in the way of notes, additions, appendices, or introductions, there are but

297, and including these the whole number does not reach 400. There are then not less than 1,650 original American works which have passed through the press during the past year, and an unusually large number of these have attained a sale of more than 10,000 copies, while a few have exceeded 50,000, and one or two 100,000 copies. The most numerous class of publications were those for juvenile readers. Of these, 420, or more than one fifth of the whole number, were issued during the year. 203 were novels, of which somewhat more than one half were reprints; 205 were theological and religious works. The number of works on military science did not exceed 65, while those on legal science numbered 75, and those on medicine, 50. Of works devoted to history—a large portion of them referring to the history of the existing war—there were 110; and about 100 biographical works. Forty-six works were devoted to physical science, and 25 to mathematics and technology. Twelve works were added to the domain of philology, of which but one was reprinted from foreign publications. Political science was discussed in 130 distinct essays and treatises. Seventy works were devoted to education. There were also 42 books in the department of art and illustrative science; 37 volumes of poems, including new poems or collections of poems by Bryant, Longfellow, Whittier, &c.; and 52 volumes of essays.[29]

The war literature itself, in the eyes of a contemporary critic, was for the most part as "shoddy" as the social antics of the war-profiteering nouveaux riches. *In successive numbers (January, February 1864),* The Round Table *commented acidly on the romances and poetry of the war. Of the romances it said:*

In the minds of most men a certain dignified solemnity connects itself inseparably with the idea of war. The gorgeous trappings of man and beast, the flapping of sanctified banners, the masses of moving humanity, the impressive effect of the

> "thunder of guns and the roll of drums
> And an army marching by,"

are all fraught with a high degree of something akin to sublimity. And especially is the battlefield a subject of awe. Beside its horrid heroism and terrible splendor all commonplace emotions seem hollow and heartless, though they may be earnest enough for everyday wear. In such company, then, flippancy becomes appalling.

Yet there is a sort of literature, based upon that prurient hunger for "sensation" which demands a nightly supper of bleeding hearts and water, that carries its flippancy and its commonplace to the battlefield, and flaunts them in affected bombast above the fallen heroes who lie there, happy, it may be, in an eternal immunity from such trash. We mean the so-called "Romances of the War" so much in vogue among magazines and "story papers" during the two sorry years just past.

Of course, there is but one wretched thread of a plot to hang the incidents upon in these romances. Of course there is a noble young gentleman, an Apollo, in a white waistcoat, with "raven curls clustering about a marble brow," and a "low sweet voice uttering burning words of love and making music richer than" various instruments, ranging from a flute to an Aeolian harp, according to the taste of the writer. Of course this young person wants to go to the war, and of course his lady-love, a maiden who lives, moves, and has her being in a "snowy tissue of crepe"—these panderers to sensation are always strong in the direction of dry-goods—"trimmed simply but tastefully with coquettish knots of blue ribbon,"—of course, we say, this gorgeous being objects most strenuously, weeping "bitter tears" upon his coat-collar and murmuring—always murmuring—"I cannot spare you *now*!"

Then something happens. The "old flag" is fired upon in Charleston Harbor; or, if that is too threadbare, the lady's great uncle gets the worst of a meeting with a rebel bullet; or a wounded soldier shows his "bronzed and haggard" physiognomy in the village and fires Angelina Sophia's heart with a "tale of lofty deeds." Thereupon she consents to the departure of Augustus, and he "takes her gently to him as if she had been a child," and "imprints" a kiss—generally of the "long, last lingering sort"—on her forehead or cheek or lips (seasoned to taste, as the cook-books say), and goes off in great splendor of uniform, and inevitably as a commissioned officer—rarely lower than a captain. There is no romance about the partings of common people. Any novelette writer will tell you that, tacitly at least.

Next comes news of the battle, which must be a splendid victory, and the said news must "flash over the wires." Augustus is reported killed, or there would be no wholesome agony to depict, and Angelina Sophia could not go about disheveled, with "stony eyes," and the "lines of her face sharper with pain." Even "jets of scalding tears" have been employed with effect.

This condition of things is continued long enough to weaken the reader-patient down to the proper state of harrowing, which operation requires a battle-scene, the blood and wound *al fresco.* Augustus is shown as he appeared while slaying small detachments of rebels usually described as "haughty foemen." Here come in such luxuries as "silver trumpet-peals and clash and clang of iron, crying voices, whistling, singing, screaming (why not fiddling?) shot, thunderous drum-rolls, sharp sheet of flame," etc., to which are tastefully added "spurts of warm blood upon the brow, the bullet rushing like a blast beside the ear, all the terrible tempest of attack trampled under the flashing hoof, climbing, clinching, slashing, back-falling, beneath cracking revolvers, hand to hand in the night"—mercy on us! We are out of breath, and fain to call for straws with which to ornament our hair after the manner of gibbering idiots upon the stage.

Naturally, Augustus is left under large "heaps of the slain," and the reader is supposed to consider him quite dead—a supposition rarely correct, if the reader has seen any two of these literary quagmires. At this juncture we are requested to "draw a veil over the sad scene" and return to Angelina Sophia, who is embroidering, or scraping lint, or meditating in black clothes, minutely described, under a sweet-apple tree in the back-garden of "her far-off Northern home."

The machinery here grows primitively simple. There is "a shadow on the sward, her name pronounced in the rich music of the voice she knew so well of old, and a burning kiss imprinted 'again' upon her brow." Arising, "she swoons in her lover's arms."

The Augustus whose name was in the list of killed was of course another Augustus; or somebody saw him fall and reported him killed, when he only had a rib or two carried away. He is pale and interesting, needs attention and gets it; and the story ends with a wedding on the part of the couple, and a yawn on the part of the reader.

This tissue of flimsy plot, dreary platitude, and sickly sentiment, floods the market of to-day, and gives us a healthy fear of opening most of the popular magazines lest Angelina Sophia may weep and Augustus bleed on every page. If there be any earnestness, any worthiness, any dignity in the profession of arms, why do not our warriors rise in protest against such a strange farrago of the namby-pamby and the disgusting? Augustus is not a type of the commissioned officer, nor Angelina Sophia a specimen of the girl he leaves behind him. The nation could well spare all romances of the war until its dreadful realities are a little draped by time; but if they must be written, let it be in wholesome English, simply constructed, with real men and women in the places of heroes and heroines, and real events in place of these musky, high scented tableaux, redolent of falsity and garished with the dissimulative rouge and plaster of prostituted literature.

If there be no other reason, this wholesale demoralization of "light writing" should weigh heavily as an inducement for the termination of hostilities. The horrors of war are numerous and great, but its romances, so-called, are hardly better; and we sincerely implore all young ladies and gentlemen of budding talent and limited experience to refrain, henceforth, from doing feeble violence to our noble language in their frantic endeavors to gild the fine gold of heroism, and paint, with unctuous carmine and rose-pink,

"the blood-red blossom of war, with a heart of fire!"[30]

On the poetry The Round Table *had this commentary:*

It may undoubtedly be accepted as a truth in literature that good subjects do not always suggest good productions. We have heretofore given sundry criticisms of the prose writings inspired by the war; we regret that we can find but little more to admire in its lyrical offspring. There have, in fact, been less than half a dozen really worthy poems written since the rebellion began having martial incidents or sentiments for their foundation. Several reasons may be ascribed for this sorry phenomenon.

When the contest began, the thinking minds of the country were too much startled, too much shocked, too fully impressed with the necessity of immediate action, to sit down quietly at verse-making. After action was concerted and organized sufficiently to allow of deliberate thought, the gigantic folly and incredible dishonesty of some who held the conduct of affairs in their hands robbed battle of its lurid splendors and made the march of victorious armies naught but a successful speculation. The humiliating and the tragi-comic do not inspire even the most temerarious poet to noble numbers. A beautiful specimen—as enthusiastic physicians say of other disgusting sights scientifically viewed—was the attempt to fudge up a presentable national anthem for a given prize, if we may so designate a prize which was never given. It was a typical demonstration, a sort of bid for poetic bounty-jumpers, since introduced into the recruiting system.

To-day the Government says, "Are you patriotic enough to fight for the Union?"

"No," says Hodge.

"Then I'll give you seven hundred and seventy-seven dollars to make you so."

And Hodge enlists, to make a very indifferent soldier, probably.

So the National Anthem Committee said, "Are you poetic enough to write for the Union?"

"No," answered the poets.

"Then I'll give you five hundred dollars to make you so."

And the poets went to work to turn out sadly indifferent verses.

These thoughts are partly suggested by a volume of poems lately published, culled from all sorts of sources, and entitled "Lyrics of Loyalty." Its purpose is, as avowed in a prefatory note, "to preserve some of the best specimens of the lyrical writings which the present rebellion has called forth." The compiler promises two more volumes to follow—one of songs and ballads, and one of "personal and political epics and rhymes," rebel as well as national. This latter bids fair to eclipse the present collection, if not the second also; for, to our shame be it said, the two most stirring war-poems of the day, which have come to our notice, are "Stonewall Jackson's Way," found on the person of a Confederate sergeant, and "Over the River," contributed to a Richmond journal by Paul Hayne, of South Carolina. These have the ring of the true metal, and bear the imprint of genuine devotion to a cause. Let the motive be good, bad, or indifferent, if the singer means what he utters, his utterance must be grand. If not, he had far better keep silence.

The only poem in this volume which seems likely to us to outlive the war which brought it forth, is Mrs. Julia Ward Howe's "Battle-Hymn of the Republic," written in the rhythmic measure of the "John Brown" chorus. The rest, for the most part, is a medley of shrieking eagles, millions yet unborn, Park Benjamin, Bungay, the thickest of the fray, swords and plowshares, Martin Farquhar Tupper, starry folds, liberty or death, and the bondsman's broken chains, with a strong dash of the "kiss me, mother, and let me go" style of sentiment.

We all know the statement attributed to Beranger, and a hundred other poets, to the effect that if he could make the songs of a nation, he was unconcerned as to who went to the legislature. This is well, perhaps, but if we had power to make the laws, almost our first enactment would be against the writing of such verses as these. . . .[31]

After the first enthusiasms for the war effort had died down, the colleges and universities, except for occasional demonstrations, orations, and the enlistment of some of their students, generally became ivory towers again to perpetuate the cultural traditions of the nation and wait out the war. Once in a while, however, as at Princeton in 1864, the political crisis of the times penetrated the ivy-clad walls.

The contributions of the colleges of the country to the war for the defence of the Union will form a most interesting feature of any truthful history of this conflict which may in after years be written. Without a single exception, so far as we know, the influence of all our great educational establishments has been from the outset on the side of the government and liberty, and thousands of young men, whose names are famous in the records of our struggle, have gone out from these institutions to battle for the country. In some colleges in the West, when the early calls for troops were made, not a single student was left, so eager were all to respond to the nation's appeal. Princeton, grave and staid as she is, has not been behind her sisters in exhibitions of patriotism; in one respect, indeed, she is in advance of many of them.

On Tuesday evening last a mass meeting was held here under the auspices of the Lincoln and Johnson Club. At this meeting we had the rare spectacle of three distinguished professors—men of studious, quiet habits, engaged in a work as remote as possible from mere politics—speaking to the people touching public questions, and urging them to support Republican candidates and measures. These professors were Alexander, McIlvaine and Guyot—the two former of whom spoke at some length with great power and earnestness as to the necessity of electing Mr. Lincoln, arguing that it is the duty of every rightminded citizen, no matter what his walk in life may be, to take the field and labor with all his strength for the sacred cause of Union and law. Professor McIlvaine has always been known as a democrat of the old school, and his course at this time will greatly affect the democracy here [i.e. at Princeton]. Professor Guyot, who was called out by the audience, electrified the hearts of all in attendance by declaring that he had that very day been naturalized in order especially that he might vote for Mr. Lincoln—a declaration which amounted in itself to a better speech than one half of our orators are wont to make.

When you remember that Princeton was once the peculiar favorite of southerners, and that it has always held an extreme "conservative" position, you will agree with me that these present signs are most significant, and justify the prediction that other writers have made in your columns—that New Jersey means, this time, to be on the side of the country and the flag which her sons are daily honoring on the bloody field. . . .[32]

Perhaps it would have been as well for the professors to spare their effort. New Jersey was one of the three Union states to cast its electoral votes for George B. McClellan.

Meanwhile, the public schools, unguarded by the privately endowed universities' ivy-clad walls, were exposed to the hot winds of patriotic politics. In Illinois and California there were movements to require teachers to take special loyalty oaths. Chicago's Board of Education, handpicked by a War Democrat-Copperhead City Council, adopted a "gag" resolution. The resolution and proceedings of the board were as follows.

L. B. Taft offered the following:

Resolved, That the teachers of the public schools shall at all times carefully abstain from introducing into the public schools or Teachers' Institutes any topic or question concerning which the opinions of different political parties are divided, and that a violation of this rule shall be considered a cause for their removal.

Dr. J. H. Foster [thought that the rule] was very general [and that it] might occasion difficulty in determining what was cause for removal.

The Chairman [Luther Haven] said that the discussion of religious and political topics had been kept out of the Board for twelve years, and they could just as well and easily be kept out of the schools.

Mr. [C. N.] Holden thought that the rule was very broad. If the Star-Spangled Banner were sung in the school, and parents found fault with it, as some had already done, it might under the rule be a cause for removal. He didn't wish to introduce religious topics, Abolitionism, or Copperheadism, in the schools, but he didn't want to remove a teacher for allowing national songs to be sung, against which some rebel might find fault. The rule exposes teachers to expulsion for committing acts which would seem wrong to eyes squinting the wrong way.

Mr. [R.] Prindiville thought the rule was clear and well defined, and would not expel a teacher for singing patriotic songs. He could see no objection to the rule.

Mr. Taft said he never heard of anyone's objecting to the singing of the Star-Spangled Banner.

Mr. [C.] Wahl said he had heard and knew people in the city who objected to it.

Mr. Holden said that inasmuch as an allusion to a matter at the last Teachers' Institute, which was neither religious nor political, had called out this resolution, he was willing that the Superintendent should examine the teachers' paper before it was read, but he was opposed to the resolution as too broad. He knew of a man in this city who had threatened to get a book out of the schools because it had a patriotic song in it.

Mr. [H. T.] Steele thought the resolution was not consistent with the position of the Board and offered the following as a substitute:

Resolved, That we recommend to the teachers of the public schools carefully to refrain at all times, from advocating and discussing, either in the schools or in the teachers' institutes, any sectarian or political question of a partisan character.

The Superintendent [William H. Wells] rose to an explanation and for instruction. He had always carefully avoided the introduction of such topics into the Board of Schools. In two or three instances he had had occasion to say such subjects were objectionable. At the last Institute two subjects were introduced on which political parties were divided—one of them negro equality. At the close of the reading of that discussion, he took occasion to say that it was not in accordance with the wishes of the Board, and that he hoped hereafter all vexed questions of this nature would be excluded from the paper. After the Institute he was almost immediately called to account by teachers. He therefore asked for instructions, and should be guided by the action of the Board.

Mr. Prindiville didn't believe in recommending to teachers. He wanted rules, if they had any, to be laid down as binding; and he moved to strike out the words in the substitute, "we recommend to." Mr. Prindiville's motion was carried. The question then arose upon the adoption of the substitute. The substitute was lost. . . .[33]

After the adoption of Taft's original "gag resolution," the Chicago Tribune *attacked it as a "compulsory rule" which defined "what teachers shall do and say in their institutes and their schools relative to political matters." Later in the war, the editor of the* Illinois Teacher *declared that Superintendent Wells tried to force a "system of espionage and gagging upon the teachers."*

Involvement, however, of the schools in the passions engendered by politics was the exception rather than the rule. In the conflict of words and ideas which preceded the war, perhaps no image more represented the virtuous claims of the North than the public school. Certainly in the definition of "freedom," the free schools were placed alongside free labor and freedom of religion as the citadel of Northern liberties.

A French pastor, Georges Fisch, found much to applaud in the public schools of the North.

. . . The most absolute obedience and the most rigid discipline prevail in all American schools. This contrast is easily explained. In ordering their schools with a sort of regimental unity of action, it is no part of their design to weaken the principle of individuality. In fact, the greater the number of children the more impersonal becomes the rule. Discipline is of itself established in the schools, which are, generally, very numerously attended. There is something in this common level to which all are subjected—in the word, the gesture, which makes a hundred wills move at once simultaneously—that pleases the imagination of the child. He vaguely understands it must be the same in the great world in which he is destined one day to take part. In this individuality-loving society, wherein the State leaves so much to the initiative of private persons, it has taken care to keep public instruction in its own hands. . . . The State offers a truly superior education to all gratuitously, and such a boon it would be madness to reject. Every child receives complete instruction, such as prepares him to enter the special schools, or the university, without its costing his parents a farthing even for pens or paper. The knowledge here acquired is solid enough for the rich man's child and sufficiently simple for the poor. At New York the son of the Irish workman may be seen seated side by side with the son of the banker of prodigious wealth. The expense of this education being defrayed by the public revenue, principally falls on those classes already the most taxed; but they willingly pay, in order that the advantages of instruction may be diffused amongst that portion of the population that are least favoured. As for themselves, they send by preference their children to the public schools, knowing that nowhere else could they find such distinguished teachers.

One of the most interesting things to be seen in America is a rural school. We teach our agricultural children little else than reading, writing, and the four rules of arithmetic. In the United States they are taught, besides, not only geography and history, which are also in our programme, but geometry, algebra, physics, chemistry, natural history, and moral philosophy as well. It is needless to say that the intention is not to transform the sons and daughters of farmers into village pedants, but to develop their intelligence, and give them a clue that may guide them in all directions. Nor is it the intelligence alone that is developed—the heart and the imagination receive their due share of attention; children are made to read and declaim the finest passages of literature. . . .

In general, the schools of the North are centres of the most intense patriotism. Children are taught songs that excite their young heads and fire their young hearts, but which are ill calculated to make a modest nation, repeating as they do upon every tone of the gamut the superiority of the Americans over all other peoples of the earth.

America, like ancient Greece, understands the importance of the education of the body, that it should keep pace with that of the intelligence and the heart. A large number of schools begin by exercises that amuse the children, while at the same time they develop their muscular force. At New York I visited a school containing fourteen hundred children. When I arrived the children were all ranged in columns along the sides of the large room. When the clock struck nine one of the mistresses took her place at the piano, which instrument fills a conspicuous part in public instruction, and performed one of Beethoven's finest marches. In an instant all the columns bounded forward, going through the most graceful movements, forming living chains interwoven into each other, now uniting, now separating, and all done with an accuracy that was really amazing. Suddenly a partition was removed, as if by enchantment, and there, upon a distant amphitheatre, hundreds of quite young children were going through the same evolutions. . . . These exercises unite the advantages of both gymnastics and dancing, and are calculated to strengthen the muscles, particularly those of the chest, and to give lightness, elasticity, and grace to the body. . . .[34]

So, in general, neither the material nor intellectual life of the people of the North was destroyed by war, and for hundreds of thousands of Northerners the daily way of life was much the same as it had been in peacetime. But it was not altogether the same. The civilian population's burden was light, compared to that of the soldier's, but there was a burden. And, on the whole, Copperheads, draft rioters, and "shoddy," notwithstanding, it was borne courageously. Some six months before Appomattox, The United States Service Magazine *summed it up:*

The first blast of the war-trumpet which announced the fall of Fort Sumter and summoned the sons of the North to the defence of the capital, awakened not only the patriotism, but the philanthropy, of the people of the Northern States. There was no withholding, no niggardliness in the offers of aid to the Union cause. Everywhere the same spirit actuated the people. Those who could go in person for the national defence offered themselves as willingly, and relinquished their usual pursuits as readily, as if the object were a pleasure-excursion instead of a fierce and deadly strife. Those who could not go contributed bountifully of money or goods for the supply of the soldier's needs, or the wants of his family in his absence; and the women of our land, while giving up, with a heroism worthy of all honor, fathers, husbands, brothers, sons, and lovers, choked down with firm resolve the tears that would come, and busied themselves with flying fingers in preparing the outfit of the brave men who were going forth to the battle-field. Day and night, Sunday and weekday, they toiled on; and the click of the sewing-machine and the sound of the hammer, as the packing cases were filled, gave signal of the vast preparations which were making for the war. At the State capitals, the Legislatures—in many cases summoned by the State Governors in extra session—voted sums far larger than their usual annual expenditure, for the equipment of troops, with a unanimity which showed the all-pervading spirit of patriotism which animated them; and, in city and country, the banks and capitalists came forward and proffered loans to large amounts, and the wealthy gave of their abundance; while everywhere, with that instinctive fondness for organization which characterizes the Anglo-Saxon mind, associations were formed to render aid to the soldiers and their families, in sickness or health. . . .

. . . The States, counties, and cities have offered as bounties sums which were almost sufficient to make the soldier independent in his circumstances; and the treasuries of the benevolent organizations have been filled to overflowing by the grateful charities of a grateful and patriotic people. For the first time in the history of civilized nations, a series of fairs, held in different cities and towns, in the course of eight months, have yielded as net results not simply hundreds of thousands, but millions, of dollars,—the aggregate net proceeds of the fairs in eight of our cities having exceeded three million six hundred thousand dollars. . . .

The several States, with but few exceptions, at the commencement of the war, advanced to their own troops the necessary uniforms, equipment, and arms to enable them to take the field promptly, the General Government agreeing to reimburse such of these expenditures as properly belonged to it. The amount thus reimbursed was about thirty millions of dollars; but there remained a further sum of nearly eleven millions of dollars . . . which had been furnished by the States in excess, or in variation from the Government regulations; and this they have paid without hesitation or complaint. . . .

In most of the large cities and towns, funds have been appropriated by the municipal authorities, and large additions made to them by corporations and individuals, for raising and recruiting regiments, the necessary expenses for this purpose ranging from fifteen thousand to forty thousand dollars, or more, per regiment.

. . . . .

Several individuals have made donations of large amount directly to the General Government. The most magnificent of these gifts was the present by Cornelius Vanderbilt, of New York, of his steamship "Vanderbilt" to the Government. The appraised value of the ship was eight hundred thousand dollars. Others (too few, indeed) have relinquished to the national treasury their commissions on purchases made for it, to the amount of fifty-five thousand dollars.

. . . We have an aggregate of more than one hundred and eighty-nine millions of dollars contributed by States, counties, cities, towns, corporations, and individuals for the equipment and organization of regiments, the payment of bounties and aid to families of volunteers, and other purposes of national defence, within the last three years.

. . . . .

There are several State organizations having for their primary object the care of the soldiers of their own States, though usually rendering assistance also to others, if in need, some of which bear the name of Sanitary Commissions. Such organizations exist in Iowa, Indiana, Illinois, and Wisconsin; and the State Soldiers' Depot of New York is somewhat analogous in character. The aggregate expenditure of these institutions since the commencement of the war has not been far from eleven hundred thousand dollars. They have accomplished a considerable amount of good; though in some cases the aid afforded would have been, perhaps, quite as judiciously administered by the United States or the Western Sanitary Commission.

Other associations, such as the "New England Soldiers' Relief" of New York, the Ladies' Aid Society of Philadelphia, the two Volunteer Refreshment Saloons of Philadelphia (which have fed all the soldiers passing through that city, either going to or returning from the field), the Soldiers' Aid Societies of Hartford, Conn., of Boston, Mass., and of many other cities and towns, and the Union Relief Associations of Baltimore, Washington, Pittsburgh, Cincinnati, and other cities East and West, deserve mention. . . . The great national religious societies, Bible, tract, missionary, and publication, as well as those of the different denominations, have contributed largely to the supplying of the army and navy with Bibles and other good books, periodicals, &c., and to the maintenance of colporteurs and missionaries in the camps, as well as among the freedmen. . . .

Other forms of aid, in which money or articles of food, clothing, or medicine stores have been sent to the soldier, have acted through what have been known as State relief organizations, in Washington, Louisville, St. Louis, and elsewhere, composed of persons who were citizens of the several States, though temporarily residing in those places. To these associations supplies have been sent from the States which they represented, and by them distributed on the field or in the hospitals. . . . Large amounts have been sent from towns or counties, throughout the country, after great battles, some prominent citizen volunteering to undertake the work of distribution without cost.

The two hundred and thirty-three general military hospitals of the country, as well as the smaller post-hospitals, have each their company of visitors, mostly, though not exclusively, ladies, who, in greater part, have a kitchen attached to the hospital, in which they prepare such delicacies as the surgeons prescribe, and, in addition, furnish the patients with books, newspapers, stationery, postage, &c., and, where they are unable to write letters to their friends, write for them.

In Philadelphia, the firemen have constructed, at their own expense, twenty-six ambulances, built in the best manner for ease and comfort for the wounded, and have procured good horses for each; and whenever a train of wounded or sick soldiers arrives at that city, they are promptly on hand to transport the poor fellows carefully and tenderly to the hospitals.

In several of the States, asylums for wounded or disabled soldiers, and homes for their widows or children, have been founded.

. . . . . .

Some . . . noble women have left homes of luxury and comfort, and, for the past two years and more, have kept in the vicinity of the camps, an ambulance or tent their home at night and the field or camp-hospital their dwelling-place by day, toiling, as few women of any rank in society toil, for the care of the wounded or fever-stricken soldier. . . . One of these heroines (Mrs. John Harris of Philadelphia) has devoted herself to this work from the time the Army of the Potomac went to the Peninsula, through all its battles and reverses till after the conflict at Gettysburg, and since that time at Chickamauga and Chattanooga, and everywhere has proved herself an angel of mercy. . . .

Another, a young and accomplished Massachusetts woman (Miss Clara Barton), has brought to the battlefields of Virginia and Maryland, and to the burning sands of Morris Island, her rare executive ability, her skilful and tender care of the wounded, and her ample supplies of those stores always needed, but rarely furnished in sufficient quantities, in such emergencies. Often in positions of deadly peril, and ever forgetful of self, in her ministrations of mercy, she has been regarded by the soldiers and officers of the Ninth and Tenth Army Corps as bearing a charmed life, and, in their almost idolatrous affection for her, they have named her "the angel of the battle-field." . . .[35]

But the most grievous of the civilian war burdens cannot be shouldered by the community, or lightened by the most furious endeavor. In the end it is borne in the heart of each individual who is bound by thongs of love to someone "gone to war." A letter, written by Sarah to Cassius Fairchild, reveals the agony of waiting. That, too, was "a way of life" of the North at war.

MADISON JULY 10, 1863
FRIDAY EVENING

I've been waiting dear Cassius in the hope of having better news to write you but I write now, fearing if I wait—it may be for worse tidings. I wrote you last Saturday morning (July 4th) the rumors we had then heard. Two or three hours later brought a dispatch from Charlie dated Baltimore Md which said "one of Gen. Cutler's staff reports Lucius wounded but slightly" The P.M. mail brought Chicago papers with lists in which his name had appended to it—"left arm amputated, doing well." We were quite inclined to think it a mistake because Charlie had not telegraphed again—heard absolutely nothing until Wednesday night. when the N. Y. Times of the 6th (page 8) in a letter from J. L. Crounse [?] (formerly of Milwaukee) had the enclosed quotation which I have marked with ink—Yesterday we rec'd an envelope from Charlie enclosing a letter from one of Lucius' "personal staff" which confirms the amputation but was written on the 1st and evidently before he was taken prisoner. A letter from Mrs. Ward in Washington, has the same intelligence but nothing further. We are resting in the faith that he did not long continue a prisoner—as Meade has recaptured them (in official dispatches) but of course there is enough doubt—to be very painful. I think his being taken prisoner has had the one good effect that if we can only hear of his being in our lines we shall be quite resigned to the dreadful loss of his arm—There seems scarcely a possibility of his having been carried off by a retreating army. Dr Ward performed the amputation, and may have been with him all the time, I hope so.

You'll not have to give the dear boy a share in your leg now & which he spoke for, you remember—You will get all the particulars of the horrible battle in the papers, so I will not attempt any details—The past three days the sun has been like a ball of fire in the heavens—and a thick smoke pervades the air. One cannot help feeling that the very elements are in horror at the dreadful sights and sounds that curse our land. I pray God constantly that He will take our affairs into his own hands—& let the right speedily prevail and peace be restored. Oh Cassius I hope you too will not fail to pray to Him who alone can protect us and ours in this world, & prepare us for a happy and sinless life in the world to come.

If I seldom speak to you of these things it is not because I do not feel the deepest interest in your welfare—but because I feel unworthy to warn one who ought to know better than I what is right —But I *do pray* constantly & most earnestly for us all, that we may love our kind Heavenly Father who has so richly blessed us and worship Him only. And I do hope dearest Cassius that you will pray for yourself and for us all if only to say that grandest and noblest of all prayers, "The Lord's Prayer"—which is sufficient for every need when felt in the heart—

We are keeping very cheerful—and hopeful—Mother almost gives up once in a while—but soon recovers. She says she cannot write until she hears from Lucius, which I think will be soon. I feel sure he will be cared for and hope for the best. Do write oftener.

Yours lovingly,
SARAH.[36]

VIII

Credos of the North

THE CIVIL WAR was a war of ideas—homegrown and European bred. Among them were those of the Puritan tradition, the evolutionary theories of Spencer and Darwin, liberalism, nationalism, and Swedenborgianism, to name only a few. Men of intellect and sensitivity were undoubtedly moved by appeals to the flag and the martial call of the drum and fife. But if they were to justify the bloodbath of war before their own consciences, they needed something more. Each must develop a system of belief—his credo. Most of them were able to do this—to find in the war some dynamic force beneficial to mankind, "which shall restore intellectual and moral power to these languid and dissipated populations."

The intellectuals were doctrinaire—often doctrinaire Radicals in their political naivete—and, in their eagerness to rationalize their position, they frequently minimized the evil results of war. But from their "private corners" they did speak out. Ralph Waldo Emerson saw the war as the suffering that was the price of redemption for the nation's "sinful years."

. . . The war, though from . . . despicable beginnings, has assumed such huge proportions that it threatens to engulf us all—no preoccupation can exclude it, & no hermitage hide us—And yet, gulf as it is, the war with its defeats & uncertainties is immensely better than what we lately called the integrity of the Republic, as amputation is better than cancer. I think we are all agreed in this, and find it out by wondering why we are so pleased, though so beaten & so poor. No matter how low down, if not in false position.

If the abundance of heaven only sends us a fair share of light & conscience, we shall redeem America for all its sinful years since the century began. At first sight, it looked only as a war of manners, showing that the southerner who owes to climate & slavery his suave, cool, & picturesque manners, is so impatient of ours, that he must fight us off. And we all admired them until a long experience only varying from bad to worse has shown us, I think finally, what a noxious reptile the green & gold thing was. . . . Their [the Southerners'] perversity is still forcing us into better position than we had taken. Their crimes force us into virtues to antagonize them and we are driven into principles by their abnegation of them. Ah if we dared think that our people would be simply good enough to take and hold this advantage to the end!—But there is no end to the views the crisis suggests, & day by day. You see I have only been following my own lead, without prying into your subtle hints of ulterior political effects. But one thing I hope, that "scholar" & "hermit" will no longer be exempts, neither by the country's permission nor their own, from the public duty. The functionaries, as you rightly say, have failed. The statesmen are all at fault. The good heart & mind, out of all private corners, should speak & save. . . .[1]

Henry James, the elder, had recently returned from Europe in 1861 when he delivered a Fourth of July address in Newport, Rhode Island. Filled with a deeply passionate love for his native land, he attempted to justify the North's cause. Profoundly influenced by Swedenborg, he, too, hailed the Civil War as one that would lead to a spiritual regeneration of the individual in American society. It was a contest between freedom and man's oppression; to James freedom meant self-realization of the individual spirit of man, and through that, a greater sense of unity with his fellow men and God.

. . . I [have] never felt proud of my country for what many seem to consider her prime distinction, namely, her ability to foster the rapid accumulation of private wealth. It does not seem to me a particularly creditable thing, that a greater number of people annually grow richer under our institutions than they do anywhere else.

. . . . .

No; what makes one's pulse to bound when he remembers his

own home under foreign skies, is never the rich man, nor the learned man, nor the distinguished man of any sort who illustrates its history . . . but it is all simply the abstract manhood itself of the country, man himself unqualified by convention, the man to whom all these conventional men have been simply introductory, the man who—let me say it—for the first time in human history finding himself in his own right erect under God's sky, and feeling himself in his own right the peer of every other man, spontaneously aspires and attains to a far freer and profounder culture of his nature than has ever yet illustrated humanity.

. . . . .

The friends of Mammon are numerous in every community; but, blessed be God, they nowhere rule in the long run. They are numerous enough to give an odious flavor to the broth; but they never constitute its body. It is impossible that we should err in this great crisis of our destiny, a crisis to which that of our national birth or independence yields in dignity and importance, as much as body yields to the soul, flesh to spirit, childhood to manhood. For this is the exact crisis we are in; the transition from youth to manhood, from appearance to reality, from passing shadow to deathless substance. Every man and every nation encounters somewhere in its progress a critical hour, big with all its future fate; and woe be to the man, woe be to the nation, who believes that this sacred responsibility can be trifled with. To every man and to every nation it means eternal life or eternal death; eternal liberty or eternal law; the heaven of free spontaneous order, or the hell of enforced prudential obedience. There is no man who hears me who does not know something of this bitter sweat and agony; whose petty, trivial cares have not been dignified and exalted by some glimpse of this hidden inward fight; who has not at times heard the still small voice of truth on the one hand counselling him to do the right thing though ruin yawn upon his hopes, counselling him *to force himself* to do the honest thing though it costs him tears of blood—and the earthquake voice of hell on the other, or the fiery breath of passion infuriated by long starvation, doing its best to drown and devour it. Our national life, believe me, is at that exact pass in this awful moment, and nowhere else. It is the hour of our endless rise into all beautiful human proportions, into all celestial vigor and beatitude, or of our endless decline into all infernality and uncleanness, and into the inevitable torments which alone discipline such uncleanness. And we must not hesitate for a moment to fight it manfully out to its smiling blissful end, feeling that it is not our own battle alone, that we are not fighting for our own country only, for our own altars and firesides as men have fought hitherto, but for the altars and firesides of universal man, for the ineradicable rights of human nature itself. Let bloated European aristocracies rejoice in our calamities; let the muttonheaded hereditary legislators of England raise a shout of insult and exultation over our anticipated downfall; the honest, unsophisticated masses everywhere will do us justice, for they will soon see, spite of all efforts to blind them, that we occupy in this supreme moment no petty Thermopylae guarding some paltry Greece, but the broad majestic pass that commands the deathless wealth and worth of human nature itself, the Thermopylae of the human mind; they will soon see, in fact, that our flags are waving, our trumpets sounding, our cannon showering their deathful hail, not merely to avenge men's outraged political faith and honor, but to vindicate the inviolable sanctity of the human form itself, which for the first time in history is Divinely bound up with that faith and honor.

This is the exact truth of the case. The political tumbledown we have met with is no accident, as unprincipled politicians would represent it. It is the fruit of an inevitable expansion of the human mind itself, of an advancing social consciousness in the race, an ever-widening sense of human unity, which will no longer be content with the old channels of thought, the old used-up clothes of the mind, but irresistibly demands larger fields of speculation, freer bonds of intercourse and fellowship. We have only frankly to acknowledge this great truth in order to find the perturbation and anxiety which now invade our unbelieving bosoms dispelled; in order to hear henceforth, in every tone of the swelling turbulence that fills our borders, no longer forebodings of disease, despair, and death, but prophecies of the highest health, of kindling hope, of exuberant righteousness, and endless felicity for every man and woman born. . . . "The Lord rules confused and disorderly things which are upon the surface *by virtue of a pacific principle in the depths or at the centre; whereby the disorderly things upon the surface are reduced to order, each being restored from the error of its nature.*" The pacific and restorative principle which in the same way underlies all our political confusion and disorder, and which will irresistibly shape our national life to its own righteous and orderly issues, is the rising sentiment of human society or fellowship, the grand, invincible faith of man's essential unity and brotherhood. The social conscience, the conscience of what is due to every man as man, having the same divine origin and the same divine destiny with all other men, is becoming preternaturally quickened in our bosoms, and woe betide the church, woe betide the state, that ventures to say to that conscience, "Thus far shalt thou go, and no further!"[2]

The Reverend Henry Whitney Bellows was not much concerned with redemption; he did not believe that the members of his "commercial" congregation of the New York City All Souls' (Unitarian) Church were lacking in grace. They were men of means and their pastor would have shared the conviction, expressed some four decades later by Bishop William Lawrence, that in the end it is only to the man of virtue that wealth comes. This is but a short step from the tenet that wealth is virtue. The Reverend Henry Whitney Bellows took that step without breaking his stride, and in doing so arrived at the text of his sermon. "The commerce and trade—not of this spring or next fall, not of this year or next year—but of the next hundred years is imperilled. . . . Your warehouses will indeed be converted into deserted palaces, and your docks into empty and sailless ditches—if the arm of your Government is not nerved with your confidence, and strung with the fibres of your loyalty and sympathy."

In this sermon, Bellows was also anticipating Andrew Carnegie's "Gospel of Wealth."

. . . I desire to speak with true respect of the material interests of society. The real progress of the world depends very much on peace and prosperous industry, and widespread, because safe and rewarding, commerce. Christianity has immensely advanced the wealth and comfort of society, and the riches and peace of the world have repaid religion by munificent support of her cause. It is not necessarily a mean and selfish instinct which makes us so sensitive to the prospects of our material interests. The bread, safety, and happiness of our wives and children; the prosperity of our social, civil, and humane institutions; the support of religion itself; the supply of labor and food to the masses of the people—all are finally dependent upon the undisturbed condition of trade, the sound basis of monetary affairs, and the pacific prospects of the world. There can be no difference among sensible men as to the vast importance of stability in the industry and commercial and fiscal affairs of the nation.

Radically and truly considered, however, there is no conflict between the moral interests of society and its material interests. What is most for the interest of piety and virtue is most for the interest of trade and commerce. What best serves God and humanity, best serves basket and store. Any seeming antagonism here is not real, but due only to shortsightedness. It is proved indisputably that public morality and piety are in the highest degree favorable to public wealth, and that the most moral and religious nations are the richest. It is with moral and spiritual truths, as it is with scientific and economical truths—they always seem to threaten disaster when they first break upon the notice of the world, but soon show themselves to be the guardians and most efficient promoters of the real interests which it is predicted they are swiftly to ruin.

. . . . .

It is idle and mischievous to think of the material and the moral interests of our own beloved country as at war with each other. Nothing immoral can be for our interest. Our people generally wish to do what is just and right, and as a rule they believe honesty the best policy, and humanity the best business. They have grown up, certainly in our own section of the land, under the conviction that the blessing of God was upon their industry, trade, and commerce; and that their material prosperity need not hinder their fidelity to conscience and their allegiance to the Almighty. And they are right in this faith. God *is* on the side of justice. Duty *is* rewarding. . . .[3]

The doctrine of wealth, however, though budding, had not yet bloomed. Bellows was a few years before his time. Most of his fellow clergymen could not justify the war as a crusade to preserve the material riches of the righteous. Nonetheless, most of them did justify it—some on grounds of Christian principles, some despite them.

Henry Ward Beecher was the most widely known minister of his time. His generation knew him as the "Great Preacher." This may have been because he did not perplex his audience with subtleties. Thus he resolved the differences between the Prince of Peace and the God of battles by dividing wars into good and bad ones. His chant of vengeance could then become a plea for a Christian cause in a sanctified conflict with the forces of evil.

. . . I agree that Christianity intends a universal peace; but it permits war. Whether it is right or wrong, depends upon whether the end is right, and the spirit in which it is waged is right. If the end is right, and we administer it with a right spirit, it is right; if not, it is all wrong. . . . What should we think of the policeman who, when he caught a thief, should pull out the Bible and read him the ten commandments? It would be much more pertinent to use the locust. It is wrong to have wars for avarice or wars for ambition, or, in short, English wars; it is wrong to have wars in which the animating spirit is cruelty; wars of national vanity, which are called wars of honor; whenever it is to augment territory—all these are wrong, not because the use of force is wrong in the hands of Government, but because the use of force with selfish ends is wrong. . . . All wars in the interest of the animal faculties are wicked; but when the end is right, and when the inspiration is just and humane, then wars are just, provided they are the last resort. The top of the head has a right to go to war, but the bottom never. . . . If you want peace, you must have justice. (Cheers.) To forbid just defensive war is to give arms to tyrants, and take them away from victims. You must stop injustice, or stop offensive war. It is very much like attempting to reform a community by turning the doctors and medicines out, without turning out the diseases. . . .[4]

Beecher's message probably represented, at least to some degree, the views of the majority of Northern clergymen. But some found it impossible to reconcile war with the Christian ethic. It must be justified on secular, not religious, grounds. The Reverend William

Rounseville Alger was one of these. He spoke thoughtfully rather than emotionally of the Christian's dilemma.

. . . War is a discord in the music of humanity, a clash in the machinery of society, the accompaniment of a fearfully imperfect civilization; not in any form an exemplification of the will of God, but the horrid work of wicked men; to be profoundly lamented, avoided whenever it consistently can be, utterly left behind as soon as possible. The natural influence of each fresh outbreak of it is to blight the industry and bankrupt the resources of a country, and to inflame and give a new lease of power to that combative spirit which is from beneath. Now, as ever—nay, more than ever—it becomes the preacher to give emphasis to the fact, that war is not a glorious opportunity, to be coveted and to feel proud of, but a tremendous evil, which good men can accept only in stern sadness, as a necessity forced on them by the savage passions of a sinful age. . . .

In the swallowing flood and tempest of patriotic fervor surging through the popular breast at a time like this, moral boundaries and lights, which ought ever to be firmly perceived and adhered to, are very apt to be blotted out by the swash of emotional sophistry. For instance: it is said, "To go to the conflict, and to cut down the foe without mercy, *is a religious duty.*" I think this is putting the matter on a false ground, confounding things wholly distinct. I say, to fight down this infamous rebellion is not religion in any sense at all, but is a civil obligation, a social necessity rising superior to everything else, and, for the time being, putting religion into abeyance. Religion is purity, prayer, and peace; to subject the passions to the conscience; to be meek and pious; to forgive injuries; to love our neighbors as ourselves, and God with all the heart. War is, to let loose the destructive elements of our nature, to brook no insult, to suppress opposition, to burn and to kill. Now, this is to be justified, not by baptizing it with the abused name of Religion, but by recognizing it as one of those emergencies in the career of a nation, where the supreme instinct of self-preservation asserts itself unto the temporary subordination of every other authority. Morality is the system of usages rightfully administering the life of a nation. Religion is the loving and reverential spirit rightfully animating those usages, and giving them celestial emphasis and direction. War is neither the rightful rule nor the rightful spirit of a nation's life, but the instinctive resources of a nation in self-defence when its life is threatened; its re-actionary self-vindication when its material existence, the government, or its spiritual vitality, the public honor, is assailed. Obviously, on the inevitable ground of instinct, life itself must take precedence both of its formal rules, or morality, and of its flowering spirit, or religion. The genuine justification of our military attitude and work in this crisis rests on the basis of civil obligation and social necessity, not on the basis of ethical right and religious duty. . . .[5]

In 1860, the Reverend Octavius Brooks Frothingham became pastor of the Third Unitarian Church in New York City. He was a humanist with a sincere belief in rational liberty. Profoundly shocked by the seeming waste wrought by war deaths, he sought to mitigate his anguish by the thought that the sacrifice would not be in vain—that it would have an immortal influence. "These deaths," he declared, "are the snapping open of so many brave caskets, and the dropping into the fruitful soil of humanity of the quick seeds of a a new national and human life." This, in turn, implied that Frothingham's humanistic faith was based upon evolutionary doctrine—the doctrine of "seeds and shells."

Of all the economies of nature, none is more beautiful than that by which the living germs of plants are kept safe in their shells till such time as they may be ready to produce new plants, and then are dropped or thrown out by the breaking of the shell, to take root in the earth and reproduce their kind.

. . . . .

The enormous heaps of ruin that lie strewn about over the fields of history are the cast-off shells which the growing thought of mankind has clipped, broken, and left behind. The breaking of the shell of State is called revolution; the breaking of the shell of Church is called reformation; in both it is new life bursting through its bark; it is the harvest springing from decay. No shell is strong enough to resist the pressure of life within it. . . .

It is the earnest hope of many, and those the most earnest people, that we, as a people, are now passing through a process of evolution, and it is this hope alone that sustains them amid the sorrows and sacrifices of the time. . . . The principle of life in our people, the sentiment of liberty, the sense of the right and human, the practical feeling of what is due to man as man, has been growing prodigiously, to many people very alarmingly, in the last twenty years. It has increased with the increasing population, it has enlarged with the enlarging territory, it has become clear and powerful by force of circumstances. It could not any longer be contained within the old social limits, and was rapidly creating a new society of its own, radically different from that of older States. It has been apparent, for a long time, that the shell of the Constitution was becoming thin and weak at the clauses that pledged the return of fugitives and guaranteed the three-fifths representation, and must soon open there; and now the ghastly split that pushes asunder the States that live by slavery, and the States that live by freedom, shows the extent to which the vital germs of our nationality have swollen, and the vigor with which they insist on making their way out into larger development and more purely human relations. . . . Think, O, think, what it would be to heave from our hearts that monstrous belching Aetna of Slavery, and to draw in, instead of its sulphurous blasts, long and deep inhalations of the pure atmosphere of Heaven. The emancipation of the black people would be the emancipation of all the white people in the land. The merchants would be free in their honor; the traders would be free in their honesty; judges would be free to be just; lawyers would be free to be conscientious; clergymen would be free to be Christian; patriots would be free to love their country sincerely; citizens would be free to consult the glorious welfare of the State; gentlemen and ladies would be free to tell the truth in parlor and street. The seeds of healthy industry and quick intelligence would be scattered broadcast over the whole country, and would come up in the shape of factories, schools, libraries, churches, clustering houses in the midst of pleasant gardens and teeming farms, flourishing villages, great cities, literature, science, art, laws fitted to the moral sentiment of the nation, institutions suited to the popular life. What luscious fruit to the Southern people themselves would not all this bring! The brain is bewildered at the dream of it: the redemption of their lands; the enormously enhanced production of free labor; the lifting of that black terror of insurrection; the

Scene in the House of Representatives, January 31, 1863

PASSAGE OF THE CONSTITUTIONAL AMENDMENT ABOLISHING SLAVERY

privilege of teaching the laboring class, and of turning to account the latent human powers, whose activity they dare not now encourage; the rescue of thousands of young men from the pit of a most abominable licentiousness, and the opening to them of a manly and honorable career—where shall we stop? There is really no end to the benefits that emancipation would confer. All that free institutions have done, where they have done most; all that free insitutions have done in Massachusetts might be freely promised in time to all the continent, if the shell, already so cracked and divided that it just hangs together by a few filaments of sentiment or policy, could be manfully struck, and nobly permitted to fall into the ground and die. . . .[6]

Frederic Henry Hedge was professor of ecclesiastical history in the Harvard Divinity School. Strongly influenced by German idealism, he had joined with Emerson and George Ripley in shaping the transcendentalist movement. In his "The Sick Woman. A Sermon For the Time," he could foresee a final solution to the problem of war only in moral regeneration of the whole people.

. . . What the country needs is to be made whole, to have its integrity re-stored and re-established on a sure foundation. How to accomplish this is the problem—a problem at which the physicians of the body politic, both before and since the disorders burst into this fever of a civil war, have been tugging and scheming with laudable zeal and honest intent, but with utter irrecognition of the real nature of the evil and the means and conditions of a radical cure. Missouri compromises and all other compromises and provisos and resolutions, and bills to pacify refractory parties that refused pacification, to keep together what was obstinately bent on disruption—all these were empiric doses, ineffectual half measures, whereby the patient "was nothing bettered but rather grew worse." The real difficulty all the while was something far more deeply inwrought in the very fabric of the national policy, which the politicians were either unable or unwilling to perceive, or too preoccupied with the paltry issues and aims of the hour, with the rivalries of faction, with the canvass of votes and the scramble for office, to confront. It was a conflict, not of sectional jealousies or party interests merely, but of fundamental principles, of the very elements of civil life. The real difficulty was, in its temporal aspect, a social discord growing out of the attempt to combine feudal and democratic principles and ideas in one polity. Viewed on the moral side it was a rupture between the national conscience and the national will, the origin of which was a contradiction in the Constitution itself—a falsification of the axioms of the Constitution by provisions of a contrary nature engrafted upon it. This rupture between the conscience and the will of the nation had gone such lengths that finally the relation of the two became completely inverted, and on the basis of this inversion a new and false union was established between them, in which the conscience was made subordinate instead of supreme—the will dictating to conscience what it should receive as right and good instead of the conscience giving law to the will. . . . The will of a faction was enthroned as absolute right, than which there could be no "higher law." Thus conscience was subsidized by reckless will; political ambition attempted to wrest Nature from her allegiance and to bend the Everlasting to its own behoof. . . .

. . . The first and most essential thing to be secured is the moral integrity of the nation. By that I do not mean the moral perfection of all the individuals composing it, but a cordial, living union of all the States on a moral basis—on the basis of a moral consent, on identity of organic principles and ideas, assent to the moral truths which lie at the basis of society, recognition of the rights of man and the Christian law of righteousness, as applicable to those rights. Without this there can be no radical cure, no restoration, no health, no peace, no nation. This moral integrity is something which neither polity nor force alone can effect. Mere victories of arms, however needful, cannot secure it, but only moral regeneration—re-birth of the national mind and heart by faith. . . .[7]

The Reverend Horace Bushnell, in "A Discourse Delivered on the Sunday after the Disaster of Bull Run," traced the origins of the Civil War to a conflict between the politico-religious experience of New England and the "unreligious" political abstractions of a "false" democracy whose prophet had been Thomas Jefferson.

. . . It is a remarkable, but very serious fact, not sufficiently noted, as far as my observation extends, that our grand revolutionary fathers left us the legacy of this war, in the ambiguities of thought and principle which they suffered, in respect to the foundations of government itself. The real fact is that, without proposing it, or being distinctly conscious of it, they organized a government, such as we, at least, have understood to be without moral or religious ideas; in one view a merely man-made compact, that without something farther, which in fact was omitted or philosophically excluded, could never have been more than a semblance of authority. More it has actually had, because our nature itself has been wiser and deeper, and closer to God, than our political doctrines; but we have been gradually wearing our nature down to the level of our doctrines; breeding out, so to speak, the sentiments in it that took hold of authority, till at last, we have brought ourselves down as closely as may be, to the dissolution of all nationality and all ties of order. Hence the war. It has come just as soon as we made it necessary, and not a day sooner. And it will stay on to the end of our history itself, unless the mistake we have suffered is, at least, practically rectified. We have never been a properly loyal people; we are not so now, save in the mere feeling, or flame of the hour. Our habit has been too much a habit of disrespect, not to persons only, but to law. Government, we say, or have been saying, is only what we make ourselves, therefore we are at least on a level with it; we too, made the nationality, and can we not as well unmake it?

That we may duly understand this matter, go back a moment to the Revolution, and trace the two very distinct, yet, in a certain superficial sense, agreeing elements, that entered into it. First, there was what, for distinction's sake, we may call the historic element, represented, more especially, by the New England people. The political ideas were shaped by religion. . . . The church, for example, was a brotherhood; out of that grew historically the notions of political equality in the state. Government was also conceived to be for the governed, just as the church was for the members; and both were God's institutes—ordinances of God. The major vote in both, was only the way of designating rulers, not the source of their sovereignty or spring of their authority. Designated by us, their investiture was from God, the only spring of authority. . . .

The other wing was prepared by sentiments wholly different; such, for example, as are sufficiently represented in the life and immense public influence of Mr. Jefferson; a man who taught abstractively, not religiously, and led the unreligious mind of the time by his abstractions. It was not his way to deal in moral ideas of any kind. Familiar with the writings of Rousseau and the generally infidel literature of the French nation, his mind was, to say the least, so far dominated by them, as to work entirely in their molds. He had no conception of any difficulty in making a complete government for the political state by mere human composition; following Rousseau's theory, which discovers the foundation of all government in a "social compact." Going never higher than man, or back of man, he supposed that man could somehow create authority over man; that a machine could be got up by the consent of the governed that would really oblige, or bind their consent; not staying even to observe that the moment anything binds, or takes hold of the moral nature, it rules by force of a moral idea, and touches, by the supposition, some throne of order and law above the range of mere humanity. Covered in by this immense oversight, he falls back on the philosophic, abstractive contemplation of men, and finding them all so many original monads with nothing historic in them as yet, he says, are they not all equal? Taking the men thus to be inherently equal in their natural prerogatives and rights, he asks their consent, makes the compact, and that is to be the grand political liberty of the world.

But the two great wings thus described can agree you will see, in many things, only saying them always in a different sense; one in a historic, the other in an abstractive, theoretic sense; one in a religious, and the other in an atheistic; both looking after consent and the major vote, both going for equality, both wanting Articles of Agreement, and finally both a Constitution. And the result is, that in the consent, in the major vote, in the equality, in the Articles of Agreement, in the Constitution, Christianity, in its solid and historic verity, as embodied in the life of a people, joins hands, so to speak, with what have been called, though in a different view, the "glittering generalities" of Mr. Jefferson. Thus in drawing the Declaration of Independence, he puts in, by courtesy, the recognition of a Creator and creation, following on with his "self-evident truths," such as that "all men are created equal," and that "governments derive their just powers from the consent of the governed," in which, too, the other wing of the revolution can well enough agree, only if they will take them, not as abstractions, but in a sense that is qualified and shaped by their history. They had nothing to do with some theoretic equality in man *before* government, in which, as a first truth of nature, governments are grounded. They were born into government, and they even believed in a certain equality under it, as their personal right. They had also elected their rulers, and so far as they could agreed to the right of a government by consent, but they never had assumed that men are *ipso facto* exempt from obligation who have not consented, or that an autocratic and princely government is of necessity void and without "just power." Their "equality," their "consent," were the divine right of their history, from the landing of the fathers downward, and before the French encyclopedists were born.

You will thus perceive that two distinct, or widely different constitutional elements entered into our political order at the beginning; that agreeing in form of words, they . . . have, in fact, been struggling in the womb of it, like Jacob and Esau, from the first day until now. . . .[8]

The discussion of war, Christianity, and morality was not limited to the pulpit. Laymen joined in. Charles Eliot Norton based his defense of the North's cause on political ethics. For him the war was a struggle between the political morality of the North and slaveholding immorality. If Northern political ethics were sublimated by war, he could see emerging from the conflict a Utopian ideal that would be close to anarchism. He wrote:

. . . Under the American system, a main feature of which is the constant potential improvement of the individual, the functions of external government are reduced to their lowest point, and under this system the way is open for the realization of the most inspiring and most promising idea of modern Christian civilization—the true brotherhood of man, in which man shall feel himself no longer an isolated individual, but shall find his completeness and perfection, his worth and his happiness, in the recognized relations of mutual dependence existing between himself and the community of which he forms an integral and essential part. Without the rest of mankind he is poor, bare, solitary, and his own nature is incomplete. . . . With them he is rich, completed, and capable of a spiritual development of which our present civilization affords but a faint and partial type.

The principles thus recognized are essentially American, the principles, namely, that politics are a subordinate branch of morals—that the people are, properly speaking, the whole community united in moral relations—that the state, politically speaking, derives its existence from the people—and that the government is but a device, determined by considerations of expediency, for the attainment of certain ends. . . . A state, founded, as ours is, on natural rights, and deriving its existence from the people, includes two controlling agencies, consisting on the one hand of a government instituted with forms and powers, and operating through organized legal and military authority, and on the other hand in the devices and arrangements adopted by the people, or growing up among them, for the preservation of the inherent good order of a well-disposed and intelligent community. . . . The government is subordinate to the arrangements for preserving good order which can and do exist independently of it. It is made, supported, and changed by proceedings outside of its own limits, save in so far as the forms of those proceedings may be regulated by it; and, instead of originating the good order of the community, itself originates from that good order. . . .[9]

Major Edward Bissell Hunt was the brother of an antebellum Governor of New York, Washington Hunt. By applying a loose interpretation of organic evolution to the development of society, and especially to the government of the United States under the Constitution, he defended the Union as a "living unity" which the South was bent upon destroying by amputation. His, however, was not a materialistic but a theistic interpretation, for in common with other theistic evolutionists, he believed that God revealed His purpose through nature. Thus the North's was the cause of evolutionary progress under God.

. . . The scientific study of nature throws much light on the question as to "what constitutes a State." Minds which have grown familiar with the organic kingdom and the grand principles of organic growth and structure, can hardly fail to recognize that nations are social and political organisms, and that the entire human family constitutes an organism of still higher generality. Germs and eggs are developed by growth into mature prolific organisms. So do nations, from germinal beginnings or colonies, develop, by vital growths, into imperial organizations, which in turn, establish colonies, and finally die of violence, disease or senility. . . . Our nation has passed through its feeble infancy, its colonial boyhood, its bold launch into independence, and its early years of young manhood. Nations, like other organisms, pass from a primal simplicity of structure to an increasing complexity of parts and functions. Nations, too, like organisms, at first manifest but slight mutual dependence of parts, but with their growth into complexity, their functions and subdivisions develop an increasing inter-dependence, until the total life at last rests on the functional perfection of each portion. Man's practical vocation is to labor. As society progresses, labor is subdivided or specialized, and the economic prosperity of a nation depends on the perfection of this labor-specialization, or on the proper correlation of its specialties. So too in plants and animals, does progress in the specialization of functions and functional organs and in their normal correlation, increasingly mark every step from germination to maturity.

. . . . .

Nothing can make the heresy of secession seem more heretical than to test its application in our government, when viewed as an organism. Were we but a polype nation, fissiparous, division would not be unnatural. Were we but some brainless, articulate organism, we might be cut in two and each half might become a living whole. That sub-cerebral states should assume superiority over the cerebral general government, is not less monstrous than the fantasy of a peaceful, painless dismembering of a high political organism. Treason seemed almost to have found an anesthetic which would enable a nation of high and sensitive structure to be cleft in twain, unconscious of the dividing edge.

Secession theories rest on the postulate of a nation *manufactured* at a certain date. *Nations grow: they are not made.* True organisms, they, like all animate beings, grow from embryo to old age. Their governments are *vital* realities; not parchments nor bargains. . . . We shall do well ever to bear in mind this living, organic nature of our government, and not to rest an unreasoning faith on the mere *verba scripta* of the Constitution. This instrument, with wondrous insight, provides for its own modification, to insure its permanent agreement with the natural, organic constitution of our people in all stages of our growth. Too exclusive an attention to the historic phases of our political organism, and too lawyer-like a concentration on the written charter which formalized it, have perhaps blinded our statesmen to the profounder organic entity, which lives in our people, and which, as it then existed, was so happily appreciated by the framers. To exalt *legal formalism* above *vital realism* is to frustrate Nature, or to breed liberating revolutions. . . .[10]

The war of ideas embraced a far broader front than Christian ethics. It was a war of cultures. New England scholars, stung by Southern taunts of "tight fisted Puritans," "mudsills," "greasy mechanics" and "shopkeepers," revived the traditions of the seventeenth-century Puritan revolution. Edmund Hamilton Sears saw in the volunteers of New England a reincarnation of the hymn-singing Roundheads who fought in Oliver Cromwell's army.

Men make a fatal mistake when they despise their enemies. That the South have persistently misunderstood the North becomes more apparent as the present controversy waxes hotter and closer. That the North would not fight; that New England men are a generation of brokers and pedlars, who would bear anything for the sake of peace; that its laboring masses are a race of boors, very easily routed, is the delusion under which the South have long acted, and which they are soon to see dispelled. The present controversy is the old one reproduced on American soil—the Saxon against the Norman, the Puritan against the Cavalier. The same prize is at stake, —liberty protected by law; liberty, not the privilege of a pampered aristocracy, but the boon and inheritance of all the people. For, complicate it as we may, this is the grand issue—whether Freedom or the Slave despotism shall possess and rule the continent.

We shall not be invincible in this controversy unless we enter upon it as a religious war. Go to it in obedience to the call of God, and the spirit of a long line of ancestry will roll through us and breathe upon us from every consecrated battle-field, from Newbury and Naseby downward. It is a most auspicious omen that a large portion of those who have enlisted are religious men. Their courage will not be inspired by rum, profane incitements, or even by the soldier's honor, but by the fear of God, and the love of his justice, and the love of humanity—motives which lift us out of ourselves and enable us to look with contempt upon death. Preach it as a religious war, from every pulpit, from the head of every regiment; let the soldiers carry it to God in their tents at night, and like Cromwell's soldiers, on the eve of battle lift up hymns against the sky, and then an arm not of flesh will smite the enemies of God and man. Let the whole Northern army be pervaded by this spirit, and we shall be saved from one of the worst consequences of war, corruption of morals. . . . And when the war is done, the religious and moral tone of society, instead of being relaxed and let down, will be found wrought up to a higher pitch than ever before. The political atmosphere about Washington, which for a long time has sweltered with corruption, will have been cleared, and become as pure and bracing as the air after a thunderstorm.[11]

Evan W. Evans, professor of natural philosophy and astronomy in Marietta College, in a slashing attack on Virginia's cherished "Cavalier tradition," carried the war to the enemy.

What Plymouth was to the North, Jamestown was to the South. Let us glance at the history of the first families of Virginia.

The numerous reputed scions of that stock are accustomed to talk boastfully of their origin; they despise the Puritans as their inferiors. On what is their claim to superiority based? . . . The three distinctive principles of American civilization, namely, constitutional democracy, religious liberty, and free popular education had their first development in New England.

On what, then, do the Virginians base their pride of ancestry? On blood, on aristocracy, on rank. They are not of plebeian origin, as the Puritans are. They are descendants of lordly cavaliers, a highborn and superior race, inheriting the blood even of those who came over to England with the Norman conqueror, to rule over the vulgar Saxon. Such is their claim, as set forth by Jefferson Davis himself. Now, waiving the question of the value of blood, considered without reference to character, let us examine into the validity of this claim. Let us see whether it be an historical fact, or only an audacious fiction.

. . . . .

Doubtless there were among them some "gentlemen born," but the great mass were of another description. Historians agree in characterizing the first settlers of Jamestown as needy adventurers, vagabond gentlemen, and servants of ill life.

. . . . .

The company sent over several ship loads of "agreeable persons, young and incorrupt," who were sold to the planters for wives. . . . It would indeed be highly uncharitable toward those ancient families to suppose that the maternal founders of any of them still remain unpaid for.

But the sale of ancestors in the Old Dominion was by no means confined to women. White servants of both sexes became a regular article of traffic. . . . What makes the whole matter more ludicrous is, that many of these loyal "cavaliers" were sold into bondage by the Puritans. The raving Judge Jeffreys did not neglect this fine opportunity of displaying righteous indignation over the sins of the austere sect. By a highly unpoetical justice, some of the Puritans themselves, upon the restoration of the Stuarts, were sold into Virginia; and we may hope they did not much thicken the blood of her population. As to Irish insurrectionists, they were sold thither by hundreds at a time. . . . It is certain that very many of the bondsmen, of different classes, after the expiration of their terms of service, became men of consideration and thrift, founders of respectable families. It is a grievous mistake to suppose that even the worst class of them gave origin only to what is known as the "poor white trash."

. . . . .

Many respectable Englishmen, as the cultivation of the soil became more profitable, came into the colony to mend their fortunes and to enjoy a social position which they could not reach at home. These were men of limited means, small farmers and tradesmen, gentlemen in reduced circumstances, rarely men of some wealth—upon the whole, a sufficiently respectable ancestry for any people, but such as our fastidious and noble friends across the water would hardly dignify with a better epithet than plebeian. . . . Moreover, large numbers of Scotch-Irish, and Pennsylvania Germans, respectable but not patrician stocks, settled in what is known as the Valley;

and if there is any necessary advantage in a mixed origin, Virginia certainly has it. Out of this heterogeneous mass there arose, in time, a prosperous community. In a country where land cost almost nothing, it was easy for the most thrifty of the inhabitants to acquire large plantations. The introduction of negro slavery served still further to elevate this fortunate class above the common level. Planters with a few hundred acres and a score or two of slaves, began to take pride in aping, in a small way, the old feudal lords of Europe with their broad territories and their thousands of retainers. Such is the true history of the rise of aristocracy in Virginia. . . .[12]

John Murray Forbes, a New Englander who had made a fortune in the China trade and Western railroads, was one of the organizers of the New England Loyal Publication Society, dedicated to the publicizing of "loyal" ideas. He saw the war as the people against aristocracy.

The negro question being settled, and the opinions of the great body of loyal people now right thereupon, the next great want is to get the public mind of the North, and of such part of the South as you can reach, right upon the true issue of the existing struggle. . . . The aristocrats and the despots of the Old World see that our quarrel is that of the people against an aristocracy. If our people of the North can be made to see this truth, the rebellion will be crushed for want of Northern support, which it has had from the wolves under the sheep's garments of sham democracy. . . . After we get military success, the mass of the southern people must be made to see this truth, and then reconstruction becomes easy and permanent. . . . Bonaparte, when under the republic, fighting despots of Europe, did as much by his bulletins as he did by his bayonets; the two went on together promising democratic institutions to the populations whose leaders he was making war upon. You have the same opportunity, and greater; for you have enemies North and South, *reading* our language, whom you can teach. . . . My suggestion then, is that you should seize an early opportunity and any subsequent chance, to teach your great audience of plain people that the war is not the North against the South, but the people against the aristocrats. . . .[13]

Charles Godfrey Leland was variously editor of the Continental Monthly, *a free-lance journalist, and a second-rank man of letters. A combination of Jeremy Bentham's utilitarianism, Henry C. Carey's economic nationalism, and his own bombast went into his credo that the war was a crusade for free labor.*

. . . Never yet—and God witnesses the truth—was the great principle of human progress so clearly and intelligently and knowingly opposed to the principle of Caste, of Aristocracy, of Immobility, as it now is in this battle. To those in this country who have for years past been reading Richmond sociologies, and New-Orleans editorials—who have seen Hammond's white Mud-Sill theory practically and theoretically endorsed as the true basis of society, and who know what "Our First Families" and "Our Aristocracy" really *mean* in the South, this accusation of a want of a definite principle is ineffably ridiculous. All Americans, of all parties, know better. Even the bitterest enemies of the Union understand that FREE LABOR represents the continued struggle of the many upward into their rights—from subordination to capital, into a harmony of interests with capital. They understand that it is virtually a strife between the endless, restless, "working and weaving in endless motion" of manufactures, and the never-moving condition of old-fashioned agriculture—and of slave agriculture at that. All of this has been more than felt or understood: it has been *expressed*—philosophically expressed—and accepted as formulising the doctrines of the North—those doctrines which Secessionism now repudiates and fights.

It was in the works of Henry Carey, of Philadelphia, that the doctrine of Labor, as a definition of Wealth, was first formally enunciated as the basis of a political economy. And it was during the Fremont campaign that these labor or free-labor doctrines, as correlative with the universal rights of man, and as opposed to the professed opposers of greasy mechanics, were first scattered broadcast among the people of America. That presidential campaign was, in all respects, the most important one which had ever taken place, for it witnessed a struggle based on a great and glorious idea—on an abstract principle—on the clearest and most distinct enunciation which the world has ever witnessed of the world's grandest and latest idea: "The greatest good for the greatest number." Hitherto, democracy had taken the crude form so popular with demagogues, of simply abusing capital—of talking as John Randolph did of old, of its oppressing labor, of a war to come between starving operatives and purse-proud factory nabobs. We have changed all that—changed it very much indeed. Capital, as it gradually learns its own interests, finds that it makes more by taking labor into partnership, than by "enslaving" it. The American world has learned that the action of Capital is democratic—science is democratic—art is democratic—in short, in this age we live in, all activity or labor, all inventiveness and novelty, tend inevitably to benefit the masses. . . .

Let us understand it, once and for all, clearly, that the principle or idea for which the North is contending, is that of the rights and dignity of Free Labor as contrasted to unprogressive aristocracy, or that inert respectability which, falling back on "blood," hereditary gifts, and mere possession, proclaims the Mud-Sill doctrine as an immutable law of human nature. It is popularly said that the negro is the real subject of contention. But it is NOT the negro. It was the question of the social standing and rights of the poor *white* man which really built up the Republican party, and which now inspires the whole body of Union men. It was the taunt of Mud-Sills and greasy Mechanics, coupled with the practical assertion of the right of a high-blooded "gentleman" to gutta-percha a "lubberly, base-blooded Yankee" which gave the North its political majority. The country has *talked* "negro" in this matter when it meant "white man"; for it was the stinging vitriol of sneers at the operatives and "bondsmen" of the North, far more than any sympathy for the black, which stirred those operatives up to opposition.

. . . . .

Every fresh strife between Conservatism and Progress has been a battle between Free Labor and Laziness, and every century has seen the fight assuming more distinctly this form. But never yet did it assume so clearly such a form as it has done in the contest between the United and Confederate States of North America. It is the real issue at stake; that which vitalizes the whole, giving it energy and strength. . . .[14]

The tide of nationalism flowed strongly in the nineteenth century. It was, therefore, a popular thesis that identified the North's cause as that of national unity pitted against the feudal particularism of the Confederacy.

France, said Louis Napoleon, at the close of the Italian campaign, is the only nation in Europe that fights for an *idea*. On this continent we are now marshaling a host greater, perhaps, than he brought into the field, to fight, like France, for an *idea*—the paramount authority of the Federal Government; the seceding States denying this authority—the loyal States affirming it.

We have only to go back one step to come at the cause of this wide divergence, which has arrayed brother against brother, and threatens to deluge the country in blood. The Southern planter, a supreme despot within his own little domain, owning his laborers, and relieved of all sense of dependence upon others, has long felt it to be intolerable that a Congress, of which the members from his State compose only one-fiftieth of the whole number, should have the power of prescribing the rule of his conduct. He feels that Government can do little for him, and his sense of obligation is measured by that of benefits received. He has no industry or enterprise off his own plantation. The sails of his ships whiten no sea. He does nothing to develop the resources of distant lands. The only thing he wants is personal protection, and for this he does not look beyond his own State; hence he views with distrust the Federal Government, which, reflecting the sentiments and interests of the whole country, the advancing spirit of the age, and a social organization entirely differing from his, he has long foreseen might some day be brought into direct collision with his fancied interests or ideas.

. . . . .

Opposed to such a sentiment, which is purely negative and hostile, and which shuts a man up in a castle from which to sally only on predatory expeditions and to retire in self-defence, is that truly expansive and cosmopolitan spirit of the North which seeks aggregation by a similarity of laws, pursuits and industries, and by that mutual dependence which a high degree of development of these is certain to produce. A New York merchant naturally desires that all his customers should be subject to the same laws as himself. Under the Constitution of the United States, it was so. The State of South Carolina having seceded from this instrument, he is cooly informed that his customers in it will *not* pay. He has no means whatever of enforcing his rights. So far, consequently, is the field of his operations curtailed. This is the reason why secession is so hateful to the Northern ear. New York today, has investments in other States to the amount of $1,000,000,000. Should all the states "shoot madly from their sphere," the greater part of this vast sum would be lost. A company of merchant princes constructed the Illinois Central Railroad, at a cost of $40,000,000, every cent of which was furnished from the Eastern States and from Europe. . . . This great enterprise, which has enriched Illinois to the amount of hundreds of millions, would be valueless to its owners, should Illinois follow the example of South Carolina. For this reason it is felt in all the Free States that secession is the destruction of property; that it is pure anarchy, threatening the subversion of society itself. This is the key-note of the great uprising, which has no parallel in history. It touches every man in his tenderest spot. It destroys not only the present but all hope for the future. . . .

. . . The North is cosmopolitan, absorbing whatever is similar in kind. It is creative, infusing with its own faculty and genius whatever it touches. It is in peace what Rome was in arms. Its field is a continent. Its mission homogeneity; but this homogeneity must be of institutions, of industries, and of charities which realize our highest idea of what man is capable. . . .

The North believes in a higher destiny. Its mission is not only to subdue a continent, but to make it homogeneous in its institutions and ideas, and to render it a fitting theatre upon which the highest drama of human life yet brought out is to be enacted. The contest in which we are engaged is not an American war, but a war of humanity, which enlists in our cause every noble sentiment and impulse. . . .[15]

As a Civil War publicist, James Russell Lowell was perhaps more articulate than profound. Nonetheless, he was influential in both forming and expressing public opinion. For him, the prime objectives of the war were to maintain order and the unity of the nation against the anarchical influence being spawned by the slaveholding Confederacy.

. . . We have no doubt of the issue. We believe that the strongest battalions are always on the side of God. The Southern army will be fighting for Jefferson Davis, or at most for the liberty of self-misgovernment, while we go forth for the defence of principles which alone make government august and civil society possible. It is the very life of the nation that is at stake. There is no question here of dynasties, races, religions,—but simply whether we will consent to include in our Bill of Rights—not merely as of equal validity with all other rights, whether natural or acquired, but by its very nature transcending and abrogating them all—the Right of Anarchy. We must convince men that treason against the ballot-box is as dangerous as treason against a throne, and that, if they play so desperate a game, they must stake their lives on the hazard. The one lesson that remained for us to teach the political theorists of the Old World was, that we are as strong to suppress intestine disorder as foreign aggression, and we must teach it decisively and thoroughly. The economy of war is to be tested by the value of the object to be gained by it. A ten years' war would be cheap that gave us a country to be proud of and a flag that should command the respect of the world because it was the symbol of the enthusiastic unity of a great nation. . . .[16]

Science applied to industry—the centripetal force building a new, progressive order—was a cliché borrowed from Herbert Spencer by an editorialist of the New York Herald. *It has remained an explanation of the North's triumph in the Civil War, although the naive assumption that "truth, reason, and justice" would accompany such a victory has withered under the hot sun of reality.*

If there ever was an age of miracles it is the present one—miracles of a positive, real, tangible character, not depending upon hearsay testimony or musty tradition for belief in their existence, but proving themselves and writing their history in ineffaceable characters on the great book of the earth's surface. Their types are interoceanic canals; railroads that traverse continents; telegraph lines that, crossing land and sea, girdle the earth; tunnels that pierce the Alps and the Appenines and bore their way under the beds of great lakes, and aqueducts that, from distant sources of supply, carry the water on which the inhabitants of great cities depend for cleanliness, life and health. These are the real miracles, appealing, not to the ear of credulity, but to the eye of reason, for proofs that man is little lower than the angels. . . .

In primitive and less advanced states of society the tendency is for communities to form themselves into classes, septs, tribes, and petty principalities; but, as civilization extends these little independencies inevitably, either through war, conquest, intermarriage or voluntary association, become blended into larger nationalities. Russia, Austria, France, England and the United States are all examples of the operation of that law, which may be defined in one sentence: "Barbarism favors the establishment of small communities, civilization that of powerful nationalities." The great internecine war in which the United States are at present engaged is but the last and greatest development of "the irrepressible conflict" between these two warring principles. We have on our side the moral as well as the physical support of this law of progress. The canals, the railroads, the telegraphs—all the great material works of the age—are co-workers with us, all tending towards the at least partial realization of that grand idea which poets have sung and prophets predicted, when all the nations of the earth shall be gathered into one fold and animated by the same principles of truth, justice, reason and civilization.[17]

The concept of the conflict as one of human progress against the forces of reaction was stretched to its uttermost limits in a New York Times *editorial. The writer viewed the American Civil War as more than a war for union and emancipation. It was a phase of the worldwide march towards liberalism and human rights.*

Whoever supposes that the conflict now waging [*sic*] in these States, is peculiar to this side of the Atlantic, or to this Continent, or that it was contingent upon, or the result of the late Presidential election, makes a very great mistake. A reference to the history of the last few decades will show that the universal drift all over the civilized world has been towards liberalism, towards the breaking up of despotisms and the advancement of human rights. The genius and spirit of the age, moving all over the face of the earth, points to the amelioration of the condition of the great masses—the millions who do the work and on whose shoulders rest the ultimate burthens of Government. . . . All over Europe is sounding the note of preparation for new movements in favor of liberalism. Underlying and impelling forward this current of events, is the great fact of a constant struggle between popular rights and despotic sway—a struggle that has been going on for decades, kept alive and strengthened by the genius and spirit of the age in which we live. . . .

In this country the conflict is intensified, because here, more than anywhere else in the wide world, is the difference between the existing forces more distinctly marked, more deeply appreciated, and in more immediate contact. On the one hand is an educated enlightened freedom that verges upon license, and on the other hand a despotism, in theory at least, whatever its practical workings may be, the mightiest and meanest that the sun or the stars ever shone upon. These two everlasting antagonisms have been approaching each other for half a century, and are at last standing face to face, with all their passions aroused and their blood up. The two systems of civilization so antipode in everything are in immediate collision. The one recognizing in all men, of whatever race, lineage or color, inalienable right as men, conceding to all the free enjoyment of life, liberty and the pursuit of happiness, regarding these great truths not as rhetorical abstractions, but as articles of living faith. The other, based upon the liberty and domination of one race, sustained by the degradation and enslaving of another; having for its leading axiom freedom for the white man—Slavery for the black. A struggle for supremacy between these systems was inevitable. . . .

The march of armies is not promotive of the safety of Slavery, and, if as an incident to this struggle forced upon the loyal States, the institution shall perish, so be it. We are drifting upon the currents of a destiny under the control of a power higher than human agencies. The path of duty is plain, and we must follow it wherever it may lead, or whatever the end may be. If the mad spirit which precipitated this conflict shall perish before the march of Liberalism, and the cause of our troubles be swept away by the onward movement of the age—a movement which we cannot control and do not choose to resist, be it so! . . .[18]

IX

Promises and Threats of Victory

THORNTON WILDER, in The Skin of Our Teeth, *has one of his characters say: "When you're at war, you think about a better life; when you're at peace, you think about a more comfortable one." The Civil War was no exception. No sooner was it under way than optimistic predictions about the postwar future—the promises of victory—began to appear. Because, however, Americans more often than not equate the "better life" with the "more comfortable one," many Northern seers peering into the future recognized no incongruity in a bright new world in which virtue and materialism were wed. Successful individuals must somehow add up to a beneficent society. But there was more. Mixed with optimism was the missionary zeal of humanitarians, the recognition of an emerging plutocracy, the hopes of a new militarism, a cry for a just vengeance—and fears and protests against all of these.*

For, as Northerners were divided during the war on such issues as the way to meet secession, emancipation, the conduct of the war, and the proper basis for a peace, so they were divided in their vision of a postwar future.

A homespun editor of a weekly newspaper in Ohio made a pithy statement of war objectives as he saw them.

"Sweet are the uses of adversity,"—There is not, nor can there be any evil without some good accompanying to mitigate its effects. The loss of an arm developes the remaining limb, so as to make it almost equal to two, the loss of hearing induces a habit of thought and self communion, so beneficial as to make it a question whether the loss of that faculty is a loss or not, particularly when one thinks of the vast amount of nonsense one escapes hearing—and the itch, though a disagreeable disease, is admirably calculated to render one thankful for the perfect scratching arrangements, nature has endowed us with. So the present war, although an undoubted evil, bears some good in its ruin.

It will:

1. Establish the supremacy of free labor upon this continent by showing the slave drivers of the South that the real strength—the actual wealth, the moral life of the nation is in the North where free labor predominates.

2. It will crush, exterminate and do away with a race of politicians, who owning men and women themselves, flattered themselves that they had an ownership of all who were not possessed of the same style of property.

3. It will dethrone Slavery, and show the worshippers of the beast that instead of controlling and ruling in the Government, it exists only upon sufferance.

4. It will disabuse the minds of many Northern men of the slightly erroneous idea that the Southern man is his superior and fitted by nature to rule.

4. [*sic*] It will ensure to the Northern man in the South all the rights and privileges belonging to an American citizen.

5. Having our institutions once placed in jeopardy, we will hereafter appreciate them better, and love them more, and whereas we have been in the habit of considering the Fourth of July a joke, and patriotism generally a very stupid thing, we shall now look at both of them as very desirable.

6. And better than all, the peace that will follow will be a permanent one—. The agitators, the disturbers will all be hung or killed—the South heretofore so full of fight, so ready to appeal to arms when matters and things did not "exactly suit her," will be combed down, cooled down, and taught her proper place in the Union, and we shall never again hear of secession as a remedy for political evils.

This will be the result of the war, and though it takes millions of treasure, and thousands of lives to accomplish it, it is well worth the sacrifice. With the elements that have been disturbing the country for thirty years, a struggle like the one now in hand was inevitable, and the country was never in better condition to stand the shock than now. When once fought out and the rebels severely whipped, there will be an abiding peace, and the country will go on in its career of prosperity at a more spanking pace than ever. The war will result in good.[1]

One publicist saw with remarkable clarity the shifts in economic and political power that the war was making inevitable.

The solution of the stupendous problem, in which we are now engaged, is sure to involve important changes, not only in the conditions of society among us, and in our modes of thought, but, very likely, in the very structure of our government. . . .

One of the most obvious changes will be that which the creation of a great national debt will effect in the conditions of the people. We must expect, as a matter of course, that the results which followed the accumulation of national indebtedness in Europe will be manifested in this country, though under somewhat different conditions, and, perhaps, in a modified form. It is clear that the actual wealth of the nation will be diminished but little, if at all, by this debt. The productive power of Europe has never been greater than since the time that great national debts were incurred. Indeed, industry seems to have thriven more rapidly and yielded richer returns than when such obligations were unknown. Under the stimulus of taxation and the stern necessities begotten of a desire to discharge these obligations, labor has been organized and economized. So far, then, as the productive industry of the country is concerned, we may feel assured that as much, nay, more wealth will be created than ever existed before. In addition to our agricultural products, from which we have heretofore derived the largest part of our national revenue, we may expect that our mineral resources will be developed in a far greater degree than ever. Mines of coal, iron, lead, copper, silver, and gold will be worked as they never have been, because under the pressure of a debt which the nation will be bound to pay. Our manufacturing interests, also, will keep pace with the development of mineral resources, and will add to the wealth of the country. Invention will be stimulated, as it was in England after the close of the great wars with Napoleon, which imposed so great a load upon the nation, and which it has borne so nobly.

Another change, and one not so pleasant to contemplate, is almost certain to follow upon the creation of an enormous national debt, and that is the concentration of wealth. The great fortunes of Europe, the houses distinguished for monetary strength, have been brought into existence simultaneously with the accumulation of government indebtedness. The Rothschilds, the Barings, the Browns, the Hopes, all attained to their position by this means. These houses first made money by their transactions with the governments of Europe, and then added to their possessions by being the media through which such governments have borrowed money of the industry of their subjects. The same process is going on here before our eyes. Those who know the history of the various houses in Wall street can point out the men who are destined to be to America what the houses just mentioned are to the governments of Europe. By perfectly legitimate transactions Mr. Chase has made Mr. Jay Cooke, and through him scores of others, immensely wealthy. Henceforth America will be as distinguished for its rich men as it has heretofore been for its traders of moderate wealth. There will be the same wealth in the country, but it will be in fewer hands; we shall have fewer traders, but more merchant princes and princely bankers. This concentration of business began, in fact, before the opening of the war. The advantage of this will be that there will be fewer non-producers and more consumers, and business, by being done by the wholesale, so to speak, will be at a less cost to the industry of the nation. . . .

These generalizations may seem startling, and the results indicated not altogether pleasing. But they are inevitable. We must accept whatever the future may have in store for us. The poor will not be as poor in this country as they are in Europe, for land is cheap and farms are easy to purchase; while productive land is open to every enterprising laborer, the wages of labor can never be very low, nor will the laborer ever be entirely at the mercy of his employer. Nor will these changes be without their compensations. The tendency to traffic and unproductive employments which has so characterized the American people will, under the pressure of necessity, be turned to more persistent and more productive labor. Then, again, the influence of the wealthy class will give greater stability to the government. Powerful as are the Rothschilds, the Barings, and other houses of equal reputation, in the courts of kings, the Jay Cookes, the Belmonts, the Ketchums, the Jeromes, as well as great banking corporations, will be still more potent in the councils of the people. Those who know the influence exerted by great railway and canal corporations, such as the New York Central and Camden and Amboy Railroads, can estimate how powerful will be the influence of our wealthy men upon the conduct of our national affairs. . . .

. . . An instructive inquiry, too, would be the probable effect of the military struggle in which we are now engaged, upon the government and the national character. Heretofore we have been governed by lawyers, by men who are fond of talk, but averse to decided action. The soldier, however, is a doer and not a talker, and soldiers will hereafter form a political class that will wield great influence. . . .[2]

The role of the military in America's future was discussed more fully and viewed with optimistic complacency by Lieutenant Colonel Cornelius W. Tolles in an article in The United States Service Magazine.

Although no measures have yet been adopted by Congress for a thorough revision and reconstruction of our military system, some comprehensive scheme is expected not only by the army, but also generally by the people. Nothing is more common than the remark, among all classes of citizens, that after the war is finished a large army must become a permanent institution. An immediate requirement for it will exist, it is thought, in the necessity of maintaining tranquility in the South; while many anticipate that the United States will hereafter be constrained to become a great military power, for the purpose of defending itself from aggression, or perhaps of carrying its principles and policy to the portions of the continent adjoining its northern and southwestern frontiers. . . .

Our civil war has effected a great change in the public sentiment in relation to the army. While, previously, the existence of an army at all had been only tolerated as an unfortunate necessity,—while all exponents of popular thought had persistently urged that ours

President Johnson, Lieutenant-General Grant, and Secretary Stanton Reviewing Sherman's Army on Pennsylvania Ave., May 24, 1865

is essentially a peaceful nation, needing no military enthusiasm and no military organization,—while we had been warned innumerable times of the dangers to republics resulting from standing armies, as exhibited in ancient history,—and while the possibility of any use for a large military force has been scouted,—now, on the contrary, the vocation of the soldier has come to be considered as the most honorable a man can adopt during our national crisis, the advantages of military instruction and accumulated materials for war are admitted, the propriety of vigorously maintaining a system which may be expanded, when occasion demands, into the full measure and complement of a vast army, is acknowledged. It is even understood that the case of turbulent, centralized, conquering Rome is not applicable to the federated United States, with their diverse interests guarded by nearly fifty independent governments, with the General Government directly responsible to the people throughout the extent of the land, with no possibility of a revolution, or the transformation of the Government, and the destruction of our institutions, whatever the army might do. This is, perhaps, the most wonderful discovery of all; for it is an overthrow of all the trite dogmatism of schoolmasters, orators, professors, divines, and statesmen, reiterated for nearly a century with the same unction and received with the same passive acquiescence.

. . . . .

The army should be constantly represented by boards or committees of officers, established by law, and with functions similar to the committees in the French system. . . . Each of the three arms should be represented, and their interests, considered separately and in their relation to each other, receive full attention and exposition. Such committees, changing their *personnel* by some rule disconnected with the changes in the political administration of the country, keeping themselves fully informed on all improvements abroad, and constantly inspecting the operation of our own system in all its departments, could, from year to year, suggest to the President measures which could become parts of a homogeneous, harmonious, and comprehensive system, in place of the isolated enactments now sporadically passed by Congress. . . .[3]

Superficially, it might have seemed that Lieutenant Colonel Tolles was a true prophet, because for nineteen years after Lincoln's death (or until Cleveland's election) every elected President at one time or another had been a general officer in the United States Army. But, it was really a false prophecy because the Civil War army of the North was a citizen's army. When the war was over, the soldier reverted to his role as a civilian. He "voted as he shot," and de-

manded and got pensions, but otherwise, after the fashion of non-veterans, he went about his private business, and between elections left government, as before, to "the trite dogmatism of schoolmasters, orators, professors, divines and statesmen." The day of the military had not yet dawned.

During the war the "dogmatism of the divines," a strong influence in American public affairs since the landing of the Pilgrims, was still making itself heard, though perhaps not felt as strongly as in the past.

The Reverend Edward Everett Hale, a prominent Unitarian clergyman and author of The Man Without a Country, *was a philanthropist zealous for social progress. He believed the antebellum South had lived by bread alone, but as the result of the war God would awaken the region from a sleep of death and give it "life more abundantly."*

. . . The mission of the continental armies to-day, and of the Government of the Union, is to introduce civilization into a region which has been living simply by physical law. People ask if it is to emancipate the slaves that we go there. The question, though so great, is still a narrow question, for, if we stopped at a decree of emancipation, the work would be useless. We are to see, that, in the future these States do "not live by bread alone." We are to compel emancipation by introducing a Christian civilization. We are to introduce manufacture, commerce, science, art, character, and religion. We are to do for them what Joshua did for Canaan, what Greece did for Sicily, what Rome did for Numidia and Gaul and Britain and what chaste and temperate Goths and Huns did for Greece and Italy in turn, when they were well-nigh dead with indolence and lasciviousness and intoxication. We are to introduce with our armies the illustrations of a higher culture, and seeds of a higher civilization. Before that Christian civilization, human slavery will die away, with or without any decree of emancipation, as the snowbanks of February, though no man commanded, have dried away before these April suns.[4]

The Iron Age, *trade journal of the iron industry, also saw "life more abundantly" because of the war.*

. . . This week we have to speak of the surrender of Lee. . . .

So glorious and complete a victory is without parallel in the history at least of modern warfare.

What will be its effect? At home—such individual activity, such commerical prosperity as the country has never witnessed. . . .

Measures will now be wisely and deliberately adopted for the management of the national finances, and the taxes rendered necessary by the war will be judiciously imposed and economically expended, and the people will not feel the burden. Meantime, such a field is opened to human industry in the great Republic—henceforth the most powerful nation on the earth—as never before was presented to toiling men. The South—purified of its foul disease—offers its illimitable resources to men of every creed and race, who come to work; and the places made solitary by slavery and blasted by the mildew of destructive war, will quickly be the dwelling-place of happy, contented freemen, through whose patient labor the land shall bloom as a garden, and smiling peace prevail on every hand. Not only to the soldiers of the republic, but to the emigrants of Europe, will the late rebellious States present a most inviting field of settlement. But not only so—they will at once offer an immense market for merchandise—indeed, on this subject we think the public attention is not sufficiently aroused—because no reasonable doubt can exist that the absolute necessities of the Southern population are such that the present stocks of goods in the country will be found utterly insufficient, and the productive power of the manufacturers will be taxed to their utmost to satisfy it. And this demand will extend to all kinds of commodities, but chiefly, of course, to those which are of indispensable necessity to working people.

Thus there will be an immediate and immense stimulus to commerce and manufactures from the present requirements of the Southern States, and a permanent and mighty development of their resources, which will inevitably produce vast national wealth, and greatly increase the taxable capacity of the country, lightening the burdens upon the loyal sections. . . .[5]

Although Northern speculation and advice regarding the American postwar future ranged far, its center was the South. What was to be done about, or to, it—the planter aristocracy, the Negro, the very fabric of its culture? The voices of the prophets were discordant.

A month after the First Battle of Bull Run, while the North was suffering from the shocking humiliation of the defeat, Sinclair Tousey wrote an article which contended that the Southerners by rebellion had forfeited their legal and constitutional rights. Tousey owned a news agency that distributed newspapers, magazines, pamphlets, and paperback novels. These reached, among other places, the army camps.

. . . Now, it is a principle of law, as well as of common-sense and common justice, that those who violate the law, do by such acts forfeit their right to enjoy the privileges the law guarantees to those who obey its provisions. Thus murderers, burglars, forgers, or any criminals who transgress the law, forfeit their rights under it, and are deprived of their liberties, or it may be of their lives, simply because they have done unpardonable violence to the law; and any attorney who should set up the plea that his murdering or thieving client was having his legal rights interfered with by the gallows or the prison, would naturally deserve and gain the contempt of the community. Violators of law forfeit their claims to the rights guaranteed to those who obey it. If such violators continued to enjoy the same privileges in society as those who never offend, there would be an end to all law, and civilization be extinguished. Force would take the place of order, and the weak yield to the strong. The distinguishing trait of civilization is, that the weakest member of the community is, in the eye of the law, strong as the strongest; were it otherwise, there could be no civilization. The South, or those living in the Southern States, *who have by their rebellion violated the Constitution, have forfeited their claims to its protection,* and are now, in their relation to the Government, in the same position as that of a convicted criminal toward society—they have no legal or constitutional rights left them, except the right of trial, and that trial is now going on from day to day in presence of the whole world, having DEITY for the presiding Judge and humanity for the jury, and must be dealt with by Government as the law and society deal with individual criminals. They must be *punished* for their transgressions, and as these have been greater than the transgressions of any single criminal, so the punishment to be awarded must be great in proportion. . . .[6]

The demand for forfeiture was supported by an uncompromising voice from the West.

Can a citizen secede from the obligations he owes to society around him? Everybody at once answers "No." But suppose he *tries* to do it, and then attempts to act as if he were no longer amenable to the laws, what is the result? Let him publish his solemn act of secession, and then gain access to the vault of the Quincy Savings Bank and carry away its bags of gold and its packages of greenbacks. And suppose then that he is arrested before he has spent a single dollar. Does any "Democrat" demand that he shall be instantly restored to his old rights as soon as the money is recovered? If not, *why* not? Why not just as safely and sensibly restore him to the bosom of an outraged community as to restore a rebellious State to its old privileges as soon as you have disarmed it? You say you cannot trust this Bank robber to go free—that *his* liberty *is* dangerous to *your* rights, and that it is your duty to punish him in order that others may shun his crime. Very well; but is a traitor State a safe member of the family of States? What guarantee have you that it may not soon again commit some outrageous and criminal act which will inflict untold misery—as this war has done—on the community at large? When you have disarmed it why not *keep* it disarmed until there is time to reform its political character? . . .[7]

The doctrine of forfeiture, based upon the thesis that the Southern states should be regarded as conquered provinces, was espoused by Republicans such as Thaddeus Stevens, who was to be the leader of the Radicals in the postwar Congress. As such, it was to be the pervading spirit of congressional reconstruction. It did not, however, represent the spirit of the whole North, or, even the majority of Northerners, during the war and prior to Lincoln's assassination.

Almost a year before the end of the war, Orestes A. Brownson published a forthright reply to those who would reshape Southern society in the image of Northern institutions. In doing so, he made a scathing attack on New Englanders who he equated with Pur-

itans. In the early 1840's Brownson had been close to the transcendental philosophy and was, himself, a Unitarian minister. Conversion to Roman Catholicism was followed by an almost complete revision of his views, and he was increasingly critical of "New Englandizing" tendencies. He supported the Union cause during the war.

We have some madmen amongst us who talk of exterminating the Southern leaders, and of New Englandizing the South. We wish to see the free labor system substituted for the slave-labor system, but beyond that we have no wish to exchange or modify Southern society, and would rather approach Northern society to it, than it to Northern society. The New Englander has excellent points, but is restless in body and mind, always scheming, always in motion, never satisfied with what he has, and always seeking to make all the world like himself, or as easy as himself. He is smart, seldom great; educated, but seldom learned; active in mind, but rarely a profound thinker; religious, but thoroughly materialistic: his worship is rendered in a temple founded on Mammon, and he expects to be carried to heaven in a softly-cushioned railway car, with his sins carefully checked and deposited in the baggage crate with his other luggage, to be duly delivered when he has reached his destination. He is philanthropic but makes his philanthropy his excuse for meddling with everybody's business as if it were his own, and under pretence of promoting religion and morality, he wars against every generous and natural instinct, and aggravates the very evils he seeks to cure. He has his use in the community; but a whole nation composed of such as he would be short-lived, and resemble the community of the lost rather than that of the blest. The Puritan is a reformer by nature, but he never understands the true law of progress, and never has the patience to wait till the reform he wishes for can be practically effected. He is too impatient for the end ever to wait [for] the slow operations of the means, and defeats his own purpose by his inconsiderate haste. He needs the slower, the more deliberate, and the more patient and enduring man of the South to serve as his counterpoise.

The South has for its natural leaders, not simply men of property, but men of large landed estates, and who are engaged in agricultural pursuits: the North has for its natural leaders, business men and their factors, who may or may not be men of wealth, or who, if rich to-day, may be poor to-morrow, and who necessarily seek to subordinate everything to business interests. They of course are less fitted, in a country like ours, to lead than the landholders, because agriculture with us is a broader and more permanent interest of the nation than trade or manufactures.

We insist that it were a gross perversion of the war to make it a war against Southern society or the Southern people. The war is just and defensible only when it is conducted as a war of the nation for its own existence and rights against an armed rebellion. In the war the nation seeks to reduce the rebels to their allegiance, not to destroy them, not to exile them, not to deprive them of their property or their franchises; it seeks to make them once more loyal citizens, and an integral portion of the American people, standing on a footing of perfect equality with the rest, not slaves or tributaries. Southern society must be respected, and any attempt to build up a new South out of the few Union men left there, Northern speculators, sharpers, adventurers, and freed negroes, is not only impolitic, but unconstitutional and wrong. Such a South would be a curse to itself and to the whole nation; we want it not. With here and there an individual exception, the real people of the South are united in the Rebellion, and under their natural leaders, and any scheme of settlement that does not contemplate their remaining with their natural leaders, the real, substantial, ruling people of the Southern States, will not only fail, but ought not to be entertained. They must have the control of affairs in their respective States, and represent them in the councils of the nation. The nation cannot afford to lose them; if it could, it need not have gone to war against them. The bringing of the negro element, except in States where it is too feeble to amount to any thing [*sic*] into American political society will never be submitted to by either the North or the South. We must suppress the Rebellion; but with the distinct understanding that the Southern States are to be restored, when they submit, to all the rights of self-government in the Union, and that no attempt in the mean time shall be made to revolutionize their society in favor of Northern or European ideas. If in our haste, our wrath, or our zeal we have said any thing that can bear a different sense, it must be retracted.

Friends of constitutional government, and of liberty with law, may justly sympathize with our Government in the present struggle; but not European radicals, democrats and revolutionists, for the principle of the struggle is as hostile to them as to the Southern rebels. In this war the nation is fighting Northern democracy or Jacobinism as much as it is Southern aristocracy, and the evidence of it is in the fact, that the people cease to support willingly the war just in proportion as it assumes a Jacobinical character, and loses its character of a war in defence of government and law. . . .[8]

Except for recognizing the demise of slavery, Abraham Lincoln was among those who had no wish to force a modification upon Southern society; he would leave that task to white Southerners, quietly suggesting what might be done in his correspondence with them. He was ready to work out a solution pragmatically, as quickly as possible. It was largely a political decision, and a quick one, that he was looking for. He expressed his views on April 11, 1865, in his last public utterances.

By . . . recent successes the reinauguration of the national authority—reconstruction—which has had a large share of thought from the first, is pressed much more closely upon our attention. It is fraught with great difficulty. . . . We simply must begin with and mould from disorganized and discordant elements. Nor is it a small additional embarrassment that we the loyal people differ among ourselves as to the mode, manner, and means of reconstruction. As a general rule, I abstain from reading the reports of attacks upon myself, wishing not to be provoked by that to which I cannot properly offer an answer. In spite of this precaution, however, it comes to my knowledge that I am much censured for some supposed agency in setting up, and seeking to sustain, the new State government of Louisiana.

. . . . .

We all agree that the seceded States, so called, are out of their proper practical relation with the Union, and that the sole object of the government, civil and military, in regard to those States, is to again get them into proper practical relation. I believe it is not only possible, but in fact easier, to do this, without deciding, or even considering, whether these States have even been out of the Union, than with it. Finding themselves safely at home, it would be utterly immaterial whether they had ever been abroad. Let us all join in doing the acts necessary to restoring the proper practical relations between these States and the Union, and each forever after innocently indulge his own opinion whether in doing the acts, he brought the States from without, into the Union, or only gave them proper assistance, they never having been out of it. The amount of constituency, so to to [*sic*] speak, on which the new Louisiana government rests, would be more satisfactory to all, if it contained fifty, thirty, or even twenty thousand, instead of only about twelve thousand, as it does. It is also unsatisfactory to some that the elective franchise is not given to the colored man. I would myself prefer that it were now conferred on the very intelligent, and on those who serve our cause as soldiers. . . .[9]

Whether Lincoln could have again outmaneuvered the Republican Radicals and rallied strong enough political support to enable him to put his moderate reconstruction program into effect, is, and must remain, one of the unanswered questions of what history "might have been." He died, and Andrew Johnson, who lacked his political following and political genius, was no match for the Radicals, who were eager to take over command. Henry Winter Davis, coauthor of the Wade-Davis Manifesto, in a letter written May 27, 1865, outlined the Radical position and proposed policy.

. . . It rests with the President, in the state in which Congress has left the question, to take the initiative, & the mode in which that is done will determine all that follows.

. . . . . .

If he permit the aggregate whole population of the South qualified to vote under the old governments abrogated by the rebellion, to organize state governments that installs [*sic*] the revolutionary faction in power in the States and fills Congress with their representatives & Senators.

That is to place the sceptre in the hand from which we have just wrested the sword.

If the President attempt to discriminate the loyal from the disloyal & exclude from voting all who have given aid and comfort to the rebellion, a mere handful of the population will remain wholly incompetent to form or maintain a State government & sure to be overwhelmed by the political counter-revolution at the next election which will restore power to the leaders of the rebellion. . . .

The whole mass of the population of the south has given aid & comfort to the rebellion. The war was made by the accession of the union men to the rebel faction . . . they never hesitated a moment which side to take. If there was to be war, they were for their states & against the United States. . . . All are willing to govern the United States again, since independence is impossible. . . . It is a great delusion to suppose them either bold or strong enough to meet & defy the united & energetic faction of revolutionists which drove them into rebellion. . . . No legal line discriminates them from the rebel mass.

If this discrimination be attempted by the oath to support the *constitution* of the United States, *every body* will take it & nobody will be excluded.

. . . . .

If either of these forms be accepted by the President & recognized by Congress, it will instantly change the balance of political power in the United States.

. . . . .

None of the white population of the Southern States is interested in paying the public debt or imposing taxes to meet its interest. They hold none of it. It was created to subjugate them to the laws. It has been consumed in their overthrow. It is to be paid in great part out of their substance. It has annihilated their public debt. It has filled the land with ostracized officers, with wounded soldiers, with an odious free negro population, lately their slaves, & still under their political control.

If the whites be restored to political power, their representatives are interested in repudiating that public debt, in refusing to pay its interest, in restoring their officers to the army & navy, in placing their wounded on the pension roll, in indemnifying their friends for losses by war or confiscation or forced tax sales, in restoring slavery under the forms of apprenticeship or fixed wages & compulsory service & discriminating & oppressive legislation. The effort has already been made in Tenness[ee]. . . .

In Congress a minority can arrest legislation. A majority of either house can compel submission to any terms—under penalty of arresting or disorganizing the government.

The representatives from the states lately in rebellion will form a powerful & hostile minority: & if they do not find enough enemies of the government from the States now represented to give them a majority in one House for some of the purposes above indicated, the near past throws no light on the near future. . . .

To expect them to join in electing a Republican President would be an [word illegible] delusion which the first election would dispel.

. . . . .

But if it be important that the *friends* & not *the enemies* of the government shall continue to govern it, other measures must be taken.

. . . . .

This can be done *only* by recognizing the negro population as an integral part of the *people* of the *Southern States; & by refusing to permit any State Government to be organized on any other basis than . . . universal suffrage & equality before the law.*

. . . . .

If organized & led by men having their confidence the negroes will prove as powerful & loyal at the polls as they have already, in the face of equal clamor & equal prejudice proved themselves under such leaders on the field of battle.

To those who say they are unfit for the franchise, I reply they are more fit than secessionists.

If they be ignorant they are not more so than large masses of the white voters of the South or the Irish rabble which is tumbled on the wharves of New York . . . & brought to the polls. . . .[10]

The greatest of the postwar problems was not to be the legal status of the conquered South, or the political reconstruction of its states. It was to be the Negro. What was his status, his role? During the war, most Northerners probably did not care very much. They were fighting to save the Union and, after the Emancipation Procla-

mation, they fought to free the slaves. That was enough. On the whole, it was neither an anti- nor a pro-Negro sentiment; it was indifference. Events were to prove that after the war a majority of Northerners voted for congressional Radicals and radical reconstruction, but when the program declined and finally was abandoned by President Hayes, they acquiesced with something like a sigh of relief. In short, during the war the Negro had but a small part in the North's vision of the future. But he was, nonetheless, part of the future, and here and there in responsible circles this was recognized. As early as October 16, 1862, the New York Times, *in discussing the coming transformation of the South, included a glance at the role of the freedmen.*

. . . The relations of one race to another, the laws of its disappearance or its increase, are as much a matter of science and investigation, as any other subject in natural history. . . . A weak race does not necessarily "disappear" before a strong; and when it does the causes are scientific, not miraculous. Sometimes the strong race disappears before the weak . . . sometimes . . . they amalgamate; sometimes . . . they live side by side for centuries. . . .

The negro, north of New York, diminishes because the climate is unsuited to him. In New York the births among the blacks just about equal the deaths; south of this latitude their number increases again under evident climatic laws. . . . But whether the competition of free white labor may not drive the negro from occupation, and so cause his extermination at the South, is quite another question. We can perhaps examine it better by supposing an individual instance. We will make the supposition that some three years from this time, the Government, having broken the rebellion, has put up at auction a fine cotton plantation, confiscated from a rebel owner on the Carolina coast. It is bought up by a shrewd enterprising Yankee. He at once hires the former slaves and black overseers, at moderate wages, and commences the very profitable cultivation of cotton. . . . The Yankee's free labor plantation yields a handsome profit, but restless, ingenious and eager for money as he is, he is not satisfied with the slow methods of the negro and their unintelligent labor. . . . He goes North, and returns with ingenious machinery and a corps of hardy, intelligent Northern "hands," tempted by the high wages he can afford to offer. The negroes, excepting a few of the most skillful, go back to their little freeholds and proceed to work there for themselves. . . . They begin to cultivate other products for the market or for export than the great staples.

In the case supposed, the negroes had begun already to appreciate the value of education, and to feel artificial wants. They desired good schools and schoolbooks; the women wanted bright dresses, and the men more respectable clothes; they had beheld and coveted the little luxuries of civilization. These wants are the preventive of idleness. They turn their labor to the thousand other products which the South is capable of producing—perhaps to the cultivation of indigo, for which South Carolina was once so celebrated. They become an industrious peasantry, on their own freeholds. But after a time the laws of climate come in to their aid, with regard to work on the neighboring cotton plantation—and by this we do not mean anything mysterious, only that after a period the hardy Northern workmen on the plantation become weakened and less energetic, from the effect of the heat, or they are taken down with coast fever, or they contract diarrhoeas, or suffer under fever and ague; while the negroes being more uniformly healthy, are found to be more steady laborers.

As time passes, the negroes, though not increasing as fast as under Slavery, are found to increase faster than the foreign white laborers, owing to their greater adaptation to the climate. . . . The negro laborer is henceforth master of the field. In the end—giving them time enough—the blacks must make up the whole industrial population. White brains and capital may direct, but black hands will do the work. . . .[11]

The Lincoln administration, too, was aware of the problem. In March 1863, Secretary Edwin M. Stanton appointed a commission to investigate the condition of the Negro freedmen, and, more important, to formulate plans for future governmental policy. The commission had as its chairman, Robert Dale Owen, eldest son of Robert Owen, the Scottish industrialist and Utopian Socialist, who had sponsored the New Harmony community in Indiana. The commission's report was close to the Radicals' interpretation of the

Negro problem but, lacking the latter's political orientation, was a thoughtful and well-balanced appraisal.

. . . As regards the question what amount of aid and interference is necessary or desirable to enable the freedmen to tide over the stormy transition from slavery to freedom, it is certain that there is as much danger in doing too much as in doing too little. The risk is serious that, under the guise of guardianship, slavery, in a modified form, may be practically restored. Those who have ceased only perforce to be slaveholders will be sure to unite their efforts to effect just such a purpose. It should be the earnest object of all friends of liberty to anticipate and prevent it. Benevolence itself, misdirected, may play into the hands of freedom's enemies; and those whose earnest endeavor is the good of the freedman may unconsciously contribute to his virtual re-enslavement.

The refugees from slavery, when they first cross our lines, need temporary aid, but not more than indigent Southern whites fleeing from secessionism—both being sufferers from the disturbance of labor and the destruction of its products incident to war. The families of colored men, hired as military laborers or enlisted as soldiers, need protection and assistance, but not more than the families of white men similarly situated. Forcibly deprived of education in a state of slavery, the freedmen have a claim upon us to lend a helping hand until they can organize schools for their children. But they will soon take the labor and expense out of our hands; for these people pay no charge more willingly than that which assures them that their children shall reap those advantages of instruction which were denied to themselves.

If we organize a Freedman's Bureau, it should be borne in mind that we need its agency as a temporary alleviation, not because these people are negroes, only because they are men who have been, for generations, deprived of their rights.

Extensive experience in the West Indies has proved that Emancipation, when it takes place, should be unconditional and absolute. The experiment of a few years' apprenticeship, plausible in theory, proved in practice a failure so injurious in its effects that the provincial legislatures, though they had been opposed to the abolition of slavery, voted, after trial, for the abolition of apprenticeship.

The freedman should be treated at once as any other free man. He should be subjected to no compulsory contracts as to labor. There should not be, directly or indirectly, any statutory rates of wages. There should be no interference between the hirers and the hired. Nor should any restrictions be imposed in regard to the local movements of these people, except such regulations incident to war, relative to vagrancy or otherwise, as apply equally to whites. The natural laws of supply and demand should be left, in all cases, to regulate rates of compensation and places of residence.

When freedmen shall have voluntarily entered into any agreement to work, they may, at first, usefully be aided in reducing that agreement to writing, and, for a time, we may properly see to it that such freedmen do not suffer from ill treatment or failure of contract on the part of their employers, and that they themselves perform their duty in the premises.

But all aid given to these people should be regarded as a temporary necessity; all supervision over them should be provisional only, and advisory in its character. The sooner they can learn to stand alone and to make their own unaided way, the better both for our race and for theirs. . . .[12]

The Freedmen's Bureau, organized as a temporary relief measure in the spring of 1865, was one attempt to carry out these suggestions.

It was left to Phillips Brooks, expressing the voice of conscience rather than business or politics, to see furthest and most clearly into the future. The war years were a time for greatness in the preaching career of young Phillips Brooks. He was trying to break down the barrier between things sacred and secular in his life. During the antebellum era he had favored abolition (although he frequently disliked the abolitionists), and in 1862 he exulted over the Emancipation Proclamation as he supported the Lincoln administration in some of his sermons. Away from the pulpit, he labored with the United States Sanitary Commission, visited camps and hospitals, and went to the Gettysburg battlefield. The indecisive course of the New York General Convention of the Episcopal Church on social issues in 1862 stirred him to scorn. His Thanksgiving Sermon of 1863 indicated his resentment of such negative attitudes.

. . . With regard to this whole slavery question . . . I may well leave to others to tell the blessings that the white man is going to feed on in this regenerated slaveless land. But speaking from the pulpit, putting this question on the highest ground, there is one distinction that belongs to us to draw. We hear so many people, even strong antislavery men, talking about the matter:—"Yes," they say, "Slavery is going fast, and we are glad of it. We shall be better off without it. The country will be richer. The Union will be safer. *Our* rejoicing is for the *white* man. It is not for the negro that we care." They make this last proviso in their creed most scrupulously. It seems to me it is a very mean, and low, and selfish one to make. It *is* for the negro that we care. It is our fault and not his, that he is here. It is our fault inherited from the fathers, that has kept in most utter bondage and most cruel bondage too, (I believe nobody doubts that now,) generation after generation of men who have proved themselves the most patient, long-suffering, affectionate, and docile race of servants that ever lived, and who now, in the little glimmer of a chance that is given them, are standing between us and the rebels, fighting battles, receiving wounds, dying deaths that belong to us more than to them; fighting splendidly, working faithfully, learning eagerly, enduring endlessly, laying hold on a higher life with an eagerness that has no parallel in savage history. Let the politicians and the economists, dear friends, do what they will with all this question. Let us put it nowhere but on the highest ground. We rejoice in emancipation because it is *right.* We hate slavery because it is *wrong.* The negro ought to be free. He has a right to be free. . . .

Not merely black men but white men have been freed this year. Slaveries have been broken that never felt an outward lash. Chains have been snapped in sunder that the wearer had never known he wore, but which had eaten unseen to within a hair's breadth of the vitals of his truth and goodness. Do you ask me where? Tell me yourself. . . . Turn over the dust at your feet and see if there are not some bits of broken prejudices yet lying there. . . . We are not all free yet. Old fragments of our servitude still cling about us; as, when a man comes out of a fever, it leaves him some memento, blindness or deafness or some kind of vexing poison in the blood. Let us get rid of these. If the negro is a man, and we have freed him in virtue of his manhood, what consistency or honor is it which still objects to his riding down the street in the same car with us if he is tired, or sitting in the same pew with us if he wants to worship God. Brethren, the world is not all saved yet. There are a few things still that "ought not so to be."[13]

The voice of conscience was a somewhat lonely one during the war; it was to be muted for a long time afterwards. But almost a century later it was to be raised again—louder in volume, harsher, sterner, more urgent in tone. The promise of the post-Civil War future, for those who in the end had the greatest stake in that war, had been too long unrealized.

"The Boys Are Coming Home Again."

Notes

NOTES TO CHAPTER I

1. [Horace Greeley], "The Right of Secession," *New York Tribune,* Dec. 17, 1860.

2. "Protection Indispensable to Our Union," Henry C. Carey to William H. Seward, Feb. 12, 1861, *New York Tribune,* Feb. 14, 1861.

3. William Lloyd Garrison in *The Liberator,* cited in Wendell Phillips Garrison and Francis Jackson Garrison, *William Lloyd Garrison* (New York: Houghton Mifflin & Co., 1894), Vol. 4, pp. 14-15.

4. "The Mayor's Message [January 6, 1861]," *New York Journal of Commerce,* Jan. 10, 1861 (weekly edition).

5. "Mayor Wood's Message—Proposal to Separate The City From The State," *New York Journal of Commerce,* Jan. 8, 1861, cited in Howard Cecil Perkins, *Northern Editorials On Secession* (New York: D. Appleton-Century Company, 1942), Vol. 1, pp. 403-4.

6. James S. Thayer, Speech in the New York Democratic State Convention which assembled Jan. 31, 1861, cited in Horace Greeley, *The American Conflict* (Hartford: O. D. Case & Company, 1864), Vol. 1, pp. 392-93.

7. James Buchanan, "Special Message to the Senate and House of Representatives, January 8, 1861," James D. Richardson, ed., *A Compilation of the Messages and Papers of the Presidents* (Washington: Government Printing Office, 1897), Vol. 5, pp. 655-58.

8. "What Is To Be Done?" Philadelphia *Press,* Dec. 27, 1860.

9. "Cincinnati and the Southern Troubles," *The* [Columbus, Ohio] *Crisis,* Jan. 31, 1861.

10. John J. Crittenden, "Compromise of the Slavery Question," Dec. 18, 1860, *Congressional Globe,* 36 Cong., 2 Sess., pp. 112-14.

11. William H. Seward, "Speech in the Senate on the Crisis," Jan. 12, 1861, *ibid.,* pp. 341-44.

12. Thaddeus Stevens to Salmon P. Chase, Feb. 3, 1861, Chase MSS, Historical Society of Pennsylvania, Philadelphia.

13. John Jay to Charles Sumner, Jan. 24, 1861, Sumner MSS, Harvard University.

14. Preston King to [John] Bigelow, Jan. 30, 1861, John Bigelow, *Retrospections of An Active Life* (New York: The Baker & Taylor Company, 1909), Vol. 1, pp. 355-56.

15. Justin S. Morrill to Ruth Morrill, Dec. 7, 1860, Morrill MSS, Library of Congress.

16. Justin S. Morrill, "Speech in the House of Representatives," Feb. 18, 1861, *Congressional Globe,* 36 Cong., 2 Sess., pp. 1005-6.

17. [Detroit *Post and Tribune*], *Zachariah Chandler: An Outline Sketch of his Life and Public Services* (Detroit: The Post and Tribune Company, 1880), pp. 192-93.

18. Lorenzo Sherwood to Salmon P. Chase, Mar. 14, 1861, Chase MSS, Library of Congress.

19. "Self Protection," *Chicago Tribune,* Mar. 25, 1861.

20. Elijah Babbitt, "Speech in the House of Representatives," Feb. 27, 1861, *Appendix to the Congressional Globe,* 36 Cong., 2 Sess., pp. 288-89. The speech was prepared for presentation on the floor of the House of Representatives; it may have been inserted in the *Appendix to the Congressional Globe* without oral delivery.

21. Hamilton Smith to Henry C. Carey, Dec. 19, 1860, Carey MSS, Historical Society of Pennsylvania, Philadelphia.

22. Abraham Lincoln, "First Inaugural Address—Final Text," Roy P. Basler, ed., *The Collected Works of Abraham Lincoln* (New Brunswick: Rutgers University Press, 1953), Vol. 4, pp. 262-71.

23. "The Resurrection of Patriotism," *New York Times,* Apr. 16, 1861.

24. "The Uprising of the Country," *New York Tribune,* Apr. 17, 1861.

NOTES TO CHAPTER II

1. "The Volunteer's Wife To Her Husband," Frank Moore, ed., *The Rebellion Record* (New York: G. P. Putnam, 1863), Vol. 6, ("Poetry, Rumors and Incidents" section), pp. 54-55.

2. Ulysses S. Grant, *Personal Memoirs of U. S. Grant* (New York: Charles L. Webster & Co., 1885), Vol. 1, pp. 230-32.

3. William Howard Russell, *My Diary North and South* (London: Bradbury and Evans, 1863), Vol. 2, pp. 108-10.

4. W[illiam] Dennison to Simon Cameron, Apr. 22, 1861, *The War of the Rebellion: A Compilation of the Official Records of the Union and Confederate Armies* (Washington: Government Printing Office, 1880-1901), Series III, Vol. 1, pp. 101-2. Hereafter cited as *O.R.*

5. "Departure of the 8th, 13th, and 69th [N. Y.] Regiments . . . ," *New York Tribune,* Apr. 24, 1861.

6. "Union Meeting," Prairie du Chien (Wisconsin) *Courier*, Apr. 25, 1861; "The Feeling Here," *ibid.;* "More Than Enough," May 9, 1861; "Departure of the Prairie du Chien Volunteers," June 27, 1861.

7. "An Hour at Camp Randall," Madison (Wisconsin) *Daily Argus and Democrat,* May 10, 1861.

8. Warren Lee Goss, "Going to the Front," *Battles and Leaders of the Civil War, Pictorial Edition* (New York: The Century Company, 1894), pp. 20-21.

9. Charles Francis Adams, Jr. to [Charles Francis Adams], Nov. 26, 1861, Worthington Chauncey Ford, ed., *A Cycle of Adams Letters* (Boston: Houghton Mifflin, 1920), Vol. 1, pp. 72-73.

10. Conrad Baker, Acting Assistant Provost Marshal General, Indianapolis, to Colonel James B. Fry, Provost Marshal General, June 11, 1863, *O.R.*, Series III, Vol. 3, pp. 338-39.

11. Peter W. Kutz, deposition, June 8, 1863, *ibid.*, pp. 332-33.

12. "The Mob in New York," *New York Times,* July 14, 1863.

13. "How to Discourage Volunteering," New York *Evening Post,* Dec. 11, 1863.

14. "The Enrollment Law," *ibid.*, Dec. 19, 1863.

15. Frank Wilkeson, *Recollections of a Private Soldier in the Army of the Potomac* (New York and London: G. P. Putnam's Sons and The Knickerbocker Press, 1887), pp. 1-2, 7-9, 12-13.

16. Simon Cameron to [Abraham Lincoln], July 1, 1861, *O.R.*, Series III, Vol. 1, pp. 305-6.

17. [Francois Ferdinand d'Orleans] Prince de Joinville, *The Army of the Potomac* (New York: Anson D. F. Randolph, 1863), pp. 13-17.

18. John Henry Crichton Erne, *A Tour in British North America and the U. S., 1863* (Dublin: Hodges, Smith and Co., Publishers to the University, 1864), pp. 55-56.

19. Jacob Dolson Cox, *Military Reminiscences of the Civil War* (New York: Charles Scribner's Sons, 1900), Vol. 1, pp. 165-71.

20. John Beatty, *Memoirs of a Volunteer, 1861-1863* (Cincinnati: Wilstach, Baldwin & Co., 1879), pp. 91-94.

21. Brigadier General Irvin McDowell to [John] Bigelow, July 30,

1861, John Bigelow, *Retrospections Of An Active Life* (New York: Baker & Taylor Co., 1909), Vol. 1, p. 361.

22. George Augustus Sala, *My Diary in America in the Midst of War* (London: Tinsley Brothers, 1865), Vol. 1, pp. 389-92.

23. [William T. Sherman], "In the field, Goldsboro, N. C.," to [Ellen Sherman], Mar. 23, Apr. 5, Apr. 9, 1865, M. A. De Wolfe Howe, ed., *Home Letters of General Sherman* (New York: Charles Scribner's Sons, 1909), pp. 335-36, 341, 343.

NOTES TO CHAPTER III

1. [Unsigned letter] to Major General George B. McClellan, July 8, 1862, McClellan MSS, Library of Congress.

2. L. A. Whiteley to James Gordon Bennett, Sept. 24, 1862, Bennett MSS, Library of Congress.

3. Jacob M. Howard, Detroit, to Charles Sumner, Oct. 31, 1862, Sumner MSS, Harvard University.

4. [Samuel F. B. Morse], "Speech of Professor Morse," *No. 1—Papers from the Society for the Diffusion of Political Knowledge* (New York: [n.p.], 1863, pp. 2-4.

5. Benjamin F. Wade [Address in the United States Senate], Apr. 21, 1862, *Congressional Globe,* 37 Cong., 2 Sess., part 2, pp. 1736-37.

6. John Sherman, Mansfield, Ohio, to [William T. Sherman], Aug. 24, 1862, William T. Sherman MSS, Library of Congress.

7. "The Carpet Bag Party," *Philadelphia North American and United States Gazette,* Mar. 14, 1861.

8. Clinton Rice to Salmon P. Chase, Oct. 29, 1863, Chase MSS, Library of Congress.

9. George W. Julian [Address in the United States House of Representatives], Mar. 18, 1864, *Congressional Globe,* 38 Cong., 1 Sess., part 2, pp. 1187-88.

10. Nathan Sidney Smith Beman, *Our Civil War. The Principles Involved. Its Causes and Cure; Being a Discourse Delivered November 27, 1862* (Troy [New York]: A. W. Scribner & Co., 1863), pp. 41-42, 50-52.

11. [Anonymous], "Song of the Secession Warrior," Frank Moore, ed., *The Rebellion Record* (New York: G. P. Putnam, 1863), Vol. 5, p. 13 ("Poetry, Rumors and Incidents" section).

12. Edgar Cowan [Address in the United States Senate], June 27, 1862, *Congressional Globe,* 37 Cong., 2 Sess., part 4, p. 2962.

13. Andrew Johnson, "Speech of Andrew Johnson at Cincinnati, Ohio, June 19, 1861," Frank Moore, ed., *The Rebellion Record* (New York: G. P. Putnam, 1862), Vol. 2, pp. 148-49 ("Documents" section).

14. John Sherman, Mansfield, Ohio, to [William T. Sherman], Nov. 16, 1862, Rachel Sherman Thorndike, ed., *The Sherman Letters* (New York: Charles Scribner's Sons, 1894), pp. 167-68.

15. Joseph Medill to Salmon P. Chase, Dec. 28, 1862, Chase MSS, Historical Society of Pennsylvania, Philadelphia.

16. James G. Blaine to Thurlow Weed, July 22, 1863, Weed MSS, University of Rochester.

17. Lucius Fairchild to Cassius Fairchild, Sept. 3, 1863, Fairchild MSS, Wisconsin State Historical Society, Madison.

18. "Correspondence of *The Times,*" *The Times,* London, Oct. 23, 1863.

19. "The Baltimore Nomination," *New York Tribune,* June 9, 1864.

20. "To the Supporters Of The Government," [The Wade-Davis Manifesto], *ibid.,* Aug. 5, 1864.

21. "TO THE PEOPLE," *Private and Official Correspondence of Gen[eral] Benjamin F. Butler During the Period of the Civil War.* (Norwood, Massachusetts: The Plimpton Press, 1917), Vol. 5, pp. 116-17.

22. J. K. Herbert, Cincinnati, to General [Benjamin F.] Butler, Aug. 27, 1864, *ibid.,* pp. 117-18.

23. Henry J. Raymond, New York City, to Simon Cameron, Aug. 21, 1864, Cameron MSS, Library of Congress.

24. Cited in *The American Annual Cyclopaedia . . . 1864* (New York: D. Appleton & Company, 1865), p. 793.

25. James W. Grimes to Adam Gurowski, Sept. 18, 1864, Gurowski MSS, Library of Congress.

26. "A National Disgrace," *Detroit Advertiser and Tribune,* Aug. 27, 1864.

27. Carl Schurz to Theodor Petrasch, Bethlehem, Pa., Oct. 12, 1864, Frederic Bancroft, ed., *Speeches, Correspondence and Political Papers of Carl Schurz* (New York: G. P. Putnam's Sons, 1913), Vol. 1, pp. 248-51.

28. "The Meaning Of It," *New York Express* cited in *New York Tribune,* Nov. 10, 1864.

29. Abraham Lincoln, "Fourth Annual Message," Dec. 6, 1864, James D. Richardson, ed., *A Compilation of the Messages and Papers of the Presidents* (Washington: Government Printing Office, 1897), Vol. 6, pp. 252-53.

NOTES TO CHAPTER IV

1. Edward Dicey, *Six Months in the Federal States* (London: Macmillan and Company, 1863), Vol. 1, pp. 68-73.

2. [no title], *The Friend*, Vol. 36 (Feb. 14, 1863), pp. 191-92.

3. Abraham Lincoln, "Address on Colonization to a Deputation of Negroes," Aug. 14, 1862, Roy P. Basler, ed., *The Collected Works of Abraham Lincoln* (New Brunswick: Rutgers University Press, 1953), Vol. 5, pp. 371-75.

4. Joseph Parrish Thompson, "African Civilization and the Cotton Trade," *The New Englander*, Vol. 19 (Oct., 1861), pp. 830, 840, 857. From 1845, Joseph Parrish Thompson (1819-79) was minister of the Broadway Tabernacle Church in New York City. He was one of the founders of *The New Englander* magazine and, until 1862, on the editorial board of the New York *Independent*. Known as a strong advocate of the slaves' welfare, he also had something of a reputation as an Egyptologist.

5. Israel Washburn to Hannibal Hamlin, Dec. 20, 1862, Israel Washburn MSS, Library of Congress.

6. Attributed to Charles G. Halpine, Horatio Pettus Batcheler [pseud. Horace P. Batcheler], *Jonathan At Home: or, A Stray Shot At the Yankees* (London: W. H. Collingridge, 1864), p. 121. Charles Graham Halpine (1829-68) was an Irish-born journalist who joined the 69th New York Volunteer regiment at the outbreak of the war, and later served on the staff of Major General David Hunter. His satirical articles and poems for the press were signed "Miles O'Reilly," a semi-literate volunteer. Halpine retired from the army in 1864.

7. Elizur Wright to Salmon P. Chase, May 4, 1861, Elizur Wright MSS, Library of Congress. This letter, somewhat altered, is in Philip Green Wright and Elizabeth Q. Wright, *Elizur Wright, The Father of Life Insurance* (Chicago: University of Chicago Press, 1937), pp. 214-15. Elizur Wright (1804-85) was a veteran antislavery advocate. In the 1830's he had been secretary of the American Anti-Slavery Society and editor of the *Massachusetts Abolitionist*, and during the decade of the of the 50's edited the *Weekly Commonwealth* in Boston. This was the organ of the Free Soil party. He was commissioner of insurance in Massachusetts.

8. Charles Carleton Coffin, *The Boys of '61, or Four Years of Fighting* (Boston: Estes and Lauriat, 1881), pp. 243-45. Coffin (1823-96)

was a war correspondent who telegraphed his dispatches from the field to the Boston *Journal* under the name "Carleton."

9. Norwood Penrose Hallowell, *Selected Letters and Papers of N. P. Hallowell* (Peterborough, New Hampshire: The Richard R. Smith Co., Inc., 1963), pp. 30-35. Norwood Penrose Hallowell, a graduate of Harvard in the class of 1861, enlisted as a private in the 4th Batt. Mass. V. M. (New England Guards) on April 25, 1861. On June 10, 1861 he was a first lieutenant in the 20th Mass. Vols., and a captain in the same regiment on Nov. 26, 1861. He fought in the Peninsula campaign, was wounded at Antietam, returned to New England, but on April 17 was commissioned Lieutenant Colonel of the 54th Mass. Vols. (a Negro regiment) ; on May 30, 1863, he became Colonel of the 55th Mass. Vols. (also a Negro regiment). He took part in the attack on Fort Wagner, and resigned because of disability on Nov. 2, 1863.

10. Report of Brig. Gen. Edward W. Hinks, Hdqtrs. Third Division, Eighteenth Corps, U. S. Army, Commanding Third Division, of operations June 15-19 [1864], to Major William Russell, Jr., Assistant Adjutant General, Eighteenth Army Corps, *O.R.*, Series I, Vol. 40, part 1, pp. 720-23.

11. George William Curtis to Charles Eliot Norton, Aug. 19, 1861, Edward Cary, *George William Curtis* (Boston and New York: Houghton Mifflin Company, 1894), pp. 149-50. George William Curtis (1824-92) was a novelist, journalist and orator. During the Civil War he wrote regular columns for *Harper's Monthly* and *Harper's Weekly* ("The Easy Chair," and "The Lounger"). In 1863, he became editor of *Harper's Weekly.*

12. Sinclair Tousey, "Emancipation: Its Influence On the Rebellion and Effect On the Whites," *The Knickerbocker,* Vol. 58 (Oct. 1861), pp. 349-50.

13. Wendell Phillips, *The War For the Union* (New York: E. B. Barker, 1862), pp. 24-25.

14. S[amuel] S. Cox, "Emancipation and Its Results—Is Ohio to be Africanized?" *Congressional Globe,* 37 Cong., 2 Sess., Appendix, p. 248.

15. John Sherman, Mansfield, Ohio, to [William T. Sherman], Aug. 24, 1862, Rachel Sherman Thorndike, ed., *The Sherman Letters* (New York: Charles Scribner's Sons, 1894), pp. 156-57.

16. Abraham Lincoln to James C. Conkling, Aug. 26, 1863, *O.R.*, Series III, Vol. 3, pp. 732-33.

17. *Proceedings of the American Anti-Slavery Society at its Third Decade, Held in the City of Philadelphia, Dec. 3rd and 4th, 1864*

[1863] (New York: American Anti-Slavery Society, 1864), p. 26.

18. "A Street Disturbance," *Philadelphia North American and United States Gazette,* Apr. 14, 1865.

19. *Douglass' Monthly,* Mar. 1862, reprinted in Philip S. Foner, *The Life and Writings of Frederick Douglass* (New York: International Publishers, 1952), Vol. 3, pp. 223-25.

NOTES TO CHAPTER V

1. "At Least One Bushel More," *American Agriculturist,* Vol. 20 (May 1861), p. 136.

2. "Present Prospects of Farmers," *ibid.,* (Sept. 1861), p. 261.

3. "Commercial Chronicle and Review," *The Merchants' Magazine and Commercial Review,* Vol. 49 (Sept. 1863), p. 220.

4. "New Helps of Agriculture In Aid of War," Cincinnati *Gazette* cited in *The Scientific American,* Vol. 7 (Nov. 1, 1862), p. 274.

5. "The War and Agricultural Implements," *American Agriculturist,* Vol. 22 (Aug. 1863), p. 233.

6. "Progressive Farming in Iowa," Davenport *Daily Gazette,* Apr. 24, 1863.

7. "Report of the Commissioner of Agriculture, January 1, 1864," House of Representatives, Exec. Doc. No. 91, 38 Cong., 1 Sess., p. 607.

8. " 'Secession' Bank Notes," [Springfield] Illinois *Daily State Journal,* citing Ottawa (Illinois) *Free Trader,* May 17, 1861.

9. M[ontgomery] C. Meigs, Quartermaster General, to Colonel D. H. Vinton, New York, Nov. 16, 1861, *O.R.,* Series III, Vol. 1, p. 649.

10. James W. Ripley, "Notes on subject of contracting for small arms," June 11, 1861, *ibid.,* pp. 264-65.

11. J[oseph] Holt and Robert Dale Owen, to E[dwin] M. Stanton, July 1, 1862, *ibid.,* Vol. 2, pp. 189-93.

12. Charles G. Nazro, Alexander H. Rice, Gardner Brewer, E. S. Tobey, T. W. Lincoln, Jr., Special Committee of the Boston Board of Trade, to Simon Cameron, Oct. 18, 1861, *ibid.,* Vol. 1, pp. 583-84.

13. Meigs to Simon Cameron, Oct. 22, 1861, *ibid.,* pp. 582-83.

14. [Gideon Welles], "Report of the Secretary of the Navy," Dec. 1, 1862, House of Representatives Exec. Doc. No. 1, 37th Cong. 3 Sess., pp. 35-36.

15. "National Workshops," *The Scientific American,* Vol. 7 (Dec. 20, 1862), pp. 393-94.

16. *Lake Superior Journal* cited in *The Merchants' Magazine and Commercial Review,* Vol. 48 (Mar. 1863), pp. 260-61.

17. Lewis B. Parsons, Colonel and Assistant Quartermaster, Quartermaster's Department, Office of Transportation, St. Louis, to Brigadier General Robert Allen, Chief Quartermaster, June 23, 1863, *O.R.*, Series III, Vol. 3, pp. 406-7.

18. "Stock Exchange and Money Market," *American Railroad Journal,* Vol. 36 (July 4, 1863), pp. 638.

19. "Commercial Retrospect of 1862," *ibid.,* (Jan. 10, 1863), p. 45.

20. Edwin M. Stanton, "Annual Report of the Secretary of War," Nov. 14, 1866, *O.R.,* Series III, Vol. 5, pp. 1042-45.

21. "Commercial Chronicle and Review," *The Merchants' Magazine and Commercial Review,* Vol. 49 (Aug. 1863), pp. 129-30.

22. "War and the Progress of Invention," *The Scientific American,* Vol. 10 (May 21, 1864), p. 329.

23. "Wants and Their Supply," Philadelphia *Public Ledger,* Nov. 4, 1862.

24. Jesse Baldwin, Youngstown, to John Sherman, Jan. 25, 1864, John Sherman MSS, Library of Congress.

25. William E. Dodge, *Influence of the War on Our National Prosperity. A Lecture Delivered in Baltimore, Md., on Monday Evening, March 13, 1865* (New York: William C. Martin, Printer, 1865), pp. 7-9. William Earl Dodge (1805-83) since 1833 had been in the firm of Phelps, Dodge & Company which played an important role in the development of copper deposits in the Lake Superior region and in the Pennsylvania iron industry. Dodge also owned pine lands in Wisconsin and had investments in the South. He was interested in various reform movements, especially temperance.

26. "The Past and Present," *Fincher's Trades Review,* July 4, 1863.

27. "Wall Street in War Time," *Harper's Monthly,* Vol. 30 (Apr. 1865), pp. 615-18.

28. "A. T. Stewart," New York correspondence of the *Boston Journal,* cited in *New York World,* Jan. 31, 1863.

29. "Oil Stock Excitement," *The Scientific American,* Vol. 12 (Jan. 2, 1865), p. 8.

30. B. Franklin, "After Petroleum," *Harper's Monthly,* Vol. 30 (Dec. 1864), p. 54.

31. "The Grain-Shovelers' Strike," *New York Times,* July 9, 1862.

32. "Effect of the War On Our Textile Industries," *The Round Table,* Vol. 1 (May 28, 1864), pp. 369-70.

33. "The Iron Trade For the Year 1862," *The Merchants' Magazine and Commercial Review,* Vol. 49 (Dec. 1863), pp. 463-64.

34. "New Rolling Mills in Pittsburgh," *The Scientific American,* Vol. 10 (Mar. 26, 1864), p. 200.

35. "Trade and Business of the United States," *New York Times,* Jan. 8, 1865.

NOTES TO CHAPTER VI

1. "A K.G.C. Dislodged," Indianapolis *Daily Journal,* Feb. 11, 1863.

2. "The Butternut Mass Meeting," *ibid.,* May 21, 1863.

3. "The Charleston Affair," Evansville (Indiana) *Daily Journal,* citing the Charleston (Illinois) *Plaindealer,* Apr. 2, 1864.

4. "The Labor Movement," Philadelphia *Press,* Nov. 16, 1863.

5. Charles Albright, Mauch Chunk, Pa., to Abraham Lincoln, Nov. 9, 1863, *O.R.,* Series III, Vol. 3, pp. 1008-9. Charles Albright was born in Berks County, Pennsylvania, in 1830. Of a prominent family, he graduated from Dickinson College in 1851, then went to Kansas to fight for the free-soilers. Returning to Pennsylvania in 1856, he settled at Mauch Chunk, practiced law, became a leading Republican, and was a delegate to the Chicago convention of 1860 that nominated Lincoln. Beginning in 1858, he engaged in the manufacture of mining machinery. When the Second National Bank was organized in Mauch Chunk in 1863, he became its president. In February 1861, he was a member of the Clay Battalion which guarded public buildings in Washington. Later he was a major in the 132nd Pennsylvania regiment, and promoted to colonel before it was mustered out in May 1863. He then organized, as colonel, the 202nd Pennsylvania volunteers. He was made a brevet brigadier general in March 1865. After the war, he was one of the lawyers who prosecuted the Molly Maguires in their 1876 trial.

6. "Employers' Associations," Detroit *Advertiser and Tribune,* July 25, 1864.

7. "Employers' Associations and Trade Unions," *Detroit Free Press,* July 31, 1864.

8. Benjamin F. Lewis, "An Address Delivered Before the Utica Typographical Union . . . December 5, 1863," *The Printer,* Vol. 5 (Jan. 1864), p. 33. Lewis was president of the union.

9. James Dawson Burn, *Three Years Among the Working-Classes in the United States During the War* (London: Smith, Elder & Co., 1865), pp. 188-89.

10. "A Subject of Much Concern—The Increased Rent of Dwelling Houses—Causes of the Rise—What Can Be Done to Provide Homes For the People," *New York Times,* Feb. 18, 1865.

11. *Report of the Council of Hygiene and Public Health . . . Upon the Sanitary Condition of the City* (New York: D. Appleton & Co., 1865), pp. lxxiv-lxxvi, xcii-xciv.

12. [Rebecca Harding Davis], "Life in the Iron Mills," *The Atlantic Monthly,* Vol. 7 (Apr. 1861), pp. 444-45. Rebecca Blaine Harding Davis (1831-1910) was from a Virginia family. She was born in Washington, Pennsylvania, and lived most of her early life in Wheeling. Largely self-taught and influenced by the success of Harriet Beecher Stowe and other feminine writers in the 1850's, she began to write short stories. Lowell, as editor of the *Atlantic,* accepted "Life in the Iron Mills," which became a landmark of literary realism. Although it is generally conceded that the life she described in her story was that which she had observed in Wheeling as a girl, the conditions were similar to those in Pittsburgh and other industrial towns in the region. Her strongly worded social criticism most certainly applied to the 1860's. In 1863, she married a journalist, L. Clark Davis, and after that lived in Philadelphia. In 1869 she joined the editorial staff of the *New York Tribune.* She was the mother of the novelist Richard Harding Davis.

13. "Opening of the Opera Season—The Age of Shoddy," *New York Herald,* Oct. 6, 1863.

14. Robert Tomes, "The Fortunes of War," *Harper's Monthly,* Vol. 29 (July 1864), pp. 230-31.

15. "A Mass Meeting At Dixon," Chicago *Times,* Nov. 29, 1862.

16. A[mory] D[wight] Mayo, *East and West* [n.p., n.d., but c. 1865], pp. 17-20. Amory Dwight Mayo (1823-1907) was a Unitarian clergyman who had served churches in Gloucester (Mass.), Cleveland, and Albany before going to Cincinnati, where he preached between 1863 and 1872. He was also a nonresident professor in Meadville Theological Seminary.

17. John Marsh, "Report of the Executive Committee, Read to the Twenty-Eighth Anniversary of the American Temperance Union, May 12, 1864," *Journal of the American Temperance Union and The New York Prohibitionist,* Vol. 28 (June 1864), pp. 81-83. John Marsh (1788-1868) was a Congregational minister and temperance reformer. A Yale graduate in 1804, he became, in 1829, secretary and general agent of the Connecticut Temperance Society, and three years later, corresponding secretary of the American Temperance Union and editor of its journal, the first number of which appeared in January 1837. He stayed

with this organization until 1865, when the American Temperance Union yielded to a new society.

18. *The Alarm Bell, No. 1, By A Constitutionalist* (New York: Baker & Godwin, 1863), pp. 3-5, 6-7, 9-10.

19. "United States Union Commission," *The American Annual Cyclopaedia* . . . 1864 (New York: D. Appleton & Company, 1865), pp. 803-5.

20. George F. Davis, Cincinnati, to John Sherman, Apr. 4, 1864, John Sherman MSS, Library of Congress. George F. Davis was a Cincinnati businessman, the proprietor of George F. Davis & Co., packers and "ham curers."

21. E[dgar] Conkling, New York City, to John Sherman, Jan. 9, 1865, *ibid.* Edgar Conkling was another Cincinnatian. Before the war, he represented in that city various promotional schemes for the development of the West, such as the Texas Western Rail Road Co. and the Sonora Exploring and Mining Company. During the war years he was much involved in projects to construct the Northern and Central Pacific Railroads across the continent.

22. "The War," *Friends' Intelligencer*, Vol. 18 (Nov. 30, 1861), pp. 600-2.

NOTES TO CHAPTER VII

1. "The Fourth of July," Lafayette (Indiana) *Daily Courier*, July 5, 1861.

2. "The Patriotism of Boston, Mass., As Exhibited August 31, 1862," Frank Moore, ed., *The Rebellion Record* (New York: G. P. Putnam, 1863), Vol. 5 ("Documents" section), pp. 600-2.

3. "Quincy," *Bellefontaine* (Ohio) *Republican*, Dec. 2, 1864.

4. New York Bible Society, *The Bible in the Army . . . 1861* (New York: The New York Bible Society, 1862), pp. 3-7. This consists of extracts from the Thirty-eighth Annual Report, relating to the military distribution of Testaments and Bibles.

5. United States Christian Commission for the Army and Navy, *First Annual Report* (Philadelphia: [n.p.], 1863), pp. 5-14.

6. "The Sanitary Commission and Our Wounded," New York *Evening Post*, May 21, 1864.

7. "Rowdyism in Springfield," [Springfield] Illinois *Daily State Journal*, May 30, 1861.

8. "Fair of the Crawford Co. Agricultural Society," *Bucyrus* (Ohio)

Journal, Aug. 16, 1861; "Our County Fair," Aug. 23, 1861; "The Fair," Sept. 27, 1861.

9. George Tuthill Borrett, *Letters From Canada and the United States* (London: J. E. Adlard, 1865), pp. 188-92.

10. "Homes For Our Citizens," *The Horticulturist,* Vol. 19 (Nov. 1864), pp. 329-30.

11. "Watering-Place Correspondence," New York *Evening Post,* Aug. 26, 1864.

12. "Trotting At the Fashion Course," *Wilkes' Spirit of the Times,* June 6, 1863.

13. "The Great Prize Battle, Joe Coburn and Mike McCool, For $2,000 and the Championship," *ibid.,* May 16, 1863.

14. Robert Ferguson, *America During and After the War* (London: Longman's Green, Reader and Dyer, 1866), pp. 44-47.

15. H. F. French, "Letter From the Homestead," *The Country Gentleman,* Vol. 24 (July 21, 1864), pp. 40-42.

16. *Chicago: A Strangers' and Tourists' Guide to the City of Chicago* (Chicago: Religious and Philosophical Publishing Association, J. S. Thompson Printers, 1866), pp. 90-95.

17. Edward Dicey, *Six Months in the Federal States* (London: The Macmillan Company, 1863), Vol. 2, pp. 127-30.

18. James Shaw, *Twelve Years in America* (London: Hamilton Adams & Co., 1867), p. 138.

19. Robert Ferguson, *America During and After the War,* pp. 51-53.

20. "Chamber Concerts," *Dwight's Journal of Music,* Vol. 20 (Nov. 30, 1861), p. 278.

21. *The New York Musical World and Review* cited in *The Musical World* (London), Vol. 42 (Aug. 27, 1864), pp. 547-48.

22. Horatio Pettus Batcheler [pseud. Horace P. Batcheler], *Jonathan At Home* (London: W. H. Collingridge, 1864), pp. 75-79, 83-85, 102-4.

23. Julia A. Layton, "American Art," *The Knickerbocker,* Vol. 58 (July 1861), pp. 48-52.

24. *The New Path,* Vol. 1 (Aug. 1863), pp. 37-42. Among the Pre-Raphaelites were Thomas C. Farrer, Clarence Cook, Clarence King, Peter B. Wight, Russell Sturgis, Charles Herbert Moore, Eugene Schuyler, Calvert Vaux, and W. T. Richards.

25. "Trade Sales," *American Literary Gazette and Publishers' Circular,* Octavo Series, Vol. 2 (Apr. 15, 1864), p. 406.

26. "Beadle's Dime Books," *The North American Review,* Vol. 99 (July 1864), pp. 303-9.

27. *Fortieth Annual Report of the Board of Managers of the Mercantile Library Company of Philadelphia, For the Year Ending December 31, 1862* (Philadelphia: William S. Young, 1863), pp. 7-10.

28. John Langdon Sibley, [Librarian's] Annual Report, 1861, Harvard College Library, John Langdon Sibley Harvard Library Journal MSS, Massachusetts Historical Society, Boston.

29. "Literature and Literary Progress in 1863," *The American Annual Cyclopaedia . . . 1863* (New York: D. Appleton & Company, 1864), p. 573.

30. "Romances of the War," *The Round Table,* Vol. 1 (Jan. 9, 1864), p. 59.

31. "War Poems," *ibid.,* (Feb. 6, 1864), p. 123.

32. "Princeton College and the Union," New York *Evening Post,* Oct. 17, 1864.

33. Proceedings of the Chicago Board of Education, cited in *Illinois Teacher,* Vol. 9 (May 1863), p. 166.

34. Georges Fisch, *Nine Months In the United States During the Crisis* (London: James Nisbet & Co., 1863), pp. 67-70.

35. L[inus P.] Brockett, "Philanthropy and the War," *The United States Service Magazine,* Vol. 2 (Oct. 1864), pp. 321-24, 328-29, 331-32.

36. Sarah to Cassius Fairchild, July 10, 1863, Fairchild MSS, Wisconsin State Historical Society Library, Madison.

NOTES TO CHAPTER VIII

1. Ralph Waldo Emerson to James Elliott Cabot, Aug. 4, 1861, Ralph L. Rusk, ed., *The Letters of Ralph Waldo Emerson* (New York: Columbia University Press, 1939), Vol. 5, p. 253.

2. Henry James, *The Social Significance of Our Institutions: An Oration Delivered By Request of the Citizens of Newport R[hode] I[sland], July 4, 1861* (Boston: Ticknor and Fields, 1861), pp. 4-6, 33-36. Henry James, the elder (1811-82), enjoying security through inherited wealth, devoted himself to a scholarly life—lecturing, writing, and traveling abroad—and settled in Newport in 1860. During the 1840's he came under the influence of Swedenborg's thinking while in England, and a few years later his social concepts were shaped to some extent by his associations with American Fourierists in New York. The central thesis of James's oration of July 4, 1861, became the theme of Lowell's hymn: "Once to every man and nation . . ."

3. Henry W[hitney] Bellows, *Duty and Interest Identical in the Pres-*

ent Crisis. A Sermon Preached in All Souls' Church On Sunday Morning, April 14th, 1861 (New York: Wynkoop, Hallenbeck & Thomas, 1861), pp. 4-5, 8-9.

4. Henry Ward Beecher, "The Camp and the Country," *New York Tribune,* Nov. 15, 1861. Henry Ward Beecher (1813-87), son of Lyman Beecher and a graduate of Amherst College, began his ministry at Plymouth Church of Brooklyn, Congregational, in 1847. By 1860, his weekly congregation had grown to about 2,500 persons. From 1861 to 1864, he was editor of the New York *Independent,* a religious newspaper of wide influence.

5. William Rounseville Alger, *Our Civil War As Seen From the Pulpit; A Sermon Preached in the Bulfinch Street Church, April 28, 1861* (Boston: Walker, Wise and Company, 1861), pp. 7-9. William Rounseville Alger (1822-1905), a graduate at the Harvard Divinity School in 1847, quickly rose to a place of leadership among New England's Unitarian intellectuals. His major work was *Critical History of the Doctrine of a Future Life,* published in 1864.

6. Octavius Brooks Frothingham, *Seeds and Shells: A Sermon Preached in New York, November 17, 1861* (New York: Wynkoop, Hallenbeck & Thomas, 1862), pp. 3, 13-15, 17-18.

7. Frederic Henry Hedge, *The Sick Woman. A Sermon For the Time* (Boston: Prentiss and Deland, 1863), pp. 8-12.

8. Horace Bushnell, *Reverses Needed. A Discourse Delivered on the Sunday After the Disaster of Bull Run, In the North Church, Hartford* (Hartford, Connecticut: L. E. Hunt, 1861), pp. 9-13. Horace Bushnell (1802-76), was pastor of the Congregational North Church in Hartford from 1833 until his resignation because of ill health in 1861. He had visited California in the 1850's. Liberal in his theology, he was the author of *Christian Nurture* (1847), the *Age of Homespun* (1851), on life in early New England, and other works. He continued to write and to publish until his death.

9. Charles Eliot Norton, "American Political Ideas," *The North American Review,* Vol. 101 (Oct., 1865), pp. 558-60. Charles Eliot Norton (1827-1908), son of Andrews Norton, lived in the family home in Cambridge. After a brief career as a merchant, young Norton traveled in Italy, became a translator of Dante, and began to develop cultural interests which eventually made him a great historian of art. During the Civil War he was coeditor of the New England Loyal Publication Society broadsides which were widely circulated among Northern newspapers.

10. Edward Bissell Hunt, *Union Foundations: A Study of American*

Nationality As a Fact of Science (New York: D. Van Nostrand, 1863), pp. 10-11, 15-17.

11. Edmund Hamilton Sears, "The Puritan and the Cavalier," *Monthly Religious Magazine*, Vol. 25 (June 1861), pp. 371-72. Edmund Hamilton Sears (1810-76), graduated at Union College, Schenectady, New York, in 1834, and at Harvard Divinity School in 1837. He was descended from Richard Sears who came from England to Plymouth Colony about 1630. His fragile health required Sears to conserve his physical strength, but for seventeen years, beginning in 1848, he was minister at Wayland, Massachusetts. He also produced a number of theological treatises, was an editor of the *Monthly Religious Magazine*, and wrote a number of hymns, of which the most famous is "It Came upon a Midnight Clear."

12. Evan W. Evans, "The American Cavaliers," *The New Englander*, Vol. 23 (Oct. 1864), pp. 651-53, 655-56.

13. Sarah Forbes Hughes, ed., *Letters and Recollections of John Murray Forbes* (Boston and New York: Houghton Mifflin & Co., 1899), Vol. 2, pp. 73-75.

14. Charles Godfrey Leland, "Have We A Principle Among Us?" *The Knickerbocker*, Vol. 58 (Aug. 1861), pp. 154-57.

15. "For What Are We Fighting?" *New York Times*, May 3, 1861.

16. [James Russell Lowell], "The Pickens-and-Stealin's Rebellion," *The Atlantic Monthly*, Vol. 7 (June 1861), p. 763.

17. "Scientific Achievements of the Age," *New York Herald*, Oct. 13, 1863.

18. "The Spirit of the Age," *New York Times*, May 8, 1861.

NOTES TO CHAPTER IX

1. "What the War Will Do," *Bucyrus* (Ohio) *Journal*, Aug. 2, 1861.

2. "After the War—What Then?" *The Round Table*, Vol. 1 (May 14, 1863), p. 337.

3. Cornelius W. Tolles, "Reorganization," *The United States Service Magazine*, Vol. 2 (July 1864), pp. 21-24.

4. Edward Everett Hale, *The Future Civilization of the South; A Sermon Preached on the 13th of April, 1862 at the South Congregational Church, Boston* (Boston: [n. p.] 1862), pp. 12-13.

5. "The Surrender of Lee," *The Iron Age*, Vol. 2 (Apr. 13, 1865), p. 2.

6. Sinclair Tousey, "Emancipation: Its Influence On the Rebellion and Effect on the Whites," *The Knickerbocker*, Vol. 58 (Oct. 1861), pp. 346-47.

7. "Restoring Traitors to their Rights," Quincy (Illinois) Daily *Whig and Republican,* Sept. 3, 1863.

8. Orestes A. Brownson, "Liberalism and Progress," *Brownson's Quarterly Review,* National Series, Vol. 1 (Oct. 1864), pp. 454-56.

9. Abraham Lincoln, "Last Public Address," April 11, 1865, Roy P. Basler, ed., *The Collected Works of Abraham Lincoln* (New Brunswick: Rutgers University Press, 1953), Vol. 8, pp. 400, 403.

10. Henry Winter Davis to Edward McPherson, May 27, 1865, McPherson MSS, Library of Congress. Henry Winter Davis (1817-65) was the son of a president of St. John's College, Annapolis, Maryland. After graduating from Kenyon College, he for a time attended law school in Virginia, and practiced law there. In the 1850's he was sent to Congress as a Know-Nothing, but in 1861 he was defeated when he ran for the House of Representatives as a Unionist in Maryland. Having swung over to the Radical point of view, he was successful in his bid for a congressional seat in 1863, and was chosen to be chairman of the House Foreign Affairs Committee. He soon was recognized as a powerful voice of the Radicals.

11. "The 'Extermination' of the Negro," *New York Times,* Oct. 16, 1862.

12. Robert Dale Owen, *The Wrong of Slavery. The Right of Emancipation and the Future of the African Race in the U.S.* (Philadelphia: J. B. Lippincott & Co., 1864), pp. 226-28.

13. Phillips Brooks, *Our Mercies of Re-Occupation. A Thanksgiving Sermon, Preached at the Church of the Holy Trinity, Philadelphia, Nov. 26, 1863* (Philadelphia: William S. and Alfred Martien, 1863), pp. 20-23.

Illustration Sources

p. xiv. *Harper's Weekly,* Vol. 5, June 8, 1861, p. 368.
3. *Ibid.,* Vol. 5, Mar. 2, 1861, p. 129.
34. *Illustrated London News,* Vol. 38, suppl., May 18, 1861, p. 471.
43. *Harper's Weekly,* Vol. 5, Aug. 31, 1861, p. 560.
61. *Ibid.,* Vol. 7, Aug. 1, 1863, p. 484.
63. *Ibid.,* p. 485.
64. *Ibid.,* p. 485.
66. *The American Soldier in the Civil War,* New York: Bryan, Taylor & Co., 1895, p. 239.
73. *Ibid.,* p. 245.
82. *Illustrated London News,* Vol. 38, June 15, 1861, p. 563.
96. *The American Soldier in the Civil War,* p. 459.
115. *Harper's Weekly,* Vol. 8, Nov. 12, 1864, p. 736.
131. *Ibid.,* Vol. 5, Jan. 26, 1861, p. 64.
139. *Ibid.,* p. 64.
148. *The American Soldier in the Civil War,* p. 307.
158. *Harper's Pictorial History of Civil War,* by Guernsey and Alden, Chicago: McDonnell bros., 1866-68, p. 752.
169. *American Agriculturist,* Vol. 24, Apr. 1865, p. 132.
177. *Harper's Weekly,* Vol. 5, Sept. 21, 1861, p. 605.
182. *American Agriculturist,* Vol. 24, May 1865, p. 168.
194. *American Agriculturist,* Vol. 23, Mar. 1864, p. 93. *Ibid.,* Vol. 24, Apr. 1865, p. 134. *Ibid.,* Vol. 24, May 1865, p. 164.
196. *Ibid.,* Vol. 23, Mar. 1864, p. 92.

205. *Ibid.*, Vol. 24, Feb. 1865, p. 60.
228. *Report of the 15th Sanitary District.* Report of the Council of Hygiene and Public Health of the Citizen's Association of New York upon the Sanitary condition of the City, New York: D. Appleton & Co., 1865, p. 178.
234. *Harper's Weekly,* Vol. 5, Apr. 13, 1861, p. 228.
251. *The American Soldier in Civil War,* p. 470.
264. *Harper's Weekly,* Vol. 8, Apr. 30, 1861, p. 276.
283. *Illustrated London News,* Vol. 38, Apr. 6, 1861, p. 306.
284. *Harper's Weekly,* Vol. 8, Aug. 6, 1864, p. 512.
289. *Ibid.*, p. 324.
328. *The American Soldier in the Civil War,* pp. 442-43.
353. *Ibid.*, p. 441.
370. *American Agriculturist,* Vol. 24, Jul. 1865, p. 224.

Index

Typefaces used in this book
are Linotype Bodoni Book, 11-point leaded 2 points,
with titles handset in Bodoni Roman and Bulmer Italic.
Printed by offset on 60-lb. Warren's 66 Antique.
The binding is Bancroft's Kennett.
Designed by Frank Mahood.

3 1398 00045 0669

973.7 Smith 67 1336
S Life in the North during the Civil War.
copy 1

28 DAYS — NOT RENEWABLE
973.7 Smith, G. 67 1336/650
S Life in the North during the Civil War.
copy 1
45 Ø669

Peninsula Public Library
280 Central Avenue
Lawrence, N. Y. 11559
Phone: 239-3262

44

DEMCO